Sefer
Yetzirah

Sefer Yetzirah

The Book of Creation

Revised Edition

ARYEH KAPLAN

WEISER BOOKS
San Francisco, CA / Newburyport, MA

Revised edition published in 1997 by
Red Wheel/Weiser, LLC
With offices at
500 Third Street, Suite 230
San Francisco, CA 94107
www.redwheelweiser.com

An index has been added to this corrected edition

ISBN: 978-0-87728-855-8

Library of Congress Cataloging-in-Publication Data
Sefer Yetzirah, English & Hebrew.
        Sefer Yetzirah = The Book of Creation : in theory and practice / Aryeh
Kaplan.—Rev. ed.
            p. cm.
        Includes bibliographical information and index.
        ISBN 0-87728-855-0 (pbk. : alk. paper)
        1. Cabala—Early works to 1800. 2. Sefer Yetzirah. I. Kaplan, Aryeh
1934–1982 or 3. II. Title.
BM525.A412K37   1997
296.1'6—dc21   96-49121

Cover design by Michael Martin
Typeset in Times

Printed in the United States of America
EB
15 14 13 12 11

The paper used in this publication meets the minimum requirements of
the American National Standard for Information Sciences–Permanence
of Paper for Printed Library Materials Z39.48–1992 (R1997).

About the Translator

Rabbi Aryeh Kaplan was a world-renowned Torah scholar who produced over 50 books in his brief lifetime, including *Meditation and the Bible, Meditation and Kabbalah* and *The Bahir*. Kaplan's works encompassed commentary and translation of ancient and obscure works by Bible scholars and Kabbalists, and works advising young Jews on the merits of study and observance. For a while he was an editor of *Jewish Life* magazine, translated an enormous commentary on the Torah by the Sephardic rabbi, Yaakov Culi, and produced an original translation-commentary of the Five Books of Moses, which he called "The Living Torah," published by Moznaim, Israel.

Aryeh Kaplan was born in the Bronx, studied at local yeshivot, and continued his education at yeshivot in Israel. For a while he entered the field of science and was, for a brief period, the youngest physicist employed by the United States government before devoting his life to Torah scholarship. He died at the age of 48 in 1983.

CONTENTS

Introduction

The *Sefer Yetzirah* is without question the oldest and most mysterious of all Kabbalistic texts. The first commentaries on this book were
written in the 10th century, and the text itself is quoted as early as
the sixth. References to the work appear in the first century, while
traditions regarding its use attest to its existence even in Biblical
times. So ancient is this book that its origins are no longer accessable
to historians. We are totally dependent on traditions with regard to
its authorship.

Equally mysterious is the meaning of this book. If the author
meant to be obscure, he was eminently successful. It is only through
the most careful analysis, studying every word with its parallels in
Biblical and Talmudic literature, that its haze of obscurity begins to
be penetrated.

There have been many interpretations of the *Sefer Yetzirah*. The
earliest commentators tried to interpret it as a philosophical treatise,
but their efforts shed more light on their own systems than on the
text. The same is true of efforts to fit it into the systems of the Zohar
or later Kabbalists. Efforts to view it as a book on grammar or pho-
netics are even more unsuccessful.

In general, the Kabbalah is divided into three categories, the theoretical, the meditative, and the magical.[1] The theoretical Kabbalah,
which in its present form is based largely on the Zohar, is concerned
mostly with the dynamics of the spiritual domain, especially the
worlds of the Sefirot, souls and angels. This branch of Kabbalah
reached its zenith in the writings of the Safed school in the 16th century, and the vast majority of published texts belong in this
category.

Meditative Kabbalah deals with the use of divine names, letter
permutations, and similar methods to reach higher states of consciousness, and as such, comprises a kind of yoga. Most of the main
texts have never been published, but remain scattered in manuscripts
in the great libraries and museums. Some of these methods enjoyed
a brief renaissance in the mid 1700's with the rise of the Hasidic
movement, but within a half century they were once again largely
forgotten.

The third category of Kabbalah–the magical–is closely related to the meditative. It consists of various signs, incantations and divine names, through which one can influence or alter natural events. Many of the techniques closely resemble meditative methods, and their success may depend on their ability to induce mental states where telekinetic or spiritual power can effectively be channeled. As with the second category, the most important texts have never been printed, although some fragments have been published. One of the best examples of these is the book Raziel.

Careful study indicates that Sefer Yetzirah is a meditative text, with strong magical overtones. This position is supported by the earliest Talmudic traditions, which indicate that it could be used to create living creatures. Especially significant are the many reports and legends in which the Sefer Yetzirah is used to create a Golem, a sort of mystical android.

The methods of the Sefer Yetzirah appear to involve meditation; and it is highly possible that it was originally written as a meditative manual. A major 12th century philosopher thus states that it does not contain philosophy, but divine mystery.[2] This comes across very clearly in the commentary of one of the greatest Kabbalists, Isaac the Blind (1160-1236), who stresses the meditative aspects of the text.

It is also particularly evident in a very ancient manuscript of Sefer Yetzirah, dating from the 10th century or earlier. The introductory colophon states, "This is the book of the Letters of Abraham our father, which is called Sefer Yetzirah, and when one gazes *(tzafah)* into it, there is no limit to his wisdom."[3] As we shall discuss in our commentary (on 1:6), the Hebrew word *tzafah* does not denote mere physical gazing, but mystical meditative insight. This very early source would therefore support the position that Sefer Yetzirah was meant to be used as a meditative text.

The commentaries which treat Sefer Yetzirah as a theoretical text, read much of it in the third person: "He combined," "He formed," and the like. According to this reading, the text is referring to God's creation. In many cases, however, the grammatical form more closely resembles the imperative.[4] The author is telling the reader to "combine" and "form" as if he was actually giving instructions. In many other cases, the text is unambiguously instructive, as in such passages as, "if your heart runs, return to the place," and, "understand with wisdom, and be wise with understanding." Rather than have the text oscillate between the third person and the imperative, it would certainly be more logical to read it all in the imperative. The Sefer Yetzirah thus becomes an instruction manual for a very special type of meditation. Out of deference to the majority of commentaries we have refrained from translating it in the imperative, but the implications of such a reading are discussed in the commentary.

What we therefore have in Sefer Yetzirah appears to be an instructional manual, describing certain meditative exercises. There is some evidence that these exercises were meant to strengthen the initiate's concentration, and were particularly helpful in the development of telekinetic and telepathic powers. It was with these powers that one would then be able to perform feats that outwardly appeared to be magical. This is supported by the Talmudical references, which appear to compare the use of Sefer Yetzirah to a kind of white magic.[5] An important 13th century commentator writes that students of Sefer Yetzirah were given a manuscript of the book Raziel, a magical text containing seals, magical figures, divine names and incantations.[6]

The Text

The Sefer Yetzirah is a very small and concise book. In its Short Version, it is only some 1300 words long, while the Long Version contains approximately 2500 words. The Gra Version used in this translation contains around 1800 words. So short is the text, that one of the earliest fragments appears to have the entire book written on a single page.[7] There is speculation that the original source may have contained as few as 240 words.[8]

The present text contains six chapters, and in some editions, these are said to parallel the six orders of the Mishnah.[9] Some ancient sources, however, state that the book contains five chapters, and it seems likely that the present fifth and sixth chapters were combined as one in these texts.[10] The earliest commentator, Saadia Gaon, in a somewhat different version, divides the book into eight chapters.[11]

The text is presented dogmatically, without substantiation or explanation. In the first chapter in particular, it is solemn and sonorous, reading like blank verse poetry. Very few Biblical passages are quoted, and with the exception of Abraham, no name or authority is mentioned.

The book seems to be divided into four basic parts. The first chapter introduces the Sefirot, speaking of them at length. After this, however, there is no mention whatsoever regarding the Sefirot in subsequent chapters. This had led to some speculation that the Sefer Yetzirah might actually be a combination of two (or more) earlier texts.

The second chapter consists of a general discussion about the letters of the alphabet. It clearly appears to be introducing their use in a meditative context. Also introduced in this chapter are the five phonetic families and the 231 Gates. Again, neither the phonetic families nor the Gates are ever again mentioned in the text.

Chapters three to five discuss the three divisions of the letters, "mothers, doubles, and elementals." These are related to the "universe, soul and year," presenting a fairly detailed astrological system. In these chapters, the entire thrust of the book is changed, and they contain virtually no hint whatsoever of its meditative aspects. This, however, can be explained by a principle found in many later Kabbalistic texts. In order to focus spiritual and mental powers, one must take into account the time and astrological environment.[12]

The sixth chapter again does not appear to have a clear connection to the earlier parts of the book, although in the Long Version, it is presented almost as a commentary. Here, for the first time, are introduced the concepts of the "axis, cycle and heart," ideas which are not discussed any place else in Hebraic or Kabbalistic literature, with the exception of the Bahir.[13] Of all the chapters, this one seems the most obscure, and it is difficult to decide if its emphasis is theoretical or meditative.

This chapter concludes with a stanza linking the Sefer Yetzirah to Abraham. It is this quote that serves as a source to the tradition that the book was authored by the Patriarch.

Authorship

The earliest source to which Sefer Yetzirah is attributed is the Patriarch Abraham. As early as the 10th century, Saadia Gaon writes that, "the ancients say that Abraham wrote it."[14] This opinion is supported by almost all of the early commentators.[15] Such ancient Kabbalistic texts as the Zohar and Raziel also attribute Sefer Yetzirah to Abraham.[16] A number of very old manuscripts of Sefer Yetzirah likewise begin with a colophon calling it "the Letters of Abraham our Father, which is called Sefer Yetzirah."[17]

This does not mean, however, that the entire book as we have it now was written by Abraham. As Saadia Gaon explains, the principles expounded in Sefer Yetzirah were first taught by Abraham, but they were not actually assembled in book form until much later.[18] Another authority notes that it could not have actually been written by Abraham, since if it had, it should have been incorporated into the Bible, or at least be mentioned in scripture.[19] Similarly, when the Zohar speaks of books antedating the Torah, it does not include the Sefer Yetzirah among them.[20]

The attribution of Abraham is supported by the final stanza of Sefer Yetzirah: "When Abraham... looked and probed... he was successful in creation..." This passage clearly suggests that Abraham actually made use of the methods found in this text.

In many editions of Sefer Yetzirah, scriptural evidence is provided by the verse, "Abraham went as God had told him, and Abraham took... the souls that they had made in Haran" (Genesis 12:5). According to some commentaries, this indicates that Abraham actually used the powers of Sefer Yetzirah to create people.[21] This would be the earliest example of the use of Sefer Yetzirah to create a Golem. According to this, Abraham would have learned how to use the mysteries of Sefer Yetzirah before God told him to leave Haran.[22]

Other authorities, however, say that "making souls" refers to converting them to belief in the one true God, and this is also supported by the Zohar.[23] Some commentaries attempt to reconcile this with the text of Sefer Yetzirah, explaining that with the miracles wrought through the Sefer Yetzirah, Abraham was able to convince people of the power of God, and thus convert them to true belief.[24]

The scripture states, "the souls that *they* made," in the plural. This would indicate that Abraham was not alone in his use of Sefer Yetzirah, but had a companion. A Midrash states that if Abraham would have engaged in the secrets of creation by himself, he would have gone too far in emulating his Creator, and he therefore worked together with Shem, son of Noah.[25] Ancient sources identify Shem with Malchizedek, who blessed Abraham and taught him many of the earlier traditions.[26]

The most important mysteries of Sefer Yetzirah involve the inner significance of the letters of the Hebrew alphabet. Here too, we find that Abraham was a master of these mysteries. A Midrash thus states that "the letters were given to none other than Abraham."[27] As we shall see in the commentary (on 1:3), the arrangement of the animals when Abraham made his covenant with God, also appears to be based on the mysteries of Sefer Yetzirah.

Further support linking Abraham to the Sefer Yetzirah is found in the Talmudic teaching that "Abraham had a great astrology in his heart, and all the kings of the east and west arose early at his door."[28] Sefer Yetzirah is one of the primary ancient astrological texts, and it is possible that it incorporates Abraham's astrological teachings. The fact that this astrology was said to be "in his heart" might also indicate that it involved various meditative techniques, as was indeed the case with ancient astrology, and is also suggested by Sefer Yetzirah. There is evidence that these mysteries were also taught to Abraham by Shem, along with the mystery of the calendar *(Sod HaIbbur)*.[29] When God revealed himself to Abraham one of the first things that He taught him was not to be overdependent on astrological predictions.[30]

Abraham was also fully aware of the magical and idolatrous uses that could be developed from these mysteries. The Talmud thus says that Abraham had a tract dealing with idolatry that consisted of 400 chapters.[31] There is also a Talmudic teaching that Abraham taught

the mysteries involving "unclean names" to the children of his concubines.[32] This is based on the verse, "to the sons of the concubines
that Abraham had, Abraham gave gifts, and he sent them away... to
the lands of the east" (Genesis 25:6). These gifts consisted of occult
mysteries, which then spread in eastern Asia.

The attribution of the mysteries of Sefer Yetzirah to Abraham
would place its origin in the 18th century before the common era.
This is not very surprising, since such mystical texts as the Vedic
scriptures date from this period, and there is every reason to believe
that the mystical tradition was further advanced in the Middle East
than it was in India at the time. Since Abraham was the greatest mystic and astrologer of his age, it is natural to assume that he was familiar with all the mysteries of ancient Egypt and Mesopotamia. Abraham was born in Mesopotamia, and he also lived in Egypt.

The next place where we find the use of Sefer Yetzirah is in a
tradition regarding the older sons of Jacob, which states that they
used it to create animals and maid servants.[33] When the scripture
states that "Joseph brought an evil report [regarding his brothers] to
his father" (Genesis 37:2), it is referring to this. Joseph's brothers had
eaten an animal without slaughtering it properly, and Joseph did not
know that the animal had been created through the Sefer Yetzirah
and did not need such slaughter. He therefore reported that his brothers had eaten "flesh from a living animal."

The mysteries of Sefer Yetzirah were used again after the Exodus, when the Israelites were building the Tabernacle in the desert.
The Talmud states that Betzalel had been chosen to build this Tabernacle because he "knew how to permute the letters with which heaven
and earth were created."[34] Such esoteric knowledge was required,
since the Tabernacle was meant to be a microcosm, paralleling both
the universe, the spiritual domain, and the human body.[35] It was not
enough merely to construct a physical building. As it was built, the
architect had to meditate on the meaning of each part, imbuing it
with the necessary spiritual properties.

The Talmud derives this from the verse where God says, "I have
called in the name of Betzalel... and I have filled him with the spirit
of God, with wisdom, understanding, and knowledge" (Exodus
31:2-3). "Wisdom, Understanding and Knowledge" (*Chakhmah,
Binah* and *Daat*) refer to states of consciousness, which we shall discuss at length. It is through the manipulation of the letters that such
states of consciousness can be attained.

The sources are silent about the Sefer Yetzirah then until the
time of Jeremiah the prophet. Here again we find a tradition that
Jeremiah wished to make use of Sefer Yetzirah, but as in the case of
Abraham, was admonished not to attempt to do so alone. He there

fore took his son, Ben Sirah, and the two explored these mysteries together.[36] Through their efforts, they were able to create a Golem, but they did not preserve it.

There might have been more than one person with the name Ben Sirah, but the one in this tradition was clearly the son of Jeremiah. Regarding his birth, there is a fascinating tradition. Jeremiah had been accosted by homosexuals in the bathhouse, and as a result, had experienced an ejaculation in the tub. His semen remained viable, and when his daughter later used the same tub, she was impregnated by it, eventually giving birth to Ben Sirah.[37] Ben Sirah was therefore the son of both Jeremiah and the latter's daughter.

Some sources say that his name was originally Ben Zera (Son of Seed), but when this name proved embarrassing, he changed it to Ben Sirah.[38] Because of the sensitive nature of his birth, he did not call himself "son of Jeremiah." There is an allusion, however, since Sirah (סירא) and Jeremiah (ירמיהו) both have a numerical value of 271. Later authorities were to bring proof from this incident that artificial insemination does not constitute adultery or incest.[39]

These traditions are of particular interest, since there are many hints that Jeremiah taught these mysteries to a certain Yosef, son of Uziel, son of Ben Sirah.[40] There is also at least one source that states that Ben Sirah actually taught the Sefer Yetzirah to Yosef ben Uziel.[41] What is even more interesting is the fact that there are hints that this very same Yosef ben Uziel may have written a commentary on Sefer Yetzirah, or even possibly one of the earliest versions of the text itself.[42]

This is important because it would date the first version of Sefer Yetzirah to the early years of the Second Temple. This was also the time of the Great Assembly, who put some of the last books of the Bible, such as Ezekiel, into writing, and then closed the Biblical Cannon.[43] Much of the regular Hebrew prayer service was also composed by this Assembly.[44] Like these prayers, the Sefer Yetzirah was not put into writing, but was taught from memory.

The Talmudic Period

Upon entering the Talmudic period, we make a transition from tradition to history. We find actual mention of Sefer Yetzirah in the Talmud, and even though it is not absolutely certain that it is identical with our version, there is no real reason to doubt that they are one and the same. In Talmudical times, the Sefer Yetzirah began as an oral teaching, and was eventually incorporated as a book, which was used by the sages.

The first reference to such use involves Rabbi Yehoshua [ben Chananya], a leading sage of the first century. He is credited with the statement, "I can take squashes and pumpkins, and with the Sefer Yetzirah, make them into beautiful trees. These will in turn produce other beautiful trees."[45] Although the phrase, "with the Sefer Yetzirah," does not occur in printed editions of the Jerusalem Talmud, it is found in manuscripts.

This reference to Rabbi Yehoshua is highly significant. Rabbi Yehoshua was one of the five main disciples of Rabbi Yochanan ben Zakkai (47 BCE-73 CE), leader of all Jewry after the destruction of the Temple, and a renowned expert in all occult arts.[46] It was Rabbi Yehoshua who was Rabbi Yochanan's main disciple in the mysteries of the Markava (Chariot), and he later gained fame as the greatest expert of his time in the occult.[47]

This also sheds light on another important mystical personality. According to one ancient source, Rabbi Yehoshua also received the tradition from Rabbi Nehunia ben HaKanah, leader of the school that produced the Bahir. In *Sefer HaTagin*, we find that the tradition regarding the mystical significance of the crowns (*tagin*) on Hebrew letters was handed down in the following manner: "Menachem gave it over to Rabbi Nehunia ben HaKanah, Rabbi Nehunia ben HaKanah gave it over to Rabbi Elazar ben Arakh, Rabbi Elazar ben Arakh gave it over to Rabbi Yehoshua, and Rabbi Yehoshua gave it over to Rabbi Akiba."[48]

Rabbi Elazar ben Arakh is best known as the greatest disciple of Rabbi Yochanan ben Zakkai.[49] It is also known that he learned the Markava mysteries from Rabbi Yochanan.[50] From the above tradition, we also see that he learned from Rabbi Nehunia, possibly after he left Rabbi Yochanan. The Talmud reports that at this point, Rabbi Elazar went to live by the river Dismas, in the town of Emmaus.[51] Emmaus, however, is also known to be the place of Rabbi Nehunia, as well as a general seat of Kabbalistic teaching.[52] It is quite possible that Rabbi Elazar became so involved in mysticism, that, as the Talmud reports, he lost his grasp of legalistic theory.

Also significant is the fact that Rabbi Nehunia is said to have received the tradition from Menachem. It is known that Rabbi Nehunia was the leading mystic of the first century, as well as a colleague of Rabbi Yochanan ben Zakkai.[53] There are, however, no records as to whom his masters were. From the *Sefer HaTagin* we learn that Rabbi Nehunia learned at least some of the mysteries from Menachem, who served as vice president of the Sanhedrin (Supreme Court) under Hillel. It was when Menachem resigned his post that Shammai was appointed in his stead.[54]

Most authorities identify this individual with Menachem the Essene, discussed by Josephus.[55] Menachem had once seen Herod as a child, and had prophesied that he would be king. Because of this, when Herod later ascended the throne, he honored Menachem as well as the other Essenes. Due to his relationship with Herod, Menachem could no longer maintain his position in the Sanhedrin.

If we accept the above tradition, Nehunia ben HaKanah might have received at least some of his mystic knowledge from Menachem the Essene. This would indicate that the Essenes were conversant in the mystical arts, and that they taught them to at least some of the Talmudic masters. Josephus states that the Essenes made use of the names of angels, and were able to fortell the future, using various purifications and methods of the prophets.[56] Even more significant, Josephus also likens the Essenes to the Pythagoreans.[57] Since the Sefer Yetzirah apparently contains some elements that resemble the teachings of the Pythagoreans, it may be that the text was preserved by the Essenes during the period that preceded the Talmud.

Rabbi Elazar taught the tradition regarding the crowns on letters to Rabbi Yehoshua, who in turn gave it over to Rabbi Akiba (12-132 ce). Rabbi Akiba excelled in this area, and the Talmud reports that he could derive many important teachings from these crowns.[58] He also received the Markava tradition from Rabbi Yehoshua, as well as other important occult lore.[59] There is no question that in his time, Rabbi Akiba was considered the greatest of all experts in the mystical realm.[60] Rabbi Shimeon bar Yochai, author of the Zohar, was also a disciple of Rabbi Akiba.

It is therefore not surprising that a number of sources attribute the authorship of Sefer Yetzirah to Rabbi Akiba.[61] Most of the early Talmudical texts originated with Rabbi Akiba, who transmitted them orally in a well defined form.[62] Although these books were not written down, they had been worded by Rabbi Akiba, and it was his wording that was taught orally.

At that time, there was a rule that the oral tradition be reviewed exactly, word for word, precisely as they had been given over. the rule was, "One should always reveiw the precise wording of his master."[63] Each master would therefore provide a program of study, which his disciples would memorize word for word. In the legalistic field, this was known as the "First Mishnah."[64] It is possible that Rabbi Akiba also produced an oral text of Sefer Yetzirah for his students of mystical lore to memorize. Besides this, personal notes may also have been kept.

In this respect, the Sefer Yetzirah would have been no different from the rest of the oral tradition. Although it was meant to be trans-

mitted by word of mouth, and was not actually published, personal
records and manuscripts were kept.[65] This was especially true of
important teachings that were not usually reviewed in the academies,
as well as esoteric texts.[66] Similarly, the heads of the academies would
keep written notes in order to accurately preserve the traditions.[67]

Although these notes were never published, they were carefully
preserved in the academies. Subsequent teachers often added marginal notes to these manuscripts, and such notes were even occasionally found in the Biblical scrolls which they used.[68] Since these notes
were preserved by private individuals and never distributed
publically, they were collectively known as "hidden scrolls" (*Megillat
Setarim*).[69] Not only such esoteric material as Sefer Yetzirah was
included in this category, but even such legalistic material as the
Mishnah, which was meant to be transmitted orally.

This might help explain why the Sefer Yetzirah exists in so many
versions. Unlike the Mishnah, which was eventually published in a
well defined edition, the Sefer Yetzirah never developed beyond the
state of being a "hidden scroll." Different versions may have been
taught by various teachers, and, since the text was never openly published, there was no way in which these versions could be compared
and corrected. Furthermore, many marginal notes may have been
incorporated into the text, also producing different versions. All this
may provide an explanation for the fact that there is no Hebrew classic that is found with so many versions and variants as the Sefer
Yetzirah.

It seems highly probable that the Sefer Yetzirah was already in
its present form when the Mishnah was redacted in the year 204 CE.
The Mishnah was edited by Rabbi Yehudah the Prince (135–220 CE),
usually referred to simply as "Rebbi." It is indeed possible that there
is a reference to Sefer Yetzirah in the Mishnah itself. In one of the
few places where it discusses esoteric lore, the Mishnah states, "The
mysteries of creation (*Maaseh Bereshit*) may not be expounded in the
presence of two disciples, and the mysteries of the Markava (*Maaseh
Markava*) may not be expounded even in the presence of one, unless
he is wise, understanding with his knowledge."[70]

The term *Maaseh Merkava* refers to the meditative methods used
to ascend to the higher spiritual realms.[71] Although such later philosophers as Maimonides claimed that this involved philosophical speculation, the most ancient sources clearly state that *Maaseh Markava* dealt
with the meditative methods used for spiritual ascent.[72] As such, it was
considered the most esoteric of all spiritual exercises.

According to many authorities, *Maaseh Bereshit* refers to the
mysteries of Sefer Yetzirah.[73] Since we know that *Maaseh Markava*
was of mystical nature, it would be logical to assume that the same
was true of *Maaseh Bereshit*. Furthermore, the assumption that

Maaseh Bereshit involves Sefer Yetzirah also clarifies a number of otherwise obscure Talmudical references. There is also evidence that Rebbi was familiar with the mysteries of the Markava, and it is logical to assume that he was also aware of Sefer Yetzirah.[74]

A generation later, we thus find an account of two of Rebbi's disciples clearly involved in the mysteries of Sefer Yetzirah. The Talmud relates, "Rabbi Hanina and Rabbi Hoshia would engage themselves in Sefer Yetzirah every [Friday] before the Sabbath, would create for themselves a prime[75] calf, and would eat it."[76] Another version of this account states that they engaged in *Hilkhot Yetzirah* (Rules of Creation), rather than Sefer Yetzirah.[77] The term *Hilkhot*, however, can apply to philosophical rules as well as legal ones.[78] In some of the most ancient manuscripts, Sefer Yetzirah is actually titled *Hilkhot Yetzirah*.[79]

There are many interpretations as to exactly what these two sages accomplished in creating such a calf, and why they did it. Some say that they did not actually create a physical calf, but created such a clear meditative image that the spiritual satisfaction was the same as eating.[80] Even such a Kabbalist as Abraham Abulafia (1240-1296) maintains that their creation was mystical rather than physical.[81] The Rashba (Rabbi Shlomo ben Aderet: 1235-1310) saw particular significance in the fact that they would engage in this on Friday, the day in which mammals were originally created.[82] This entire question will be discussed further in our commentary.

Evidently, Rebbi also taught these mysteries to his disciple Rav (Abba Arikhta), who in turn taught them to Rav Yehudah (220-299 CE), founder and first master of the Babylonian academy in Pumpadita. This Rav Yehudah, together with Rav Aina, were called the "elders of Pumpadita."[83] The Talmud relates that the "elders of Pumpadita were versed (*tanu*) in *Maaseh Bereshit*."[84] From the use of the word *tanu* here, it is evident that *Maaseh Bereshit* already existed in a definite form, most probably as a written book.[85] This would suggest that Sefer Yetzirah had already been put in writing.

There is also other evidence that Rav Yehudah learned the mysteries of Sefer Yetzirah from Rav. The teaching, "Betzalel knew how to permute the letters with which heaven and earth were created," is attributed to "Rav Yehudah in the name of Rav."[86] Also attributed to him is the statement that God told Abraham to "go out of your astrology."[87] This indicates that he had some evidence that Abraham was versed in astrology, a position clearly found in Sefer Yetzirah. There is also evidence that Rav Yehudah learned the mysteries of the 42 letter Name from Rav.[88]

As an initiate into the mysteries of Sefer Yetzirah, Rav Yehudah would also have a deep understanding of the mystical significance of the Hebrew language. We thus find that he emphasized the use of the

Hebrew language, even in his daily conversation.[89] Rav Yehudah also maintained that prayer should be voiced in Hebrew, and not in the Aramaic vernacular.[90]

The Talmud relates that Rav Yosef knew the mysteries of the Markava, while the "elders of Pumpadita" were versed in the mysteries of creation. Rav Yosef got the elders to teach him the mysteries of creation, but would not entrust them with the Markava mysteries in return.[91]

This indicates that the mysteries of the Markava and those of Sefer Yetzirah were taught by different schools, and that members of one school did not know the teachings of the other. The two involved different disciplines, and care was taken to keep them separate. This also answers the question as to why the Sefer Yetzirah is never mentioned in the *Hekhalot*, the classic of Markava literature.[92] The Markava literature developed in a school that might have not had access to Sefer Yetzirah, even though certain of its members were definitely versed in it. In the same context, Sefer Yetzirah is mentioned but a very few times in the Zohar, and then, not in the main text.[93]

In that period, there were some sages who eschewed these mysteries completely. Such an individual was Rabbi Elazar ben Padat, who headed the academy in Tiberius after the death of Rabbi Yochanan in the year 279 CE. When Rabbi Yochanan had offered to teach him the Markava mysteries, he deferred on the grounds that he was too young. After Rabbi Yochanan's death, when Rabbi Assi wished to impart these mysteries to him, he again deferred, saying, "If I would have been worthy, I would have learned them from Rabbi Yochanan your master."[94]

Instead, Rabbi Elazar adopted a position somewhat opposed to the esoteric schools, accepting the viewpoint of Rabbi Yosi ben Zimra. Denying that the Sefer Yetzirah could be used to actually create life, he said in the name of Rabbi Yosi, "If all the people in the world came together, they could not create a gnat and imbue it with a soul."[95] It was not that Rabbi Elazar doubted that such powers existed. Rather, he felt that they were no longer known. These powers, however, did exist in the Torah. Rabbi Elazar thus said, "The paragraphs of the Torah are not in order. If they were in [correct] order, anyone who read them would be able to [create a world,] resurrect the dead, and perform miracles."[96]

A generation later, we find two important sages actively engaged in the mysteries of Sefer Yetzirah. The first was Rava (299-353 CE), founder and first master of the Babylonian academy in Mechuza, who is credited with saying, "If the righteous desired, they could create a world."[97] His partner was Rav Zeira, who was known as the "saint of Babylon."[98] So great were Rav Zeira's meditative powers that he was able to place his feet in fire without burning them. He would test himself each month to see if this power was unabated. On one occasion, the other sages distracted him, and he failed, whereupon he was called, "The little man with the burned feet."[99]

An ancient tradition states that Rava and Rav Zeira worked together for three years, meditating on the Sefer Yetzirah. When they finally mastered it, they created a calf and slaughtered it, serving it at a feast celebrating their accomplishment. They then lost their powers and had to work for another three years to restore them.[100]

The Talmud relates that "Rava created a man" and sent him to Rav Zeira. When the latter saw that this android would not answer his questions, he realized that it was a Golem, and told it to "return to the dust."[101] The Bahir remarks that the Golem could not speak because Rava was not completely free from the taint of sin, and as long as man sins, he cannot partake of the powers of the Creator.[102] Only God can make a man who can speak. This is the first mention of the creation of a Golem in Hebraic literature, but in the middle ages, several other instances are reported.[103]

Even the expression, "Rava created a man," has mystical connotations. In the original, it is *RaBhA BaRA GaBhRA* (רבא ברא גברא), and, as an early Kabbalist notes, the second word is nothing other than the reverse of the first.[104] The third word adds a Gimmel, the third letter of the alphabet, to the word before it. This yields a phrase consisting of ten letters, with a numerical value of 612, one less than 613, the number of bones and blood vessels in the human body.[105] The man created by Rava was thus something less than human. In many ways, this expression is reminiscent of the word Abracadabra (*ABRA K'ADaBRA*–אברא כאדברא), which literally means, "I will create as I speak."[106]

During the Talmudic period, there were many sages who engaged in these mysteries.[107] With the close of this era, however, a blanket of silence was cast over all occult activities. It appears that a number of mystical books were written during the subsequent Gaonic period, but their origins are shrouded in mystery. Still, knowledge of these practices clearly existed as late as the 10th century, and Hai Gaon (939-1038) speaks of people engaged in the mystical permutation (*tzeruf*) of letters.[108]

Texts and Commentaries

It is not until the post-Talmudic period that we find actual quotations from the Sefer Yetzirah. One of the earliest such references is in a

Table 1. Historical opinions as to when *Sefer Yetzirah* was written.

Before 100 BCE	Lazarus Goldsmidt, *Das Buch der Schöpfung*, Frankfurt, 1894, p. 12. Israel Weinstock, *Temirin I*, Jerusalem, 1972, p. 21. (for earliest parts).
100 BCE-100 CE	Adolphe Franck, *Die Kabbalah*, Leipzig, 1844, p. 65. Israel Weinstock, *loc.cit.* (for second layer).
1-100 CE	Adolph Jellinek, Introduction to *Die Kabbalah*, pp.6-9. Yohann Friedrich von Meyer, *Das Buch Yezirah*, Leipzig, 1839, p. v. Heinrich Graetz, *Gnosticismus*, Krotoschin, 1846, pp. 102-103.
100-200 CE	Isadore Kalish, *Sefer Yetzirah*, New York, 1877, p. 3. David Castelli, *Commenti di Donolo*, Firenze, 1880, p. 14. Abraham Epstein, *Beitrage zur Judischen Alterthumskunde*, Vienna, 1887, 1:46 49. *Idem., Rescherche sur le Sefer Yecira, Revue des Edut es Juives* 29:75-76 (1894). Gershom Scholem, *Ursprung und Anfänge*, Berlin, 1962, pp. 21, 25 (note 45). Avraham Meir Habermann, *Sinai* 10:141 (1947).
200-400 CE	Louis Ginzberg, *Jewish Encylopedia*, New York, 1904, 12:605. Gershom Scholem, *Encyclopedia Judaica*, Berlin, 1932, 9:109.
400-600 CE	Leo Baeck, *Aus drei Jahrtausende*, Berlin, 1938, p. 382.
600-800 CE	Hermann L. Strack, *Einleitung in Talmud und Midras*, Munich, 1921, p. 221. Sh. Morg, *Sheva Kefalot, BGD KRPT, Sefer Tur Sinai*, Jerusalem, 1960, pp. 233-236. Nehemia Aloni, *Historische Grammatik*, Hali, 1922, p. 92. *Idem., Temirim I*, p. 96.

Table 1. Historical opinions as to when *Sefer Yetzirah* was written (continued).

800-900 CE	Leopold Zunz, *Die Gottensdienlichen Vorträge der Juden*, Berlin, 1892, p. 175. Mortiz Steinschneider, *Judische Literatur*, p. 401. Heinrich Graetz, *Geschechte der Juden* (1875) 5:297. Ph. Bloch, *Mystik und Kabbalah*, Trier, 1896, p. 244. Israel Weinstock, *loc cit.* (for latest additions).

poem written by Rabbi Elazar Kalir, who lived in the fifth or sixth century, and perhaps even earlier. He writes:[109]

Then, from eternity, with Ten Sayings You gouged
With Scribe, script and scroll–Ten,
You finished them in six directions,
    Ten words.

There are also allusions to the teachings of Sefer Yetzirah in *Bereita deShmuel HaKatan*, which, according to internal evidence, was written in or around 776 CE.[110] There is also a mention of the "Ten Sefirot of Nothingness" in a late Midrash, which could have been redacted around this time.[111]

The absence of any unambiguous references to Sefer Yetzirah in earlier literature has led some historians to speculate whether or not the Talmudic citations are referring to our text. Some maintain that our version was written much later than the Talmud. A list of such estimates in given in Table 1.

The most careful analysis, however, reveals a number of strata in the text. The earliest parts of the book appear very ancient, possibly antedating the Talmudic era.[112] A considerable amount of the text appears to have been added later on, possibly as a glossary or commentary. As some of the earliest commentators on Sefer Yetzirah note, commentaries and marginal notes were occasionally incorporated into the text.[113] In the 10th century, Rabbi Yaakov ben Nissim writes, "People write Hebrew comments on the book, and other foolish people come later and comment on the commentary. Between them, truth is lost."[114] This is not surprising, since in Talmudic times, such marginal notes were even common in Biblical scrolls, although enough was known of their text, that the comments were not incorporated into it.

Several strata are evident in Sefer Yetzirah, some apparently added in the late Talmudic period, and others in the Gaonic era.

Thus, critical estimates as to its age would depend on which parts were studied.

The earliest commentaries on Sefer Yetzirah were written in the 10th century. The first was written in 931 by Saadia Gaon, one of the most important religious leaders and philosophers of his time. The second, *Chakamoni*, was written by Rabbi Shabbatai Donnelo in 946, while the third was written by Donash ibn Tamim a decade later.[115] All of these are philosophical, rather than mystical, in content.

Most significant is the fact that each of these commentaries was written on a different version of Sefer Yetzirah. The commentary by Donash was written on what is now generally referred to as the Short Version. With minor variations, it was this version that was printed in 1562 in the Mantua edition, and it is dominant in all subsequent printed editions.

The commentary of Shabbatiai Donnelo was written on what is now referred to as the Long Version. Many printed editions included this Long Version as a sort of appendix. A complete manuscript, dating from the 10th century, also exists of this version. Although there are important differences in the assignment of values to letters and planets, the Long Version is very much like the Short Version with an additional commentary. This is particularly evident in the sixth chapter, where we find a commentary on the first stanza of the book. Also significant are some recaps (4:14, 5:20), which are actually revisions of the previous text. The existence of both a Short and Long Version was noted as early as the 13th century by Abraham Abulafia.[116]

The third version is that of Saadia Gaon, which is also found in some early Geniza fragments. This is very much like the Long Version, except that the stanzas are in completely different order. This variant, usually called the Saadia Version, has been virtually ignored by the Kabbalists, even though it was apparently used by Rabbi Yehudah HaLevi in his Kuzari.

As early as the 10th century, Saadia Gaon remarked about the many variants of Sefer Yetzirah, saying, "It is not a common book, and many people have been careless in changing or transposing the text."[117] A century later, Rabbi Yehudah Barceloni likewise notes that, "there are many versions, some very confused."[118] In 1562, the printers of the first Mantua edition remarked how they had to sift through many manuscripts to find a dependable text.

If all the variants found in manuscripts are counted, there are literally dozens of different variants in the text of Sefer Yetzirah. No other Judaic text exists in so many versions. Some of these might have come from different schools, who, because these teachings were secret, did not communicate with each other. Different marginal notes and commentaries also apparently became incorporated into the text, producing different variants. Furthermore, if the text was preserved orally for a long time, variants in its ordering may have also developed.

Besides this, there is another possibility, suggested by the fact that, in essence, the Kabbalists rejected all the above mentioned versions. It is known that during the Gaonic period (6th-10th centuries), the Kabbalists restricted their teachings to very small secret societies. Great stress was placed on maintaining secrecy so that their teachings should not fall into improper hands. Since Sefer Yetzirah is such a small book, it presented the greatest danger. The leaders of these schools may have deliberately released spurious versions, so as to confuse those who would be tempted to penetrate their mysteries. With several versions in circulation, the uninitiated would not know which to choose.

It was the Kabbalists themselves who preserved the correct text, initially concealing it from outsiders. Around 1550, Rabbi Moshe Cordevero, leader of the Safed school and the greatest Kabbalist of the day, sifted through the ten best manuscripts available, choosing the one most closely fitting the tradition of the Kabbalists.[119] A generation later, the text was further refined by the Ari (Rabbi Yitzchak Luria), one of the greatest Kabbalists of all time. This text, known as the Ari Version, was published a number of times, usually as part of some other collection. It resembles the Short Version in many ways, but there are some very significant differences in assignment. In general, the Ari Version is the only one which is in agreement with the Zohar.

A number of variations were found even in this version, and a final edited text was finally produced by the Gra (Rabbi Eliahu, Gaon of Vilna) in the 18th century.[120] This is known as the Gra-Ari Version, or simply, as the Gra Version.

Thus, there are four important versions of Sefer Yetzirah. They are:

1) The Short Version
2) The Long Version
3) The Saadia Version
4) The Gra Version.

Since the Gra Version was considered the most authentic by the Kabbalists, this is the one that we have chosen for the initial translation and commentary. The other three versions are presented in Appendix I.

Over eighty commentaries have been written on Sefer Yetzirah. Some, especially the earliest, were primarily philosophical. With the emergence of Kabbalah as a public teaching, a number of Kabbalistic and mystical commentaries were also written. When the Bahir and the Zohar were published, commentators worked to fit the Sefer Yetzirah into the system of these texts. The same was true of the teachings of the Ari, which dominates the later commentaries. A history of the commentaries on Sefer Yetzirah reads very much like a history of the Kabbalah in general. A list of the major commentaries is found in the Bibliography.

Our commentary on Sefer Yetzirah takes into account most of these, as well as our other research into the methods of the Kabbalists, much of which has been published in my *Meditation and Kabbalah*. While the various theoretical approaches are important, I have focused primarily on the mystical techniques outlined in Sefer Yetzirah, as well as the meditative methods that they imply.

3 Kislev, 5737

Sefer
Yetzirah

CHAPTER ONE

1 : 1 בשלשים ושתים נתיבות פליאות חכמה
חקק יה יהוה צבאות אלהי ישראל אלהים
חיים ומלך עולם אל שדי רחום וחנון רם ונשא שוכן
עד וקדוש שמו מרום וקדוש הוא וברא את עולמו
בשלשה ספרים בספר וספר וספור:

> *With 32 mystical paths of Wisdom*
> > *engraved Yah*
> > > *the Lord of Hosts*
> > > *the God of Israel*
> > *the living God*
> > > *King of the universe*
> > *El Shaddai*
> > > *Merciful and Gracious*
> > > *High and Exalted*
> > > *Dwelling in eternity*
> > > *Whose name is Holy —*
> > > > *He is lofty and holy —*
> *And He created His universe*
> > *with three books (Sepharim),*
> > > *with text (Sepher)*
> > > *with number (Sephar)*
> > > *and with communication (Sippur).*

With 32

As the next stanza will explain, these 32 paths are manifest as the 10 digits and the 22 letters of the Hebrew alphabet. The 10 digits are also manifest in the Ten Sefirot, which are the most basic concepts of existence.

The letters and digits are the basis of the most basic ingredients of creation, quality and quantity.[1] The qualities of any given thing can be described by words formed out of the letters, while all of its associated quantities can be expressed by numbers.

Numbers, however, cannot be defined until there exists some element of plurality in creation. The Creator Himself is absolutely

Table 2. The 32 Paths in Genesis I.

1.	In the beginning God created	Keter	Sefirah 1
2.	The spirit of God hovered	Heh	Elemental 1
3.	God said, let there be light	Chakhmah	Sefirah 2
4.	God saw the light that it was good	Bet	Double 1
5.	God divided between the light and darkness	Vav	Elemental 2
6.	God called the light day	Zayin	Elemental 3
7.	God said, let there be a firmament	Binah	Sefirah 3
8.	God made the firmament	Alef	Mother 1
9.	God called the firmament heaven	Chet	Elemental 4
10.	God said, let the waters be gathered	Chesed	Sefirah 4
11.	God called the dry land earth	Tet	Elemental 5
12.	God saw that it was good	Gimel	Double 2
13.	God said, let the earth be vegetated	Gevurah	Sefirah 5
14.	God saw that it was good	Dalet	Double 3
15.	God said, let there be luminaries	Tiferet	Sefirah 6
16.	God made two luminaries	Mem	Mother 2
17.	God placed them in the firmament	Yud	Elemental 6
18.	God saw that it was good	Kaf	Double 4
19.	God said, let the waters swarm	Netzach	Sefirah 7
20.	God created great whales	Lamed	Elemental 7
21.	God saw that it was good	Peh	Double 5
22.	God blessed them, be fruitful and multiply	Nun	Elemental 8
23.	God said, let the earth bring forth animals	Hod	Sefirah 8
24.	God made the beasts of the field	Shin	Mother 3
25.	God saw that it was good	Resh	Double 6
26.	God said, let us make man	Yesod	Sefirah 9
27.	God created man	Samekh	Elemental 9

Table 2. The 32 Paths in Genesis I (continued).

28.	In the form of God He created him	Eyin	Elemental 10
29.	God blessed them	Tzadi	Elemental 11
30.	God said, be fruitful and multiply	Malkhut	Sefirah 10
31.	God said, behold I have given you	Kuf	Elemental 12
32.	God saw all that He had made	Tav	Double 7

simple, containing no plurality whatsoever. He is the most absolute unity imaginable. Therefore, plurality only came into existence with the advent of creation. Only then could numbers be defined.

The first elements of plurality in creation involved the Ten Sefirot. Hence, it was the Sefirot that defined the numbers, and therefore, the concept of quantity in general.

Most of Sefer Yetzirah will deal with these 32 paths, as they are manifest in the letters and numbers. The 32 paths, themselves, however, will not be mentioned again. The early Kabbalists define these 32 paths as different states of consciousness. A list of these is given in Appendix II.

According to the Kabbalists, these 32 paths are alluded to in the Torah by the 32 times that God's name Elohim appears in the account of creation in the first chapter of Genesis.[2] In this account, the expression "God said" appears ten times, and these are the Ten Sayings with which the world was created.[3] These Ten Sayings parallel the Ten Sefirot.[4] The first saying is said to be the verse, "In the beginning God created the Heaven and the Earth" (Genesis 1:1). Even though "God said" does not appear here, it is implied and understood.[5]

The other 22 times that God's name appears in this account then parallel the 22 letters of the alphabet. The three times in which the expression "God made" appears parallel the three Mothers. The seven repetitions of "God saw" parallel the seven Doubles. The remaining twelve names parallel the twelve Elementals. See Table 2.

In general, none of the names of God refer to the Creator Himself. The Creator is only referred to as Ain Sof, which means the Infinite Being, or simply, the Infinite. The names used in scripture and elsewhere merely refer to the various ways through which God manifests Himself in creation.

The name Elohim, which is used throughout the first chapter of Genesis, refers to the manifestation of delineation and definition. Each of the 32 paths therefore served to delineate and define a partic-

Table 3. The Hebrew alphabet.

Final	Form	Represented by	Hebrew name	Sounded as	Signification of the names	Numerical value
	א	Silent	אָלֶף	A'-lĕph	Ox	1
	ב	b, bh	בֵּית	Bēth	House	2
	ג	g, gh	גִּימֶל	Gī-măl	Camel	3
	ד	d, dh	דָּלֶת	Dâ'-lēth	Door	4
	ה	h	הֵא	Hē	Window	5
	ו	v	וָו	Vâv	Hook	6
	ז	z	זַיִן	Zā'yĭn	Weapon	7
	ח	ch	חֵית	Chēth	Fence	8
	ט	t	טֵית	Tēth	Snake	9
	י	y (i)	יוֹד	Yōdh	Hand	10
ך	כ	k, kh	כַּף	Kāph	The hand bent	20
	ל	l	לָמֶד	Lâ'-mĕdh	Ox-goad	30
ם	מ	m	מֵם	Mēm	Water	40
ן	נ	n	נוּן	Nūn	Fish	50
	ס	s	סָמֶךְ	Sâ'-mĕkh	Prop	60
	ע	Silent	עַיִן	Ā-yĭn	Eye	70
ף	פ	p, ph	פֵּא	Pē	Month	80
ץ	צ	ts	צָדִי	Tsâ-dhē'	Fish-hook	90
	ק	k (q)	קוֹף	Qōph	Back of the head	100
	ר	r	רֵישׁ	Rēsh	Head	200
	שׁ	sh, s	שִׁין	Shīn	Tooth	300
	ת	t, th	תָּו	Tâv	Cross	400

ular aspect of creation. Man is seen as a microcosm, with each thing in his body paralleling something in the forces of creation. Thus, for example, the six days of creation have parallels in man's two arms, two legs, torso and sexual organ. This is the significance of the Torah's statement that God formed man "in the image of God" (Genesis 1:27). Note that the word for "God" here is Elohim. This is because man's form parallels the structure of the delineating forces that define creation.

The Kabbalists note that the 32 paths of Wisdom have their parallel in the human nervous system.[6] Thirty-one of these paths then parallel the 31 nerves that emanate from the spinal cord. The thirty-second and highest path corresponds to the entire complex of cranial nerves, which are twelve in number.

The nervous system serves a double purpose. First, it transmits messages from the brain to all parts of the body, allowing the mind to control the limbs and organs. Secondly, the nervous system transmits information from the various senses to the brain. Four of the senses, sight, hearing, taste and smell, come directly through the cranial nerves, which are entirely in the brain. The impulses that come from the lower 31 nerves deal primarily with the sense of touch and feeling.

Like the nerves, each of the 32 paths is a two way street. First it is the channel through which the Mind exerts control over creation. Secondly, however, it is also the path through which man can reach the Mind. If an individual wishes to attain a mystical experience and approach the Mind, he must travel along the 32 paths.

In Hebrew, the number 32 is written Lamed Bet (לב). This spells Lev, the Hebrew word for heart.[7] It is in the heart that the action of the Mind is manifest in the body. As soon as the influence of the mind ceases, the heart ceases to function, this being the definition of death.

The heart also provides lifeforce to the brain and nervous system. When the heart stops pumping, the nervous system can no longer function, and the mind no longer exerts influence on the body. The heart therefore serves as a causal link between mind and body.[8]

It is for this reason that Sefer Yetzirah calls the heart "the king over the soul" (6:3). It also describes the mystical experience as a "running of the heart" (1:8).

The Torah is seen as the heart of creation. The first letter of the Torah is the Bet (ב) of *Bereshit* (בראשית)—"In the beginning." The last letter of the Torah is the Lamed (ל) of *Yisrael* (ישראל)—"Israel." Together, these two letters also spell out Lev (לב), meaning heart.[9] The 32 paths are contained in the Torah, which is the means through which the Mind is revealed. It is also the link between the Mind and the physical universe. The Torah is therefore expounded in 32 different ways, as taught by Rabbi Yosi of Galili.

The two letters Lamed (ל) and Bet (ב) also share another unique distinction. As a prefix, Lamed means "to," and Bet means "in." The three letters of the Tetragrammaton, Yud (י), Heh (ה), and Vav (ו), can also serve as suffixes for personal pronouns. The suffix Yud means "me," Heh means "her," and Vav means "him."

In the entire alphabet, there are only two letters to which these
suffixes can be joined, and these are Lamed and Bet. These then spell
out the words:

Li	לי	to me	*Bi*	בי	in me
Lah	לה	to her	*Bah*	בה	in her
Lo	לו	to him	*Bo*	בו	in him

The two letters, Lamed and Bet, are the only ones in the entire alphabet which combine with the letters of the divine name in this
manner.[10]

The number 32 is the fifth power of two (2^5). As the Sefer
Yetzirah explains (1:5), the Ten Sefirot define a five dimensional
space. The 32 paths correspond to the number of apexes on a five
dimensional hypercube.[11]

This is not as difficult as it might seem. A line, which has one
dimension, has two (2^1) apexes or ends. A square, having two dimensions, has four (2^2) apexes or corners. A cube, which has three dimensions, has eight (2^3) corners. We thus see that with the addition of
each dimension, the number of apexes is doubled. A four dimensional hypercube has 16 or 2^4 apexes, while a five dimensional
hypercube has 32 or 2^5 apexes.

Paths

The Hebrew word for "paths" here is *Netivot* (נתיבות), a word that
occurs only rarely in scripture. Much more common is the word
Derekh (דרך). As the Zohar states, however, there is an important difference between these two words. A *Derekh* is a public road, a route
used by all people. A *Nativ*, on the other hand, is a personal route, a
path blazed by the individual for his personal use.[12] It is a hidden
path, without markers or signposts, which one must discover on his
own, and tread by means of his own devices.

The 32 paths of Wisdom are therefore called Netivot. They are
private paths, which must be blazed by each individual. There is no
open highway to the mysteries—each individual must discover his
own path.

The numerical value of *Nativ* (נתיב) is 462. This is twice the number of the 231 Gates discussed below (2:4). These gates are a means
through which one ascends and descends along the 32 paths.

Mystical

These paths are said to be mystical, *Peliyot* (פליאות) in Hebrew. This comes from the root *Pala* (פלא), which has the connotation of being hidden and separated from the world at large.[13] Not only are these paths individual, but they are hidden, concealed and transcendental.

This is very closely related to the word *Peleh* (פלא), meaning a miracle. A miracle is *separated* and independent from the laws of the physical world. It is also influenced by *hidden* forces. As such, it is a link with the mystical and transcendental plane. The same is true of the paths of Wisdom.

According to the Zohar, the word *Peleh* specifically relates to the paths of Wisdom.[14] The type of miracle denoted by the word *Peleh* is specifically one that is accomplished through the manipulation of these paths. The methods of manipulating these paths is one of the important teachings of Sefer Yetzirah.

The Sefer Yetzirah later calls the three Mothers, "a great mystical (*muPhLA*) secret" (3:2). The first of the three Mothers is Aleph (א). When spelled out, Aleph (אלף) has the same letters as Peleh (פלא).[15]

According to the Kabbalists, the letter Aleph denotes Keter (Crown), the highest of the Sefirot.[16] It is with regard to Keter that Ben Sirah said, "In what is mysterious (*muPhLA*) for you, do not seek."[17]

The Kabbalists call Keter the level of Nothingness (*Ayin*).[18] It is on this level that the laws of nature cease to exist, and can therefore be altered.

As the book *Raziel* points out, the three letters of *Peleh* (פלא) represent increasingly hidden values.[19] According to the phonetic families defined by Sefer Yetzirah (2:3), the first letter, Peh (פ), is pronounced with the lips, the second letter, Lamed (ל), with the middle of the tongue, and the final Alef (א), with the throat. Thus, the first letter is pronounced with the outermost revealed part of the mouth, while the last is voiced with the innermost concealed part. The word *Peleh* thus denotes the transition from the revealed to the concealed.

Wisdom

These 32 paths are said to be paths of Wisdom (*Chakhmah*). In a Kabbalistic sense, Wisdom is seen as pure, undifferentiated Mind.[20] It is pure thought, which has not yet been broken up into differentiated ideas. Wisdom is the level above all division, where everything is a simple unity.

It is in recognition of this that the Talmud states, "Who is wise (*Chakham*)? He who learns from every man."[21] It is on the level of Wisdom that all men are one. Hence, if one is on this level, he must learn from every human being, and indeed, from all creation. According to the Baal Shem Tov, this means that a person on the level of Wisdom must even learn from Evil.[22] It is only on levels below Wisdom that people are separated into different individuals. Only on lower levels does the division between good and evil exist.

The Talmud likewise states, "Who is wise? He who perceives the future."[23] This is because Wisdom is the pure mind force that transcends time. On the level of Wisdom, past, present and future have not yet been separated. Hence, on this level, one can see the future just like the past and present.

The antithesis of Wisdom is Understanding. The Hebrew word for Understanding is *Binah* (בינה), which comes from the root *Beyn* (בין), meaning "between."[24]

Understanding is the level immediately below Wisdom. It is on the level of Understanding that ideas exist separately, where they can be scrutinized and comprehended. While Wisdom is pure undifferentiated Mind, Understanding is the level where division exists, and where things are delineated and defined as separated objects.

On the level of Wisdom, all men are included in a single world soul. Understanding is the level of *Neshamah*, where the soul of each individual assumes a distinct identity, and each one is seen as a separate entity.

The divine name associated with Understanding is Elohim.[25] This is a plural word, since Understanding implies a plurality of forces. It is the name Elohim that is used throughout the entire first chapter of Genesis in describing the act of creation. The 32 times that this name occurs correspond to the 32 paths of Wisdom.

This resolves an important difficulty. If Wisdom is a simple undifferentiated Mind, how can it be manifest as 32 distinct paths? But actually, Wisdom is undifferentiated, and it is only through the power of Understanding that it is divided into separated paths. These paths are therefore designated by the name Elohim, the name associated with Understanding.

An example would be water flowing through a system of pipes. Water itself is an undifferentiated fluid, having no essential (macroscopic) structure. Structure is only imposed on it when it flows through the system of pipes. In the analogy, Wisdom is the water, while Understanding represents the pipes that channel it.

The 32 paths are expressed as the letters and numbers. Since these represent division, they are manifestations of Understanding.[26] Hence, Wisdom represents nonverbal thought, while Understanding is its verbalization.

In this respect, Wisdom and Understanding are seen as being male and female respectively. In the Kabbalah, Wisdom is seen as the Father (Abba), while Understanding is the Mother (Immah). The male represents unchanneled creative force. This can only be brought into fruition when delineated, enclosed and channeled by the female womb. It is for this reason that the Sefer Yetzirah (1:2) calls the primary letters "Mothers."

This also resolves another difficulty. Earlier, we said that the 32 paths represent the heart, since the Hebrew word for heart, *Lev*, actually spells out the number 32. The heart, however, is normally associated with Understanding, while these paths are said to pertain to Wisdom.[27] But the paths merely channel Wisdom, while the substance of the paths themselves is Understanding.[28]

Engraved

The text states that the Creator used these 32 paths to "engrave" so as to create His universe.

The Hebrew word here is *Chakak* (חקק). This usually has the connotation of removing material, as in the verse, "Engrave *(chakak)* yourself a dwelling in a rock" (Isaiah 22:16). Derived from this root are the words *Chok* (חוק) and *Chukah* (חוקה), meaning "rule" and "decree," since rules and laws serve to remove some of the individual's freedom of action.[29] Thus, the word *Chakak* is closely related to *Ma-chak* (מחק), meaning "to erase," as well as to the root *La-kach* (לקח), meaning to "remove" or "take."[30]

The word *Chakak* is very closely related to the concept of writing.[31] The main difference between engraving *(chakak)* and writing is that when one writes, one adds material such as ink to the writing surface, while when one engraves, one removes material. When the Bible uses the work *Chakak* to designate writing, it is referring to such systems as cuneiform, where the text was written by removing wedges of clay from a tablet.

To understand why the author uses the term "engraved" here, we must understand the idea of creation. Before a universe could be created, empty space had to exist in which it could be made. But initially, only God existed, and all existence was filled with the Divine

Essence, the Light of the Infinite (*Or Ain Sof*). It was out of this undifferentiated Essence that a Vacated Space had to be engraved. The process, known to the Kabbalists as the *Tzimtzum* (Constriction), is clearly described in the Zohar:[32]

> In the beginning of the King's authority
> The Lamp of Darkness
> Engraved a hollow in the Supernal Luminescence. . .

The hollow engraved in the Supernal Luminescence was the Vacated Space, in which all creation subsequently occured.

The undifferentiated Light of the Infinite which existed before the Constriction is on the level of Wisdom, which is pure undelineated Mind. The power of constriction is that of Understanding, this being what the Zohar calls the "Lamp of Darkness." It is negative light, or negative existence, which can engrave a hollow in the Divine Essence.

This Constriction or hollowing of the Divine Essence did not occur in physical space, but rather, in conceptual space. It is "hollow" insofar as it contains the possibility for information, but not actual information. As such, it is the "Chaos and Void" (*Tohu* and *Bohu*) mentioned in the account of creation, where the Scripture states, "the earth was chaos and void" (Genesis 1:2). Chaos is a state where information can exist, but where it does not exist.[33]

The hollow was made through the 32 paths, since letters and digits are the basic bits of information. While random letters and numbers do not actually convey information, as long as they exist, it is also possible for information to exist. The Vacated Space is therefore the state where it is possible for information to exist, but where this possibility has not yet been realized.

These letters were subsequently combined into words, forming the Ten Sayings of creation. Each of these sayings brought information into the Vacated Space, through which creation could take place there.

The order was therefore first "engraving," and then "creation." The Sefer Yetzirah therefore states that the Creator "engraved. . . and created His universe."

Engraved Yah

Many of the Kabbalistic commentaries translate this as "He engraved Yah. . . ." In Hebrew, the word "he" is often not written out, but understood from the verbal form. The "He" here refers to the Infinite Being (*Ain Sof*) who is above all the divine Names.[34]

According to this, the Sefer Yetzirah is saying that the Infinite Being began creation by engraving the divine Names through the 32 paths of Wisdom. The Names are written with letters, and they could only come into being after the letters had been created.

It is in the same vein that some of the early Kabbalists interpret the first verse in Genesis to read, "In the beginning He created Elohim, along with the heaven and the earth."[35] The first thing that the Infinite Being created was the name Elohim, which is associated with the Constriction.

The divine Names also parallel the Sefirot. Once the Vacated Space had been engraved, the Sefirot could be created inside it. The "engraving" of this Space was therefore intimately related to these Names.

This can also be read in the imperative, "With 32 mystical paths of Wisdom, engrave Yah... and create His world." The term "engrave" here would mean to form a clear mental image of the Name, so as to meditate on it, as we will discuss later (1:14). The method is alluded to in Rava's saying, "If the righteous desired, they could create a world."[36]

Yah

Saadia Gaon translates this as, "the Eternal."

The Kabbalists normatively associate the name Yah (יה) with Wisdom (Chakhmah). Actually, however, only the first letter of this name, the Yud (י), designates Wisdom. The second letter, Heh (ה) designates Understanding, the feminine principle.

The reason why this name as a whole is used to designate Wisdom is because Wisdom cannot be grasped except when it is clothed in Understanding. For this reason, the Yud alone is not used as the name for Wisdom, but rather, the Yud combined with the Heh.

There are a number of reasons why these two letters represent Wisdom and Understanding respectively. Yud has the primary form of a simple point. This alludes to the fact that Wisdom is simple and undifferentiated. The numerical value of Yud is 10, indicating that all Ten Sefirot are included in the simple nature of Wisdom.

At the beginning of a word, the letter Yud indicates the masculine future. This is related to the teaching, "Who is wise? He who perceives the future."[37]

At the end of a word, when used as a suffix, the letter Yud means "me" or "my." Wisdom is the essential nature of the individual, belonging to him alone. As such, it is the ultimate "my." The same is true of the Sefirah of Wisdom (Chakhmah) with respect to the Infinite Being.

Heh has a numerical value of 5, alluding to the five fingers of
the hand. As such, it represents Understanding, the hand that holds
Wisdon, distributing and channeling it.[38]

At the beginning of a word, the prefix Heh means "the." It is the
definite article, that specifies and delineates an object. Like a hand,
the definite article holds and specifies a concept that is specific rather
than general. At the end of a word, Heh indicates the feminine pos-
sessive, "her." This is because Understanding is the domain of the
Feminine Essence.

Heh is one of the two letters in the Hebrew alphabet that is written as two disjunct parts. This alludes to the fact that Understanding
represents the beginning of separation.

There is some disagreement in the Talmud as to whether or not
Yah is a divine name.[39] The Sefer Yetzirah clearly takes the position
that it is.

Yah, the Lord...

In Hebrew, this is written as YH YHVH (יה יהוה). It was with these
six letters that God created all things. It is thus written, "Trust in
God for eternity of eternities, for with YH YHVH He formed universes" (Isaiah 26:4).[40]

The Lord of Hosts

This name usually designates the Sefirot which are associated
with revelation and prophecy. These are Netzach (Victory) and Hod
(Splendor).[41]

This name, however, also contains the Tetragrammaton
(YHVH), here translated as "the Lord." The Tetragrammaton designates the totality of all the Sefirot. Hence, the phrase, "YHVH of
Hosts," actually represents all the Sefirot as they are revealed to
man.[42]

This is the reason for the designation, "YHVH of Hosts." It
refers to revelation, the state in which God associates Himself with
beings that are lower than Himself, namely, His "hosts."

According to the Talmud, the first person to use the designation,
"Lord of Hosts," was Hannah, when she prayed, "O Lord of Hosts,
if You will look at the affliction of Your servant" (1 Samuel
1:11).[43]

God of Israel

This is connected to "Lord of Hosts." While revelation in general is to all of God's hosts, in particular, it is granted to Israel. As we shall see (2:4), the name Israel is closely associated with the 231 gates.

The Hebrew word for "God" here is Elohim. This alludes to Understanding, the concept that divides and delineates.

The Living God

The name is associated with the essential creative forces, represented by the Sefirah of Yesod (Foundation). In man, this force parallels the sexual organ.

In Hebrew, this phrase is *Elohim Chaim*. This Sefirah takes all the forces, collectively referred to as Elohim, and presents them in an active, procreative mode. Life is defined as that which is active and procreates, and hence, this is the connotation of "Living God."[44]

King of the Universe

This is the mode in which God relates to the universe as a king, and it is associated with the Sefirah of Malkhut (Kingship). Of all the Sefirot, this is the only one which comes into direct contact with the lower stages of creation.

The first five designations, "Yah, the Lord of Hosts, God of Israel, the Living God, King of the Universe," thus designate the Ten Sefirot in their downward mode, as they are the source of all creative force.

El Shaddai

These two names are usually translated as "Almighty God." Saadia Gaon, however, translates them as "Omnipotent Almighty."

Here the Sefer Yetzirah begins designating the Sefirot in an upward mode. In the Bahir, the disciples thus ask, "From above to below we know. But from below to above we do not know."[45]

The designation El Shaddai is also related to the procreative force represented by Yesod (Foundation), and corresponding to the sexual organ in man.

We therefore have two designations for Yesod (Foundation), "Living God" (*Elohim Chaim*), and El Shaddai.

"Living God" is the designation of this Sefirah from a God's eye view, while El Shaddai is its designation from a man's eye view. God thus told Moses, "I appeared to Abraham, Isaac and Jacob as El Shaddai" (Exodus 6:3).

The first five designations represented the downward process, from God to the universe, through which the creative force is channeled. The author, however, is now designating the names that relate to the upward process, through which man approaches the Divine. "King of the Universe," the lowest stage, applies to both directions.

Merciful and Gracious

These are the second and third of the Thirteen Attributes of Mercy, expressed in the verse, "El, merciful and gracious" (Exodus 34:6).[46]

On this level, one can comprehend the inner workings of the six Sefirot, Chesed (Love), Gevurah (Strength), Tiferet (Beauty), Netzach (Victory), and Hod (Splendor). It is through these Sefirot that God expresses His mercy to the world. This level was gained by Moses when God told him, "I will have mercy upon whom I will have mercy, and I will be gracious to whom I will be gracious" (Exodus 33:19).

High and Exalted

The next designations are all taken from the verse, "For thus says [God], High and Exalted, dwelling in Eternity, and whose Name is Holy, I dwell lofty and holy..." (Isaiah 57:15).

"High and Exalted" refers to the level of Understanding (Binah). The lower seven Sefirot correspond to the seven days of creation. Understanding (Binah) is above these seven Sefirot, and hence, it is the level preceding action and creation. This is the level where God is seen as being utterly transcendental, separated from all the worldly, and high above everything mundane.

"Dwelling in eternity" speaks of the level of Wisdom (Chakhmah). This is the level that is above time. Here one perceives God as transcending not only space, but time as well.

"His Name is Holy" alludes to the level of the Crown (Keter), the highest of the Sefirot.

The Kabbalists note that the expression, "His Name," which in Hebrew is *Sh'mo* (שמו), has a numerical value (*gematria*) of 346. This is the same as the value of Ratzon (רצון), meaning "will."[47] Will is even higher than Wisdom, since it is the impluse that gives rise to all things, even thought. In Kabbalistic terms, Will is designated as Crown (Keter). Just as a crown is worn above the head, so is the Will above and outside all mental processes.

The word Holy (*Kadosh*) denotes separation, and its general sense implies separation from the mundane.[48] The expression, "His Name is Holy," indicates that the Crown is a level that is separated and removed from every imaginable concept. Since it is above the mental processes, it cannot be grasped by them.

The last expression, "lofty and holy" is not found in many versions of Sefer Yetzirah. It possibly relates to the Infinite Being (Ain Sof), which is lofty above all concepts, even Will.

The last five designations thus refer to the rungs which man must climb to reach the Infinite. These are the Sefirot in their upward mode.

The impulse of creation first went downward through the Sefirot, and then it went upward again, returning to the Infinite. Only then could creation take place.

With three books

Sefer Yetzirah now begins to define the word Sefirah, the Hebrew designation for the divine emanations that form the basis of creation.

The Hebrew word for book, *Sepher* (ספר), has the same root as the word *Sephirah* (ספירה), except that the former is masculine and the latter is feminine.

These three books are said to be "text, number, and communication." The Hebrew word for "text" here is *Sepher* (ספר), which literally means "book." "Number" is *Sephar* (ספר), from which the English word "cipher" is derived. "Communication" is *Sippur* (סיפור), which more literally is "telling."

These three divisions respectively represent quality, quantity, and communication. These are the letters, numbers, and the manner in which they are used.[49]

These three books correspond to the three divisions of creation defined by Sefer Yetzirah, namely, "Universe, Year, and Soul." In

Table 4. The three books.

Text (*Sepher*)	World (space)	Form of Letters
Number (*Sephar*)	Year (time)	Numerical Value
Communication	Soul (spirit)	Pronunciation and
(*Sippur*)		Name of letters

more modern terms, these would be called space, time and spirit. "Universe" refers to the dimensions of space, "year" to time, and "soul" to the spiritual dimension. See Table 4.

As we shall see, the Sefer Yetzirah speaks of a five-dimensional continuum, defined by the Ten Sefirot. The first three are the three dimensions of space, the fourth dimension is time, while the fifth is the spiritual dimension.

Since the three spacial dimensions comprise a single continuum, the three of them together constitute the first "book." Time is the second "book," while the spiritual dimension is the third.

The three books define the three ways in which the array of the 32 paths can be presented. First, one can draw a diagram representing them, as one would picture them in a book. This is the aspect of "text." This is also the aspect in which they appear in the Book of the Torah, in the first chapter of Genesis.

Secondly, one can express the numerical sequences and distributions of these paths. Thus, for example, as the Sefer Yetzirah states (1:2), the 32 paths consist of ten Sefirot, and 22 letters, the latter which consists of three Mothers, seven Doubles, and twelve Elementals. This is the aspect of number in the 32 paths. This is also related to their affinity to certain geometrical forms.

Finally, one can speak of the relationships between these paths as they convey information. This is the level of "communication." It is closely related to the 32 paths where they represent states of consciousness, as presented in Appendix II.

These three aspects are most apparent in the letters of the alphabet.[50] There are three primary ways in which the letters can be interpreted. First, there is the physical form of the letters, as they are written in a book. This is the aspect of "text" (Sepher), which literally means book. Secondly, there is the numerical value or gematria of the letter, this being "number." Finally, there is the sound of the letter, as well as the way its name is pronounced, this being "communication" or "telling." See Table 5 on page 22.

"Text" (*Sepher*), the physical form of the letter, pertains to the continuum of space, since form only can be defined in space. This is "Universe." Number (*Sephar*), implies sequence, and this is the sequence of time, which is the continuum of the "Year." Finally, communication (*Sippur*) applies to the mind, and this is in the spiritual continuum, which is "Soul."

These three words also define the term Sefirah. First, the word Sefirah shares the root with *Sefer*, meaning book. Like a book, each Sefirah can record information. The Sefirot thus serve as a memory bank in the domain of the Divine. A permanent record of everything that has ever taken place in all creation is thus made on the Sefirot.

Secondly, the word Sefirah shares a root with *Sephar*, meaning number. It is the Sefirot that introduce an element of number and plurality into existence. The Creator, the Infinite Being, is the most absolute unity, and the concept of number does not apply to Him in any manner whatever. In speaking of the Infinite Being, the Sefer Yetzirah therefore asks, "Before one, what do you count" (1:7)? It is only with the creation of the Sefirot that the concept of number comes into being.

In this mode, every event and action is measured and weighed by the Sefirot, and the appropriate response is conceived and calculated. Using the computer as an analogy, the Sefirot function as the processing unit of the Divine domain in this mode.

Finally, the word Sefirah shares a root with *Sippur*, which means "communication" and "telling." The Sefirot are the means through which God communicates with His creation. They are also the means through which man communicates with God. If not for the Sefirot, God, the Infinite Being, would be absolutely unknowable and unreachable. It is only through the Sefirot that he can be approached.

Of course, as all the Kabbalists warn, one should not in any way worship the Sefirot or pray to them.[51] One may, however, use them as a channel. Thus, for example, one would not think of directing a petition to the postman, but one could use him to deliver a message to the king. In a mystical sense, the Sefirot form a ladder or tree through which one can "climb" and approach the Infinite.

Thus, when the Sefer Yetzirah presents the words *Sepher, Sephar* and *Sippur* here, it is not doing so accidentally. Rather, the book is deliberately presenting roots which define the concept of the Sefirot. This is all the more obvious, since this entire chapter deals with the Sefirot.

The three aspects, "text, number and communication," are the keys to the methods of Sefer Yetzirah.

If one wishes to influence anything in the physical universe (space), he must make use of the physical shape of the letters. If this involves a meditative technique, one would contemplate the appropriate letters, as if they were written in a book. The method involves

Table 5. The numerical value of letters.

Letter	Name		Sound	Value	Designation	Phonetic Family
א	Alef	אלף	silent	1	mother	guttural
ב	Bet	בית	B,Bh	2	double	labial
ג	Gimmel	גמל	G,Gh	3	double	palatal
ד	Dalet	דלת	D,Dh	4	double	lingual
ה	Heh	הא	H	5	elemental	guttural
ו	Vav	וו	V (W)	6	elemental	labial
ז	Zayin	זין	Z	7	elemental	dental
ח	Chet	חית	German ch	8	elemental	guttural
ט	Tet	טית	T	9	elemental	lingual
י	Yod	יוד	Y (I)	10	elemental	palatal
כ,ך	Kaf	כף	K,Kh	20	double	palatal
ל	Lamed	למד	L	30	elemental	lingual
מ,ם	Mem	מם	M	40	mother	labial
נ,ן	Nun	נון	N	50	elemental	lingual
ס	Samekh	סמך	S	60	elemental	dental
ע	Eyin	עין	silent	70	elemental	guttural
פ,ף	Peh	פא	P,Ph	80	double	labial
צ,ץ	Tzadi	צדי	Tz	90	elemental	dental
ק	Kuf	קוף	K (Q)	100	elemental	palatal
ר	Resh	ריש	R,Rh	200	double	dental
ש	Shin	שין	Sh (S)	300	mother	dental
ת	Tav	תיו	T,Th	400	double	lingual

making each particular letter combination fill the entire field of vision, eliminating all other thoughts from the mind.

Finally, if one wishes to influence the spiritual realm, he must make use, either of the sounds of the letters, or of their names. This technique, which we shall describe, is the one that is used when making a Golem.

1:2

עשר ספירות בלי מה ועשרים ושתים אותיות
יסוד שלש אמות ושבע כפולות ושתים עשרה
פשוטות:

Ten Sefirot of Nothingness
And 22 Foundation Letters:
Three Mothers,
Seven Doubles
And twelve Elementals.

Ten Sefirot

The Sefer Yetzirah now defines the 32 paths as consisting of 10 Sefirot and 22 letters.

The word *Sefirah* literally means "counting." It is thus distinguished from the word *Mispar*, meaning "number." Although the Sefirot are said to represent the ten basic digits, they are not actual numbers. Rather, they are the sources from which the numbers originate. Although the Sefer Yetzirah does not name the Ten Sefirot, their names are well known from the classical Kabbalah. They are given in Table 6. The Sefirot are usually presented in an array consisting of three columns, as in the figure.

The names of the Sefirot are all derived from scripture. In recounting Betzalel's qualifications, God says, "I have filled him with the spirit of God, with Wisdom, with Understanding, and with Knowledge" (Exodus 31:3). As the Sefer Yetzirah later states (1:9), the "spirit of God" refers to Keter (Crown), the first of the Sefirot. Wisdom and Understanding then refer to the next two Sefirot.

The first two Sefirot are likewise alluded to in the verse, "With Wisdom, God established the earth, and with Understanding, He established the heavens, and with His Knowledge, the depths were broken up" (Proverbs 3:19,20). It is likewise written, "With Wisdom a house is built, with Understanding it is established, and with Knowledge its rooms are filled" (Proverbs 24:3,4).

Table 6. The ten Sefirot.

1.	Keter	Crown
2.	Chakhmah	Wisdom
3.	Binah [Daat]	Understanding [Knowledge]
4.	Chesed	Love
5.	Gevurah	Strength
6.	Tiferet	Beauty
7.	Netzach	Victory
8.	Hod	Splendor
9.	Yesod	Foundation
10.	Malkhut	Kingship

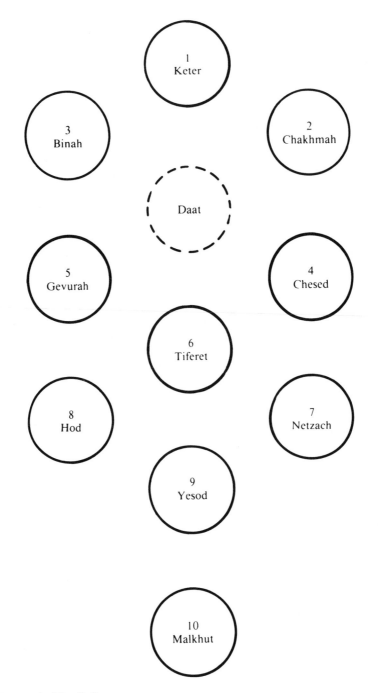

Figure 1. The Sefirot.

All of these sources list three qualities—Wisdom, Understanding, and Knowledge. Knowledge, however, is not a Sefirah, but merely the point of confluence between Wisdom and Understanding. In many ways, however, it behaves as a Sefirah, and it is thus often included among them.[52]

The next seven Sefirot are named in the verse, "Yours O God are the Greatness (4), the Strength (5), the Beauty (6), the Victory (7), and the Splendor (8), for All (9) in heaven and in earth; Yours O God is the Kingdom (10)..." (1 Chronicles 29:11).[53] It is here that the names of all the lower Sefirot are defined. See figure 1 on page 24. In most sources, however, the first of these is called Chesed (Love) instead of Gedulah (Greatness). Similarly, the sixth is called Yesod (Foundation) rather than "All." In older Kabbalistic texts, however, both designations are used.

According to some Kabbalists, the Ten Sefirot also parallel the 10 Hebrew vowels.[54] Together with the 22 letters, they then comprise the totality of the Hebrew language.

Of Nothingness

The Hebrew word here is Beli-mah (בלימה). This word can also be translated as meaning closed, abstract, absolute or ineffable.

This word occurs only once in scripture, in the verse, "He stretches the north on Chaos, He hangs the earth on Nothingness (*Beli-mah*)" (Job 26:7). According to many commentaries, the word *Beli-mah* is derived from the two words, *Beli*, meaning "without," and *Mah*, meaning "what" or "anything." The word *Beli-mah* would then mean "without anything," or "nothingness."[55]

According to this interpretion, the designation "Sefirot of Nothingness" is used to indicate that the Sefirot are purely ideal concepts, without any substance whatever. Unlike letters which have form and sound, the Sefirot have no intrinsic physical properties. As such, they are purely conceptual.

Other sources state that *Belimah* comes from the root *Balam* (בלם), meaning "to bridle." This is found in the verse, "Do not be like a horse or mule, who do not understand, whose mouth must be bridled (*balam*) with bit and rein" (Psalms 32:9).[56]

This second interpretation seems to be indicated by the Sefer Yetzirah itself, since it later says, "Bridle (*balom*) your mouth from speaking of them" (1:8). According to this, *Belimah* would be translated as "ineffable." The text is speaking of "Ten Ineffable Sefirot," indicating that they cannot be described in any manner whatever.

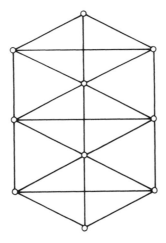

Figure 2. Ten points linked by 22 lines. There are three horizontals, seven verticals, and twelve diagonals.

Similarly, the Biblical verse, "He hangs the earth on the ineffable," would mean that the forces which uphold creation cannot be described.[57]

According to both interpretations, the Sefirot are distinguished from the letters. While the letters are primarily modes of expression, the Sefirot are inexpressible by their very nature.

A leading Kabbalist, Rabbi Issac of Acco (1250-1340), points out that *Belimah* has a numerical value of 87. God's name Elohim, on the other hand, has a value of 86. *Belimah* thus represents the stage immediately following the pure essence of the Divine.[58]

22 Foundation Letters

In the simplest sense, these are called Foundation letters because it was through the letters of the Hebrew alphabet that the universe was created.[59]The Sefer Yetzirah itself therefore says of the letters, "with them He depicted all that was formed, and all that would ever be formed" (2:2). This is also alluded to in what the Talmud says of the builder of the Tabernacle, "Betzalel knew how to permute the letters with which heaven and earth were made."[60]

With each act of creation, the Torah reports that "God said." Thus, "God said: let there be light," and "God said, let there be a firmament." The decrees through which God brought creation into being consisted of sayings. These in turn consisted of words, and these words were formed out of letters. Hence, it was through the letters of the alphabet that the universe was created.

These letters of creation were not only responsible for the inception of the world, but they also constantly sustain it. It is thus written, "Forever, O God, Your word stands in the heavens" (Psalms 119:89). The very words and letters with which the universe was created are also the ones which constantly sustain it. If these words and letters were withdrawn for even an instant, the universe would cease to exist.[61]

Thus, if one knows how to manipulate the letters correctly, one can also manipulate the most elemental forces of creation. The methods of doing this comprise the main subjects of Sefer Yetzirah.

In Hebrew, "Foundation Letters" is *Otiot Yesod*. This can also be translated, "Letters of Foundation."

In the Kabbalah, Foundation (Yesod) is the Sefirah that corresponds to the sexual organ. It therefore has the connotation of coupling and pairing, usually for the purpose of procreation.

The letters are said to pertain to Foundation (Yesod), since it is only through the letters that Wisdom and Understanding can come together and be coupled. As discussed earlier, Wisdom is pure nonverbal thought. Understanding, on the other hand, can only be verbal, since if an idea cannot be expressed verbally, it cannot be understood. The only link between nonverbal Wisdom, and verbal Understanding, consists of the letters of the alphabet.

This is also evident from the above mentioned Talmudic teaching. The Talmud states that, "Betzalel knew how to permute the letters with which heaven and earth were made." This is derived from the verse where God says of Betzalel, "I will fill him with the spirit of God, with Wisdom, with Understanding, and with Knowledge" (Exodus 31:3).

We therefore see that the ability to manipulate the letters of creation depends on "Wisdom, Understanding, and Knowledge." Knowledge (*Daat*), however, is the point at which Wisdom and Understanding come together. If has the connotation of joining and intercourse, as in the verse, "Adam *knew* his wife Eve" (Genesis 4:1).[62] Knowledge therefore serves in the place of Foundation between Wisdom and Understanding. It is in this same context that the Sefer Yetzirah speaks of "Letters of Foundation."

In a more general sense, the letters serve to pair off and connect all the Sefirot. This is particularly true in the "Tree of Life" shown in figure 1 (page 24), which shall be discussed in detail.

Three Mothers

These are the three letters, Alef (א), Mem (מ), and Shin (ש). They will be discussed at length in Chapter Three. These letters are called

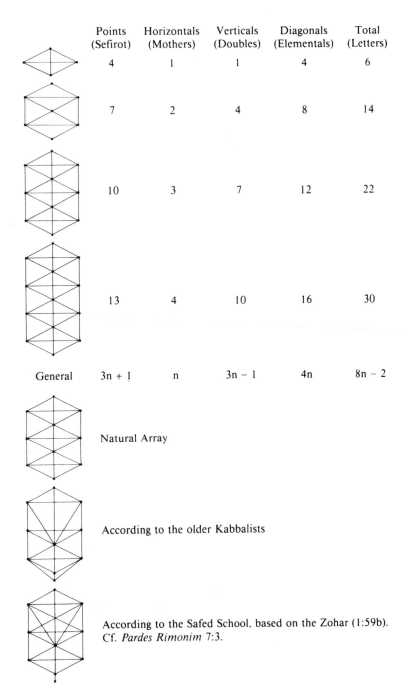

	Points (Sefirot)	Horizontals (Mothers)	Verticals (Doubles)	Diagonals (Elementals)	Total (Letters)
	4	1	1	4	6
	7	2	4	8	14
	10	3	7	12	22
	13	4	10	16	30
General	$3n + 1$	n	$3n - 1$	$4n$	$8n - 2$

Natural Array

According to the older Kabbalists

According to the Safed School, based on the Zohar (1:59b). Cf. *Pardes Rimonim* 7:3.

Figure 3. Family of diagrams.

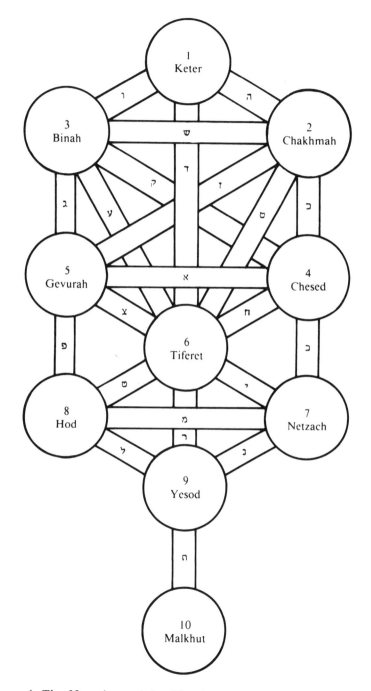

Figure 4. The 32 paths as defined by the Ari.

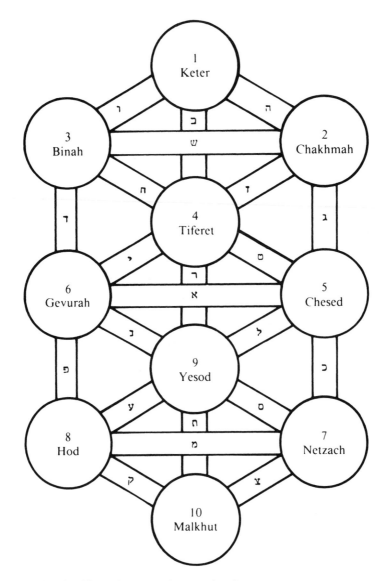

Figure 5. The 32 paths according to the Gra.

"Mothers" because they are primary. Essentially, Alef is the first letter of the alphabet, Mem is the middle letter, and Shin is the second
from the last.[63] The reason why Tav (ת) — the last letter of the alphabet — is not used is because it is one of the Doubles.

One reason why these letters are called "Mothers" is because, in
general, the letters are derived from Understanding (Binah). As discussed earlier, Understanding is the primary feminine principle, and
is therefore called Mother. This is alluded to in the verse, "For you
shall call Understanding a Mother" (Proverbs 2:3).[64] Since these are
the primary letters, they are called the "Mothers."[65]

These letters are also called mothers (Imot) in the same sense
that a crossroad is called a "mother of the road" (Ezekiel 21:26).[66]
These three letters are called "crossroads," since they form the horizontal links between the Sefirot in the Tree of Life diagram. On a
more basic level, these are "mothers," because the number of horizontal links defines the order of the array, as discussed below.

Seven Doubles

These are the seven letters that can express two sounds: Bet (ב),
Gimel (ג), Dalet (ד), Kaf (כ), Peh (פ), Resh (ר), and Tav (ת).

The Elementals are the twelve remaining letters, which have a
single sound. These two groups will be discussed in chapters four and
five, respectively.

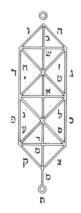

*Figure 6. The paths defined by the Gra, as they appear in the Warsaw,
1884 edition, (p. 26b of Part Two).*

If we draw ten points in three columns in the simplest manner, we see that they are automatically linked by 22 lines. Of these, three are horizontal, seven are vertical, and twelve are diagonal as shown in figure 2 on page 26. The division presented by Sefer Yetzirah is therefore a natural consequence of the array. This figure can actually be looked upon as a member of a family of diagrams. The order of the diagram is then determined by the number of horizontal links.

In practice, for reasons dealing with the basic nature of the Sefirot, they are not arranged in this natural order, but have the middle line lowered somewhat. There are several different ways that the Kabbalists assign the letters in these diagrams. These are shown in figures 3-6.

1:3   עשר ספירות בלימה במספר עשר אצבעות חמש
כנגד חמש וברית יחיד מכוון באמצע במילת
הלשון ובמילת המעור:

> Ten Sefirot of Nothingness
> in the number of ten fingers
> five opposite five
> with a singular covenant
> precisely in the middle
> in the circumcision of the tongue
> and in the circumcision of the membrum.

The number of ten fingers

Creation is said to have been accomplished with God's fingers, as it is written, "When I see Your heavens, the work of Your fingers" (Psalms 8:4). The 10 numerical digits similarly parallel the ten fingers in man. The five fingers of the hand contain a total of fourteen bones. This is the numerical value for Yad (יד), the Hebrew word for hand.

Five opposite live

Although the Sefirot are usually divided into three columns, they can also be arranged in two arrays, one to the right, and the other to the left. The "masculine" Sefirot on the right side would then be all those normally on the right, as well as the upper two center Sefirot. The "feminine" Sefirot on the left would include the three normally on the left, together with the lower two center Sefirot.[67]

The five masculine Sefirot are often referred to as the five Loves (*Chasadim*), since they are on the side of *Chesed* (Love). The five feminine Sefirot are similarly called the five Strengths (*Gevurot*) because they are on the side of Gevurah (Strength). See figure 7 on page 34.

When the Sefirot are in their normal state, arrayed in three columns, they are in a state of equilibrium. But when the Sefirot of the central column are moved to the right and left, so as to divide the Sefirot into two arrays, a powerful tension is produced. When they are in such a mode, powerful spiritual forces can be directed and channeled.

Therefore, in many places where God interferes directly with the physical world, the scripture speaks of God's fingers or hands. The most obvious case occurs with reference to creation itself, which the Psalmist calls "the work of Your fingers," as quoted above. We similarly find, "My [left] hand has founded the earth, and My right hand has spread out the heavens" (Isaiah 48:13). Before such a creative act could take place, all the Sefirot had to be polarized to male and female sides, generating tension and force. Just as human procreation involves male and female, so does Divine creation.

Very closely related to this are the various actions that use the hands to channel spiritual forces. These include the laying of hands, the lifting of the hands in the Priestly Blessing, and the spreading of the hands in prayer. In all these cases, the intent is to channel the power of the Ten Sefirot through the ten fingers.[68] In making them correspond to the two hands, the Sefirot are polarized, creating spiritual tension. See figure 8 on page 34. Once such tension exists, through meditation and concentration, the powers of the Sefirot can be focused and channeled.

And a singular covenant

The Hebrew here is *Brit Yachid*. Some read *Brit Yichud*, "a unifying covenant," but the meaning is similar.[69] A similar concept is found in the last chapter with regard to Abraham (6:7). In general, a covenant (*brit*) is something that comes between two separate parts. The paradigm of a covenant is that which God made with Abraham when he commanded him, "Take to Me a prime heifer, a prime female goat, a prime ram, a turtle dove, and a young pigeon" (Genesis 15:9).[70] These five animals paralleled the five fingers. Three of the animals were divided in half, so that the six halves represented the six Sefirot that are normally to the right and left. The four halves of the birds, which were not divided, represented the four Sefirot which are normally in the center line. See figure 9.

Feminine Strengths (Left)   Masculine Loves (Right)

	Keter
Binah	Chakhmah
Gevurah	Chesed
Hod	Tiferet
Yesod	Netzach
Malkhut	

Figure 7. Masculine and feminine Sefirot.

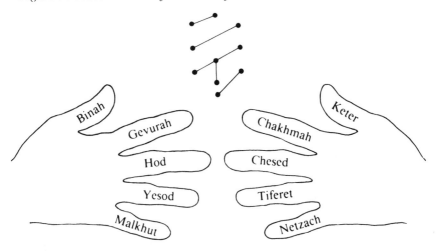

Figure 8. Polarizing the ten Sefirot through the ten fingers.

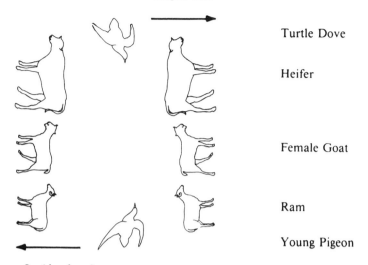

Turtle Dove

Heifer

Female Goat

Ram

Young Pigeon

Figure 9. Abraham's covenant.

The two tablets containing the Ten Commandments were also called the "Tablets of the Covenant" (Deuteronomy 9:9). It was for this reason that they were given as two tablets, rather than as a single one.

When the Ten Sefirot are divided into this double array, the place in the middle becomes the focus of spiritual tension. This place is then called the "singular covenant" or "unifying covenant."

Circumcision of the Tongue

The Hebrew word for "circumcision" is *Milah*. This same word, however, also means "word," as we find, "God's spirit speaks in me, and His word (*milah*) is on my tongue" (2 Samuel 23:2). Hence this can also be translated, "a word of the tongue." The "circumcision of the tongue" refers to the ability to utilize the mysteries of the Hebrew language.[71] It also refers to the ability to probe the mysteries of the Torah.[72]

In a more general sense, such circumcision denotes a fluency of speech. One who cannot speak properly is said to have "uncircumcised lips." Moses thus said, "How will Pharoah listen to me, when I have uncircumcised lips?" (Exodus 6:12). When one is given the power of proper speech, his tongue is said to be circumcised. This is both the "circumcision" and the "word" of the tongue.

A good example of this is found in the Priestly Blessing. Here, the priests raise their hands and pronounce the blessing outlined in scripture (Numbers 6:22-27). The priests must raise their hands so that they are precisely level with the mouth, as it is written, "Aaron lifted up his hands toward the people, and he blessed them" (Leviticus 9:22).[73] The cohen-priest must concentrate on the fact that his ten fingers represent the Ten Sefirot. As a result of the focus of spiritual force between his two hands, his tongue is "circumcised," and his blessing has its proper effect.

The same is true of raising one's hands in prayer. Here again, the two hands focus spritual power so as to "circumcise" the tongue, allowing the individual to pray effectively. In some Kabbalistic meditative systems, the raised hand position was likewise used to focus spiritual energy.[74] It was for a very similar reason that the cohen-priests had to wash their hands and feet before engaging in the divine service.[75]

This also provides insight into the significance of the two Cherubim that were on the Ark of the Covenant in the Holy of Holies. These two Cherubim were the source of all prophecy. Prophecy involves a particularly intense focusing of spiritual energy, allowing the prophet to actually speak in God's name. Prophecy was thus the ultimate level of "circumcision of the tongue."

In describing the Ark, God told Moses, "I will commune with you, and I will speak to you from above the ark-cover, from between the two Cherubim, which are on the Ark of Testimony" (Exodus 25:22).[76] What was true of Moses was also true of the other prophets, and the influx of prophecy was channeled primarily through these two Cherubs in the Holy of Holies. There is some evidence that at least in some cases, the prophetic experience was the result of intense meditation of these two Cherubim.[77] When the Cherubim were removed from the Holy of Holies with the destruction of the First Temple, prophecy as such ceased to exist.

According to the Zohar, the two Cherubim represented the Sefirot divided into a masculine and feminine array.[79] These were placed on the Ark, which contained the original Tablets of the Ten Commandments. There were five Commandments on each tablet, so the two represented a similar array of the Sefirot. This created a permanent state of tension, through which the spiritual force associated with prophecy could be focused.

Circumcision of the Membrum

Just as the fingers of the two hands represent the Ten Sefirot, so do the toes of the two feet. Between the legs is the circumcision of the sexual organ.

In order to understand the significance of this circumcision, one must realize why God commanded that it be done on the eighth day. The Torah states, "On the eighth day, the flesh of his foreskin must be circumcised" (Leviticus 12:3).[80] The covenant of circumcision was originally given to Abraham.

The world was created in six days, representing the six primary directions that exist in a three-dimensional universe. The seventh day, the Sabbath, is the perfection of the physical world, and it represents the focal point of these six directions, as discussed below (4:4). The eighth day then represents a step above the physical, into the realm of the transcendental.[81]

Through the covenant of circumcision, God gave Abraham and his desendents power over the transcendental plane. The most obvious case in which this occurs is in conception, where a soul is brought down into the world. Since the mark of the covenant is on the sexual organ, it gives the individual access to the highest spiritual realms, from which he can draw down the most lofty souls.

By meditating on the fact that the ten toes represent the Ten Sefirot, one is able to concentrate spiritual energy into the sexual organ.[82] Through such methods, one can gain complete control over one's sexual activities, even in the midst of intercourse.[83] By sanctifying oneself in this manner during sexual intercourse, one is able to determine the qualities of the child that will be conceived.[84]

The covenant of circumcision also represents the channeling of sexual energy. The sexual drive is one of the most powerful psychological forces in man, and when it is channeled along spiritual lines, it can help bring one to the highest mystical states. In giving the commandment of circumcision, God indicated that the emotions and desires associated with sex could be used for the mystical quest of the Divine on a transcendental plane.

The juxtaposition between the "circumcision of the tongue" and the "circumcision of the membrum" explains the prophetic position favored by Elijah. The scripture states, "Elijah went up to the top of the Carmel, entranced himself on the ground, and placed his face between his knees" (1 Kings 18:42). This position was used for the intense concentration of spiritual energy. According to the Midrash, this position was used because it placed the head in conjunction with the mark of circumcision.[85]

When one is in this position, all of these forces are brought together. The ten fingers, ten toes, tongue and sexual organ comprise a total of 22 elements, paralleling the 22 letters of the Hebrew alphabet.[86] The individual's body itself thus becomes an alphabet, with which he can "write" in the spiritual realm.

1:4

עשר ספירות בלימה עשר ולא תשע עשר ולא
אחת עשרה הבן בחכמה וחכם בבינה בחון
בהם והקור מהם והעמד דבר על בוריו והשב יוצר
על מכונו:

Ten Sefirot of Nothingness
    ten and not nine
    ten and not eleven
Understand with Wisdom
Be wise with Understanding
    Examine with them
    and probe from them
Make [each] thing stand on its essence
And make the Creator sit on His base.

This section speaks primarily of the first three Sefirot, Keter (Crown), Chakhmah (Wisdom), and Binah (Understanding). Later, we find a similar discussion with regard to the lower seven Sefirot (4:5).

Ten and not nine

The highest faculty in man is will. This corresponds to the first of the Sefirot, Keter (Crown).

If one were to attempt to describe God, it would be tempting to say that He is pure Will. This would be very much like saying that God is "spirit," or that He is "love," since all such descriptions attempt to depict God in terms of human traits. If any human trait were to be used, however, it should be will since this is the highest of all human faculties.

If we would say that God was pure Will, however, then we would be saying that He is identical with Keter. Keter, however, is merely a Sefirah, and as such, it is something created by God and inferior to Him. We therefore cannot even say that God in pure Will. Even Will is among His creations, and is inferior to Him. Therefore, there is no word that can be used to describe God's essence.

The author consequently states that the Sefirot are "ten and not nine." For if we were to say that God is Will, then Keter would be identical to God, and only nine Sefirot would remain. But since there are ten Sefirot, then even Will is nothing more than a Sefirah, and it is something that is inferior to the Creator.

The Sefer Yetzirah also warns, "ten and not eleven." This is to teach that God Himself, the Infinite Being, is not to be included among the Sefirot. If He were, then there would be eleven rather than ten.[87]

God belongs to a totally different category than the Sefirot, and is not to be counted among them. As a result, we cannot even describe Him by such purely abstract qualities as will, wisdom, love or strength. When the Bible makes use of any of these qualities in relation to God, it is speaking of the Sefirot created by God, and not of the Creator Himself.

This is particularly important for the mystic. As a person reaches the highest levels, he might think that he is actually reaching God Himself. The Sefer Yetzirah therefore warns that when one climbs the ladder of the Sefirot, there are only ten steps, and not eleven. The Creator is always beyond our grasp.

It is for this reason that God is called Ain Sof, literally "the Infinite." One can climb higher and higher, reaching toward infinity, but one can never attain it. Infinity may remain a goal, but it is only a goal that points to a direction, but not a goal that acually can be reached. The same is true of the Infinite Ain Sof.[88]

Understand with Wisdom

As discussed earlier, Understanding (Binah) involves verbal thought, while Wisdom (Chakhmah) is pure nonverbal thought. Understanding consists of the normal reverie, where the person thinks out things so as to understand and organize the thoughts. Wisdom, on the other hand, is pure thought, and in particular, it refers to a state of consciousness where the mind is not engaged in reverie.

It is very difficult to experience pure, nonverbal thought. As soon as a person attempts to clear his mind of thought, he immediately begins to think, "Now I am not thinking of anything." The state of Wisdom or Chakhmah consciousness is one of pure nonverbal thought, which is very difficult to attain.

It is in an attempt to attain the state of Chakhmah consciousness that the various meditative methods are used. Thus, mantra meditation attempts to clear the mind of reverie by filling it with the repeated words of the mantra. Similarly, contemplation pursues the same goal by filling the mind with the contemplated object.

Wisdom is associated with the nonverbal right hemisphere of the brain, while Understanding is associated with the verbal left hemisphere. As the Kabbalists explain, Wisdom is normally only experienced when it is clothed in Understanding. One may be able to experience the workings of the nonverbal areas of the mind, but only when one clothes them with verbal thoughts.

It is here that the Sefer Yetzirah begins instruction on how to grasp the Sefirot.[89]

The first step is to, "Understand with Wisdom, and to be wise with Understanding." This involves a deliberate oscillation between Understanding and Wisdom, between verbal Binah consciousness, and nonverbal Chakhmah consciousness.

Try for a moment to stop thinking. You remain completely conscious, but there are no verbal thoughts in your mind. If you are an average person, you may be able to maintain such a state for a few seconds, but immediately your mind begins to verbalize the experience. You might say to youself, "I am not thinking of anything." But as soon as you do this, of course, you actually are thinking of something.

For those few seconds, however, you have experienced nonverbal Chakhmah consciousness. If you work at this exercise, you can gradually learn how to extend the time in which you are in this state. It is like a heavy pendulum, the longer you push it back and forth, the further it will swing. Similarly, the more you learn to oscillate between verbal Binah consciousness and nonverbal Chakhmah consciousness, the deeper you will reach into the latter, and the longer you will be able to maintain this state.

Chakhmah consciousness is particularly important in reaching the Sefirot. As mentioned earlier (1:2), the Sefirot are ineffable, and cannot be understood verbally. As the Sefer Yetzirah itself says, they must be reached by "paths of Wisdom," that is, through the paths of nonverbal Chakhmah consciousness.

Examine with them

A similar expression is later used with regard to the lower Sefirot (4:5).

Once an individual is able to experience the Sefirot, he must make use of them to examine and test them. The author does not say "examine them," but "examine *with* them." The Hebrew word used here is *Bachan*, and it means that one is to test things for their intrinsic quality as they are at the immediate moment.[90]

When a person has an awareness of the Sefirot, he can then "examine" anything in creation and determine the Sefirah to which it pertains. As he becomes proficient in doing this, he can use various things to strengthen his attachment to their associated Sefirah. When the Sefer Yetzirah was first written, each individual had to do this on his own. Now, however, there are many lists which associate various things and ideas with their appropriate Sefirot, and these can be used as aids in binding oneself to them.[91]

Probe from them

The Hebrew word for "probe" here is *Chakar*, which usually indicates attaining the ultimate knowledge of a thing.[92]

The Sefer Yetzirah says that one should "probe *from* them." As a result of the spiritual power that one attains from the Sefirot, one should probe each thing to its ultimate depth. Through one's experience of the Sefirot, one is to gain the deepest possible insight into everything in the world.

Note carefully that the Sefer Yetzirah does not tell us to contemplate the Sefirot themselves. Rather, it instructs us to use them in developing an inner sight with which to view the world.[93]

Make [each] thing stand on its essence

In this manner, one can learn how to perceive the essential nature of each thing.[94] The Sefer Yetzirah says, "make each thing stand on its essence" so as to parallel the next phrase, "make the Creator sit on His base."

The Sefer Yetzirah is also indicating here that when a person perceives the true spiritual nature of a thing, he also elevates that thing spiritually. "Standing" refers to such elevation. The expression, "make each thing *stand*" therefore says that when one "probes from them," he elevates the things that he probes.

Make the Creator sit on His Base

The Hebrew word for "base" here is *Makhon*, and in a number of places it is seen as the place where God "sits." Thus, in his prayer, Solomon speaks of "the heaven, the base (*makhon*) of Your sitting" (1 Kings 8:39). The scripture likewise states, "Righteousness and

Table 7. The four universes.

Universe	Content	Level
Atzilut (Nearness, Emanation)	Sefirot	Nothingness
Beriyah (Creation)	The Throne	Something from Nothing
Yetzirah (Formation)	Angels	Something from Something
Asiyah (Making, Action)	Shade of the physical	Completion

judgement are the base (*makhon*) of Your Throne" (Psalms 89:15). In other places, the Bible speaks of the Temple as being the "base" upon which God sits.[95]

The word *Makhon* (מכון) comes from the root *Kon* (כון), which is also the root of the word *Hekhin* (הכין), meaning "to prepare."[96] Hence, *Makhon* refers not merely to a physical base, but to one that is specifically prepared for a special purpose. The Scripture thus says, "He founded the earth on its base (*makhon*)" (Psalms 104:5). This verse indicates that everything in the physical world has a specific spiritual counterpart and basis, through which it can be elevated.[97]

In general, the anthropomorphism "sit," when used with respect to God, indicates a sense of lowering.[98] When a person sits down, he lowers his body. Similarly, when God "sits," He "lowers" His essence so as to be concerned with His creation. When the Bible speaks of God's Throne, it is speaking of the vehicle through which He expresses such concern.

In Kabbalah, there is general rule that every "awakening from below" motivates an "awakening from above." Thus, when a person mentally elevates each thing to its spiritual essence, he also brings spiritual sustenance (*shefa*) down to that particular object. This sustenance can then be channeled and used by the individual. Under some conditions, this can be used to actually bring about physical changes in the world.[99]

The term *Makhon* is also interpreted by the Talmud to indicate a parallelism between the spiritual and the physical domains.[100] The "prepared basis" (*makhon*) through which God "sits" and channels His spiritual influence to the world is precisely this *Makhon*—the parallelism between the spiritual and the physical. This is the aspect through which God "sits," and the scripture therefore speaks as the "base (*makhon*) of Your sitting."

In this context, the Sefer Yetzirah here calls God the *Yotzer*. We have translated this as "the Creator," but a more accurate rendition would be "the Former," or the "One who forms."

In Hebrew, there are three words which have similar meaning. They are *Bara*, meaning "to create," *Yatzar*, meaning "to form," and *Asah*, meaning "to make." According to the Kabbalists, *Bara* indicates creation *ex nihilo*, "something from nothing." *Yatzar* denotes formation of something from a substance that already exists, "something from something." *Asah* has the connotation of the completion of an action.[101]

The Kabbalists teach that stages parallel the three supernal universes, which are called Beriyah (Creation), Yetzirah (Formation), and Asiyah (Making). They are alluded to in the verse, "All that is called in My Name, for My Glory (Atzilut), I have created it (Beriyah), I have formed it (Yetzirah), and I have made it (Asiyah)" (Isaiah 43:7).[102]

The highest universe is Atzilut, the domain of the Sefirot themselves. Below this is Beriyah, the domain of the Throne. Since Beriyah (Creation) is "something from nothing," Atzilut is often referred to as "Nothingness" (*Ayin*). Hence, the Sefirot, which are in Atzilut, are called Sefirot of Nothingness.

Below Beriyah is the universe of Yetzirah (Formation), which is the world of the angels. Finally, there is the universe of Asiyah (Making), which consists of the physical world and its spiritual shadow. See Table 7.

Here, Sefer Yetzirah is speaking primarily about establishing a link between the two lower worlds, Yetzirah and Asiyah. The methods of Sefer Yetzirah involve the manipulation of the forces of the Universe of Asiyah, and this is the reason for the name of the book. The text therefore speaks of God as the *Yotzer*, the Former, indicating His manifestation in the world of Yetzirah.

From the above mentioned verse, "He founded (*yasad*) the earth on its base (*Makhon*)," we see that *Makhon* refers to a spiritual level that is close to the physical world, namely, the lowest level of Yetzirah.[103] *Makhon* is on the level corresponding to Yesod (Foundation), which has the connotation of connecting and binding. Hence, it binds Yetzirah to Asiyah. By elevating objects in the physical world, one can then draw upon the forces of Yetzirah, the world of the angels.

It is for this reason that the Sefer Yetzirah uses the term *Makhon* (Base) rather than Throne (*Kisey*). The term "Throne" would indicate the Universe of Beriyah, which is the world of the Throne. *Makhon*, on the other hand, is a level of Yetzirah.

1:5

עשר ספירות בלימה מדתן עשר שאין להם סוף
עומק ראשית ועומק אחרית עומק טוב ועומק
רע עומק רום ועומק תחת עומק מזרח ועומק מערב
עומק צפון ועומק דרום אדון יחיד אל מלך נאמן
מושל בכולם ממעון קדשו עד עדי עד:

Ten Sefirot of Nothingness:
   Their measure is ten
   which have no end
A depth of beginning
   A depth of end
A depth of good
   A depth of evil
A depth of above
   A depth of below
A depth of east
   A depth of west
A depth of north
   A depth of south
The singular Master
   God faithful King
dominates over them all
   from His holy dwelling
   until eternity of eternities.

Here the Sefer Yetzirah defines the five dimensional continuum which is the framework of its system. These five dimensions define ten directions, two opposite directions in each dimension. See Table 8 on page 46.

The space continuum consists of three dimensions, up-down, north-south, and east-west. This continuum is defined by six directions, and is called "Universe." The time continuum consists of two directions, past and future, or beginning and end. This is called "year." Finally, there is a moral, spiritual fifth dimension, whose two directions are good and evil. This is called "soul."

According to the later Kabbalists, these ten directions parallel the Ten Sefirot in the following manner:

Beginning   Chakhmah (Wisdom)

End   Binah (Understanding)

Good	Keter (Crown)
Evil	Malkhut (Kingship)
Up	Netzach (Victory)
Down	Hod (Splendor)
North	Gevurah (Strength)
South	Chesed (Love)
East	Tiferet (Beauty)
West	Yesod (Foundation)[104]

The Ten Sefirot are thus seen as consisting of five sets of opposites. These are the "five opposite five" discussed above (1:3). The opposites parallel the five fingers on each of the two hands.[105]

Wisdom is always defined as the beginning by the Kabbalists. This is based on such verses as "The beginning is Wisdom" (Proverbs 4:7).[106] This corresponds to the beginning of existence, before creation was defined, articulated, or verbalized.

God then created the world with ten sayings. This represents the power of Understanding (Binah), which is the aspect of verbal thought. As discussed earlier, the name Elohim, used in the account of creation, represents Understanding. "Sayings" can only come about through Understanding, denoted by the name Elohim.

Psychologically, Wisdom also represents the past in another manner. Memory is not verbal, but is stored in the mind in a nonverbal mode. It is only when one brings a memory to the surface that it becomes verbalized. Since pure memory is completely nonverbal, it is in the category of Wisdom.

The future, on the other hand, cannot be imagined at all, except in verbal terms. One can remember the past, but not the future. The future can only be conceived when it is described. The main way in which we know the future is by extrapolating from our knowledge of the past, or, in the language of the Talmud, "Understanding one thing from another."[107]

Past and future are also the counterparts of Wisdom and Understanding insofar that they are respectively male and female. The past is said to be male, since it directly influences the future. In this manner, it is as if the feminine future is impregnated by the past.

Keter is said to be "good," since it is the Sefirah closest to God. For the same reason, Malkhut, the Sefirah furthest from God, is said to be evil. This does not mean that Malkhut itself is actually evil, since all the Sefirot are completely and absolutely good. However,

Table 8. The ten directions.

	Ari[1]	Raavad[2]	Isaac the Blind[3]	Ramak[4]
Beginning	Chakhmah	Chakhmah	Chakhmah	Keter
End	Binah	Binah	Binah	Malkhut
Good	Keter	Chesed	[Chesed]	Chakhmah
Evil	Malkhut	Gevurah	[Malkhut]	Binah
Up	Netzach	Keter	[Keter]	Netzach
Down	Hod	Malkhut	Yesod	Hod
East	Tiferet	Tiferet	Tiferet	Tiferet
West	Yesod	Yesod	Netzach	Yesod
North	Gevurah	Netzach	Gevurah	Gevurah
South	Chesed	Hod	Hod	Chesed

1. See note 104 in text.
2. Raavad, Ramban (2), *Otzar HaShem, ad loc., Pardes Rimonim* 3:4.
3. *Yitzchak Sagi Nahor, ad loc.*
4. *Pardes Rimonim* 3:5 end, from *Tikuney Zohar* 15a,b, 70 (125a).

since Malkhut points in the direction away from God, it is said to denote the direction of evil.

The entire array of the Sefirot is often called the "Tree of Life." The center line, from Keter to Malkhut, when taken alone, is called the "Tree of Knowledge." It is on this line that good and evil come together, this being the mystery of the "Tree of Knowledge of Good and Evil" (Genesis 2:9), of which Adam and Eve were commanded not to partake.[108] It is in the quasi-Sefirah of Knowledge (Daat) that good and evil converge. Because of this, some of the later Kabbalists place the "depth of good and depth of evil" both in Knowledge (Daat).[109]

There are 32 hyperquadrants that can be defined in a five-dimensional hyperspace. These correspond to the 32 apexes on a five-dimensional hypercube, as discussed above (1:1). These in turn are related to the 32 paths of Wisdom. See Table 9.

In general, a knife or cutting blade has one dimension less than the continuum that it cuts. In our three-dimensional continuum, a blade is essentially a two-dimensional plane. Therefore, in a five-dimensional continuum, one would expect a blade to have four dimensions. Such a blade would be a four-dimensional hypercube, having 16 apexes. The Midrash states that God's sword has 16 edges, indicating that it is indeed a four-dimensional hypercube.[110]

Table 9. The 32 hyperquadrants.

1	Keter	Chakhmah	Chesed	Tiferet	Netzach
2	Keter	Chakhmah	Chesed	Tiferet	Hod
3	Keter	Chakhmah	Chesed	Yesod	Netzach
4	Keter	Chakhmah	Chesed	Yesod	Hod
5	Keter	Chakhmah	Gevurah	Tiferet	Netzach
6	Keter	Chakhmah	Gevurah	Tiferet	Hod
7	Keter	Chakhmah	Gevurah	Yesod	Netzach
8	Keter	Chakhmah	Gevurah	Yesod	Hod
9	Keter	Binah	Chesed	Tiferet	Netzach
10	Keter	Binah	Chesed	Tiferet	Hod
11	Keter	Binah	Chesed	Yesod	Netzach
12	Keter	Binah	Chesed	Yesod	Hod
13	Keter	Binah	Gevurah	Tiferet	Netzach
14	Keter	Binah	Gevurah	Tiferet	Hod
15	Keter	Binah	Gevurah	Yesod	Netzach
16	Keter	Binah	Gevurah	Yesod	Hod
17	Malkhut	Chakhmah	Chesed	Tiferet	Netzach
18	Malkhut	Chakhmah	Chesed	Tiferet	Hod
19	Malkhut	Chakhmah	Chesed	Yesod	Netzach
20	Malkhut	Chakhmah	Chesed	Yesod	Hod
21	Malkhut	Chakhmah	Gevurah	Tiferet	Netzach
22	Malkhut	Chakhmah	Gevurah	Tiferet	Hod
23	Malkhut	Chakhmah	Gevurah	Yesod	Netzach
24	Malkhut	Chakhmah	Gevurah	Yesod	Hod
25	Malkhut	Binah	Chesed	Tiferet	Netzach
26	Malkhut	Binah	Chesed	Tiferet	Hod
27	Malkhut	Binah	Chesed	Yesod	Netzach
28	Malkhut	Binah	Chesed	Yesod	Hod
29	Malkhut	Binah	Gevurah	Tiferet	Netzach
30	Malkhut	Binah	Gevurah	Tiferet	Hod
31	Malkhut	Binah	Gevurah	Yesod	Netzach
32	Malkhut	Binah	Gevurah	Yesod	Hod

Their measure is ten, which have no end

The Sefer Yetzirah does not say, "their number is ten," but, "their measure is ten." What it is saying is that the Sefirot define a continuum of ten directions or five dimensions.

Each of these directions is said to be infinite and endless. Indeed, in saying that "they have no end," the Sefer Yetzirah uses the term, *"Ain (la-hem) Sof."* This is the term usually used for God, the Infinite Being. Each direction extends without limit, and in this respect, the Sefirot share a property with the Infinite Being.[111]

The initiate is here given an allegory through which he or she can perceive his or her path to the Infinite Being. The allegory consists of any of the directions. Thus, for example, "up" has no end. One can continue to travel in an upward direction, but can never actually reach "up." The same is true when one travels "up" spiritually.

A depth of beginning

The Sefer Yetzirah does not speak of directions, but of depths. In general, the concept of depth indicates something at a great distance, as when one looks down a deep well, gazing at its "depth." It therefore denotes great distance, both physical and mental. Therefore, an idea that is difficult to understand, and far from one's comprehension, is also said to be deep.

There are many examples of this in scripture. We thus find, "The heavens for height, the earth for depth, and the heart of kings has no probing" (Proverbs 25:3). Regarding Wisdom, Kohelet likewise said, "It is deep, deep, who can find it" (Ecclesiastes 7:24). In particular, the word "depth" is used in relation to the Divine, as in, "How great are your works, O God, Your thoughts are very deep" (Psalms 92:6). These ten depths therefore represent the ten directions extended to infinity.

It is written, "Counsel in man's heart is like deep water, but a man of understanding will draw it out" (Proverbs 20:5). Although the depth of these directions is infinite, it can be described mentally. The first technique involves verbal thought, through being "a man of Understanding." Gradually, then, one can also learn to depict these infinite depths nonverbally.

The first exercise is to try to depict the "depth of beginning." Attempt to picture an infinity of time in the past. Let the mind travel back to a minute ago, and hour ago, a day ago, a year ago, continuing until you reach a level where you are trying to imagine an infinity ago. Then do the same with regard to the future.

The next exercise involves trying to imagine infinite good and infinite evil. The limits are pure ideas, which cannot be verbalized.

Finally, one must imagine the limits of the spacial dimensions. One must perceive the height of the sky and beyond the sky, the depth of the earth and beyond the earth.[112]

In this manner, one gradually trains the mind to depict the infinite. Since the Sefirot themselves are also infinite, this exercise can help one attain communion with the Sefirot.[113]

The individual can then learn how to climb the Tree of the Sefirot, and eventually approach the loftiest spiritual heights. This is accomplished through these depths. It is written, "A song of steps, from the depths I call You O God" (Psalms 130:1). One calls out to God by meditating on the depths, and then one can ascend through a series of steps. The psalm is therefore called "a song of steps."[114]

The singular Master

This can also be read, "The Master is singular," and a similar expression is found below (1:7).

After describing the five dimensional continuum defined by the Sefirot, the Sefer Yetzirah specifically refers to God as the "singular Master." The Hebrew for "singular" here is *Yachid*, indicating a complete and absolute unity.

The unity of God is absolute. He is not like a person who consists of many parts. He is not even like the most simple physical object, since even such an object has three dimensions. To say that God is bound by dimensions would in itself introduce an element of plurality in His essence, and this is excluded.

After the Sefer Yetzirah has defined the five-dimensional continuum, one might be misled to think that God Himself is a five-dimensional being. The text therefore stresses His unity at this point. The concept of dimensionality does not apply to God at all.

God faithful King

In Hebrew, this is *El Melekh Ne'eman* (אל מלך נאמן). The initial letters of this phrase spell out Amen (אמן), and according to the Talmud, it is this phrase that defines the word Amen.[115]

The statement here that God is "faithful" means that He is accessible only through faith. The human intellect can only grasp concepts within the five-dimensional continuum of space-time-spirit. God, the Infinite Being, however, is beyond this. He may relate to the universe as "King," but He Himself is above the grasp of our mentality.

Dominates them all

The Hebrew word for "dominate" here is *Moshel*. There are two synonyms that indicate dominance — *Melekh* and *Moshel*. A *Melekh* is a king who interacts with his subjects, and is therefore affected by them. A *Moshel*, on the other hand, is a tyrant and dictator, who rules, but is in no way influenced by his subordinates.[116]

God is sometimes called a *Melekh*, but this refers only to His actions through Malkhut (Kingship), the lowest of the Sefirot. The Infinite Being, however, is actually a *Moshel*, an absolute ruler who is in no way affected by His creation. The scripture thus says, "If you are righteous, what do you give Him? What does He receive from your hand" (Job 35:7).[117] This is particularly true of God's relationship to the Sefirot. He is in no way affected or defined by them.

From His holy habitation

The Hebrew word for "habitation" here is *Ma'on* (מעון). The expression "Holy habitation" (*Ma'on Kadosh*) occurs a number of times in the Bible.[118] It is also used again below (1:12).

The word *Ma'on* is defined by the verse, "O God, You have been a habitation (*ma'on*) for us" (Psalms 90:1). The Midrash interprets this to indicate that "God is the habitation of the world, and the world is not His habitation."[119] God is the "place" of the world, defining the space-time-spirit continuum, and He is not defined by any continuum whatever. The continuum is contained in God, as it were, and He is not contained in the continuum.

The word *Ma'on* is very closely related to the word *Makom* (מקום), meaning "place." *Makom* comes from the root *Kom* (קום), meaning "to stand." Hence, *Makom* denotes a place in physical space, where something can "stand." *Ma'on* (מעון), on the other hand, comes from the same root as *Onah* (עונה), meaning a "time" or "period." Just as *Makom* defines a point in space, so *Ma'on* defines a point in the space-time continuum.[120]

Thus, when the Sefer Yetzirah says that God dominates the Sefirot from His "Holy *Ma'on*" it is indicating that He is the "place" and "habitation" of the five-dimensional continuum. Not only does

God circumscribe the universe of space, but He even defines time and spirit. This is said to be "holy," and as discussed above (1:1), the word "holy" (*Kadosh*) denotes separation from the mundane. The Infinite Being is separated from all the Sefirot, and in relation to Him, even the Sefirot are mundane.

Until eternity of eternities

In Hebrew, this is *Adey Ad* (עדי עד), and this expression occurs numerous times in the Bible.[121]

There are two synonyms which denote eternity. The first is *LeOlam*, usually translated as "forever," which indicates the end point of the time continuum. Often used is the expression *LeOlam VaEd* (לעולם ועד), which means "forever and eternity." The expression "eternity," here denotes the realm outside the time continuum, where the concept of time does not exist at all.

Even in such a timeless domain, however, there is still a kind of hypertime, where events can occur in a logical sequence. The Midrash calls such hypertime, the "order of time" (*seder zemanim*).[122] The expression "eternity of eternities" (*Adey Ad*) denotes a domain that is beyond even such hypertime.

1:6 עשר ספירות בלי מה צפייתן כמראה הבזק
ותכליתן אין להם קץ ודברו בהן ברצוא ושוב
ולמאמרו כסופה ירדופו ולפני כסאו הם משתחוים:

> *Ten Sefirot of Nothingness*
> *Their vision is like the "appearance of lightning"*
> *Their limit has no end*
> *And His Word in them is "running and returning"*
> *They rush to His saying like a whirlwind*
> *And before His throne they prostrate themselves.*

Their vision

The word for "vision" here is *Tzafiyah*, which usually denotes a prophetical or mystical vision. The Hekhalot, an ancient mystical text which might be contemporary to Sefer Yetzirah, speaks of the "vision (*tzafiyah*) of the Markava."[123] The Markava is the divine

Chariot seen in Ezekiel's vision, and the term is used to denote the mystical experience on its highest levels.

The Sefer Yetzirah is now describing how the Sefirot appear in a mystical vision. In earlier sections, the text spoke of the exercises used to visualize the Sefirot, and now it describes their appearance.

The Bahir, another very ancient text, explains that the word *Tzafiyah*, derived from the root *Tzafah*, indicates that one is looking down from a high place.[124] In the previous section, the Sefer Yetzirah spoke of the Sefirot as ten "depths." When one looks into a depth, however, one is usually looking downward. In the Hekhalot, the mystical experience is often described as a descent in a downward direction, and it is called "descending to the Markava."[125]

One reason why gazing at the Sefirot is called a "descent" is because, in order to accomplish this, one must first attain Chakhmah consciousness, as discussed earlier. In the array of the Sefirot, however, Chakhmah is the highest, at least of those which are approachable. In climbing the Tree of the 32 paths of Wisdom, one must begin by attaching himself to Chakhmah (Wisdom). When this is accomplished, one then looks down at the other Sefirot. Only then does one begin climbing the Sefirot, beginning at the lowest.

Like the appearance of lightning

This is taken from the verse, "And the Chayot, running and returning, like the appearance of lightning (*bazak*)" (Ezekiel 1:14).

The word *Bazak*, which is found only in this one place in the Bible, is usually translated as "lightning" or "a spark."[126] According to other interpretations, *Bazak* denotes a flashing meteor or a bursting bubble.[127] According to all these opinions, the Sefer Yetzirah is stating that the Sefirot can only be visualized for an instant, and then they vanish.

The great Kabbalist, Rabbi Moshe de Leon (1238-1305), best known as the publisher of the Zohar, offers an interesting analogy.[128] When the Sefirot are seen in a mystical vision, their appearance is like sunlight reflected on a wall from a bowl of water. As long as the bowl is absolutely still, the reflected image is clear, but the slightest vibration causes it to break up and oscillate wildly.

Similarly, a clear vision of the Sefirot would be possible in theory, but only if the mind were absolutely still and calm. The slightest exterior thought, however, destroys the image completely. When the mind is in a state where it can visualize the Sefirot, it is disturbed by the most minute distractions.

Their limit has no end

This is obviously derived from the verse, "For every limit I have seen an end, Your commandment is very broad" (Psalms 119:96).

The Hebrew word for "limit" here is *Takhlit* (תכלית), which also means "completion" and "ultimate."[129] It is derived from the root *Kalah* (כלה), meaning to "complete" or "finish," as in "the heaven and earth were finished (*kalah*)" (Genesis 2:1). The word *Takhlit* also denotes purpose, since when something fulfills its purpose it is said to be completed and fulfilled.

The expression, "their limit has no end (*ketz*)," can be compared to the earlier expression, "their measure. . . has no end (*sof*)" (1:5). Both words, *Ketz* and *Sof,* denote an end, but the shade of meaning is somewhat different.

The word *Sof* (סוף) is derived from the root *Safah* (ספה), meaning "to cease to exist." The term *Ketz* (קץ), on the other hand, comes from *Katzatz* (קצץ), meaning "to cut off."[130] Hence, the end implied by *Sof* is where something ceases to exist, while *Ketz* implies the point where it is "cut off," that is, its extreme boundary or limit. As one authority puts it, *Sof* is the end in relation to that which follows it, and *Ketz* is the end with regard to that which precedes it.[131]

When the Sefer Yetzirah spoke earlier of the Sefirot as extensions, the text says that they have no *Sof.* This indicates that there is no place where they cease to exist, no matter how far out one goes. This is the infinity of extension. Similarly, when God is called Ain Sof, literally "without *Sof,*" it also means that there is no place where He ceases to exist.[132]

Here, on the other hand, the Sefer Yetzirah is speaking of the Sefirot as they are seen in a mystical vision. The text then says that their purpose, completion and outcome have no limit (*ketz*). Even though the Sefirot are seen only as a flash, there is no limit to the insight that they can imbue to the individual.

His word in them is "running and returning"

This also alludes to the verse, "And the Chayot running and returning, like the appearance of lightning" (Ezekiel 1:14). It is discussed again later (1:8).

The phrase "His word" is Devaro (דְּבָרוֹ). Others, however, vocalize this Dabru (דָּבְרוּ), which means "they speak." This line then reads, "They speak of them as running and returning."[133]

This teaches that one cannot focus for any length of time on any of the Sefirot. The mind can concentrate and see them as a "flash of lightning," but only for an instant. Then one must return. One oscillates between "running" and "returning," peeking for an instant, and then immediately returning to one's normal mental state.[134]

The Kabbalists note that "running" denotes Chakhmah, while "returning" implies Binah.[135]

As discussed earlier, one can only visualize the Sefirot with Chakhmah consciousness, through the nonverbal part of the mind. Such Chakhmah consciousness is very difficult to maintain, since the mind normally functions in a state of verbal Binah consciousness. As mentioned earlier (1:4), the only way to attain Chakhmah consciousness is to swing back and forth between Chakhmah and Binah. It is only during the instant of pure Chakhmah consciousness that the Sefirot can be perceived.

In Hebrew, the word "run" is usually Rutz (רוּץ). Here, however, the commentaries note that the root of the word is Ratza (רצא), and this is apparently the only place in the entire Bible where this root is found.[136] According to the Midrash, this root is related both to Rutz, "to run," and to Ratzah (רצה), meaning to "will" or "desire."[137] The word Ratza (רצא) therefore has the implication of "running with one's will," or impelling the will to concentrate on something beyond its grasp. This indicates the mental effort through which the Sefirot are visualized.

The Sefer Yetzirah relates "running and returning" to speech. Speech exists only in relation to Binah consciousness, since this is the verbal part of the mind. As long as a person is normally in a state of Binah consciousness, he can only visualize the Sefirot as a flash, "running and returning."

They rush to His saying like a whirlwind

The Sefer Yetzirah says that God's "speech in them runs and returns." God's speech can be visualized through the Sefirot, but it "runs and returns."

"Speech" (Davar) refers to the general concept, while a "saying" (Ma'amar) denotes a particular statement. It is only with regard to the generic "speech" that the Sefirot oscillate, "running and return ing." But when there is a *Ma'amar*, a specific saying or edict, they no longer oscillate, but rush "like a whirlwind."

According to the reading, "His speech in them runs and returns," this entire section is speaking of the Sefirot. One normally sees the Sefirot "running and returning," like flashes of lightning. But when a particular edict from God is present, they no longer oscillate, but pur sue it "like a whirlwind."

According to the commentaries who interpret this line as "they speak of them running and returning," the entire text is speaking of "they," namely the masters and prophets. Although they normally only visualize the Sefirot "running and returning," when a specific edict from God was heard, they would pursue it like a whirlwind, going far beyond their normal bounds.

The Hebrew word for whirlwind here is *Sufah*, a term that occurs many times in the Bible.[138] The word *Sufah* (סופה) comes from the root *Safah* (ספה), meaning "to annihilate." Thus, according to many commentaries, it is the most powerful and destructive wind possi ble.[139] It is also related to the word *Sof* (סוף), meaning a limit or boundary. As one authority explains, a *Sufah* is a wind that exceeds the normal bounds of natural weather.[140]

This teaches that when there is an edict from God, the mystic can go far beyond the normal bounds to pursue it. The fact that he is pursuing a divine "saying" allows him to have access to much higher states of consciousness than the normally can attain.

It is for this reason that many mystics would engage in medita tions related to the observance of various commandments. They were making use of God's "saying" and edict, and in this manner, were able to reach much higher levels than usual. The divine "saying" asso ciated with the commandment would also serve to attract the Sefirot and make them more accessible.

There are two types of storm wind, a *Sa'arah* and a *Sufah*.[141] A *Sa'arah* is a wind that merely agitates (*Sa'ar*), while a *Sufah* is a hurri cane that sweeps away everything in its path.[142]

At the beginning of the mystical experience, Ezekiel says that he saw a "storm wind (*sa'arah*) coming from the north" (Ezekiel 1:4). According to some commentaries, this refers to the agitation of the mind when one enters the transcendental realm.[143]

The vehicle through which one rises and enters the mystical realm is called a Markava (chariot), and the art of engaging in this practice is called "working in the Chariot" (*Ma'aseh Markava*).[144] It is therefore highly significant that the scripture states, "His Chariot (*markava*) is like a whirlwind (*sufah*)" (Isaiah 66:15).[145] This indicates

that the *Sufah* wind acts like a Chariot, conveying one into the mysti
cal realm. It is a force that carries one beyond the normal limit (*sof*)
into the transcendental.

Saadia Gaon interprets *Sufah* to denote the dust devils that one
sees in small whirlwinds, where the dust assumes many shapes and
forms. These forms constantly change, and a distinct form lasts only
for a moment. Similarly, when one visualizes the Sefirot, one can see
them in many forms, but like sand devils, they last only for an
instant, and then dissolve.

Before His Throne they prostrate themselves

As discussed earlier (1:4), when we speak of God as "sitting," it
means that He is lowering His essence so as to be concerned with His
creation. His Throne is the object upon which He sits, and hence, it
denotes the vehicle of such lowering and concern.

While "sitting" is a lowering that one does on one's own initia-
tive, prostrating oneself and bowing is a lowering that one does
because of a higher power. The tools of God's concern are the Sefirot,
since it is through them that He directs the universe. As a result of
the concept of God's Throne, the Sefirot must also lower their
essence and interact with the lower world. The Sefer Yetzirah therefore says, "before His Throne they prostrate themselves."

The universe of the Sefirot is called Atzilut. Below it is Beriyah,
the world of the Throne. As Ezekiel describes it, "Above the firmament that was over their heads was the likeness of a Throne. . . and
upon the likeness of the Throne, was a likeness of the appearance of
a Man" (Ezekiel 1:26). The Throne is in the universe of Beriyah,
while the "Man" on the Throne represents the anthropomorphic
array of the Sefirot in Atzilut.

The highest universe that can actually be visualized is Yetzirah,
the world of the angels. In this world, one can visualize a reflection
of the Throne, and hence, Ezekiel said that he saw "the *likeness* of a
Throne." One can also see a "reflection of a reflection" of the Sefirot,
and he therefore saw, "the likeness of the appearance of a Man."

When the Sefer Yetzirah says that the Sefirot "prostrate them-
selves," he is indicating that they are reflected in the lower universes.
Since they prostrate themselves before God's Throne, which is in
Beriyah, they are even visible in Yetzirah. It is in the universe of
Yetzirah that a reflection of the Sefirot is visualized.

1:7

עשר ספירות בלימה נעוץ סופן בתחלתן ותחלתן
בסופן כשלהבת קשורה בנחלת שאדון יחיד ואין
לו שני ולפני אחד מה אתה סופר:

Ten Sefirot of Nothingness
   Their end is imbedded in their beginning
   and their beginning in their end
     like a flame in a burning coal
For the Master is singular
   He has no second
And before One, what do you count?

Their end is imbedded in their beginning

According to most commentaries, the "beginning" is Keter (Crown), while the "end" is Malkhut (Kingship). These are the two end points of the spiritual dimension.

In the most basic level, Keter is seen as the concept of Cause, while Malkhut is the archetype of Effect. Since a cause cannot exist without an effect, and an effect cannot exist without a cause, the two are interdependent on each other.

The Sefer Yetzirah likens this to a "flame bound to a burning coal." A flame cannot exist without the coal, and the burning coal cannot exist without the flame. Although the coal is the cause of the flame, the flame is also the cause of the burning coal. Without the flame, it would not be a *burning* coal.

Since Cause cannot exist without Effect, Effect is also the cause of Cause. In this sense, Effect is the cause, and Cause is the effect. Since beginning and end are inseparable, "their end is imbedded in their beginning, and their beginning in their end."

Thus, even though Keter is Cause and Malkhut is Effect, there is also a sense in which Malkhut is the cause of Keter. Often in Kabbalah, where such a situation exists, Keter is seen as existing on a lower level than Malkhut. Thus, for example, Keter of Beriyah is below Malkhut of Atzilut, and Keter of Yetzirah is below Malkhut of Beriyah.

As discussed earlier, there is no term that can be used to describe God. God Himself cannot even be called the Cause.[146] A cause is to some degree dependent on its effect, and God cannot be dependent on anything. The Kabbalists therefore teach that before creating any-

N

O

Figure 10. A circle with O and N as two antipodal points.

thing else, God created the concept of "Cause." This is the Sefirah of Keter (Crown). Keter is also often identified with Will. This, however, is an anthropomorphism, since in man, will is the *cause* of all action.[147]

The Sefer Yetzirah therefore states that "the Master is singular, He has no second." The Sefirot may be interdependent, but this does not include the Infinite Being. Since God is absolutely unitary, He cannot even be called the Cause, since this would imply an effect as a "second."

When we view the Sefirot as being ten directions in a five-dimensional continuum, we can also interpret this in another manner. Every pair of Sefirot defines an infinite line, extended infinitely in both directions. The end points of such an infinite line, however, come together and meet once again at the "point at infinity." This is a fact recognized by mathematicians, and considerable use of the "point at infinity" is found in complex analysis, the calculus of complex numbers.

Although this is a highly abstract concept, it is not that difficult to understand. Imagine a circle, with two antipodal points, O and N. Obviously, two lines extending outward from O will once again come together at point N. But then what happens if we make the circle infinitely large? The larger the circle, the closer the curve approaches a straight line. In the limit where the circle becomes infinitely large, the lines extending outward from point O actually become straight. But still, they come together at point N. This point at infinity is where all endpoints meet.[148] See figure 10.

In our three-dimensional continuum, we can likewise extend all lines outward infinitely. The end points of all these lines would then be an infinite sphere surrounding all space. However, each opposing pair of lines would meet at the point at infinity, and therefore, all outgoing lines must meet at this point.[149]

Thus, in one sense, the entire three-dimensional space continuum can be seen as surrounded by an infinite sphere. In another sense, however, this entire infinite sphere can also be represented by a single point — the point at infinity. A point, however, is infinitely small. Thus, the point at infinity can be seen as being both infinitely large and infinitely small at the same time.

The same argument can easily be extended to the five-dimensional hyperspace discussed in Sefer Yetzirah.

Thus, if every pair of Sefirot defines an infinite line, the beginning of each line is "imbedded" in its end. This is true of all the Sefirot. All opposites, in their extreme case, become joined as one.

One can use this as a meditation. Try to imagine the sphere at infinity and the point at infinity, and attempt to perceive how they are actually one. You will then see that your usual conception of space and extension are not as simple as you believe.

In particular, this is true of the Keter-Malkhut line. In the direction of Keter, this line extends infinitely toward God, the ultimate Good. In the Malkhut direction, it extends infinitely away from God, toward ultimate evil. These two end points can also be viewed as the ultimately spiritual and the ultimately physical. In this sense, we must therefore say that the ultimately physical and the ultimately spiritual are "imbedded" in each other.

In order to understand this more deeply, we must first ask some questions. The most basic question is: Why did God create a physical world? God created the universe to bestow good to His creation, but this good is purely spiritual. This being true, what need is there for a physical world? Before we can answer this question, we must first ask another question. What is the difference between the material and the spiritual?

We speak of the material and the spiritual as two different concepts. We know that the spiritual is not material. But precisely what is the difference? The answer should be obvious. The main difference between the material and spiritual involves space. Physical space only exists in the physical world. In the spiritual, there is no space as we know it.

Although concepts of distance and closeness exist in the spiritual realm, they do not have the same meaning as they do in the physical world. In a spiritual sense, closeness involves resemblance. Two things that resemble each other are said to be spiritually close. Two things that differ, on the other hand, are far apart in a spiritual sense.

This has very important implications. In the spiritual world, it is utterly impossible to bring two opposites together. Because they are opposite, they are by definition, poles apart.

Thus, for example, God and man are worlds apart—"as the heavens are higher than the earth." On a purely spiritual plane, it would be totally impossible for the two ever to be brought together. It was for this reason that God created the concept of space. Spiritual things can be bound to the material, just as, for example, the soul is bound to the body.

Two opposites can then be brought together by being bound to physical objects. In the physical world, space exists, and two opposites can literally be pushed together. Furthermore, two spiritual opposites can even be bound to the same material object.[150]

Thus, for example, man has both an urge for good and an urge for evil, the *Yetzer Tov*, and the *Yetzer HaRa*. In a purely spiritual sense, these are poles apart. Without a physical world, they could never be brought together in a single entity.

The archetype of the spiritual being is the angel. Since an angel has no body, it can never contain both good and evil in its being. Our sages therefore teach us that angels have no *Yetzer HaRa*.[151]

It is only in a physical being that both good and evil can exist together. Although they are at opposite poles spiritually, they can come together in the physical man. One reason why God created man in a physical world was to allow him to have full freedom of choice, with both good and evil as part of his makeup. Without a physical world, these two concepts could never exist in the same being.[152]

The fact that good and evil can exist in the same physical space also allows good to overcome evil in this world. Here again, this is only possible in a physical world. In a purely spiritual arena, good could never come close enough to evil to have any influence over it. In the physical world, however, good and evil can exist together, and good can therefore overcome evil. Our sages thus teach us that one of the main reasons why man was placed in the physical world was to overcome the forces of evil.[153] The Zohar expresses it by stating that we are here "to turn darkness into light."[154]

The entire concept of the nonphysical is very difficult to comprehend, and may be clarified by a remarkable teaching of our sages. The Midrash tells us, "One angel cannot have two missions. Neither can two angels share the same mission."[155]

This teaching brings our entire discussion into focus. The angel is the archetype of the nonphysical being. When we speak of an angel, we are speaking of an entity that exists purely on a spiritual plane. Angels can be differentiated only by their mission, that is, by their involvement and attachment to some physical thing.

Two angels therefore cannot share the same mission. It is only their different missions that make the two angels different entities. They cannot be separated by space like physical objects.[156] Therefore, if they both had the same mission, there would be nothing to differentiate them, and they would be one. Similarly, one angel cannot have two missions. On a purely spiritual plane, two different concepts cannot exist in a single entity. If an angel had two missions, then it would be two angels.

We can also understand this in terms of the human mind. In a sense, the mind is a pure spiritual entity, bound to man's physical brain. Many thoughts and memories may be bound together by man's physical brain, but the mind can only focus on one of them at a time. In simple terms, a person can only think of one thing at a time. A thought is a spiritual entity, and as such, can only contain a single concept. Since both a thought and an angel are basic spiritual entities, this is very closely related to the fact that an angel can only have a single mission.[157]

For a similar reason, angels have no way of knowing anything that does not pertain to their particular mission. An angel may be created initially with a vast storehouse of knowledge, but it has no way of increasing it, at least, not beyond its own sphere of activity. Thus, for example, we find one angel asking another a question: "And one [angel] said to the Man dressed in linen. . . 'How long shall it be until the end of these wonders'" (Daniel 12:6)? One angel had to ask the other, because he himself could not know something outside of his own domain.[158]

In the physical world, we can learn things through our five senses. We can hear, feel, smell and taste. Our knowlege of things comes from our physical proximity to them. In the spiritual worlds, however, this does not exist. The only way that one can learn about a thing is to come into spiritual proximity with it. An angel cannot do this outside of his own realm.

Man therefore has an advantage over an angel. The very fact that he exists in this lower world enables him to reach up ever higher.

There are concepts of good decreed by God, and as His decrees, they are intimately bound to Him. When a man physically involves himself with these good concepts, he literally binds himself to God. He thus achieves a closeness that no angel could ever hope to reach.[159]

This is a major difference between a man and an angel. An angel is assigned to one spiritual station, and has no way to rise any higher. Thus, when the prophet speaks of angels, he says, "Around Him, the seraphim stood" (Isaiah 6:2). Angels are described as standing and stationary. But when God speaks to man, He tells him, "If you walk in My ways. . . then I will give you a place to move among those who stand here" (Zechariah 3:7). God was showing the prophet a vision of stationary angels, and telling him that he would be able to move

Table 10. Unification of the Sefirot.

׳	Apex of Yud	Keter
׳	Yud	Chakhmah
ה	Heh	Binah
ו	Vav	Chesed, Gevurah, Tiferet, Netzach, Hod, Yesod
ה	Heh	Malkhut

among them. Man can move from level to level, but angels are bound to their particular plane.[160]

There are many levels in the spiritual world. If only the spiritual would exist, there would be no way for these to come together. The only thing that can possibly unify these levels is their relationship to the physical world.

In order to reach the highest levels of holiness, man must therefore become part of the physical world. When he obeys God's commandments, he attaches himself to the same physical objects as the One who gave the commandments. In obeying these commandments, man therefore attaches himself to God to the greatest possible degree. He is thus able to scale the highest spiritual heights.

This is the symbolism of Jacob's dream in which he saw, "A ladder standing on earth, whose top reached the heavens" (Genesis 28:12). It is only through earthly deeds that we can climb the loftiest heights. The different levels of the spiritual world, the rungs of the "ladder," can only be bound together when they are "standing on the earth."[161]

The Sefirot are not physical, and do not appear to be attached to any physical concept. Since they represent different concepts and levels, the question then arises: How can they interact? Obviously, the only possible way is through some relationship with the physical world. It is only when two different Sefirot come together and interact with the same physical object that they can also interact with each other. The Kabbalists therefore engage in many physical activities with the primary intent of "unifying the Sefirot."

Another way in which the Sefirot are unified is through the Divine Names. This is especially true of the Tetragrammaton, YHVH (יהוה). According to the Kabbalists, the apex of the Yud (׳) represents Keter, the Yud itself, Chakhmah, the initial Heh (ה), Binah, the Vav (ו), which has a numerical value of six, the next six Sefirot, and the final Heh, Malkhut. See Table 10.

The very fact that this Name can be written on a physical piece of paper, where the letters representing the Sefirot are brought together, serves to unify the Sefirot. Each Sefirah is associated with a letter, and when these letters are physically brought together, the Sefirot can also interact. Specific interactions involving the Sefirot can also be brought about when various names are combined. The same is also true of other Kabbalistic diagrams and representations of the Sefirot.

Even though the Sefirot were created before the physical world, they exist in a domain that is above time, where past, present and future are one. The very fact that they would have physical counterparts in the future provided them with a link with the physical world. Since God willed that at some future time, the letters of the Name would be able to be represented by physical forms and be written on a physical medium, they had an association with the physical even before it was created. This allowed the Sefirot to interact, even before the creation of the physical universe.[162]

The same is true of the other letters of the alphabet. Although the letters are best known as they are written down physically, they actually also represent spiritual forces. Through various combinations of the letters, the spiritual forces associated with them are brought together in various effective combinations. These spiritual forces are the "letters with which heaven and earth were created."

From all this, we see that there is an important link between the physical and the spiritual. Even Keter, the highest of the Sefirot, has a physical representation in the apex of the Yud of the Divine Name.

This is also realted to our earlier discussion of cause and effect. The highest level of Keter is the ultimate cause, while the physical world is the ultimate effect.

Like a flame in a burning coal

In describing the relationship between the physical and the spiritual, the Zohar uses an expression very similar to that used here. The Zohar states: "If one wishes to know the wisdom of the holy unification, let him look at the flame rising from a burning coal or from a kindled lamp. The flame cannot rise unless it is unified with something physical."[163]

From the context, it is evident that the Zohar is speaking of the different parts of the flame. The only way in which the flame can rise is for all of these parts to come together. This is only possible when the flame is attached to the physical coal or wick. In a similar manner, all the spiritual levels cannot function or interact unless they are bound to the physical.

The Sefer Yetzirah therefore states that "their end is imbedded in their beginning. . . like a flame in a burning coal." The only way in which the end and beginning can interact is because both are bound to related physical concepts.

This can also be used as a meditation.[164] The wick itself represents the physical world, while the blue flame nearest to the wick is the counterpart of Malkhut.[165] Surrounding this is the bright yellow flame, corresponding to the next six Sefirot: Chesed, Gevurah, Tiferet, Netzach, Hod and Yesod. Above this is the barely visible exterior flame, the hottest part of all, paralleling Binah. Then comes the light radiating from the candle, which is Chakhmah. Finally, there is the concept of flame itself, and this corresponds to Keter.

All of these parts are unified only through the wick. By contemplating a flame in this manner, one can bind himself to the Ten Sefirot.

It is for this reason that the Sefer Yetzirah states that the Ten Sefirot parallel the ten directions. Even though the Sefirot are purely spiritual, the very fact that they are associated with the physical directions serves to unify them. Then, as it were, the point at infinity in the five-dimensional hyperspace would represent the unapproachable Infinite.

The great Kabbalist, Rabbi Abraham Abulafia, notes that the Hebrew word for "coal," *Gachelet* (גחלת), has a numerical value of 441. This is the same as the value of *Emet* (אמת), meaning "truth."[166] It is Truth that binds all opposites together. This is indicated by the word itself. The word *Emet* begins with an Alef (א), the first letter of the alphabet, and ends with a Tav (ת), the last letter. Thus, the "end is imbedded in the beginning." This is accomplished through the Mem (מ), the middle letter of the alphabet.

Another master Kabbalist, Rabbi Joseph Gikatalia (1248-1323), points out that Alef and Tav are also the first letters of the word *Atah* (אתה), meaning "Thou." The Heh (ה) at the end of this word, which has a numercial value of five, represents Binah, as expressed in the five books of the Torah, and in the five phonetic families of the alphabet.[167] In order to address God as "Thou," we must first "imbed the beginning (Alef) in the end (Tav)." Only then can we address Him through the letters of the Torah, represented by the Heh.

For the Master is Singular

Besides being brought together by their association with the physical world, the Sefirot are also unified by God Himself. In his prayer, Elijah thus says regarding the Sefirot, "You bind them, and You unify them."[168]

When the Ten Sefirot are represented as the ten directions, the physical can be taken as the zero point, from which they all emanate. God, as it were, can be said to parallel the point at infinity, where they all converge. Of course, God has no representation whatever, but this is the closest that the human mind can come to imagining a representation. By contemplating the point at infinity, one can approach a conception of the Infinite Being.

This point at infinity is both infinitely large and infinitely small. It does not have any defined place in the continuum of space, time, or the spiritual. It has neither shape nor form, yet, at the same time, it is defined as a single, unitary, undifferentiated point. All of this is also true of God. Of course, God is much more than this.

In describing God here, the Sefer Yetzirah does not say that He is one (Echad), but that He is singular (Yachid). It is saying that God is so absolutely singular that there is no quality whatever that can be attributed to Him. As the philosophers state, we cannot describe God with any quality or adjective whatever, only with negative attributes or attributes of action.[169] Although we cannot say what God *is*, by using negative attributes, we can say what He *is not*. Similarly, with attributes of action, we can speak of what God does.

This also implies that God is absolutely simple. In the domain that existed before creation, there was nothing other than God. As mentioned earlier, even such simple concepts as Cause and Effect had to be created. The same is true of number.

If the concept of "oneness" existed in God, this would imply that the concept of number exists in His essence. This in itself would introduce an elelment of plurality. One could then speak of God and His "oneness," that is, His association with the number one. "God" and "His oneness" would then be two concepts.

The Hebrew word *Echad* denotes an association with the number one. *Yachid*, on the other hand, is a negative attribute, indicating the absence of any plurality whatever.

He has no second

This is based on the verse, "There is One, He has no second, He has neither son nor brother" (Ecclesiastes 4:8).

Before one, what do you count

How can one count before the concept of "one" came into existence. As the Sefer Yetzirah later says, "one" parallels Keter, the first Sefirah (1:9). As discussed earlier (1:1), the concept of numbers did not come into existence until the creation of the Sefirot, which were the first elements of numerality and plurality in creation. The concept of "one" did not come into being until the Sefirah of Keter was created. God, the Infinite Being, existed before Keter came into being.

1:8   עשר ספירות בלימה בלום פיך מלדבר ולבך
מלהרהר ואם רץ פיך לדבר ולבך להרהר שוב
למקום שלכך נאמר (יחזקאל א') והחיות רצוא
ושוב ועל דבר זה נכרת ברית:

Ten Sefirot of Nothingness
  Bridle your mouth from speaking
  and your heart from thinking
And if your heart runs
  return to the place.
It is therefore written,
  "The Chayot running and returning." (Ezekiel 1:24)
Regarding this a covenant was made.

Bridle your mouth

The Sefer Yetzirah defines the word *Belimah*, which we translate as "nothingness." It says that it also has the connotation of bridling (*balam*).

The essence of the Sefirot can only be attained when one bridles one's lips from speaking, and closes one's mind to all verbal and depictive thought. Only when one makes the mind completely blank can the Sefirot be experienced.

This is particularly important, since many techniques of Kabbalah meditation involve the recitation of a mantra-like device or various types of contemplation. All such techniques, however, are only a means through which the mind is cleared of all thought. The actual experience of the Sefirot only comes after one stops using the technique and remains absolutely still, with all the thought processes hushed.[170]

And your heart from thinking

In Kabbalah, the term "heart" usually denotes Binah.[171] It indicates the verbal part of the mind, which is the seat of Binah consciousness. This Binah consciousness must be "bridled" so the Sefirot can be experienced with Chakhmah consciousness alone.

And if your heart runs

Here, "heart" again refers to Binah consciousness. The Sefirot must be experienced with Chakhmah consciousness. If one tries to depict them with Binah (the "heart"), then the mind can become engulfed in a profusion of symbolism. As the Kabbalists explain, this is very dangerous, since the mind can be swallowed up in this kaleidescope of symbolism, and not be able to emerge from it.[172] This is what happened to Ben Zomah, who lost his mind when he entered Paradise.[173]

This "running" consists of a rapid profusion of symbolism, either verbal or visual.[174] If the "heart runs," the Sefer Yetzirah warns that one should "return to the place." He must focus on something physical, so as to restore spiritual equilibrium.[175]

In this respect, one must emulate the Chayot, the "living angels" seen by Ezekiel in his vision. One must oscillate between "running and returning." Since one can only think with Binah consciousness, one must use it to swing into Chakhmah consciousness. This state can only be maintained for a short time, whereupon Binah consciousness returns, and one tries to depict his experience. At this point, one must immediately return to the physical. In this manner, one can oscillate back and forth, reaching higher each time.[176]

A covenant was made

From the context, this covenant is a mutual agreement between God and the mystic. The mystic promises that he will not attempt to depict the Sefirot with Binah consciousness, and God promises that if one runs back immediately, then he will be able to return.

It is in this context that the Kabbalists advised those who were attempting to reach the highest levels to bind their soul with an oath that it should return to their body.[177] Besides such individual oaths, there is also a general covenant that implies that the soul will be able to return, even from the highest levels.

In more general terms, a covenant is something that comes between two things and joins them. This is the covenant that joins the spiritual and the physical.

In particular, as the Sefer Yetzirah states (1:3), a covenant denotes circumcision. One of the reasons for circumcisions is to indicate that one should be able to control one's sexual passions.[178] Communion with the spiritual is also sexual in a sense, and the covenant of circumcision also helps to control this passion. A person who can control his sexual passions even at the height of desire, can also control his mind when it enters the spiritual realm.

According to some critical studies, this line is the end of the most ancient part of the text. The Sefer Yetzirah (6:7) also appears to indicate that the covenant mentioned here was that which God made with Abraham. What the text might be saying is that, regarding everything that has been written up to this point, a covenant was made, possibly with Abraham.

1:9   עשר ספירות בלימה אחת רוח אלהים חיים
ברוך ומבורך שמו של חי העולמים קול ורוח
ודבור והוא רוח הקודש:

Ten Sefirot of Nothingness:
One is the Breath of the Living God
Blessed and benedicted is the name
of the Life of Worlds
The voice of breath and speech
And this is the Holy Breath.

One

The Sefirah alluded to here is Keter (Crown). This is the number one. It is the first of the numbers to come into existence.[179]

The breath of the Living God

This is based on the verse, where God says of Betzalel, builder of the tabernacle in the desert, "I will fill him with the Breath of God (*Ruach Elohim*), with Wisdom, Understanding, and Knowledge" (Exodus 31:3). We therefore see that the "Breath of God" comes before Wisdom and Understanding. Among the Sefirot, then, this corresponds to Keter.[180] As the Talmud says, it was through this "Breath of God" that Betzalel was able to manipulate the letters of creation.

The word *ruach*, which we translate here as "breath," is also the word for wind, and the Sefer Yetzirah also apparently uses it as the term for air. This word, however, is often used in the Bible to denote spirit, and this is the sense that it is used here.

In general, the word *ruach* indicates motion and communication. It is related to the words *O-rach*, meaning a path, and *O-reach*, meaning a guest. The spirit (*ruach*) of life in an animal is the power that causes it to move.

Normally, the air is invisible and undetectable. It is only when it moves that one can feel it as a wind or breath. Similarly, the spiritual continuum is undetectable, except when it moves. It is then experienced as spirit (*ruach*). Hence, *ruach* is the word for wind, breath, and spirit.

This is also describing the act of creation. The analogy would be the formation of a glass vessel.[181] First the breath (*ruach*) emanates from the mouth of the glassblower. The vessel is shaped through the interaction of the breath, where the wind bounding off the walls causes pressure. The vessel then expands in all spacial directions.

Living God

As mentioned above (1:1), the term "Living God" (*Elohim Chayim*) denotes Yesod (Foundation), when this Sefirah is in a pro-creative mode, disbursing all the forces of creation. The "spirit" here, which is from Keter, is that which is ultimately disbursed by Yesod. Since Keter itself cannot be experienced, it is referred to in terms of Yesod, since that is where it is experienced.[182]

Blessed and Benedicted

In other ancient Kabbalah texts, such as the Bahir, these adjectives are also used with regard to Keter.[183]

In Hebrew, the two terms here are *Barukh* (ברוך) and *MeBhorakh* (מבורך). Both words actually mean "blessed." *Barukh* denotes that God is intrinsically blessed, while *MeBorakh* implies that He is blessed by others in prayer.

When we say that God is "blessed," this means that His essence is brought down, so as to interact with His creation and "bless" it.[184] Hence, it is related to the word *Berekh* (ברך), meaning "knee." Just as the knee, when it is bent, serves to lower the body, so a blessing serves to lower the Divine. This is closely related to the concept of sitting, discussed above (1:4).

God has an intrinsic mode through which He brings His essence to bear on His creation. In this respect, He is called *Barukh*. His essence is also brought to bear to a greater degree as a result of prayer and similar actions. In this respect He is said to be *MeBhorakh*.

Life of Worlds

This also refers to the Sefirah of Yesod (Foundation), but in a mode where it bestows spiritual influx and life to the universes below Atzilut. It is therefore called "Life of *Worlds*."

Voice of Breath and Speech

These were the tools of creation, as it is written, "With the Word of God, the heavens were made, and with the Breath (*Ruach*) of His mouth, all their hosts" (Psalms 33:6). According to the Talmud, this alludes to the first Saying of creation, that is, to Keter.[185]

Voice (*kol*) is pure inarticulate sound, and as such, it is related to Chakhmah. Speech, on the other hand, is articulate and related to Binah. These two opposites are then connected by "Breath" (Ruach).

This can also be interpreted in terms of creation. "Voice" is pure, inarticulated creative force. It is alluded to in the first verse of the Torah, "In the beginning God created the heaven and the earth." The Talmud states that this was the first of the Ten Saying with which the world was created.[186] This is an inarticulate Saying, since only the accomplishment, and not the saying, is recorded in the Torah.

Right after this, the Torah reports, "The breath of God (*Ruach Elohim*) hovered on the face of the water" (Genesis 1:2). This is "Breath" or Spirit (*Ruach*). It is only after this that God speaks and says, "Let there be light" (Genesis 1:3). This is the reason for the sequence in Sefer Yetzirah: "Voice, breath, speech."[187]

This is the Holy Breath

In Hebrew, this is *Ruach Hakodesh*, usually translated as "Holy Spirit." This is the usual term for divine inspiration, which in its higher forms also includes prophecy.

This "Holy Spirit" can be seen as the intermediate between Voice and Speech. It is thus also intermediate between Chakhmah and Binah consciousness. *Ruach HaKodesh* is the divine inspiration and information that one can bring back from a state of Chakhmah consciousness to one's normal state of Binah consciousness.

Such *Ruach HaKodesh* is like Keter, which stands between Chakhmah and Binah, but which is above them. Both Chakhmah and Binah are functions of the mind itself, while *Ruach HaKodesh* comes from without. It is therefore likened to Keter, since a crown is worn above the head and is external to it. This *Ruach HaKodesh* is the "breath of God" mentioned in the verse, "I will fill him with the Breath of God, with Wisdom, Understanding, and Knowledge."[188]

1 : 10 שתים רוח מרוח חקק וחצב בה עשרים ושתים
אותיות יסוד שלש אמות ושבע כפולות ושתים
עשרה פשוטות ורוח אחת מהן:

Two: Breath from Breath.
With it He engraved and carved
22 Foundation Letters
Three Mothers
Seven Doubles
and Twelve Elementals
And one Breath is from them.

Breath from Breath

This is Malkhut (Kingship), the lowest of the Ten Sefirot.[189]

It is counted right after Keter, following the above mentioned dictum, "imbed their end in their beginning." Keter is Cause, while Malkhut is Effect, and Cause cannot exist without Effect.

In the language of the later Kabbalists, the first Breath from Keter is called Direct Light (*Or Yashar*). This second "Breath from

Breath," associated with Malkhut is called Reflected Light (*Or Chozer*).[190] Using the analogy of the glassblower above, this is the breath that bounces off the walls of the vessel being formed.

In a conceptual sense, the Direct Light is the concept of causality, where Keter is the Cause of all things. As mentioned above, however, Cause cannot exist without Effect, and hence, Effect is also the cause of Cause. Malkhut, the Effect, is therefore also the Cause, and this the concept of Reflected Light.

The Kabbalists often speak of Lights and Vessels. "Light" denotes the concept of giving, while Vessels indicate that of accepting and receiving. The Kabbalists also teach that the Vessels came into being through the "collision" between Direct Light and Reflected Light.[191] These Vessels are the letters of the alphabet.[192]

The Sefer Yetzirah therefore speaks of "Breath" and of "Breath from Breath." The first "Breath" denotes the simple breath that emanates from the lungs and throat. "Breath from Breath" is that which is reflected by the various parts of the mouth to produce the sounds of speech.[193] It is through the interaction of direct and reflected breath that sounds are produced.

In man, this takes place in the mouth, while in the Sefirot, it occurs in Malkhut. It is for this reason that the Tikkuney Zohar speaks of Malkhut as the "Mouth."[194] It is also through Malkhut that all images of the higher Sefirot are reflected so that they should be visualized.[195]

The Sefer Yetzirah therefore says that the 22 letters were created through this second Sefirah.

Engraved and carved

As discussed earlier (1:1), the word *Chakak*, which is translated as "engrave," denotes the removal of material. The letters came into existence when the reflected breath removes portions of the direct breath. This takes place through the various motions of the mouth.

The second process is *Chatzav*, which is translated as "carve" or "quarry." This denotes separating material from its source, as in the verse, "From its mountains, you quarry (*chatzav*) copper" (Deuteronomy 8:9). It also refers to "quarrying" in a spiritual sense, as in, "Look at [God] the Rock from which you were quarried (*chatzav*)" (Isaiah 51:1).[196]

The word *Chatzav* thus denotes the process wherein the letter sounds leave the mouth and are expressed independently. In this context, "Engrave" (*chakak*) indicates the articulation and pronunciation of the sounds, and "carve" (*chatzav*) denotes their expression.[197]

From the last section of Sefer Yetzirah (6:7), we also see that "engraving" and "carving" denote meditative process. This shall be discussed later.

And one breath is from them

All letters that are expressed involve the same breath. In a spiritual sense, this means that the same inspiration comes from all letters. This is the *Ruach HaKodesh* that emanates from Malkhut. Since Malkhut is called the "Mouth," the spirit emanating from it is called "speech." Just like physical speech, this consists of "words," which in turn are comprised of "letters."

Some authorities interpret this phrase, "And breath is one of them." This is because Breath (*Ruach*) is associated with the letter Alef, as below (3:7).[198]

1:11 שלש מים מרוח חקק וחצב בהן כ"ב אותיות
מתהו ובהו רפש וטיט חקקן כמין ערוגה
חצבן כמין חומה סיבבס כמין מעזיבה ויצק עליהם
שלג ונעשה עפר שנאמר כי לשלג יאמר הוא ארץ:

Three: Water from Breath.
With it He engraved and carved
[22 letters from]
chaos and void
mire and clay
He engraved them like a sort of garden
He carved them like a sort of wall
He covered them like a sort of ceiling
[And He poured snow over them
and it became dust
as it is written
"For to snow He said, 'Become earth'" (Job 37:6).]

Water from Breath

This is Chakhmah (Wisdom).[199] The Midrash thus says, "Breath (*Ruach*) gave birth to Wisdom."[200] Wisdom is represented by water,

since water is an undifferentiated fluid, as discussed earlier (1:1).
Structure must be imposed on it from without.

The process described by Sefer Yetzirah is alluded to in the
verse, "He makes His breath (*ruach*) blow, the waters flow" (Psalms
147:18).[201]

The analogy is rain, which is formed when warm, moist air col-
lides with cold air. Similarly, the interaction of direct and reflected
breath creates the Sefirah of Chakhmah. Just as rain falls in all things
alike, so Chakhmah bestows God's blessing on all things without distinction.[202] Just like air can hold moisture, so Chakhmah is implied
in the "Breath" that is Keter.

The parallel between Chakhmah and rain is described in the
verses (Isaiah 55:9-11):

> *As the heaven is higher than the earth*
>   *so are My ways higher than your ways*
>   *and My thoughts, than your thoughts.*
> *But as the rain and snow descend from heaven*
>   *and return not there*
>   *without watering the earth*
>   *making it bloom and bud*
>   *giving seed to the sower and bread to he who eats.*
> *So the word that emanates from My mouth*
>   *shall not return to me emptyhanded*
>   *without accomplishing that which I please*
>   *and succeeding in its mission.*

Here God is saying that His "thought," which is Chakhmah, is
as far above the human mind as the sky is above the earth. But just
as rain can descend from the sky, so can God's Wisdom come down
to man, accomplishing what He desires.

The difference between breath and water is that breath must be
blown downward, while water falls on its own.[203] The spiritual
essence implied by Keter can only be granted by God's direct intervention and will.[204] That implied by Chakhmah, on the other hand,
descends to lower levels on its own.

In a psychological sense, Keter represents *Ruach HaKodesh*, the
divine inspiration that can only be granted by God. Wisdom, on the
other hand, can be gained by man on his own. If man makes himself
into a vessel for Chakhmah, it comes down to him automatically. In
this respect, it is like rain, which can be used by anyone who has a
proper vessel to hold it.

Breath also alludes to the process whereby God imposes His will
on creation deliberately, so as to change natural events. Chakhmah,
on the other hand, involves the natural course of events, which pre-

cede without any divine intervention. It is because of Chakhmah that the course of nature can exist. In a physical sense, water is said to allude to the undifferentiated primeval matter.[205]

With them He engraved

Here the Sefer Yetzirah is speaking about the beginnings of written letters. The spoken letters arise from breath, but for the written letters to exist, there must exist a writing fluid, such as ink. This implies the liquid state, of which the prototype is water. The writing fluid is spoken of as "mire and clay."

Chaos and Void

Tohu and *Bohu* in Hebrew. This alludes to the initial state of creation, as it is written, "The earth was chaos and void" (Genesis 1:2). The Sefer Yetzirah later says that it was out of this chaos (*tohu*) that substance was formed (2:6).

Tohu denotes pure substance that does not contain information. *Bohu* is pure information that does not relate to any substance.[206] Both are undifferentiated, and are therefore included in Chakhmah. With *Bohu* (information), the alphabet letters could be engraved on *Tohu* (substance).

The scripture states that, "the *earth* was chaos and void." The Kabbalists note that "earth" (*eretz*) is a feminine word, and teach that it alludes to Malkhut, the archetype of the feminine. "Chaos and void," which related to Chakhmah, did not come into existence until after Malkhut. This is the same as the order of the Sefer Yetzirah, which also places Chakhmah after Malkhut.[207]

Mire and clay

In Hebrew, mire is *Refesh*, and clay is *Tyt*. The only place in the Bible where the two are mentioned together is in the verse, "The wicked are like the troubled sea. It cannot rest, and its waters cast up mire and clay" (Isaiah 57:20).

In describing the original state of creation, the Torah states, "The earth was chaos and void, and darkness on the face of the deep (*tehom*)" (Genesis 1:2). According to the commentaries, the word *Tehom* denotes the mud and clay on the bottom of the sea.[208]

"Chaos and void" allude to the interaction between Chakhmah (water) and Keter (Breath). "Mire and clay" allude to the interaction between Chakhmah (water) and Malkhut (earth). Mire consists mostly of water, and therefore represents the dominance of Chakmah. Clay consists mostly of earth, and represents the dominance of Malkhut. The mire is the writing fluid, while the clay is the medium upon which it is written.

He engraved them...

The Hebrew letters have three basic parts, a top, center, and bottom. The top and bottom usually consist of heavy horizontal lines, while the center consists of thinner vertical lines.

The bottoms of the letters were "engraved like a garden." This is where material is removed from the matrix, leaving a hollow. The sides of the letters are then "carved like a wall." These are the vertical lines which separate the letters from each other like walls. Finally, the tops of the letters are added, like a ceiling covering the letters.[209] According to some authorities, this also alludes to the creation of space.[210]

As we shall see later (2:4), this can also be an instruction for a meditation.

He poured snow over them

This is omitted in some versions, but the idea is found in the Midrash.[211]

The liquid state represents fluidity and change, whereas the solid state represents permanence. When the Torah speaks of instability, it uses water as an example, as in the verse, "unstable like water" (Genesis 49:4).[212] Thus, when Chakmah is in a state of flux, it is represented by water, but when it is in a state of permanence, it is represented by snow.

As mentioned earlier, Chakmah has two modes. The first is that of Chakmah consciousness, while the second is that of memory. Chakhmah consciousness is fluid, and is represented by water. Memory, on the other hand, is fixed, and is denoted by snow.

The letters themselves represent the fluid state. Like a fluid, at this point, they can be combined in any way that one desires. Only after snow is poured over them do they become set and immutable in the solid state. A similar idea is found in the Bahir, which states that before it was given to Israel, the Torah was likened to water, but after it was given, it was likened to stone.[213]

Although Chakhmah is nonverbal. and nonvisual, it still represents the *source* of the letters. It is only after the letters are combined into words that they represent verbal Binah consciousness. The letters themselves are the "paths of Wisdom," but, as explained earlier (1:1), they are expressed primarily through Understanding.

1:12

ארבע אש ממים חקק וחצב בה כסא הכבוד
שרפים ואופנים וחיות הקודש ומלאכי השרת
ומשלשתן יסד מעונו שנאמר עושה מלאכיו רוחות
משרתיו אש לוהט:

Four: Fire from Water
With it He engraved and carved
*   the Throne of Glory*
*   Serafim, Ophanim, and holy Chayot*
*   and Ministering angels*
From these three He founded His dwelling
*   as it is written:*
"He makes His angels of breaths,
*   His ministers of flaming fire" (Psalms 104:4).*

Fire from Water

This is Binah (Understanding).[214] The process described here is alluded to in the verse, "Fire kindles water" (Isaiah 64:1).[215]

We can use the same analogy as before, where rain is brought about by the confluence of warm and cold air. "Fire from Water" would then denote the lightning that accompanies a rainstorm.[216] The process would then be alluded to in the verse, "God's voice carves out (*chotzev*) flames of fire" (Psalms 29:8).[217]

Other commentaries state that this refers to fire kindled by a globe of water used as a burning glass.[218]

According to both interpretations, the fire is seen as one that is finely focused on one particular place. It is very different than rain, which falls everywhere without distinction. This, however, is an important difference between Binah and Chakhmah. Binah focuses on a single object, while Chakhmah encompasses everything.

There is also another important difference between fire and water. Water naturally flows downward, while fire tends to ascend upward.[219] Fire also causes the air above it to move upward, and prevents it from descending. In a similar manner, Binah tends to restrict and curtail the flow of spiritual sustenance (*shefa*) downward to the lower spheres. In this respect, it is the precise opposite of Chakhmah. If Chakmah is the source of giving, then Binah is the source of restraint.

The analogy of fire and water also refers to the mental states implied by Chakhmah and Binah. The Midrash states, "Water conceived and gave birth to Gloom (*Afelah*), Fire conceived and gave birth to Light, Breath (*Ruach*) conceived and gave birth to Wisdom."[220] From the statement, "Breath gave birth to Wisdom," we see that this entire passage is speaking of mental states.

Water, which represents Chakhmah consciousness, thus gives birth to Gloom and darkness. This is the hushing and nullification of the senses, as well as the cessation of all normal mental processes. Fire, which represents Binah consciousness, then gives rise to light, since it is in this state that visible images are perceived.

Just like water is calm and cool, so Chakhmah consciousness is perfectly calm. Indeed, the experience of entering this state may be very much like descending into calm, deep water. It is for this reason that when Rabbi Akiba and his companions entered into the mysteries, he warned them not to say, "Water, water."[221] They should not be misled into thinking that they were actually experiencing physical water.

In the realm of Chakhmah consciousness, even the letters only exist in a state of pure information. This information exists as "chaos and void," which cannot be grasped at all, or as "mire and clay," which are totally opaque. As explained earlier, the information and letters in Chakhmah can only be grasped through the imagery of Binah (1:1). It is while in a state of Binah consciousness that this information can be described using such imagery as angels and the Throne of Glory.

The Sefer Yetzirah also implies that the physical world came into being through Chakhmah, while the spiritual world has its roots in Binah. This is because Chakhmah, the concept of giving freely, is the root of mercy, while Binah, the concept of restraint, is the root of justice. Since evil exists in the physical world, if can only be sustained through God's mercy, as the Psalmist sang, "I have said, the world is built on mercy" (Psalms 89:3). In the spiritual world, on the other hand, pure judgment prevails.[222]

According to the philosophers, Water represents the primeval matter, while Fire represents the primitive aether.[223]

The Throne of Glory

This is the vehicle through which God "sits" and "lowers" His essence so as to be concerned with His creation, as above (1:4). According to the Kabbalists, this Throne represents the Universe of Beriyah. It is in this universe that the power of Binah is dominant.

Serafim

This is the highest species of angels, which exist in the Universe of Beriyah. Other Kabbalists refer to them as Powers, Forces or Potentials

Table 11. The angels and Sefirot.

Universe	Angels	Parallel Sefirot	Inhabitant
Atzilut	[Akatriel]	Chakhmah	Sefirot
Beriyah	Serafim	Binah	Throne of Glory
Yetzirah	Chayot	Next Six	Angels
Asiyah	Ophanim	Malkhut	Shade of Physical World

(*Kochot*), rather than angels.[224] The prophet thus said, "I saw the Lord sitting on a high and exalted Throne. . . Serafim stood around Him" (Isaiah 6:1-2). The prophet Isaiah was visualizing Beriyah, the world of the Throne, and he saw the Serafim, the angels of that universe.[225]

The word "Serafim" comes from the root *Saraf,* meaning "to burn." They are given this name because they are in the world of Beriyah, where Binah, which is represented by fire, is dominant.[226]

The Chayot are the angels of Yetzirah, and these were the beings that were visualized by Ezekiel. He therefore said, "Above the firmament that was over the heads [of the Chayot] was the likeness of a Throne. . ." (Ezekiel 1:26). Finally, the Ophanim are the angels of Asiyah. These were therefore seen below the Chayot, as the prophet said, "There was an Ophan on the earth near the Chayot" (Ezekiel 1:15).

"Ministering angels" are those which appear to man on earth. While other angels can only be seen prophetically, ministering angels can also be seen physically.[227] Table 11 shows the angels in relation to the Sefirot.

From these three

That is, from Breath, Fire and Water.

He founded His dwelling

The word for "dwelling" here is *Ma'on,* which we encountered previously (1:5). This term relates to God as He encompasses all creation, including time and the spiritual dimension.

Breath, Fire and Water are the sources of the spiritual (Keter-Malkhut) and time (Chakhmah-Binah) continuums, and these encompass all creation.

As it is written...

The complete verse is, "He lays the beams of His upper chambers with water. . . He makes breaths His angels, His ministers of flaming fire."

God's "upper chambers" are the spiritual universes, while His lower chamber is the physical world. The ceiling beams of His upper chambers are said to be made of water. This refers to the level above Beriyah, which is Atzilut. In Atzilut, Chakhmah is dominant, and Chakhmah is represented by water.

The verse says that the angels are made of "breaths" (*ruchot*), in the plural. This alludes to both direct and to reflected breath. The word for angel here is *Malakh*, which also means "messenger." Just as breath descends and ascends through God's will, so do these angels. They therefore carry out the function of direct and reflected Breath.

The second kind of angel functions as a minister, remaining in a single universe. These are visualized as fire.

1:13

בירר שלש אותיות מן הפשוטות בסוד שלש
אמות אמ״ש וקבעם בשמו הגדול וחתם בהם
ששה קצוות. חמש חתם רום ופנה למעלה וחתמו
ביה״ו. שש חתם תחת ופנה למטה וחתמו בהי״ו.
שבע חתם מזרח ופנה לפניו וחתמו בוי״ה. שמונה
חתם מערב ופנה לאחריו וחתמו בוה״י. תשע חתם
דרום ופנה לימינו וחתמו ביו״ה. עשר חתם צפון
ופנה לשמאלו וחתמו בהו״י:

He chose three letters
    from among the Elementals
      [in the mystery of the three Mothers
        Alef Mem Shin (אמש)]
And He set them in His great Name
    and with them, He sealed six extremities.
Five: He sealed "above" and faced upward
    and sealed it with Yud Heh Vav (יהו).
Six: He sealed "below" and faced downward
    and sealed it with Heh Yud Vav (היו).
Seven: He sealed "east" and faced straight ahead
    and sealed it with Vav Yud Heh (ויה).
Eight: He sealed "west" and faced backward
    and sealed it with Vav Heh Yud (והי).
Nine: He sealed "south" and faced to the right
    and sealed it with Yud Vav Heh (יוה).
Ten: He sealed "north" and faced to the left
    and sealed it with Heh Vav Yud (הוי).

He chose three letters

The Sefer Yetzirah stresses the importance of the fact that these letters were chosen from among the Elemental letters. This provides one reason why the letters Yud Heh Vav (יהו) were chosen.

As the Sefer Yetzirah will later explain (2:3), in alphabetical order, the first three phonetic families are:

Gutturals:	Alef Heh Chet Eyin	אההע
Labials:	Bet Vav Mem Peh	בומפ
Palatals:	Gimel Yud Kaf Kuf	גיכק

It is immediately obvious that the first letters on these groups are the first three letters of the alphabet. Of these, Alef is one of the three Mothers, while Bet and Gimel are among the Doubles. In these three groups, therefore, the first simple letters are Heh, Vav and Yud. These are the letters of the Tetragrammaton.

The primary ordering of these letters is Yud Heh Vav. According to the book *Raziel*, this is because Yud includes the first four letters of the alphabet. Yud has a numerical value of 10, and this is the sum of the first four letters (1 + 2 + 3 + 4 = 10). After 4 comes 5, the numerical value of Heh, and then 6, the numerical value of Vav.[228]

Further significance of these letters is discussed above (1:1).

In the mystery of the three Mothers

The three letters of the Divine Name, Yud Heh Vav (יהו), parallel the three Mothers, Alef Mem Shin (אמש). See Table 12.

As the Sefer Yetzirah later explains (3:4), Mem is water, Shin is fire, while Alef is breath-air. However, we also know that Yud represents Chakhmah, which is the archetype of water, and Heh represents Binah, which is fire. We therefore have a relationship between Yud and Mem, as well as between Heh and Shin.

Vav has numerical value of 6, and therefore represents the six basic spacial directions.[229] It also represents the six Sefirot: Chesed, Gevurah, Tiferet, Netzach, Hod, and Yesod. Among the elements, Vav is said to represent Air and Breath. Indeed, in Hebrew, the word

Table 12. The three Mothers.

Mem	מ	Water	Chakhmah	Yud	י
Shin	ש	Fire	Binah	Heh	ה
Alef	א	Air Breath	The Six	Vav	ו

for "direction" is *Ruach*, the same as that for Breath. Vav is therefore derived from Alef.

As we shall see, the three Mothers (Alef Mem Shin) represent thesis, antithesis and synthesis, the basic triad of Sefer Yetzirah (3:1). Here the text explains how a three-dimensional space is produced from these three concepts.

Thesis and antithesis represent two opposite directions in a one dimensional line. Together with synthesis, they yield three elements. Since these three elements can be permuted in six different ways, they define a three-dimensional space having six directions.[230]

He sealed "above"...

There are a number of ways in which the directions are represented by the letters. In the Gra version, we have the following:

up	YHV	יהו
down	HYV	היו
east	VYH	ויה
west	VHY	והי
south	YVH	יוה
north	HVY	הוי

In this system, the axis is determined by the neutral letter Vav (ו). As mentioned earlier, Yud is thesis, Heh is antithesis, and Vav is synthesis. Since it represents synthesis, Vav is therefore the zero point, which is the point on the axis. See Table 13 and figure 11.

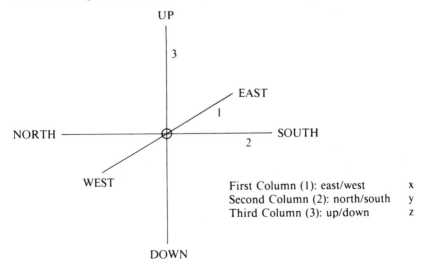

First Column (1): east/west   x
Second Column (2): north/south   y
Third Column (3): up/down   z

Figure 11. The Gra version.

Table 13. Various ways the directions are symbolized.

Direction	Gra[1]	Short[2]	Long[3]	Saadia[4]	Ari[5]	Zohar[6]	TZ[7]	
Up	YHV	YHV	HYV	YHV	YVH	YVH	VYH	5
Down	HYV	YVH	YVH	YVH	HYV	HYV	HYV	6
East	VYH	HYV	VYH	HVY	VYH	VHY	VHY	7
West	VHY	HVY	VHY	HYV	VHY	VYH	YVH	8
South	YVH	VYH	YVH	VYH	YHV	YHV	YHV	9
North	HVY	VHY	HVY	VHY	HVY	HVY	HVY	10

[1] Gra Version, *Shaarey Tzion, etc.*
[2] *Chakamoni,* Donash, Raavad, Ramban, Botril, Eliezer of Wormes (1), *Chayay Olam HaBah* (end), *Otzar Eden HaGanuz* 171b.
[3] There might be a mistake in this version, since YVH is repeated twice. It probably should be like the Gra version.
[4] Saadia Version 4:8, *Kuzari* 4:24 (63b).
[5] *Shaar HaKavanot, Kavanot Naanuim* (p. 310), *Siddur HaAri.*
[6] *Zohar* 3:17a.
[7] *Tikuney Zohar* 15a,b, *Pardes Rimonim* 3:5. See Gra on *Tikuney Zohar* 16b.

The position of the Vav thus determines the axis. The up down axis is reresented by the last column, the east west axis by the first column, and the north south axis by the middle column.

The direction is then determined by the remaining two letters, Yud and Heh. If they are in direct order, YH (יה), then they define the positive direction on the axis. If they are in reverse order, HY (הי), then they define the negative direction.

The second important system is found in the Short Version, and used by most of the commentaries. Here, the system is:

up	YHV	יהו
down	YVH	יוה
east	HYV	היו
west	HVY	הוי
south	VYH	ויה
north	VHY	והי

Here, the axis is determined by the letter in the first column. The assignment is

Yud	י	up down
Heh	ה	east west
Vav	ו	up down

The positions of the last two letters then determine whether it is in the positive or negative direction along the given axis.

The system found in the Long Version is very similar to that of the Gra, except for the up down direction. Examining it carefully,

Table 14. Directions based on the Ari, *Zohar*, and *Tikuney Zohar*.

Sefirah	Direction		Ari	Zohar	TZ
Chesed	south	right	YHV	YHV	YHV
Gevurah	north	left	HVY	HVY	HVY
Tiferet	east	front	VYH	VHY	VHY
Netzach	up	up	YVH	YVH	VYH
Hod	down	down	HYV	HYV	HYV
Yesod	west	back	VHY	VYH	YVH

one suspects that it originally was the same as the Gra version, except that the first two combinations were confused. This is supported by the fact that the permutation YVH is repeated twice.

The Saadia version is very much like the Short Version, except that the permutations representing east and west are interchanged.

Highly significant is the system of the Ari, presented in his discussion of the mystical meditations associated with the Four Species. The Four Species consist of the citron (*etrog*), palm (*lulav*), myrtle (*hadas*), and willow (*aravah*). The are taken on the festival of Succot (tabernacles), following the commandment, "On the first day, you shall take fruit of the citron tree, branches of palm trees, boughs of myrtle trees, and willows of the brook" (Leviticus 23:40). These species are waved in all six directions, and according to the Ari, the appropriate letter combination must be meditated upon for each direction.[231] Each of these directions is also paired with its appropriate Sefirah.

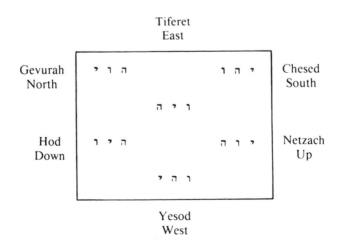

Figure 12. *The Ari's representation.*

The Ari begins with Chesed (Love), the first Sefirah, which represents the south, taking the letters of the Name in their natural order, YHV (יהו). See Table 14.

To determine the order for the opposite direction, the Ari then makes use of a system used by the Sefer Yetzirah itself. (2:4). The text states that the two prime opposites are *Oneg* (ANG ענג) meaning "delight," and Nega (NGA נגע), meaning a "plague." In forming an opposite, it takes the first letter and places it at the end. This is precisely what is done to produce Gevurah (Strength), which represents the north. The Yud (י), which was at the beginning, is now placed at the end, producing the combination HVY (הוי). The north south axis is then represented by the two letters HV (הו).

The up down axis is similarly defined by the letters YV (יו), with the position of the H (ה) determining the direction.

In this system, the first letter is also significant. For south and up, the initial letter is Y (י), while for north and down, it is H (ה). Both of these are opposites in the three column representation.

The east west axis is on the neutral zero point on both the up down line and on the north south line. In the three column representation, Tiferet (east) and Yesod (west) are both in the middle line. Since both the middle line and the letter V (ו) represent synthesis, the representation of both these directions begins with a Vav.[232] See figure 12.

The system of the Zohar is exactly the same as that of the Ari, except that east and west are interchanged. The system of the Tikuney Zohar uses a similar principle, but somewhat differently.

Later we shall see that the twelve possible permutations of YHVH represent the twelve diagonal boundaries (5:2). Each of the six basic directions can include two of the diagonal boundaries. The first of these is represented by the second Heh at the end of the triplet, and the second, with this Heh at the beginning.

• • •

We can now understand the conceptual nature of the Sefirot. The most primary relationship possible is that which exists between Creator and creation. This is the cause effect relationship. Cause is Keter, while Effect is Malkhut.

Once the concepts of Cause and Effect exist, another concept comes into being, namely that of opposites. If opposites exist, similarities must also exist.

Two new concepts therefore come into being. These are Similarity and Oppositeness. In the language of philosophy these are thesis and antithesis. In our terminology, Similarity is Chakhmah, while

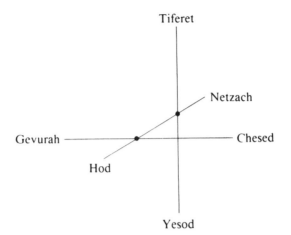

Figure 13. The six directions in space.

Oppositeness is Binah. These are the Yud and initial Heh of the Tetragrammaton.

Once Similarity and Opposition exist, another concept comes into being, namely Relationship. In philosophic terms, this is the synthesis between thesis and antithesis. In our present terminology, this is the Vav of the Tetragrammaton. The word "Vav" means a hook, and the letter Vav as a prefix means "and." In both senses, it denotes connection and relationship.

At this point in the logical sequence, we have five concepts: Cause and Effect, Similarity and Opposition, and Relationship. These, respectively are Keter and Malkhut, Chakhmah and Binah, and the Vav.[233]

Until the concept of Relationship was introduced, only four abstract points existed: Keter and Malkhut, and Chakhmah and Binah. It is with the concept of Relationship that a three-dimensional conceptual continuum comes into existence. This defines six directions, and hence, the numerical value of Vav is 6.

Each of the four abstract concepts then gives rise to a relationship. Chakhmah gives rise to Chesed (Love), Binah gives rise to Gevurah (Strength), Keter gives rise to Tiferet (Beauty), and Malkut gives rise to Yesod (Foundation).

As discussed earlier, in a spiritual sense, Similarity is closeness, while Opposition is distance. In order to give, the giver must be close to the recipient. In a spiritual sense, there must be an element of similarity between giver and recipient.

Therefore, Chakhmah, which is Similarity, gives rise to Chesed, which is the concept of giving. Conversely, Binah, which is Opposition, gives rise to Gevurah, the concept of witholding.

Tiferet is similarly derived from Keter, the concept of Cause. In order to have the relationship of Cause, an element must give the precise amount of existence or motivation required for the effect. This is the concept of measured giving, represented by Tiferet. Tiferet is beauty, the golden mean.

Since Tiferet is derived from Keter, it would be expected to be above Chesed and Gevurah. However, since Tiferet is also the synthesis between Chesed and Gevurah, it is usually represented as being below them.

Malkhut, the concept of Effect, is usually said to be the feminine archetype of creation. Since Yesod is derived from Malkhut, Yesod is naturally drawn to it and motivated to attach itself to it. It is for this reason that Yesod is said to parallel the sexual organ. It is called Yesod (Foundation) because it is the lowest of the six.

Derived from the original four, there are now four new concepts: Chesed, Gevurah, Tiferet and Yesod.

Once the concept of Relationship has been introduced, these four concepts are no longer merely abstract points in conceptual space. They are connected by the concept of Relationship. The two pairs, Chesed-Gevurah and Tiferet-Yesod are like two crossing lines. This yields four directions in a two-dimensional continuum.

These two dimensions can be represented in physical space. The Tiferet-Yesod axis can represent east-west, while the Chesed-Gevurah axis can represent south-north. This then yields a two-dimensional continuum.

Since the concept of Relationship exists, the relationship between the two dimensions themselves is also significant. In the conceptual space depiction, this would be represented as a line drawn between the two existing lines.

The Cause-Effect or Keter-Malkhut relationship is that which is primary. This is represented by the Tiferet-Yesod axis. The thesis-antithesis relationship was introduced only to make the cause-effect relationship possible. The thesis-antithesis or Chakhmah-Binah relationship is therefore secondary. This is represented by the Chesed-Gevurah axis.

The Tiferet-Yesod axis is therefore the primary dimension, while the Chesed-Gevurah axis is the secondary dimension. This yields a totally new concept, namely the quality of being primary or secondary. These, in turn, form a new, third dimension, which can be related to the up down direction. This is the axis linking Netzach (Victory) and Hod (Splendor). See Figure 13.

With the introduction of these two concepts, the six Sefirot represented by the Vav are complete. These are Chesed, Gevurah, Tiferet, Netzach, Hod and Yesod. These six Sefirot represent the six directions in space. Together with the original four, these six yield the Ten Sefirot.

1:14   אלו עשר ספירות בלימה (אחת) רוח אלהים
              חיים רוח מרוח מים מרוח אש ממים רום ותחת
                        מזרח ומערב צפון ודרום:

These are the Ten Sefirot of Nothingness:
The Breath of the Living God
Breath from Breath
Water from Breath
Fire from Water
Up down east west north south.

Aside from their theoretical implications, the Ten Sefirot also have
important mystical and meditative significance. The Sefer Yetzirah,
in this first chapter, has presented a system of meditating on the
Sefirot and of binding oneself to them.

One may use the letters to climb the Tree of Life, but the Sefirot
are the points where one must rest.

There is actually an important apparent contradiction in the text.
In one section (1:6), the text says, "Their vision is like the appearance
of lightning. . . they speak of them 'running and returning.'" This
would imply that it is impossible to see the Sefirot for more than an
instant, just like a flash of lightning. Later, however, the text states,
"If your heart runs, return to the place, as it is written, 'The Chayot
running and returning'" (1:8). This appears to say that one can go
further, but that one should refrain from doing so.[234]

What the text is actually doing, however, is describing two distinct stages of initiation into the mysteries of the Sefirot.

The first stage begins with the exercise where the initiate must
"understand with Wisdom, and be wise with Understanding" (1:4).
Here he learns how to oscillate between Binah consciousness and
Chakhmah consciousness. On this level, he can meditate on the
Sefirot as ten depths, allowing the mind to reach out to the infinity
of each of these depths. Since he is still in a state of oscillating mentality, he sees the Sefirot like flashes of lightning, "running and
returning."

The ten infinite directions, however, represent a state of separation and disunity. This is the essence of Binah. The initiate must

therefore "imbed their end in their beginning" (1:7). He must contemplate the point at infinity, where all these opposing directions come together as one.

This, however, is something that cannot be accomplished with Binah consciousness. This state of consciousness can only imagine things verbally, or depict things in physical terms. The point at infinity is both infinite and infinitesimal, and therefore, cannot be depicted. It can only be contemplated with Chakhmah consciousness.

As the text notes, this represents the unity that preceded the concept of number. It introduces a device very much like a Zen *koan*, asking, "Before one, what do you count"? What is the number that precedes all number?

Both the point at infinity and the *koan* are meant to train the mind to visualize absolute nothingness. The Ari notes that Keter, the highest of the Sefirot, is often designated by the word *Ayin*, meaning "nothing." The Infinite Being, the level above Keter, cannot even be designated by this word. The only word that can be used is *Effes*, which, according to the Ari, denotes a nothingness that thought (Binah) cannot grasp at all.

It has been said that the best way to describe absolute nothingness is to speak of it as "what you see behind your head." Since vision does not exist in the back of the head, what one sees there is absolute nothingness. If I ask you what you see behind your head, you answer that you see nothing. Contemplating on what one sees behind one's head is therefore a good way to learn how to visualize absolute nothingness.

In general, the soul is said to consist of five parts: Nefesh, Ruach, Neshamah, Chayah and Yechidah. Of these, only the first three, Nefesh, Ruach and Neshamah, have any effect on the mind. The last two, Chayah and Yechidah, are called "envelopments" (*makifin*), which cannot enter the mind.[235]

Neshamah, the highest part of the soul that "enters" the mind, parallels the Sefirah of Binah. See Table 15 on page 90. Chakhmah consciousness is above thought, and is like something that exists outside the mind. Or, as in the analogy used earlier, it is like what we "see" behind our heads. Just like something behind the head can only be seen if reflected in a mirror, so Chakhmah consciousness can only be grasped when reflected and clothed in Binah. With relation to conscious thought, Chakhmah consciousness is called "nothingness."[236]

It is in this context that the text says, "Bridle your mouth from speaking and your heart from thinking." "Heart" denotes Binah consciousness, and hence, it is saying that on this level, the initiate must blank out Binah consciousness completely. This is accomplished by

Table 15. Levels of the soul.

Yechidah	Keter		
Chayah	Chakhmah	Nothingness	Atzilut
Neshamah	Binah	Thought	Beriyah
Ruach	The Six	Speech	Yetzirah
Nefesh	Malkhut	Action	Asiyah

contemplating nothingness. He must maintain this level, and is accordingly instructed, "If your heart runs" back to Binah, "return to the place." This "place" is Chakhmah consciousness, which the initiate has already attained. Once the initiate has reached a point where he can maintain a state of Chakhmah consciousnes, he is ready to actually begin climbing the Tree of Life, which is the ladder of the Sefirot.

Hebrew is written without vowels, and therefore, the third person and the imperative are written exactly the same. We have translated the last paragraph, "He sealed north and faced to the left, and He sealed it with VHY." This, however, can also be read in the imperative: "Seal north, face to the left, and seal it with VHY."

In a similar manner, the expression, "He engraved it and He carved it," can also be read in the imperative, "Engrave it and carve it." If understood in this manner, sections 1:9-13 can be read as instructions rather than as a theory of creation. (In Appendix I, I have translated the Short Version completely in the imperative, to demonstrate how it reads.)

The supposition that this is describing a technique is supported by the last section of the Sefer Yetzirah itself, which says of Abraham, "He bound the 22 letters of the Torah in his tongue. . . He drew them in water, kindled them with fire, agitated them with breath" (6:7).

The initiate begins by meditating on Keter, the initial "Breath of the Living God." This Breath must be brought down to the level of Yesod (Foundation). In doing this, he must contemplate the essence of "Voice, Breath and Speech."

Ordinary thought is verbal, and hence, consists of words. These words consist of letters. These are not physical letters, but mental, conceptual letters. These conceptual letters, however, are built out of "Voice, Breath, Speech." Hence, in meditating on these concepts, one is actually contemplating the very roots of thought.

In the Long Version, the text concludes, "Speech is *Ruach HaKodesh* (Divine Inspiration)." *Ruach HaKodesh*, however, is above thought. Hence, the "speech" which the text is speaking of, is a "speech" that precedes thought.

The second step is "Breath from Breath." The text states, "with it engrave and carve 22 letters." The Kabbalists explain that "engraving" and "carving" denote meditative techniques. This is supported by the last section (6:7), which states that Abraham "looked, saw, understood, probed, engraved, and carved, and was successful in creation."

They teach that "engraving" denotes a process where one depicts a letter in one's mind. "Carving" then means that this letter is separated from all other thoughts, so that the entire mind is filled with it.[237] One may do this by contemplating a letter or letter combination until all other images and thoughts are banished from the mind. Alternatively, this may be accomplished by chanting a letter in a manner that shall presently be described.

This is the stage of Malkhut, where one stands at the bottom of the Tree of Life. It is at this stage that the initiate must work with the letter that he wishes to use. He must then "draw it in water, and kindle it with fire" (6:7). The subsequent instructions therefore indicate how the letter is to be charged with spiritual power.

The third step, then, is "Water from Breath." At first, the initiate depicts the letter in transparent air, visualizing it clearly. Now he must reach up to the level of Chakhmah, returning to a state of Chakhmah consciousness. He then begins to see the letter as if he were looking at it through water. This is "drawing it through water." The letter begins to blur and fade, as if it were being viewed through increasingly deep water.

The initiate must then "engrave and carve chaos and void, mire and clay." At this stage, the form breaks up and dissolves completely, like something seen through turbulent water. This is "chaos and void."[238] The image then fades away completely, as if it were being viewed through muddy water. This is "mire." Finally, all that is left is inky blackness, as if one were buried in totally opaque mud and clay.

The text describes this process saying, "Engrave them like a garden, carve them like a wall, cover (or surround) them like a ceiling." First visualize this blackness beneath your feet. Your feet may then appear to dissolve, a phenomenon that is also mentioned in other ancient mystical texts.[239] Slowly, make this blackness creep over you, surrounding you completely like a wall. Finally, let it cover and surround you like a ceiling of inky black mire. At this point, you will have no visual sensation whatever, neither physical nor mental.

All through this process, you are constantly aware of the feeling of water, cool and absolutely calm. It is the dark, wet feeling of the womb, where you are totally isolated from all sensation.

It is with respect to this state that the Midrash states, "Water conceived and gave birth to absolute darkness (*afelah*)."[240] This is the level of Chakhmah consciousness.

Figure 14. The letters Yud Heh Vav in Ashurite script.

The initiate then reaches the fourth step, where he returns to a state of Binah consciousness. This is depicted as fire and blinding light, as the Midrash continues, "Fire conceived and gave birth to Light." This is the stage where one "kindles them with fire."

Here, the initiate must "engrave and carve out the Throne of Glory, Serafim, Ophanim, and holy Chayot." He depicts (engraves) and fills the mind (carves) with these images, these being the same as the ones visualized by the prophets.[241] He must start with the Throne, and then continue through the various levels of angels, ending with the Chayot in the Universe of Yetzirah, which corresponds to the Six Directions. The influx is thus brought to the level of Binah.

Now the initiate must bring it to the other six Sefirot — Chesed, Gevurah, Tiferet, Netzach, Hod, and Yesod. These are associated with the six directions of the physical world, which have their counterpart in the six days of creation. By associating the Sefirot with the six physical directions, one actually brings the influx into the physical domain.

The method of drawing the influx into these lower Sefirot involves contemplating the three letters Yud Heh Vav (יהו). These should be visualized as if written in the Ashurite script, with black fire on white fire. See figure 14. These letters should appear huge, filling the entire mind.[242]

The idea of black fire is not just the absence of light, but negative light.[243] The black must be so intense that it is brilliantly black, just as a light is brilliantly white. This is the black fire with which the letters must be depicted.

While contemplating the letter combinations, one should face in the appropriate direction, either physically or mentally. After completing all six directions and permutations, this part of the exercise is complete.

What still remains are the astrological applications of this technique, which will be described in chapters 4 and 5. This is the process described in the case of Abraham, "He ignited them with the Seven [Planets], he directed them with the Twelve constellations" (6:7).

CHAPTER TWO

2:1 עשרים ושתים אותיות יסוד שלש
אמות ושבע כפולות ושתים עשרה
פשוטות. שלש אמות אמ"ש יסודן כף זכות וכף חובה
חק מכריע בינתים. שלש אמות אמ"ש מ' דוממת
ולשון ש' שורקת א' אויר רוח מכריע בינתים:

Twenty-two Foundation Letters:
   Three Mothers
   Seven Doubles
   and Twelve Elementals.
The Three Mothers are Alef Mem Shin (אמש),
Their foundation is
   a pan of merit
   a pan of liability
   and the tongue of decree deciding between them.
[Three Mothers, Alef Mem Shin (אמש)
   Mem hums, Shin hisses
   and Alef is the Breath of air
   deciding between them.]

Twenty-two Foundation Letters

Having completed the initiation into the Ten Sefirot, the text now discusses the 22 letters of the Hebrew alphabet.

Three Mothers

The first set of letters are the Three Mothers, which will be discussed in further detail in chapter 3. Here they are introduced because they define the thesis-antithesis-synthesis structure that is central to the teachings of Sefer Yetzirah. They also serve as an introduction to the meditative techniques involving the letters.

These three letters represent the three columns into which the Sefirot are divided. The right hand column, headed by Chakhmah, is represented by Mem. The left column, headed by Binah, is repre-

sented by Shin. The center column, headed by Keter, is represented
by Alef. As discussed earlier, Chakhmah is water (which is here represented by Mem), Binah is fire (which is Shin), and Keter is breath-air
(which is the Alef).

A pan of merit

The Hebrew word for "pan" here is *Kaf.* This word can denote
the pan of a scale, but it also denotes the palm of the hand. Likewise,
the word *Lashon* can be used for the tongue of a balance, the pointer
which indicates when the two pans are in equilibrium. Its usual
meaning, however, is the tongue that is in the mouth.[1]

Therefore, on one hand, the letters Alef Mem Shin (אמש) represent the two pans and tongue of a balance. On the other hand, they
represent the two hands, and the "covenant between them" (1:3),
which is the tongue.

The tongue of decree

The Hebrew word for "decree" here is Chok (חק). This comes
from the root Chakak (חקק), meaning to "engrave." It is the "tongue
of balance" that "engraves" the letters. This is represented by the letter Alef (א), the basis of the alphabet.

In the most elemental terms, Mem, Shin and Alef represent thesis, antithesis, and synthesis.

The analogy is that of a scale. (See figure 15.) There is a pan of
merit   and   a   pan   of   liability.   This   is   very   much   like
the scale used to weigh one's merits and sins, which is mentioned in
the Talmud.[2] In the center is the fulcrum and pointer, both represented by the Alef, which is the "tongue of decree."

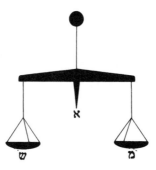

Figure 15. The scale that weighs merits and sins.

In practical application, these letters can also be used. If one wishes to create a situation in which he himself or another person is to be brought to the side of merit, one does so by making use of the letter Mem (מ).[3] The techniques shall be discussed later. Similarly, if one wishes to bring an enemy to the side of liability, so that he should be judged harshly on high, one makes use of the letter Shin (ש). Alef (א) is used to bring a person to be judged fairly and evenly.

These qualities also come into play in popular usage. Humming, which involves pronouncing the letter Mem, is usually seen as a happy, pleasant, positive activity. Conversely, one hisses at a villain or enemy, pronouncing the letter Shin.

Mem hums, Shin hisses

The Hebrew word for "hum" here is *Damam* (דמם), in which the letter Mem is dominant. Similarly, the word for "hiss" is *Sharak* (שרק), which begins with a Shin.[4]

The humming sound associated with Mem is very calm, and it is thus, the sound associated with water and Chakhmah consciousness. If one wishes to attain Chakhmah consciousness, one repeats this sound in the manner described like the Kabbalists. The resemblance between this and the "Om" chant is certainly more than coincidental.

This sound is also closely associated with prophecy, which involves Chakhmah consciousness. The Kabbalists say that the "fine still (*damamah*) voice" (1 Kings 19:12), heard by Elijah, was actually a "fine humming sound."[5] This humming sound is used to attain such a state of consciousness, and as such, it is experienced when one is in a prophetic state.

Just as telling is a passage in Job, which, incidentally, also describes the prophetic experience very graphically (Job 4:12-16):

> *A word was stolen to me*
> > *My ear caught a touch of it*
> *In meditations from night visions*
> > *When a trance falls on man*
> *Terror called me and I shuddered*
> > *It terrorized most of my bones*
> *A spirit passed before my face*
> > *Made the hair of my flesh stand on end*
> *It stood and I did not recognize its vision*
> > *A picture was before my eyes*
> > *I heard a hum (damamah) and a voice.*

Table 16. Shin and Mem as pronounced with the five primary vowels.

ShoMo ShoMa ShoMe ShoMi ShoMu	שֹׁמוֹ	שֹׁמִי	שֹׁמֵ	שֹׁמַ	שֹׁמֹ
ShaMo ShaMa ShaMe ShaMi ShaMu	שַׁמוֹ	שַׁמִי	שַׁמֵ	שַׁמַ	שַׁמֹ
SheMo SheMa SheMe SheMi SheMu	שֶׁמוֹ	שֶׁמִי	שֶׁמֵ	שֶׁמַ	שֶׁמֹ
ShiMo ShiMa ShiMe ShiMi ShiMu	שִׁמוֹ	שִׁמִי	שִׁמֵ	שִׁמַ	שִׁמֹ
ShuMo ShuMa ShuMe ShuMi ShuMu	שֻׁמוֹ	שֻׁמִי	שֻׁמֵ	שֻׁמַ	שֻׁמֹ

The letter Shin has the hissing sound of sh or s. This sound is associated with fire and Binah consciousness.

The two sounds, M and Sh, may also be used as a device for oscillating between Binah and Chakhmah consciousness. One invokes a strong state of Binah consciousness by pronouncing the Shin, and then swings to Chakhmah consciousness by voicing the Mem. The pronunciation of these two letters can also include the five primary vowels, in a manner that will be described below (2:5) in greater detail.

It is significant to note that these two sounds are dominant in the word Chashmal (חשמל), which, according to the Kabbalists, is the interface between the physical and the spiritual. In his vision, Ezekiel thus says that he saw, "The appearance of Chashmal in the midst of the fire" (Ezekiel 1:4). It was only after visualizing the Chashmal that Ezekiel was able to perceive the Chayot and enter into the state of prophecy. In our present terminology, Chashmal would be the interface between Binah consciousness and Chakhmah consciousness. It therefore appears out of the "midst of the fire," since it arises from a state of Binah consciousness.

Since M and Sh are the dominant consonants in Chashmah, it is possible that the word itself was used as a mantra when the prophet swung between Binah and Chakhmah consciousness. "The appearance of Chashmal" would then be the visual experience that one would have during such a state of oscillation. Even the more advanced prophets, who could enter a state of chakhmah consciousness at will, would use the term Chashmal to describe this interface.[6]

According to the Talmud, the word Chashmal comes from two words, Chash, meaning "silence," and Mal, indicating speech. It can therefore be translated as "speaking silence."[7] It is a double sensation, where one is experiencing the "silence" of Chakhmah consciousness, and the "speech" of Binah consciousness at the same time. The two parts of the mind are experiencing different things simultaneously.

Such double sensation can be easily experienced. Take a red glass and place it over the right eye, and place a green glass over the left

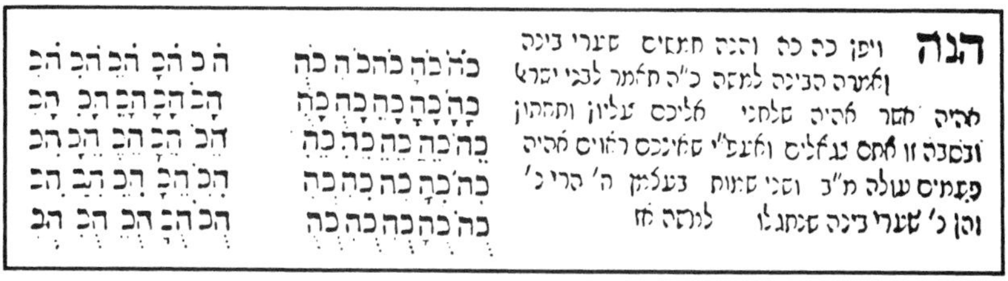

Figure 16. The word Koh in an array with the five primary vowels.
From Shoshan Sodot (The Rose of Mysteries).

eye. When you look through both eyes, you will perceive two opposite sensations simultaneously. The world will take on a surrealistic, almost spiritual, appearance. The interface between Chakhmah and Binah is even more etherial.

The Kabbalists also note that the two letters Shin and Mem spell out *Shem* (שם), the word for "name."[8] It is through the "names" of objects, and in particular, through divine Names, that one can make the transition between Chakhmah and Binah consciousness. As the Baal Shem Tov taught, it is through a name that one can grasp the spiritual essence of a person or object.[9]

The Zohar also says that the letters Mem and Shin define the mystery of Moses, whose Hebrew name, Mosheh, is spelled Mem Shin Heh (משה).[10] This would be an allusion to the fact that the two consonants, Mem and Shin, represent Chakhmah and Binah. The Heh has a numerical value of 5, and this would represent the five primary vowels, with which the combination of consonants is pronounced. See Table 16.

A somewhat similar idea is taught explictly by the early Kabbalists. The Torah states that Moses killed an Egyptian who was striking an Israelite, and the Midrash explains that this was accomplished with a divine Name.[11] When he struck the Egyptian, the Torah reports that Moses "looked here (*koh*) and there (*koh*)" (Exodus 2:12). In Hebrew, both "here" and "there" are *Koh* (כה), a word which has a numerical value of 25. The Kabbalists say that this represents the twenty-five combinations between two letters that are possible with the five primary vowels.[12] See figure 16.

Alef is the Breath of air

Alef is a silent consonant, and as such, it represents a simple breath of air. This does not draw one toward either state of consciousness.

Normally, breathing is an unconscious act, and hence, it pertains to Chakhmah consciousness. However, one can also control one's breathing, and it is then in the domain of Binah consciousness.

Consciously controlling the breath is therefore a valid technique for bringing together these two states of consciousness. It is also useful in making the transition between the two states. Thus, the Kabbalists make use of controlled breathing in association with such techniques as pronouncing two consonants with the five primary vowels.[13] In particular, such a breath comes between the pronunciation of the Mem and the Shin.

2:2

עשרים ושתים אותיות יסוד חקקן חצבן צרפן
שקלן והמירן וצר בהם את כל היצור ואת כל
העתיד לצור:

Twenty-two Foundation letters:
He engraved them, He carved them,
He permuted them, He weighed them,
He transformed them,
And with them, He depicted all that was formed
and all that would be formed.

He engraved them

First the letters are "engraved" out of nothingness. Then they are "carved" out and separated. They are then "permuted," so that a given combination appears in different sequences. They then are "weighed" and manipulated according to their numerical values. Finally, they can be "transformed" through the various standard ciphers.[14] These ciphers are shown in Table 17.

Each letter represents a different type of information. Through the various manipulations of the letters, God created all things.[15]

The final expressions of creation were therefore the Ten Sayings, found in the first chapter of Genesis. Each Saying consisted of words, which in turn consisted of letters.

This section can also be read in the imperative: "Engrave them, carve them, permute them, weigh them, and depict all that was formed . . ."

When interpreted in this manner, this section is teaching a technique discussed by various Kabbalists.[16] The initiate must first depict

Table 17. The standard ciphers.

א"כ ג"ד	א"ט ב"ח	אי"ק בכ"ר	א"ל ב"ם	אח"ס בט"ע	א"ת ב"ש	משקל	אות
ב	ט	י	ל	ח	ת	1	א
ג	ח	כ	מ	ט	ש	2	ב
ד	ז	ל	נ	י	ר	3	ג
ה	ו	מ	ס	כ	ק	4	ד
ו	ה	נ	ע	ל	צ	5	ה
ז	ד	ס	פ	מ	פ	6	ו
ח	ג	ע	צ	נ	ע	7	ז
ט	ב	פ	ק	ס	ס	8	ח
י	א	צ	ר	ע	נ	9	ט
כ	צ	ק	ש	פ	מ	10	י
ל	פ	ר	ת	צ	ל	20	כ
מ	ע	ש	א	ק	כ	30	ל
נ	ס	ת	ב	ר	י	40	מ
ס	נ	ר	ג	ש	ט	50	נ
ע	מ	ם	ד	ת	ח	60	ס
פ	ל	ן	ה	א	ז	70	ע
צ	כ	ף	ו	ב	ו	80	פ
ק	י	ץ	ז	ג	ה	90	צ
ר	ת	א	ח	ד	ד	100	ק
ש	ש	ב	ט	ה	ג	200	ר
ת	ר	ג	י	ו	ב	300	ש
א	ק	ד	כ	ז	א	400	ת
		ה				(500)	ך
		ו				(600)	ם
		ז				(700)	ן
		ח				(800)	ף
		ט				(900)	ץ

the letters, "engraving" them in his mind. Then he must "carve" them out, making them fill his entire consciousness. After this, he can permute them in various ways. He can also manipulate them through their numerical values and the standard ciphers.

Another important technique involved meditating on the letters by writing them.[17] The simplest method was to take a word and permute it in all possible ways. If one used a set system to permute these letters, this was called *Gilgul*, or "cycling" of the letters.[18] In more advanced systems, one would also use Gematria (numerical values) and the ciphers to extend the process.

In effect, writing or reciting these letter combinations was very much like repeating a mantra. It serves to blank out all thought from the mind and allow it to reach a state of Chakhmah consciousness. Visualizing the letters is very much like some of the more advanced contemplative methods of meditation, and it has a similar effect.

In all, there are five basic techniques mentioned here. These parallel the five phonetic families discussed in the next section.[19]

2:3 עשרים ושתים אותיות יסוד חקקן בקול חצבן
ברוח קבען בפה בחמשה מקומות אחה"ע בגרון
גיכ"ק בחיך דטלנ"ת בלשון זסשר"ץ בשינים בומ"ף
בשפתים:

Twenty-two Foundation Letters
  He engraved them with voice
  He carved them with breath
  He set them in the mouth
In five places

Alef Chet Heh Eyin (אחהע) *in the throat*		*(Gutturals)*
Gimel Yud Kaf Kuf (גיכק) *in the palate*		*(Palatals)*
Dalet Tet Lamed Nun Tav (דטלנת)		
in the tongue		*(Linguals)*
Zayin Samekh Shin Resh Tzadi (זסשרץ)		
in the teeth		*(Dentals)*
Bet Vav Mem Peh (בומף) *in the lips.*		*(Labials)*

He engraved them with voice

As explained earlier, "engrave" means to sound a letter, while "carve" means to express it. Some versions add, "He bound them to the tongue like a flame is bound to a burning coal." This is similar to an expression used above (1:7).

In five places

The division of the letters into five groups is presented here, but this is the only time that this is mentioned in Sefer Yetzirah. No apparent reason or application for this division is given.

One hint may come from what we have written above (1:13). The three letters of the Name, Yud Heh Vav (יהו), are the first of the Twelve Elementals to be found in the first three phonetic families when taken in alphabetical order: gutturals, labials, and palatals. See Table 18.

There are two basic ways in which these families are ordered. The first way is that which is presented here, which starts from the throat, the most internal part of the mouth, and then continues outward to the lips.[20] The second ordering, found in the older commentaries, takes the groupings in alphabetical order.[21] See Table 19 on page 104.

The most obvious reason for the five phonetic families would be so that the divisions of the alphabet should parallel the divisions in the five dimensional continuum defined by Sefer Yetzirah. Indeed, the Kabbalists teach that these five groups parallel the Five Loves and Five Strengths (see 1:3), which are the end points of these dimensions.[22] The assignment of these families to specific dimensions, however, is not indicated, although it may be derived indirectly.

It is significant to note that all five families are present in Bereshit (בראשית), the first word of the Torah.[23]

One of the mysteries of the Sefer Yetzirah is the fact that the double letters are not mentioned. These double letters are the ones which have different forms in the middle and at the end of a word: Mem (מם), Nun (נן), Tzadi (צץ), Peh (פף), and Kaf (כך). As the Talmud states, the forms of these letters were forgotten, and later re-instituted by the prophets.[24] There is absolutely no reference to these doubles in Sefer Yetzirah.

The Kabbalists, however, draw a parallel between the five phonetic families and the five doubled letters. According to the Ari, the letters paralleling the phonetic families in the order presented here are: Tzadi, Nun, Kaf, Mem, Peh.[25] See Table 20 on page 104.

Another concept that is conspicuously missing in the Sefer Yetzirah is that of the vowels. Here again, they form a group of five, the main vowels being Cholam (o), Kametz (a), Tzereh (e), Chirik (i), and Shurek (u). See Table 21 on page 104. These are often alluded to in the mnemonic Pituchey Chotam (פִּתְחֵי חֹתָם), the "signet engraving" (Exodus 28:11) of the Bible.[26] Another mnemonic is

Table 18. Phonetic division of the alphabet.

	Mothers	Doubles	Elementals	(Finals)
Gutturals	א		חהע	
Labials	מ	בפ	ו	סף
Palatals		גכ	יק	ך
Linguals		דת	טלנ	ן
Dentals	שׁ	ר	זסצ	ץ

Table 19. Ordering of the families.

	Gra-Ari		Short Version		Donash	
1.	Gutturals	אחהע	Gutturals	אחהע	Gutturals	אחהע
2.	Palatals	גיכק	Labials	בומף	Labials	בומף
3.	Linguals	דטלנת	Palatals	גיכק	Palatals	גיכק
4.	Dentals	זסשרצ	Linguals	דטלנת	Dentals	זסשרצ
5.	Labials	בומף	Dentals	זסשרצ	Linguals	דטלנת

Table 20. Parallel between phonetic families and doubled letters.

1.	Gutturals	אחהע	Tzadi	צץ
2.	Palatals	גיכק	Nun	נן
3.	Linguals	דטלנת	Kaf	כך
4.	Dentals	זסשרצ	Mem	מם
5.	Labials	בומף	Peh	פף

Table 21. The primary vowels.

1.	Cholam	O	X
2.	Kametz	A	X
3.	Tzereh	E	X
4.	Chirik	I	X
5.	Shuruk	U	X

Table 22. Ordering of the vowels.

Tikuney Zohar[1]	a e o i u	
Tikuney Zohar[2]	i u e o a	order of *Pituchey Chotam*
Rabbi Elazar Rokeach[3]	u a e i o	order of *Nutareyikon*
Rabbi Elazar Rokeach[4]	a e i o u	
Rabbi Abraham Abulafia[5]	o a e i u	
Rabbi Joseph Gikatalia[6]	o u i e a	
Emek HaMelekh[7]	u a i e o	
Rabbi Moshe Cordevero[8]	o i u a e	

[1] *Tikuney Zohar*, Introduction (4b), 5 (20a), 19 (38a, 41a).
[2] *Ibid.* Introduction (14a), 70 (135b).
[3] Commentary on Sefer Yetzirah 4b. See *Pardes Rimonim* 21:2.
[4] *Ibid.* p 14b.
[5] *Or HaSekhel* 8:1, quoted in *Pardes Rimonim* 21:1 as *Sefer HaNikkud*.
[6] *Ginat Egoz* 25a.
[7] *Emek HaMelekh* 9c.
[8] *Pardes Rimonim* 30:2.

Table 23. Phonic groups and Sefirot.

	Ari	Ramak	Vowel	Final Letter	
Gutturals אחהע	Hod	Chesed	i	Tzadi	צץ
Palatals גיכק	Netzach	Gevurah	e	Nun	נן
Linguals דטלנת	Tiferet	Tiferet	o	Kaf	כך
Dentals זסשרצ	Gevurah	Netzach	a	Mem	מם
Labials בומף	Chesed	Hod	u	Peh	פף

Nutareyikon (נְטָרִיקוֹן).[27] Although there are other vowels in Hebrew, these five are considered to be the root vowels, both by the grammatarians and by the Kabbalists.

The Zohar clearly draws a parallel between the five phonetic families and the five prime vowels, and this is echoed by other Kabbalists.[28] The five primary vowels would then also represent the five dimensions of the Sefer Yetzirah.

In general, the five vowels are very important in the use of the Sefer Yetzirah. The usual procedure is to take a pair of letters, pronouncing them with the twenty-five possible combinations of the five vowels. This appears in the system of Rabbi Abraham Abulafia, as well in various techniques of making a Golem. There appear, however, to be a number of different opinions as to the ordering of the vowels, and a few of these are presented in Table 22.[29]

Some of the later Kabbalists also assign the five phonetic families to the five Sefirot: Chesed, Gevurah, Tiferet, Netzach and Hod. Yesod is not included, since, in this respect, Yesod and Tiferet are counted as one.[30] Furthermore, Yesod pertains to melody rather than to sound.[31] There is, however, a difference of opinion between the Ari and the Ramak as to whether the Sefirot are to be taken in descending or in ascending order.[32] The five main vowels are also assigned to these same Sefirot.[33] See Table 23.

The first clue as to how to assign these to the five-dimensional continuum comes from the ordering of the final letters in the Talmud: Mem Nun Tzadi Pen Kaf (מנצפך). In all sources, both Talmudic and Kabbalistic, the letters are presented in this order. The correct alphabetical order of the letters, however, would be: Kaf Mem Nun Peh Tzadi (כמנפץ). See Table 24 on page 106. The question then arises: why are these letters usually not presented in their alphabetical order?[34]

Earlier (1:3), however, we have spoken of the division of the Ten Sefirot into two groups representing the two hands. These are the Five Loves and the Five Judgments. In the order of the Sefirot, they are:

Five Loves: Keter, Chakhmah, Chesed, Tiferet, Netzach.
Five Judgments: Binah, Gevurah, Hod, Yesod, Malkhut.

It is immediately obvious that each group represents a set of end points in the five-dimensional continuum. The pairing in this continuum is:

Keter-Malkhut	Good-Evil
Chakhmah-Binah	Past-Future
Chesed-Gevurah	South-North
Tiferet Yesod	East-West
Netzach-Hod	Up-Down

If we now take the final letters in alphabetical order and line them up with the Five Loves in order, we have the following assignment:

ך	Kaf	= Keter	(Malkhut)
ם	Mem	= Chakhmah	(Binah)
ן	Nun	= Chesed	(Gevurah)
ף	Peh	= Tiferet	(Yesod)
ץ	Tzadi	= Netzach	(Hod)

We now must take the Five Strengths as the opposite end points in the five-dimensional continuum. Placing them in order, we then have:

Binah	= Mem	ם
Gevurah	= Nun	ן
Hod	= Tzadi	ץ
Yesod	= Peh	ף
Malkhut	= Kaf	ך

Table 24. The correct alphabetical order of the letters.

Dimension	Sefirot	Final Letter	Phonetic Family	Vowel
Spiritual	Keter-Malkhut	Kaf	דטלנת	o
Time	Chakhmah-Binah	Mem	זמשרץ	a
North-South	Chesed-Gevurah	Nun	גיכק	e
East-West	Tiferet-Yesod	Peh	כומף	u
Up-Down	Netzach-Hod	Tzadi	אחהע	i

Table 25. Parallel ordering of the letters.

Five loves		Five strengths	
o	דטלנת	a	זסשרץ
a	זסשרץ	e	גיכק
e	גיכק	i	אחהע
u	בומף	u	בומף
i	אחהע	o	דטלנת

This is the precise order in which these letters are usually presented, and this hardly appears to be coincidental. Also significant is the fact that the Ari states that the usual order MNTzPKh (מנצפך) only applies to these letters when they parallel the Five Strengths. When they relate to the Five Loves, they are in direct alphabetical order.[35] See Table 25.

Since each of the final letters represents one of the phonetic families, these can also be assigned to their appropriate dimension.

In relating the five primary vowels to these phonetic families, the Zohar presents them in the order i u e o a, this being the order that they appear in PiTuCheY ChoTaM (פְּתֻחֵי חֹתָם).[36] Since the Zohar here presents the phonetic families in alphabetical order, a parallel can immediately be drawn:

Gutturals	אחהע	i	Chirik
Labials	בומף	u	Shurek
Palatals	גיכק	e	Tzereh
Linguals	דטלנת	o	Cholam
Dentals	זסשרצ	a	Kametz

We now have three groups of five: the phonetic families, the final letters, and the primary vowels. All these can be related to the five dimensions.

As all the sections, this one can also be read in the imperative, providing an important technique. The text then says, "Engrave them with voice, carve them with breath, and set them in the mouth in five places."

The instruction is to carefully pronounce each letter of these five families. This is "engrave them with voice." Then one must "carve them with breath," contemplating each letter carefully, and concentrating on the breath that is exhaled while it is pronounced. Finally, one must "set them in the mouth," meditating on the place in the mouth with which the letter is pronounced.

In this exercise, each family may also be pronounced with its appropriate vowel. This yields a chant that can be used for this exercise. See Table 26 on page 108.

The purpose of this exercise is to make the initiate highly aware of the physical processes involved in pronouncing the letters. While speech itself involves Binah consciousness, the pronunciation of the letters is an automatic activity, and hence, it involves Chakhmah consciousness.

With this exercise, the initiate learns to make use of the letters with Chakhmah consciousness. By pronouncing them physically, he then clothes them in Binah. It is through this exercise that he learns to use the letters as "paths of *Wisdom*."

Table 26. A chant utilizing the five phonetic families.

A Cha Ha 'A	אָ חָ הָ עָ
Ge Ye Ke Ke	גֶ יֶ כֶ קֶ
Do To Lo No To	דֹ טֹ לֹ נֹ תֹ
Zi Si Shi Ri Tzi	זִ סִ שִ רִ צִ
Bu Vu Mu Pu	בֻ וֻ מֻ פֻ

In the first section of this chapter, the two Mothers, Mem and Shin, were used as an exercise to oscillate between Chakhmah and Binah consciousness. The second section presented an exercise involving the pronunciation and permutation of letters, making them fill the entire mind. Now we have a third exercise, where one meditates on the physical processes involved in pronouncing the letters, drawing all of them into Chakhmah consciousness.

Once this has been mastered, the initiate is ready to embark on the more advanced techniques involving the 231 Gates.

2:4   עשרים ושתים אותיות יסוד קבען בגלגל כמין
חומה ברל"א שערים וחוזר הגלגל פנים ואחור
וסימן לדבר אין בטובה למעלה מענג ואין ברעה
למטה מנגע:

Twenty-two Foundation Letters:
He placed them in a circle
  like a wall with 231 Gates.
The Circle oscillates back and forth.
A sign for this is:
    There is nothing in good higher than Delight
(Oneg—ענג)
    There is nothing evil lower than Plague (Nega—נגע).

In a circle

The word for "circle" here is *Galgal*. This can also be translated as "sphere" or "cycle." Later, the Sefer Yetzirah speaks of the *Galgal* again, saying, "The cycle (*galgal*) in the year is like a king in the provence" (6:3).

The first chapter spoke of the 32 paths of Wisdom. As discussed there (1:1), the number 32, when written out, spells *Lev*, meaning "heart." The text later speaks of the mystical experience by saying, "If your *heart* runs" (1:8). It also warns, "Bridle your... *heart* from thinking" (1:8).

The first chapter thus speaks of one aspect of kingship, which is the heart. As the text later says, "The heart in the soul is like a king in war" (6:3). The heart therefore dominates the continuum of the spiritual. Now, in the second chapter, the text is turning to a second aspect of kingship, the Cycle (*galgal*), which dominates time.

In general, if a number of points are placed in a circle, the number of possible lines that can connect any pair of points can be easily calculated. If we let *n* be the number of points, and *L* the number of lines, the formula is:

$$L = n \, (n - 1)/2$$

Take the number, multiply it by the number below it, and divide by two.

Thus, three points in a circle can be joined by three lines, four points by six lines, five points by ten lines, and six points by fifteen lines. See figure 17 on page 110. A given number of points can always be joined by the number of lines provided by the above formula.

The number of lines that can connect the 22 letters placed in a circle is therefore $(22 \times 21)/2$. See figure 18 on page 111. Making the calculation, we find that there are 231 such lines. These are the 231 Gates.

Like a wall...

This can also be read in the imperative: "Place them in a circle, like a wall with 231 gates."

The Kabbalists present an important meditation regarding these gates.[37] This is based on a text in the first chapter: "Engrave them like a garden, carve them like a wall, deck them like a ceiling" (1:11).

The initiate must contemplate the ground, visualizing it as murky black mud. He must then "engrave" the 22 letters, forming each one in his mind. These should make a circle in the ground.

Then he must "carve them like a wall." He must "carve" each letter out of the ground and stand each one up, making a circle of letters, surrounding him like a wall. One of the major Kabbalists, Rabbi Isaac of Acco, speaks of a similar meditation, where the letters are visualized on the horizon.[38]

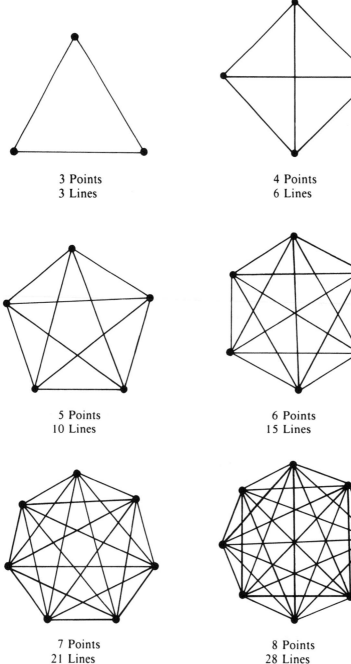

3 Points
3 Lines

4 Points
6 Lines

5 Points
10 Lines

6 Points
15 Lines

7 Points
21 Lines

8 Points
28 Lines

Figure 17. Lines connecting points in a circle.

Figure 18. The 231 Gates.

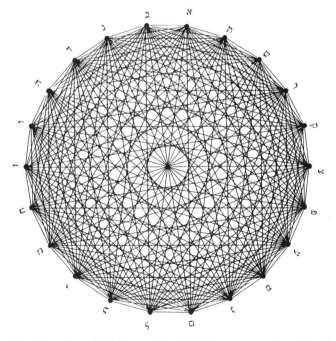

Figure 19. 22 points, 231 lines. The 231 lines connecting the 22 letters are the 231 Gates.

אב בג גד דה הו וז זח חט טי יך כל	לם מן נס סע עף פץ צק קר רש שת
אג בד גה דו הז וח זט חי טך יל כם	לן מס נע סף עץ פק צר קש רת
אד בה גו דז הח וט זי חך טל ים כן	לס מע נף סין עק פר צש קת
אה בו גז דח הט וי זך חל טם ין כס	לע מף נין סק ער פש צת
או בז גח דט הי וך זל חם טן יס כע	לף מץ נק סר עש פת
אז בח גט די הך ול זם חן טס יע כף	לץ מק נר סש עת
אח בט גי דך הל ום זן חס טע יף כץ	לק מר נש סת
אט בי גך דל הם ון זס חע טף יץ כק	לר מש נת
אי בך גל דם הן וס זע חף טץ יק כר	לש מת
אך בל גם דן הס וע זף חץ טק יר כש	לת
אל בם גן דס הע וף זץ חק טר יש כת	
אם בן גס דע הף וץ זק חר טש ית	
אן בס גע דף הץ וק זר חש טת	
אס בע גף דץ הק ור זש חת	
אע בף גץ דק הר וש זת	
אף בץ גק דר הש ות	
אץ בק גר דש הת	
אק בר גש דת	
אר בש גת	
אש בת	
את	

Figure 20. The 231 Gates in a triangular array. Logical Method.

1	א ב ג ד ה ו ז ח ט י כ ל מ נ ס ע פ צ ק ר ש ת
2	א ג ה ז ט כ מ ס פ ק ש א ג ה ז ט כ מ ס פ ק ש
3	א ד ז י מ ע ק ת ג ו ט ל ס צ ש כ ה ח כ נ פ ר
4	א ה ט מ פ ש ג ז כ ס ק א ה ט מ פ ש ג ז כ ס ק
5	א ו כ ע ש ד ט נ ק ב ז ל פ ת ה י ס ר ג ח מ צ
6	א ז מ ק ג ט ס ש ה כ פ א ז מ ק ג ט ס ש ה כ פ
7	א ח ס ת ז נ ש ו מ ר ה ל ק ד כ צ ג י פ ב ט ע
8	א ט פ ג כ ק ה מ ש ז ס א ט פ ג כ ק ה מ ש ז ס
9	א י ק ו ס ב כ ר ז ע ג ל ש ח פ ד מ ת ט צ ה נ
10	א כ ש ט ק ז פ ה ס ג מ א כ ש ט ק ז פ ה ס ג מ
11	א ל א ל א ל א ל א ל א ל א ל א ל א ל א ל א ל
12	א מ ג ס ה פ ז ק ט ש כ א מ ג ס ה פ ז ק ט ש כ
13	א נ ה צ ט ת מ ד פ ח ש ל ג ע ז ר כ ב ס ו ק י
14	א ס ז ש מ ה ק כ ג פ ט א ס ז ש מ ה ק כ ג פ ט
15	א ע ט ב פ י ג צ כ ד ק ל ה ר מ ו ש נ ז ת ס ח
16	א פ כ ה ש ס ט ג ק מ ז א פ כ ה ש ס ט ג ק מ ז
17	א צ מ ח ג ר ס י ה ת פ ל ז ב ק נ ט ד ש ע כ ו
18	א ק ס כ ז ג ש פ מ ט ה א ק ס כ ז ג ש פ מ ט ה
19	א ר פ נ כ ח ה ב ש צ ס ל ט ו ג ת ק ע מ י ז ד
20	א ש ק פ ס מ כ ט ז ה ג א ש ק פ ס מ כ ט ז ה ג
21	א ת ש ר ק צ פ ע ס נ מ ל כ י ט ח ז ו ה ד ג ב

Figure 21. Initial array used in the Kabbalistic Method.

Next, the initiate must "deck them like a ceiling." He must imagine the 231 lines connecting the 22 letters, and depict them like a ceiling over his head.

Once he has completed this exercise, he is ready to make use of the circle. If he wishes to use it to create, he must proceed in direct order, beginning with the Alef. Focusing the mind on the Alef, he then follows each of the 21 paths emanating from it to the other letters, from Bet to Tav. He continues in this manner, using all the other letters. See figure 19 on page 111.

According to some, this is also a technique for making a Golem. If one wishes to destroy it, one proceeds in the precise opposite direction, beginning with Tav, and ending with Aleph.

Some commentaries present a more primitive method, where the initiate actually draws a circle around the object that he wishes to form.[39] Proceeding in a circle, he chants the letter combinations, first Alef with all the other letters, then Bet, until the alphabet is completed. If one wishes to destroy the creation, he proceeds in the opposite direction.

It is also related that the disciples of the Riva[40] attempted to use the Sefer Yetzirah to make a creature. They went in the wrong direction, however, and sunk in the earth up to their waists through the power of the letters. Trapped, they cried out for help. The Riva was finally contacted, and he told his other disciples to recite the alphabets while proceeding in the opposite direction, until the others were freed.[41]

There is some question as to whether "proceeding" here means that one should actually walk around the circle, or whether it means that one must merely move around it mentally and meditatively.

With 231 Gates

The number 231 represents the number of ways in which two different letters of the Hebrew alphabet can be connected. This number also is the number of two letter words that can be formed with the letters, provided the same letter is not repeated, and provided that order is not considered. These combinations may be arranged in a triangle.[42]

This first method is called the Logical Method (figure 20). Besides this, there is also a Kabbalistic Method (figure 21), which is somewhat more complex.[43]

In the Kabbalistic Method, one begins by writing the entire Hebrew alphabet, from Alef to Tav. On the second line, one writes every other letter, ending with Shin. One then skips the Tav and begins once again with Alef. The sequence therefore repeats itself.

שת	קר	פצ	סע	מנ	כל	טי	זח	הו	גד	אב
קש	ספ	כמ	זט	גה	שא	פק	מס	טכ	הז	אג
פר	כנ	הח	שב	סצ	טל	גו	קת	מע	זי	אד
סק	זכ	שג	מפ	הט	קא	כס	גז	פש	טמ	אה
מצ	גח	סר	הי	פת	זל	קב	טנ	שד	כע	או
כף	שה	טס	קג	זמ	פא	הכ	סש	גט	מק	אז
טע	פב	גי	כצ	קד	הל	מר	שו	זנ	סת	אח
זס	מש	קה	גכ	טפ	סא	שז	המ	כק	פג	אט
הנ	טצ	מת	פד	שח	גל	זע	כר	סב	קו	אי
גמ	הס	זפ	טק	כש	מא	סג	פה	קז	שט	אכ
אל	אל	אל	אל	אל	אל	אל	אל	אל	אל	אל
שכ	קט	פז	סה	מג	כא	טש	זק	הפ	גס	אמ
קי	סו	כב	זר	גע	של	פח	מד	טת	הצ	אנ
פט	כג	הק	שמ	סז	טא	גפ	קכ	מה	זש	אס
סח	זת	שנ	מו	הר	קל	כד	גץ	פי	טב	אע
מז	גק	סט	הש	פכ	זא	קמ	טג	שס	כה	אפ
כו	שע	טד	קנ	זב	פל	הת	סי	גר	מח	אצ
טה	פמ	גש	כז	קס	הא	טמ	שפ	זג	סכ	אק
זד	מי	קע	גת	טו	סל	שצ	הב	כח	פנ	אר
הג	טז	מכ	פס	שק	גא	זה	כט	סמ	קפ	אש
גב	הד	זו	טח	כי	מל	סן	פע	קץ	שר	את

Figure 22. The 231 Gates according to the Kabbalistic Method.

0	1	2	3	4	5	6	7	8	9
0	2	4	6	8	0	2	4	6	8
0	3	6	9	2	5	8	1	4	7
0	4	8	2	6	0	4	8	2	6
0	5	0	5	0	5	0	5	0	5
0	6	2	8	4	0	6	2	8	4
0	7	4	1	8	5	2	9	6	3
0	8	6	4	2	0	8	6	4	2
0	9	8	7	6	5	4	3	2	1

Figure 23. A number array resembling the initial array used in the Kabbalistic Method.

In the third line, one writes every third letter, in the fourth, every fourth letter, continuing until the 21 lines have been completed. One then has the initial array.

The eleventh line is particularly interesting. Since 22 is divisible by eleven, the two letters, Alef and Lamed, repeat themselves for the entire line.

The next step is to take the array and break it into pairs. This yields 21 lines and 11 columns, producing a total of 231 pairs. These are the 231 Gates according to the Kabbalistic Method. See figure 22.

This system is actually not as complex as it first appears. To understand it more thoroughly, we can take a similar array, using the numbers from 0 to 9 instead of letters.

It is quite simple to make such an array. See figure 23. In the first line, one merely counts from 0 to 9. In the second line, one counts by two. As soon as we reach 10, we merely use the last digit. In the third line, we do the same, counting by three and using only the final digit. The rest of the array is formed using subsequent numbers.

What we actually have then is a simple multiplication table, where only the last digits have been retained. Clearly obvious in this array is the diagonal symmetry, which is also found in the alphabetical array.

The fifth line is particularly significant. When one counts by 5, one obtains the numbers 5, 10, 15, 25, and so on. Therefore, when only the last digits are taken, 5 and 0 alternate on this line. The same is true of the eleventh line in the alphabetical array, where the Alef and the Lamed alternate.

One then divides the array into double columns, to form a numerical analogue of the 231 Gates. The only difference is that when working with the alphabet, we are, in effect, using a number base of 22. See figure 24 on page 116.

One thing that is immediately apparent is the fact that even though we obtain 45 pairs, they do not correspond exactly to the 45 unique pairs that can be obtained from 10 digits. See figure 25 on page 116. We actually find that 14 pairs are missing, while an equal number are repeated. The most glaring example of this is the repetition of the combination 05, which occurs five times. Another redundancy is 80, which is merely the reverse of 08.

Just as one can begin each sequence from Alef, so one can also begin it from Bet. One would then have a similar array, with each line beginning with a Bet instead of an Alef. Each letter of the Bet array would be one higher than the corresponding letter in the Alef array. One can make similar arrays with all the letters of the alphabet.

Very important is the eleventh line, where the letter pairs repeat themselves. In the Alef array, the letters Alef and Lamed repeat themselves in this line. In the Bet array, the letters Bet and Mem will repeat themselves. As subsequent arrays are constructed, the repeating letters continue to conform to those in the ALBaM (בם אל) cipher. See figure 26 on page 116.

01	23	45	67	89
02	46	80	24	68
03	69	25	81	47
04	82	60	48	26
05	05	05	05	05
06	28	40	62	84
07	41	85	29	63
08	64	20	86	42
09	87	65	43	21

Figure 24. A numerical analogue of the 231 Gates as formed by the Kabbalistic Method.

01	02	03	04	05	06	07	08	09
12	13	14	15	16	17	18	19	
23	24	25	26	27	28	29		
34	35	36	37	38	39			
45	46	47	48	49				
56	57	58	59					
67	68	69						
78	79							
89								

Figure 25. The 45 unique pairs obtainable from ten digits.

לא	אל
מב	במ
נג	גנ
סד	דס
עה	הע
פו	ופ
צז	זצ
קח	חק
רט	טר
שי	יש
תכ	כת

Figure 26. The ALBaM cipher.

This holds true until one reaches the Kaf array, where the letters Kaf and Tav repeat. In the Lamed array, the letters Alef and Lamed repeat, so that this is the reverse of the Alef array. The repeating letters in the subsequent arrays are the reverse of those in the first eleven arrays.

Therefore, there are eleven arrays where the eleventh line has the pairs in the ALBaM sequence repeating. The next eleven arrays have their reverse repeating.

A number of somewhat similar arrays are used by the later Kabbalists.[44] Instead of using the Kabbalistic Method, however, they merely skip a number of letters in the second column, and then proceed with the alphabet in its usual order. It is not clear if these later Kabbalists did this so as to conceal the true method, or if it actually represents a completely different procedure. See figure 27 on page 118.

According to either procedure, there are eleven arrays in which the pairs represented by ALBaM are dominant. Then, there are another eleven arrays where the reverse of these pairs are dominant.

The first eleven arrays are said to represent the eleven Sefirot when the quasi-Sefirah Daat (Knowledge) is also included. The sequence is: Keter, Chakhmah, Binah, Daat, Chesed, Gevurah, Tiferet, Netzach, Hod, Yesod, Malkhut.

The first eleven arrays, where the pairs of ALBaM are in direct order, represent the "front" of these eleven Sefirot. The second set of eleven, where these pairs are reversed, represent the "back" of the Sefirot. These arrays are presented in Appendix III.

Although the Sefer Yetzirah says, "Ten and not eleven" (1:4), this is only speaking of the inner essence of the Sefirot. When we speak of their representation as letter arrays, we are speaking of their outer essence, and here Daat (Knowledge) is also counted, making eleven.[45]

These arrays are very important in binding oneself to the Sefirot. They are also used in the creation of a Golem.

According to the early Kabbalists, the 231 Gates are alluded to in the name Israel.[46] In Hebrew, Israel is spelled YiSRAeL (ישראל). These letters can also spell out YeSh RLA (יש רלא), which literally means, "there are 231."

The Midrash states that at the beginning of creation, "Israel rose in thought."[47] The name "Israel" thus alludes to the fact that creation took place through these 231 Gates. According to the later Kabbalists, these 231 gates are what remained in the Vacated Space that preceded creation.[48]

When the Sefer Yetzirah speaks of the "32 Paths of Wisdom," it uses the word *Nativ* for "path." The numerical value of Nativ (נתיב)

י	שת	קר	פצ	סע	מנ	כל	טי	זח	הו	גד	אב
ו	תב	רש	צק	עפ	נס	למ	יכ	חט	וז	דה	אג
ד	בן	שת	קר	פצ	סע	מנ	כל	טי	זח	הו	אד
ה	גד	תב	רש	צק	עפ	נס	למ	יכ	חט	וז	אה
י	דה	בג	שת	קר	פצ	סע	מנ	כל	טי	זח	או
ו	הו	גד	תב	רש	צק	עפ	נס	למ	יכ	חט	אז
י	וז	דה	בג	שת	קר	פצ	סע	מנ	כל	טי	אח
ו	זח	הו	גד	תב	רש	צק	עפ	נס	למ	יכ	אט
ה	חט	וז	דה	בג	שת	קר	פצ	סע	מנ	כל	אי
י	טי	זח	הו	גד	תב	רש	צק	עפ	נס	למ	אכ
יה	יכ	חט	וז	דה	בג	שת	קר	פצ	סע	מנ	אל
י	כל	טי	זח	הו	גד	תב	רש	צק	עפ	נס	אמ
ו	למ	יכ	חט	וז	דה	בג	שת	קר	פצ	סע	אנ
ד	מנ	כל	טי	זח	הו	גד	תב	רש	צק	עפ	אס
ה	נס	למ	יכ	חט	וז	דה	בג	שת	קר	פצ	אע
י	סע	מנ	כל	טי	זח	הו	גד	תב	רש	צק	אפ
ו	עפ	נס	למ	יכ	חט	וז	דה	בג	שת	קר	אצ
א	פצ	סע	מנ	כל	טי	זח	הו	גד	תב	רש	אק
ו	צק	עפ	נס	למ	יכ	חט	וז	דה	בג	שת	אר
ה	קר	פצ	סע	מנ	כל	טי	זח	הו	גד	תב	אש
י	רש	צק	עפ	נס	למ	יכ	חט	וז	דה	בג	את

Figure 27. The 231 Gates according to the later Kabbalists. This is the Alef array corresponding to Keter. (Note how the letters of the Tetragrammaton spelled out, are lined up with the lines.)

is 462, exactly twice 231. Since each of the 231 Gates contains two letters, there are a total of 462 letters in each array.[49] It is therefore evident that the "Paths of Wisdom" are related to these arrays. In some versions of Sefer Yetzirah, the actual reading is "462 Gates."[50]

There is, however, a very ancient tradition which reads 221 Gates rather than 231.[51] This is the reading favored by Rabbi Eliezer Rokeach of Wormes, who learned it by tradition from Rabbi Yehudah HaChasid.[52] See figure 28.

The Kabbalists note that this number is based on the Talmudic teaching that in the Future World, King David's cup will hold 221 measures.[53] This is based on the verse, "You have annointed my head with oil, my cup is overflowing" (Psalms 23:5). In Hebrew, "overflowing" is Revayah (רויה), which has a numerical value of 221.

The term Revayah is later used by Sefer Yetzirah to denote the "temperate" season, paralleling the letter Alef (3:5, 7). Just as the Alef serves as the intermediate between Shin and Mem, these arrays might

אב	גד	הו	זח	טי	כל	מנ	סע	פצ	קר	שת
אג	הז	טכ	מס	פק	שא	גה	זט	כמ	ספ	קש
אד	זי	מע	קת	גו	טל	סצ	שב	הח	כנ	פר
אה	טמ	פש	גז	כס	קא	הט	מפ	שג	זכ	סק
או	כע	שד	טנ	קכ	זל	פת	הי	סר	גח	מצ
אז	מק	גט	סש	הכ	פא	זמ	קג	טס	שה	כפ
אח	סת	זנ	שו	מר	הל	קד	כצ	גי	פב	טע
טא	פג	כק	המ	שז	סא	טפ	גכ	קה	מש	זס
אי	קו	סב	כר	זע	גל	שח	פד	מת	טצ	הנ
אכ	שט	קז	פה	סג	מא אל	כש	טק	זפ	הס	גמ
אמ	גס	הפ	זק	טש	כא	מג	סה	פז	קט	שכ
אנ	הצ	טת	מד	פח	של	גע	זר	כב	סו	קי
אס	זש	מה	קכ	גפ	טא	סז	שמ	הק	כג	פט
אע	טב	פי	גצ	כד	קל	הר	מו	שנ	זת	סח
אפ	כה	שס	טג	קמ	זא	פכ	הש	סט	גק	מז
אצ	מח	גר	סי	הת	פל	זב	קנ	טד	שע	כו
אק	סכ	זג	שפ	מט	הא	קס	כז	גש	פמ	טה
אר	פנ	כח	הב	שצ	סל	טו	גת	קע	מי	זד
אש	קפ	סמ	כט	זה	גא	שק	פס	מכ	טז	הג
את	שר	קצ	פע	סנ	מל	כי	טח	זו	הד	גב

Figure 28. The 221 Gates according to Rabbi Eliezar Rokeach of Wormes (1160–1237).

serve as a means of transition between Binah and Chakhmah consciousness.

Also significant is the context of this teaching. The beginning of this verse is, "You have annointed my head with oil." This alludes to the feeling of being bathed in oil which is frequently encountered during the mystical experience.[54] Attaining such an experience is therefore associated with these 221 Gates.

The number 221 is also significant as being the product of two primes, 17 and 13. The numbers can therefore be placed in a unique array.

This system follows logically from the Kabbalistic Method discussed earlier. In the array produced by this method, the two letters, Alef and Lamed, are repeated eleven times. Since this is a single combination, such repetition is redundant. In Eliezer Rokeach's system, the Alef-Lamed pair is used only once. Since ten such pairs are omitted, instead of 231 Gates, one is left with 221.

Similar arrays can be made beginning with the other letters. These are presented in Appendix III.

לם	כן	יס	טע	חפ	זצ	וק	הר	דש	גת	אב
במ	לן	כס	יע	טפ	חצ	זק	ור	הש	דת	אג
מנ	לס	כע	יפ	טצ	חק	זר	וש	הת	בג	אד
גנ	מס	לע	כפ	יצ	טק	חר	זש	ות	בד	אה
נס	מע	לפ	כצ	יק	טר	חש	זת	גד	בה	או
דס	נע	מפ	לצ	כק	יר	טש	חת	גה	בו	אז
סע	נפ	מצ	לק	כר	יש	טת	דה	גו	בז	אח
הע	ספ	נצ	מק	לר	כש	ית	דו	גז	בח	אט
עפ	סצ	נק	מר	לש	כת	הו	דז	גח	בט	אי
ופ	עצ	סק	נר	מש	לת	הז	דח	גט	בי	אכ
פצ	עק	סר	נש	מת	וז	הח	דט	גי	בכ	אל
זץ	פק	ער	סש	נת	וח	הט	די	גכ	בל	אמ
צק	פר	עש	סת	זח	וט	הי	דכ	גל	במ	אנ
חק	צר	פש	עת	זט	וי	הכ	דל	גמ	בן	אס
קר	צש	פת	חט	זי	וכ	הל	דמ	גן	בס	אע
טר	קש	צת	חי	זכ	ול	המ	דן	גס	בע	אפ
רש	קת	טי	חכ	זל	ומ	הן	דס	גע	בפ	אצ
יש	רת	טכ	חל	זמ	ון	הס	דע	גפ	בצ	אק
שת	יכ	טל	חמ	זנ	וס	הע	דפ	גץ	בק	אר
כת	יל	טמ	חן	זס	וע	הפ	דצ	גק	בר	אש
כל	ימ	טן	חמ	זע	ופ	הץ	דק	גר	בש	את

Figure 29. Abulafia's array of the 231 Gates.

01	29	38	47	56
02	39	48	57	16
03	12	49	58	67
04	13	59	68	27
05	14	23	69	78
06	15	24	79	38
07	16	25	34	89
08	17	26	35	49
09	18	27	36	45

Figure 30. Numerical analogue of Abulafia's array.

Another important representation of the 231 Gates is that of Rabbi Abraham Abulafia.[55] This is somewhat like the Logical Array, but it is set in a rectangle, with the upper right side arranged so as to fill in the missing letters (figure 29). The structure is discernable when one studies its numerical analogue (figure 30). Close examination shows some redundancy in this array. Certain combinations are

לם	כנ	יס	טע	חפ	זצ	וק	הר	דש	גת	אב
כמ	לן	כס	יע	טפ	חצ	זק	ור	הש	דת	אג
מנ	לס	כע	יפ	טצ	חק	זר	וש	הת	בג	אד
ינ	מס	לע	כפ	יץ	טק	חר	זש	ות	בד	אה
נס	מע	לפ	כץ	יק	טר	חש	זת	גד	בה	או
טס	נע	מפ	לץ	כק	יר	טש	חת	גה	בו	אז
סע	נפ	מץ	לק	כר	יש	טת	דה	גו	בז	אח
חע	ספ	נץ	מק	לר	כש	ית	דו	גז	בח	אט
עפ	סץ	נק	מר	לש	כת	הו	דז	גח	בט	אי
זפ	עץ	סק	נר	מש	לת	הז	דח	גט	בי	אכ
פצ	עק	סר	נש	מת	וז	הח	דט	גי	בכ	אל
יץ	פק	ער	סש	נת	וח	הט	די	גכ	בל	אמ
צק	פר	עש	סת	זח	וט	הי	דכ	גל	במ	אנ
הק	צר	פש	עת	זט	וי	הכ	דל	גמ	בנ	אס
קר	צש	פת	חט	זי	וכ	הל	דמ	גנ	בס	אע
דר	קש	צת	חי	זכ	ול	המ	דן	גס	בע	אפ
רש	קת	טי	חכ	זל	ומ	הנ	דס	גע	בפ	אצ
גש	רת	טכ	חל	זמ	ונ	הס	דע	גפ	בצ	אק
שת	יכ	טל	חמ	זנ	וס	הע	דפ	גצ	בק	אר
בת	יל	טמ	חנ	זס	וע	הפ	דצ	גק	בר	אש
כל	ים	טנ	חמ	זע	ופ	הצ	דק	גר	בש	את

Figure 31. Abulafia's array modified to remove redundancies.

01	29	38	47	56
02	39	48	57	46
03	12	49	58	67
04	13	59	68	37
05	14	23	69	78
06	15	24	79	28
07	16	25	34	89
08	17	26	35	19
09	18	27	36	45

Figure 32. Numerical analogue of Abulafia's array modified to remove redundancies.

repeated, while others are omitted. This array can be modified, however, so that its redundancies are removed and all combinations are represented. See figure 31 and figure 32.

Even with the redundancies removed, however, the extreme left column is anomalous and complex. This anomaly can be removed,

כמ	ין	טס	חע	זפ	וץ	הק	דר	גש	כת	אב
לם	כנ	יס	טע	חפ	זצ	וק	הר	דש	גת	אג
לן	כס	יע	טפ	חצ	זק	ור	הש	דת	בג	אד
מנ	לס	כע	יפ	טצ	חק	זר	וש	הת	בד	אה
מס	לע	כפ	יץ	טק	חר	זש	ות	גד	בה	או
נס	מע	לפ	כץ	יק	טר	חש	זת	גה	בו	אז
נע	מפ	לץ	כק	יר	טש	חת	דה	גו	בז	אח
סע	נפ	מץ	לק	כר	יש	טת	דו	גז	בח	אט
ספ	נץ	מק	לר	כש	ית	הו	דז	גח	בט	אי
עפ	סץ	נק	מר	לש	כת	הז	דח	גט	בי	אכ
עץ	סק	נר	מש	לת	וז	הח	דט	גי	בכ	אל
פץ	עק	סר	נש	מת	וח	הט	די	גכ	בל	אמ
פק	ער	סש	נת	זח	וט	הי	דכ	גל	במ	אנ
צק	פר	עש	סת	זט	וי	הכ	דל	גמ	בן	אס
צר	פש	עת	חט	זי	וכ	הל	דמ	גן	בס	אע
קר	צש	פת	חי	זכ	ול	המ	דן	גס	בע	אפ
קש	צת	טי	חכ	זל	ומ	הן	דס	גע	בפ	אצ
רש	צת	קת	טכ	זמ	ונ	הס	דע	גפ	בצ	אק
רת	יכ	טל	כמ	זן	וס	הע	דפ	גצ	בק	אר
שת	יל	טמ	כן	זס	וע	הפ	דצ	גק	בר	אש
כל	ימ	טנ	כס	זע	ופ	הץ	דק	גר	בש	את

Figure 33. Abulafia's array modified and simplified.

01	19	28	37	46
02	29	38	47	56
03	12	39	48	57
04	13	49	58	67
05	14	23	59	68
06	15	24	69	78
07	16	25	34	79
08	17	26	35	89
09	18	27	36	45

Figure 34. Numerical analogue of Abulafia's array modified and simplified.

and the array is then further simplified. See figures 33 and 34.

The number 231 represents the total number of combinations of two letters. The number of combinations of three letters is 1540. Rabbi Abraham Abulafia notes that this is equal to 22 times 70. The number 70 represents the 70 primary languages. If each of these lan-

Table 27. Combinations of letters.

Letters	Combinations	Letters	Combinations
0	1	11	705,432
1	22	12	646,646
2	231	13	479,420
3	1,540	14	319,770
4	7,315	15	170,544
5	26,334	16	74,613
6	74,613	17	26,334
7	170,544	18	7,315
8	319,770	19	1,540
9	479,420	20	231
10	646,646	21	22
		22	1

guages had an alphabet of 22 letters, there would be a total of 1540 letters.[56]

In general the number of combinations of *n* letters is given by the formula:

$$C = 22!/[n!(22-n)!].$$

Values of the numbers from zero to 22 are provided in Table 27.

There is nothing in good higher than Delight...

This is because the Bible refers to the most direct experience of God using the word "delight" (*Oneg*). It is thus written, "Then you will delight upon God" (Isaiah 58:14).[57]

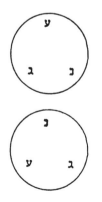

Figure 35. The word nega is obtained from Oneg by notation.

The word for "plague," *Nega* (נגע), is obtained from *Oneg* (ענג) by simple rotation. The term *Nega* denoted especially a leprosy like plague, which was a sign of disapproval by God. See figure 35 on page 123.

In an earlier section (1:13), we discussed how permutations such as these can result in opposites.

A very similar permutation is presented by the Kabbalists. The highest spiritual level to which one can aspire is the Sefirah of Keter (Crown). The further one climbs, however, the more rarified the atmosphere, and the greater the spiritual danger. By a simple permutation, the word *Keter* (כתר) becomes *Karet* (כרת), the Hebrew word for excision, where a person is completely cut off spiritually.[58]

One of the early 10th century mystics, Hai Gaon, noted that many people who embarked on the mysteries were successful, but then met with untimely death.[59] The higher the climb, the more dangerous the fall.

A person would not attempt to climb a dangerous mountain without the proper training and equipment. Any novice who would attempt a climb without an experienced guide would be courting disaster. Climbing spiritual heights can be equally dangerous. One needs the proper training and mental equipment, as well as an experienced spiritual guide.

2:5

כיצד צרפן שקלן והמירן א' עם כולם וכולם עם
א' ב' עם כולם וכולם עם ב' וחוזרות חלילה
ונמצאות ברל"א שערים ונמצא כל היצור וכל הדבור
יוצא משם אחד:

How?
He permuted them, weighed them, and transformed them,
  Alef with them all
    and all of them with Alef,
  Bet with them all
    and all of them with Bet.
They repeat in a cycle
  and exist in 231 Gates.
It comes out that all that is formed
  and all that is spoken
    emanates from one Name.

One Name

According to the Kabbalists, this Name is the Tetragrammaton, YHVH (יהוה). Each letter must be permuted with the Tetragrammaton in an appropriate manner.

The technique for doing this is outlined by Rabbi Eliezer Rokeach of Wormes, particularly in the context of creating a Golem.[60] This brings us to some of the most powerful meditative techniques of the Sefer Yetzirah.

When one is working with a letter, he must combine that letter with the letters of the Tetragrammaton, using all five vowels.

Thus, for example, if one were using the Alef, one would begin by combining it with the Yud of the Tetragrammaton, using all five vowels. See figure 36 on page 126. There is, however, some question as to how one is to go about this. From the words of Rabbi Eliezar Rokeach, it would appear that one simply makes use of all the vowels in sequence:

AuYuAaYaAiYiAeYeAoYo   אֹ אֶ אֵ אִ אַ אֻ

As discussed earlier, there is some question regarding the sequence of the five primary vowels (2:3). There are at least a half dozen different opinions. If the proper sequence is crucial, much dangerous experimentation would have to be done to determine the proper sequence. It is possible, however, that the sequence is not overridingly important.

In any event, following the system of Rabbi Eliezer Rokeach, the initiate must then proceed in this manner, completing all four letters of the Tetragrammaton. One can proceed in the same manner using any other letter of the alphabet.

The initiate continues in this manner, pronouncing all the letters in the array of the 221 (or 231) Gates.

Since Alef is the letter associated with the thorax, the entire Alef array would pertain to this part of the body. Next the initiate would proceed to the head, for which he would use the Shin array, as explained below (3:9). He would form an array of the 221 Gates where every line begins with a Shin. He would then continue in this manner through all the parts of the body, using the letters that the Sefer Yetzirah associates with each part.

For each letter, one must go through the entire sequence of 221 (or 231) Gates. Each such sequence contains 442 letters, and therefore, in completing all 22 letters of the alphabet, one will have made use of 4862 letters. Each of these letters will have been pronounced with the five primary vowels and the four letters of the Tetragramma-

Alef	
AuYu AaYa AiYi AeYe AoYo	אַיְ אָיְ אִיְ אֵיְ אֹיְ
AuHu AaHa AiHi AeHe AoHo	אַהְ אָהְ אִהְ אֵהְ אֹהְ
AuVu AaVa AiVi AeVe AoVo	אַוְ אָוְ אִוְ אֵוְ אֹוְ
AuHu AaHa AiHi AeHe AoHo	אַהְ אָהְ אִהְ אֵהְ אֹהְ
Bet	
BuYu BaYa BiYi BeYe BoYo	בַּיְ בָּיְ בִּיְ בֵּיְ בֹּיְ
BuHu BaHa BiHi BeHe BoHo	בַּהְ בָּהְ בִּהְ בֵּהְ בֹּהְ
BuVu BaVa BiVi BeVe BoVo	בַּוְ בָּוְ בִּוְ בֵּוְ בֹּוְ
BuHu BaHa BiHi BeHe BoHo	בַּהְ בָּהְ בִּהְ בֵּהְ בֹּהְ

Figure 36. The sequence for Alef and Bet.

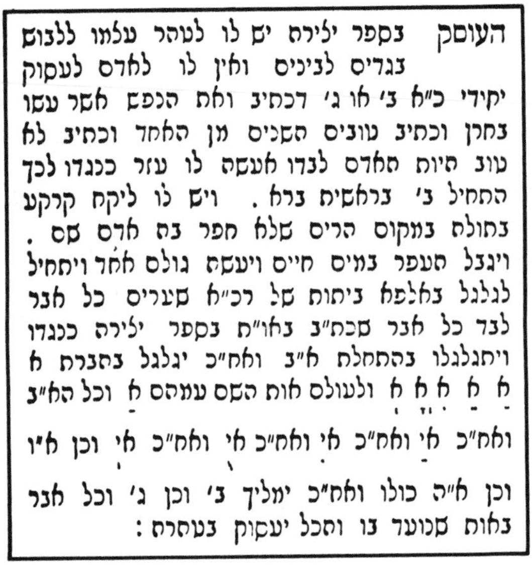

Figure 37. Instructions for making a Golem, from Rabbi Eliezar Rokeach's commentary on Sefer Yetzirah.

ton, a total of twenty pronunciations for each letter. This means that the entire exercise makes use of 97,240 pronunciations. Assuming that one can pronounce four syllables a second, it would take approximately seven hours to complete this entire process.

The method of creating a Golem is outlined by Rabbi Eliezer Rokeach in his commentary on Sefer Yetzirah, and presented in

אם תרצה לכרוא ' גולם אחד או ענלא תלחא

כנון אבי ורב' ז ל' שיעשו זה כרשו'ממ'ה שהשינו שלום מסתיכה'
רק'כה ר'ל שהככים עמהם ש'שחטשו בכתרו של ממ'ח ואם לא
יגניש בוד'אי ודרך הפועל לצרף עם הא' כ' כולם השם של הויח
בחכישהתנוינו'שהם   אי א' אי אי או   וילנ ל קורס פרצוף
ואל' ף 'עם כל אות'ות'ה הכחוברים אליה כתנרגת אַ'י ואח'ן
פעם שנית אַ'י ואחר כך א' ואח'כן אַ'י ואח'כן א' ער תשל'ום
אות'יות האל'ף 'עם ה'ור של הוי'ח ואח'כן כסדר הזה 'עם אות ה'
של השם הויה ואח'כ 'עם היו'ו ואח'כ 'עם ה' הה' וכפרר הזה לכל
האות'יות של השאר כ'א פרצופים וצריך אחת שלא תטעוה כהם
ותי'ענט ואם תאבר אותם מהיםכים 'בל'יען הארץ ' וצריך שהדיע
ג'כ כשחן'עשה הנוף תאמר אלו ואאות'ות הנג' דהיינו כשחן'עשה
הנויה האם' פרצוף של א'לף 'עם אות'יות 'כאשר הריחין וכשחן'עש'
הנכ מ'עם חצרף אַוות מם וכשחן'עשה הראש חצרף פרצוף ש'ן
וכשחן'עשה הם 'ח תצרף הב'ח ' ועין ימין פרצוף נ'מל ' ועין
שב'אל ח'   אף יס'ן כ'ף ואף שמאל פא אוז 'מין ר'ש א'ון
שמאל חו 'י יר 'מן ה'יד שמאל ו'רגל 'מין ז'רנל שמל'ח 'כוליא
ימין ט'כוליא שמ'אל ו' כנר ל' ·   פרה נ' ·   טחול ס' הסכם
ע' ק'נה צ' קורקנן ק' 'והי'עכק בספר 'צירה 'ס'הר עמון כנגני'
לננ'ם תק'יפ ואל ' 'עכוק 'ח'די אלא בשנים או'ם בשלשה
רכתי'כ ואת הנפש אשר ע'שו כחן וכתיב טוב'ים הטנ'ים כן האח'

וכתכ לא טוב היות האדם לכרו' · ולכן התחיל התורה באות ב'
שנ' כראשית כרא וגו' וי'עשה תינ'ניות הידוע' לנו עם שאר כוונות
הש'יכים לזאת הפ'עולה ואח'כ יקח קרקיע כתול'כמקן'הרים שלא
חפר בה אדם וינכל ה'עפר בכהרה במ'ם חיים וי'עשה גולם אחר
על גלגל כצירופו הא'כא ב'יחא של רל'א ש'עָרים כל אות אחת
לכרו' באורת הש'ם והנקורה הנזכר למ'עלה הות'ח'יל' כו וילגלנו
בהתחלת א' כ' כנו' ואח'כ יגלגלנו נהברת · או אח' אי אַ' אַ' או
ולי'עולם תגלגל את השם 'עמהם אַ'י וכל האלפא ב'חא ואחר' כך
אַ'י ואח'כ אַ' ואח'כ א' ואח'כ א' ואח'כ. ·א' וכן או
וכן אי וכן אַה' וכ. וכ. כל האות'ורת כלם 'עם השם ה'ה היה כדרך הנג'
ער תשל'ום פרצו'ף אות הא' וכן ה'צי'ף אות ב' ''עם ה'שם וכן אות
ופרצ'ף אות ג וכן כלם 'ער כ א א'רב'ב · ב'יה'וֹת ש'י אות חיוזכל'
אנר כאיח הנועד כו ויהל'יעכ'ק   נכרהרה ולא 'ט'נה ה' 'ו'דל'אא
באות'יות ולא כהנקרות וכל 'ש'שלא 'ט'ענה בגלגול א'ת'היה השם
שנ'כי 'ישרים דרכ'י ידוד צד'יק'ם 'לכו   כם ופושי'ע'ים 'כשלו כס
ומי ש'יורע' כדר הפ'עולו'של כפר 'צירה 'ה'ה · נאהב לט'על'ולכטה
ונוחל שג' 'עולמים שנ'להנח'ל אוהב' 'יש ואו'גרותיה 'אב'לא ונהם
כרא א'ס כל כל ה'עולמ'ורת וכל' סרר ה'צירה הנשכ' והרוחני זהו
האכור כס' ובר בהם כל ה'צור וכו' שנ' 'כל הנקרא כשמ'לכבורי
כראח'י יצרת'י אף 'עש'ית'י ונאמר כי כיה ידו ד צור 'עולמים
ילא'ו ':

Figure 38. *Instructions for making a Golem from* Emek HaMelekh.

somewhat greater detail by the author of *Emek HaMelekh* (Depths of the King).[61] See figure 37 on page 126 and figure 38. An initiate should not do it alone, but should always be accompanied by one or two colleagues. The Golem must be made of virgin soil, taken from a place where no man has ever dug. The soil must be kneaded with pure spring water, taken directly from the ground. If this water is placed in any kind of vessel, it can no longer be used. The people making the Golem must purify themselves totally before engaging in this activity, both physically and spiritually. While making the Golem, they must wear clean white vestments.

These authors also stress that one must not make any mistake or error in the pronunciation. They do not say what must be done if one errs, but from other sources, it would appear that at very least, one would have to begin the array from the beginning. During this entire procedure, no interruption whatsoever may occur.

These authors also intimate that they are only revealing the outline of the method, and are not presenting it in its entirety. This also appears evident from other sources.

There is also evidence that creating a Golem was primarily not a physical procedure, but rather, a highly advanced meditative technique.[62] By chanting the appropriate letter arrays together with the letters of the Tetragrammaton, the initiate could form a very real mental image of a human being, limb by limb. This possibly could be used as an astral body, through which one could ascend to the spiritual realms.

The formation of such a spiritual body, however, would also result in a tremendous spiritual potential. Once the conceptual Golem was completed, this spiritual potential could be transferred to a clay form and actually animate it. This was the process through which a physical Golem would be brought to life.

In introducing this method, the Sefer Yetzirah said, "Engrave them like a garden, carve them like a wall, deck them like a ceiling" (1:11). There is some question as to what role this meditation plays in the technique of making a Golem. According to some early sources, one must proceed in a circle around the creature that one is creating. This might refer to the mental structuring of this "garden," "wall," and "ceiling," before the Golem is formed.

Pronunciation with the Yud (י):	
AoYo AoYa AoYe AoYi AoYu	אֹי אֹי אֹי אֹי אֹי
AaYo AaYa AaYe AaYi AaYu	אָי אָי אָי אָי אָי
AeYo AeYa AeYe AeYi AeYu	אֵי אֵי אֵי אֵי אֵי
AiYo AiYa AiYe AiYi AiYu	אִי אִי אִי אִי אִי
AuYo AuYa AuYe AuYi AuYu	אֻי אֻי אֻי אֻי אֻי
YoAo YoAa YoAe YoAi YoAu	יֹא יֹא יֹא יֹא יֹא
YaAo YaAa YaAe YaAi YaAu	יָא יָא יָא יָא יָא
YeAo YeAa YeAe YeAi YeAu	יֵא יֵא יֵא יֵא יֵא
YiAo YiAa YiAe YiAi YiAu	יִא יִא יִא יִא יִא
YuAo YuAa YuAe YuAi YuAu	יֻא יֻא יֻא יֻא יֻא

Pronunciation with the Heh (ה):	
AoHo AoHa AoHe AoHi AoHu	אֹה אֹה אֹה אֹה אֹה
AaHo AaHa AaHe AaHi AaHu	אָה אָה אָה אָה אָה
AeHo AeHa AeHe AeHi AeHu	אֵה אֵה אֵה אֵה אֵה
AiHo AiHa AiHe AiHi AiHu	אִה אִה אִה אִה אִה
AuHo AuHa AuHe AuHi AuHu	אֻה אֻה אֻה אֻה אֻה
HoAo HoAa HoAe HoAi HoAu	הֹא הֹא הֹא הֹא הֹא
HaAo HaAa HaAe HaAi HaAu	הָא הָא הָא הָא הָא
HeAo HeAa HeAe HeAi HeAu	הֵא הֵא הֵא הֵא הֵא
HiAo HiAa HiAe HiAi HiAu	הִא הִא הִא הִא הִא
HuAo HuAa HuAe HuAi HuAu	הֻא הֻא הֻא הֻא הֻא

Figure 39. Abulafia's system.

Also important was the system taught by Rabbi Abraham Abulafia, which is apparently rooted in earlier techniques. See figure 39 on pages 128-129. It is not certain, however, whether Abulafia is expanding upon the methods of Rabbi Eliezar Rokeach, or if he is drawing from an entirely different tradition. This technique is also quoted by a number of later Kabbalists.[63]

In this system, the initiate pronounces the letters together with those of the Tetragrammaton, just as in the system of Rabbi Eliezar Rokeach. However, instead of merely using the five primary vowels alone, he must use every possible combination of these vowels, twenty-five in all.

Pronunciation with the Vav (ו):

AoVo	AoVa	AoVe	AoVi	AoVu	אֹו אֹו אֹו אֹו אֹו
AaVo	AaVa	AaVe	AaVi	AaVu	אֹו אֹו אֹו אֹו אֹו
AeVo	AeVa	AeVe	AeVi	AeVu	אֹו אֹו אֹו אֹו אֹו
AiVo	AiVa	AiVe	AiVi	AiVu	אֹו אֹו אֹו אֹו אֹו
AuVo	AuVa	AuVe	AuVi	AuVu	אֹו אֹו אֹו אֹו אֹו
VoAo	VoAa	VoAe	VoAi	VoAu	וֹא וֹא וֹא וֹא וֹא
VaAo	VaAa	VaAe	VaAi	VaAu	וָא וָא וָא וָא וָא
VeAo	VeAa	VeAe	VeAi	VeAu	וֵא וֵא וֵא וֵא וֵא
ViAo	ViAa	ViAe	ViAi	ViAu	וִא וִא וִא וִא וִא
VuAo	VuAa	VuAe	VuAi	VuAu	וֻא וֻא וֻא וֻא וֻא

Pronunciation with the final Heh (ה):

AoHo	AoHa	AoHe	AoHi	AoHu	אֹה אֹה אֹה אֹה אֹה
AaHo	AaHa	AaHe	AaHi	AaHu	אָה אָה אָה אָה אָה
AeHo	AeHa	AeHe	AeHi	AeHu	אֵה אֵה אֵה אֵה אֵה
AiHo	AiHa	AiHe	AiHi	AiHu	אִה אִה אִה אִה אִה
AuHo	AuHa	AuHe	AuHi	AuHu	אֻה אֻה אֻה אֻה אֻה
HoAo	HoAa	HoAe	HoAi	HoAu	הֹא הֹא הֹא הֹא הֹא
HaAo	HaAa	HaAe	HaAi	HaAu	הָא הָא הָא הָא הָא
HeAo	HeAa	HeAe	HeAi	HeAu	הֵא הֵא הֵא הֵא הֵא
HiAo	HiAa	HiAe	HiAi	HiAu	הִא הִא הִא הִא הִא
HuAo	HuAa	HuAe	HuAi	HuAu	הֻא הֻא הֻא הֻא הֻא

Figure 39. Abulafia's system (continued).

Cholam		Begin straight ahead and raise head upward.
Kametz		Begin at right and move head to left.
Tzereh		Begin at left and move head to right.
Chirik		Begin straight ahead and lower head downward.
Shurek		Move head directly forward.

Figure 40. Head motions.

If this method were used with an entire array of 221 letter pairs, completing a single array would be a major task, taking over an hour and a half to complete. It would take over 35 hours to complete the entire sequence of 22 letters. It is questionable if this was ever actually done in practice, but it is not impossible. Forming a Golem was considered to be the most advanced—and dangerous—of all meditative techniques. An initiate advanced enough to attempt it might also have the discipline necessary for over thirty hours of continuous meditation.

Besides this, Abulafia also prescribes specific breathing exercises to be used while chanting these letters. Between each letter one is to take a single breath. Between pairs, one is to take no more than two breaths, between lines, no more than five, and between each letter of the Tetragrammaton, no more than twenty-five.

Specific head motions are also prescribed for this exercise. These head motions are to be made slowly and deliberately, while one pronounces the letter and exhales. See figure 40. These motions correspond to the shape of the vowel. While doing this exercise, one is seated, facing toward the east.

There is evidence that the names and shapes of the Hebrew vowel points were used for mystical puposes long before they were used in writing and grammar. The earliest non-mystical use of the vowels dates from the eighth or ninth century, while mystical uses are found in Kabbalistic sources that date as early as the first century. It is highly possible that the shapes of the written vowels were taken from the head motions associated with their sounds.

Abulafia uses his system of breathing exercises and head motions with the letter Alef, since Alef (with a numerical value of 1) expresses unity with God. The same system can also be used with other letters. There is no evidence, however, that this method was ever used with an entire array of 221 letter pairs. To use it with even a single letter is a major effort. It is possible, however, that this method could be used with various letters to attain specific results with them.[64]

Golem-making was merely the most advanced and spectacular use of the methods of Sefer Yetzirah. Each letter individually, however, is also associated with a part of the body. The array associated with the particular letter could be used as a meditation to affect that specific limb. This could be used to strengthen the spiritual energy of that limb, or even for curative puposes.

The letters are also associated with various times and astrological signs. Using the system of Sefer Yetzirah one can also construct meditations associated with these.

2:6

יצר ממש מתהו ועשה את אינו ישנו וחצב
עמודים גדולים מאויר שאינו נתפש וזה סימן א'
עם כולם וכולם עם א' צופה וממיר ועשה את כל היצור
ואת כל הדבור שם אחד וסימן לדבר עשרים ושתים
חפצים בגוף אחד:

He formed substance out of chaos
  and made nonexistence into existence
He carved great pillars from air
  that cannot be grasped.
This is a sign
  [Alef with them all, and all of them with Alef]
He forsees, transforms and makes
  all that is formed and all that is spoken:
    one Name.
A sign for this thing:
  Twenty-two objects in a single body.

He formed substance out of chaos

Earlier, the Sefer Yetzirah stated that chaos (*tohu*) was "engraved and carved" from water (1:11). As we explained there, "Water" alluded to Chakhmah and the basis of all physical creation. The "water" mentioned there denoted the most primitive spiritual root of water, as it exists in the universe of Atzilut, the realm of the Sefirot. It was out of this that the first stage of matter, "Chaos" (*tohu*), was formed. The text here therefore states that it was out of this "chaos" that matter was formed.

The word for "substance" here is Mamash (ממש). This comes from the root *Mashash* (משש), meaning "to touch." What is produced is a reality that can not only be seen, but which is physical enough to be touched.

And made nonexistence into existence

Chakhmah, however, is on the level of Nothingness. It is from this Nothingness, however, that all things were created. From this "nonexistence," Binah and Beriyah, which are called "existence" (*Yesh*), were brought into being.

He carved great pillars

The reference here is obviously to the verse, "Wisdom has built its house, it has carved its seven pillars" (Proverbs 9:1). This is further evidence that this section is speaking of Chakhmah (Wisdom).[65]

There is some discussion at to the meaning of the "seven pillars" in this verse. In one place, the Talmud says that they are the seven days of the week.[66] Elsewhere, the Talmud states that they refer to the seven pillars upon which the world stands, an interpretation that is also mentioned in the Zohar.[67] Others identify them with the seven sciences: grammar, rhetoric, logic, arithmetic, music, geometry, and astronomy.[68]

The Kabbalists teach that these seven pillars represent the lower seven Sefirot.[69] These correspond to the seven pillars of creation and the seven days of the week, so this does not contradict the Talmudic interpretation.

In the system of the Sefer Yetzirah, it is obvious that these seven pillars represent the seven Doubles. They are called "pillars" because they are represented by vertical lines in the Tree of Life diagram.

These seven Doubles are derived from the three Mothers. This would support an ancient version, which instead of "substance" (Mamash—ממש), read AMSh (אמש), the three Mothers.[70] The text would then read, "He formed AMSh (אמש) out of chaos ... and carved great pillars ...."

From air that cannot be grasped

These pillars are carved from "air which cannot be grasped." Air was earlier identified with Breath, which in turn is associated with the first Sefirah, Keter. Air is also identified with the letter Alef (2:1, 3:4).

The Sefer Yetzirah states that water is below, fire above, and air is in the middle. This may initially be somewhat difficult to understand, since air is associated with Breath and Keter, the highest Sefirah.[71] It is also associated with Alef, the first letter of the alphabet.

As explained earlier (1:9), however, the Breath associated with Keter is not graspable, since this Sefirah represents a level above the intellect. The only place where this Breath can become manifest is in the lower Sefirot. Therefore, even though it is on a level above Chakhmah and Binah, it is only manifest on a level that is below them.

The "air that cannot be grasped" is therefore the Breath coming from Keter. This cannot be grasped until it enters the realm of the "pillars," that is, the lower seven Sefirot.

This section is actually best understood in a mystical sense. The previous section explained how to use the letter arrays together with the divine Name as a meditative device. One of the manifestations of higher meditative states (as well as some drug-induced states) is hallucinogenesis, where one can voluntarily form mental images. These mental images appear to be real and substantial. When a person is in a normal state of consciousness, he may be able to form mental images, but they are weak, transient, and blurred by mental static. In contrast, the images formed in a meditative state appear solid, substantial, and real.

In an ordinary state of Binah consciousness, the mind is filled with static. If you wish to see this static, merely close your eyes. You will see a rapidly changing kaleidoscope of images, one imposed on another. Even if you can grasp a single image for a short while, it is intermingled with mental static, and you have little control over the image. You cannot make it come and go at will, and you cannot determine how it behaves. Even when you can exert some influence over it, the image will seem to have a mind of its own.

This static also exists even when our eyes are open, but it is overshadowed by the images of the real world. In a darkened room, however, it does remain visible to some degree. This static impairs our perception of the outside world, and clouds our mental processes.

The perception of the spiritual world is even more tenuous than that of the physical. In a normal state of consciousness, mental static makes it absolutely impossible to visualize the spiritual world.

Here this state of mental static is called "chaos" (*tohu*). As both
the Kabbalists and linguists teach, the word *Tohu* (תהו) comes from
the verb *Tahah* (תהה), meaning to be "astounded" or "confused."[72]
This is the normal state of mental confusion, where the mind is
clouded with static. This is also associated with Binah consciousness,
and accordingly, a number of Kabbalists associate *Tohu* with Binah.[73]
The Zohar also teaches that *Tohu* is associated with the *Klipah*
(Husk), the forces that prevent one from visualizing the spiritual
realm.[74]

It is out of this *Tohu*, this state of confused Binah consciousness,
that one must create a palpable image. There are many images that
can be produced, but the most common is the mental Golem, the
astral body. The initiate thus "forms palpable substance (*mamash*)
out of chaos." This implies attaining a state of Chakhmah consciousness. The Kabbalists thus note that the word Golem (גלם) has a
numerical value of 73, the same as that of Chakhmah (חכמה).[75]

One must then "make nonexistence into existence." Earlier, in stating, "form substance out of chaos," the text uses the word "form," while
here it uses the word "make." In Hebrew, especially according to the
Kabbalists, the word "form" (*yatzar*) denotes the initial forming of
"something from something." The term "make" (*asah*), on the other
hand, refers to the completion of the process. Thus, in "*forming* substance
out of chaos," one begins the mental act of creation. In "*making* nonexistence into existence," one completes it.

The term "formation" also implies an activity taking place in
Yetzirah, the lower spiritual universe. Thus, when one "forms substance out of chaos," one is bringing about a purely spiritual result
in the universe of Yetzirah. "Making," on the other hand, refers to
the universe of Asiyah, which borders on the physical. This implies
results that may actually be manifest in the physical world.

In order to accomplish this, one must enter fully into the realm
of Nothingness. This is the highest level of Chakhmah consciousness,
bordering on Keter. One therefore begins with "nonexistence," which
is Nothingness.

When one reaches this level, he can actually make something
"that actually is" (*yeshno*) or "existence." He can actually bring about
results in the universe of Asiyah, which can then be reflected in the
physical world. In making a Golem, this would correspond to the
state of consciousness required before the mental image could be
imposed on the clay, bringing it to life.

A very similar process is described by the great Hassidic master,
Rabbi Dov Baer, the Maggid of Mezritch (1704-1772). He writes that
when a person contemplates a physical object completely and totally,
he can actually bring that object onto his thought. If his thought is

then bound to the supernal Mind, he can elevate that object to the level of Mind. From there, it can be further elevated to the level of Nothingness, where the object ceases to exist. When this object is then once again brought back to the level of Mind, it can be brought back in any form that the initiate desires. Thus, when he finally brings it back to its normal physical state, the object can be changed in any manner he desires. As the Maggid states, "he can even transform it into gold."[76]

It is in this state of consciousness that one can visualize the Sefirot as "great pillars." One "carves" them out, this meaning that the image of the Sefirah is seen separately, totally filling the consciousness. Even though the Sefirot are totally ineffable and indescribable, when a person is in this state of consciousness, he can "carve" them out. They are then perceived as solid pillars, made of transparent air. Like the air, the Sefirot are still invisible, but in this state of consciousness, even the air can become visible.

This is a sign...

The Sefer Yetzirah describes a sign through which one knows that he has attained this state. He must go through the entire array, "Alef with them all, and all of them with Alef." This means that he permutes the array forward and backward, which respectively are the modes of creating and destroying.

The initiate then "forsees, transforms and makes." The word for "foresee" here is *tzofeh*, and as discussed earlier (1:6), this word denotes mystical insight and foresight. If the initiate has attained the proper state, he attains a mystical insight through which he can perceive the inner essence of all things. He can then engage in the process described earlier, where the Sefer Yetzirah said, "discern with them, and probe from them" (1:4).

When the initiate reaches this high level, he can also "transform," actually changing physical things. He can even "make," bringing things to existence in the physical world.

Most important is the final realization: "All that is formed and all that is spoken is one Name." The initiate not only knows this intellectually, but he can actually visualize and see that all creation is nothing more than one Name, the Tetragrammaton.

A sign for this thing, 22 objects . . .

This goes back and refers to the entire chapter. "Twenty-two objects in a single body," is a sign that the initiate has completed this discipline and has mastered it fully.

He uses each of the 22 letters to form a mental image of a different part of the body. Each part of the body can thus be formed separately. The ability to complete separate parts, however, does not prove mastery of the method of Sefer Yetzirah. The final proof of mastery is the ability to assemble all these 22 objects into a single body.[77]

This is the process of completing a mental Golem. The initiate must not only form all the parts, but he must actually assemble them. This means that while he is engaged in the meditation to create one part, he must not lose his mental image of the parts that he formed earlier. As each part of the image is formed, it must be retained in the mind, with subsequent images added to it, part by part. The amount of mental discipline, as well as the advanced nature of the meditative technique required for this, is virtually beyond description.

The creation of a mental Golem is therefore a culmination of the arts of Sefer Yetzirah, as well as a test to determine if one has mastered them. This did not involve the actual creation of a physical Golem, since this was only done on very special occasions. As the Kabbalists warn, such an undertaking should not be attempted without permission from on high.[78]

CHAPTER THREE

3:1

שלש אמות אמ"ש יסודן כף זכות
וכף חובה ולשון חק מכריע בינתים:

Three Mothers: Alef Mem Shin (אמש)
Their foundation is
   a pan of merit
   a pan of liability
     and the tongue of decree deciding between them.

This repeats part of a previous section (2:1), and it has already been discussed. Chapters one and two spoke of the basic meditative methods involving the Sefirot and letters. Now the letters are treated separately.

Thus, in the beginning of chapter two, the three Mothers were introduced. The main idea there, however, was to teach that "Mem hums and Shin hisses," one of the first meditative practices using the letters.

Here, the same concept is repeated, but as introduction to the idea of thesis, antithesis, and synthesis. It is similar to an ancient tradition of homiletic interpretation: "Two scriptures that contradict one another, until a third scripture comes and decides between them."[1] In both cases, the same expression, "decides between them." (*Makhria Beynehem*), is used. It is significant to note that the homiletic rule is expressed by Rabbi Ishmael, a leader of an important first century mystical school, who apparently received it from Rabbi Nehuniah ben HaKana.[2]

The simplest interpretation is that Mem is thesis, Shin is antithesis, and Alef is synthesis. These three elements then form the three vertical columns into which the Sefirot are divided. Mem represents the right hand column (headed by Chakhmah), Shin, the left hand column (headed by Binah), and Alef, the central column (headed by Keter).[3]

There is, however, another interpretation, and this follows the arrangement of the letters on the Tree of Life according to the Ari.[4] Here, Alef, Mem and Shin are the horizontal lines, connecting opposing Sefirot. Shin is between Chakhmah and Binah, Alef between Chesed and Gevurah, and Mem between Netzach and Hod.

Following this, the text is saying that the "foundation" of all three of these Mother letters is the synthesis that connects thesis and antithesis. Thesis is the Sefirah to the right, antithesis is the one to the left, and synthesis is the Mother letter connecting the two.

3:2 שלש אמות אמ״ש סוד גדול מופלא ומכוסה
וחתום בשש טבעות ויצאו מהם אויר מים
אש ומהם נולדו אבות ומאבות תולדות:

Three Mothers: Alef Mem Shin (אמש)
A great, mystical secret
*   covered and sealed with six rings*
And from them emanated air, water and fire
And from them are born Fathers,
*   and from the Fathers, descendents.*

A great mystical secret

The word for "mystical" here is *MuPhla* (מופלא).[5] This is very closely related, and shares the same root with the word Peliyah (פליאה), used in relation to the Thirty-two Paths of Wisdom (1:1). One reason for this, as discussed earlier (2:1), is because it is through these Mother letters that one can enter into the realm of Chakhmah consciousness, which is the portal to the transcendental.

These three Mother letters are also related to the mystery of the divine Name. The Sefer Yetzirah earlier said, "He chose three letters ... in the mystery of the three Mothers, AMSh (אמש)" (1:13). Thus, the letters AMSh (אמש) are the roots of the letters of the Tetragrammaton, YHV (יהו). According to the Kabbalists, Yud is derived from Mem, Heh from Shin, and Vav from Alef.[6] These three Mothers therefore represent an even deeper mystery than the Tetragrammaton.

The Tetragrammaton actually only relates to the Ten Sefirot. There is, however, an aspect of creation that existed before the Sefirot. In this stage, the proto-Sefirot existed as simple non-interacting points. In the language of the Kabbalists, this is known as the Universe of Chaos (*Tohu*). In this state, the Vessels, which were the proto-Sefirot, could neither interact nor give to one another. Since they could not emulate God by giving, they were incomplete, and could therefore not hold the Divine Light. Since they could not fulfill their purpose, they were overwhelmed by the Light and "shattered." This is known as the "Breaking of Vessels."

The broken shards of these Vessels fell to a lower spiritual level, and subsequently became the source of all evil. It is for this reason that Chaos (*Tohu*) is said to be the root of evil.

After having been shattered, the Vessels were once again rectified and rebuilt into Personifications (*Partzufim*). Each of these Partzufim consists of 613 parts, paralleling the 613 parts of the body, as well as the 613 commandments of the Torah. These Partzufim were then able to interact with each other. More important, through the Torah, they were also able to interact with man. This is the stage where the Sefirot become givers as well as receivers.

In this rectified state the Vessels (or Sefirot) became fit to receive God's Light. In Kabbalistic terminology, this state is called the Universe of Rectification (*Tikkun*).

The Kabbalists teach that the letters of the Tetragrammaton, YHV (יהו), only pertain to the Universe of Rectification. In the Universe of Chaos (*Tohu*), the divine Name consisted of the letters AMSh (אמש).[7]

When a person enters into the mysteries, he must parallel the sequence of creation.[8] First he enters the Universe of Chaos (*Tohu*). Here his mind is filled with confused transient images. If he perceives the Sefirot, they are "like lightning, running and returning" (1:6). The Sefirot are perceived as disconnected images, where no relationship between them can be seen. This is the state of consciousness attained through the letters AMSh (אמש), as discussed earlier (2:1).

The initiate can then enter the Universe of Rectification, where the Sefirot are connected and assume the form of Partzufim. Each Partzuf is a human-like form, very closely related to the conceptual Golem. The creation of this mental Golem-Partzuf is accomplished through the letters of the name YHVH together with various letters, as described above (2:5). This is the Name associated with the Universe of Rectification.

Here, one must combine all the Sefirot to form "a single body" (2:6). One also becomes aware of the lines connecting the Sefirot, which are included in the Thirty-two Paths of Wisdom. Hence, when these Thirty-two Paths are discussed, the Sefer Yetzirah uses the names YH YHVH.

The three Mother letters, AMSh also spell out the Hebrew word *Emesh* (אמש), meaning "yesternight." This occurs in the verse, "You slept last night (*emesh*) with my father" (Genesis 19:34). The word *emesh* also denotes deep impenetrable gloom, as in the verse, "Gloom (*emesh*), waste and desolation" (Job 30:3).[9] This is the inky gloom that existed before creation, in the Universe of Chaos, the "yesternight" before the Sefirot were brought into being.

There is also evidence that the word *emesh* was also used as a mystical name of God. Thus, Laban said to Jacob, "The God of your fathers last night (*Emesh*) said to me" (Genesis 31:29). This can just as easily be read, "The God of your fathers, Emesh, said to me." Similarly, Jacob said, "And Emesh gave judgment" (Genesis 31:43).[10]

According to some authorities, the letters Alef Mem Shin (אמש) also conceal a deeper mystery, which is Alef Vav Yud (אוי).[11]

Another element of the mystery of the letters AMSh is the fact that they represent the reconciliation of opposites. Logically, there is no way in which opposites can be reconciled. These letters therefore represent a mystery that cannot be penetrated by logic.

One commentator states that the letters AMSh contain the mystery through which one can walk on fire.[12] The reason for this may be because these letters have the power to reconcile opposites. It is possible that Rav Zeira made use of this technique to prevent his feet from being burned in fire, as related in the Talmud.[13]

Sealed with six rings

The obvious scriptural source is the verse, "The script which is written in the King's name and *sealed* with the King's *ring*, cannot be reversed" (Esther 8:8).

According to this, the "rings" here would be the rings of the King's name, that is, the letters YHV (יהו). The Kabbalists therefore say that these six rings are the six directions, which, as the Sefer Yetzirah (1:13) earlier says, were "sealed" with the letters YHV (יהו).[14] Behind the permutations of the letters YHV is the deeper mystery of the permutations of the letters AMSh, now under discussion.

These six directions, which comprise the physical universe, are what hide the deeper mysteries. It is thus written, "He has set the universe in their heart, so that man cannot find out the work that God has done, from the beginning to the end" (Ecclesiastes 3:10). As the commentaries point out, the word "universe" here in Hebrew is *Olam* (עולם). It comes from the root *Alam* (עלם), meaning "occlusion," and also has this connotation. As long as a person can only think in terms of the physical dimensions of space, the inner reality is concealed from him.

Also significant is the fact that a ring is normally worn on the finger. As the Sefer Yetzirah states (1:3), the Ten Sefirot are represented by the ten fingers. The six rings are thus worn on the six "fingers" corresponding to the six Sefirot, which represent the six directions.[15]

The "six rings" here also allude to the "six rings of the throat," mentioned in the Zohar.[16] It is from these rings that all sound and speech are derived. These six rings, which are the source of physical speech, conceal the mystery of AMSh, which relates to the root of speech. This mystery can only be penetrated when one transcends the realm of physical speech.

From them emanated air, water and fire

This is the process described in detail in chapter one (1:9-12).

From them are born Fathers

The three Mother letters, AMSh (אמש), represent cause, effect and their synthesis. Shin (ש) is cause, Mem (מ) is effect, and Alef (א) is the synthesis between these two opposites. In the Tree of Life diagram, these are represented by three horizontal lines.

These three horizontal lines give rise to the three vertical columns in the Tree of Life diagram, headed by Keter, Chakhmah, and Binah. These are represented by "air, water, and fire."

We therefore begin with a dialectic triad: "Creator," "object of creation," and "act of creation." This gives rise to a second triad: love, judgment, and mercy. This second triad defines the three columns into which the Sefirot are arranged.[17]

The three horizontal lines are the three Mothers. The three columns define the three Fathers, which are the letters Yud Heh Vav (יהו). It was from these letters that space is defined, as the Sefer Yetzirah states earlier (1:13). Once space is defined, then creation can take place.

This can also be understood in a meditative sense. Through the pronunciation of the letters AMSh, one enters the realm of Chakhmah consciousness, and passes through the Chashmal. One then passes through the domains of Breath, water and fire, as described earlier (1:14). At this time, one must be in a totally receptive mode, which is an aspect of the feminine. Hence, the letters AMSh are called "Mothers."

After this, however, one can enter into a creative mode through the letters YHV. These letters are therefore called "Fathers." Only then can one produce "descendents."

3:3

שלש אמות אמ"ש חקקן חצבן צרפן שקלן
והמירן וצר בהם שלש אמות אמ"ש בעולם
ושלש אמות אמ"ש בשנה ושלש אמות אמ"ש בנפש
זכר ונקבה:

Three Mothers: Alef Mem Shin (אמש)
He engraved them, He carved them,
He permuted them, He weighed them,
He transformed them,
And with them He depicted
Three Mothers AMSh (אמש) in the Universe,
Three Mothers AMSh (אמש) in the Year,
Three Mothers AMSh (אמש) in the Soul,
male and female.

He engraved them...

The beginning of this section is exactly the same as 2:2, except that all the letters were being discussed there, and here only the three Mother letters are under consideration. In both cases, there are five processes: engraving, carving, permuting, weighing, and transforming.

When, as in chapter two, all 22 letters are given equal status, then all five dimensions as the five phonetic families (2:3). Here, on the other hand, the three Mothers are taken separately. The five dimensions are therefore also divided into three domains: Universe, Year, and Soul. The Universe consists of the three spacial dimensions, Year consists of the time dimension, while Soul consists of the spiritual dimension.

A similar division into three domains was encountered earlier, in chapter one, when the Sefirot were first enumerated. First enumerated was the domain of Soul, the spiritual dimension, which consisted of "Breath," and "Breath from Breath" (1:9,10). Then came the domain of Year, the time dimension, consisting of Water and Fire (1:11-12). Finally came the domain of Universe, the three spacial dimensions, represented by the six permutations of the letters YHV (1:13).

The Sefer Yetzirah stated earlier (1:13) that the three letters YHV, which define the space continuum, are derived from AMSh.

Therefore, it is the letters AMSh which separate the space continuum from that of time and the spiritual.

There is an important difference between the space continuum and the other two. It is only in space that one can move voluntarily. In time, one moves in one direction at a predetermined rate. In the spiritual dimension, a physical body cannot move at all. Only the soul can move through the spiritual dimension, and it is for this reason that this domain is called Soul.

The letters AMSh differentiate space from time and soul. These same letters can therefore be used to do away with this differentiation.

3:4 שלש אמות אמ"ש בעולם אויר מים אש שמים
נבראו מאש וארץ נבראת ממים ואויר מרוח
מכריע בינתים:

Three Mothers, AMSh (אמש),
in the Universe are air, water, fire.
Heaven was created from fire
Earth was created from water
And air from Breath decides between them.

In chapter one, the text discussed the spiritual aspect of "Breath, water and fire," in terms of the original four Sefirot. Here it is speaking of how these three are also manifest in the physical world.

In the simplest physical terms, "water" repesents matter, "fire" is energy, and "air" is the space that allows the two to interact.[18]

On a somewhat deeper physical level, fire, water and air represent the three basic physical forces. "Fire" is the electromagnetic force, through which all matter interacts. The atomic nucleus, however, consists of like positive charges, which would repel each other if only electromagnetism existed. There must therefore exist another force which can bind the nucleus together. This is the "strong nuclear" or pionic force, which binds the nucleus together, repre-

Figure 41. From Maaseh Toviah (Cracow, 1908) p. 45a.

sented by "water." If this nuclear force were to interact with all particles, however, all matter would be mutually attracted together, forming a solid lump denser than a neutron star. On the other hand, even
within each elementary particle, there is a need for a cohesive force
to counteract the electromagnetic repulsion within the particle itself.
This force can be neither electromagnetic nor pionic. This is the
"air," which represents the "weak nuclear" force, which "decides
between" the other two. It is this force that allows light particles (lep-
tons) such as electrons to exist. See figure 41.

The fourth force, gravity, corresponds to "earth." Earth, however
is not a basic element, but a confluence of the other three.[19] It is
therefore represented by the final Heh in the Tetragrammaton, which
is actually a repetition of the first Heh in this name.

On an even more elementary level, these three elements represent the three axes in the unitary symmetry, SU(3), which is the most
basic property of matter.

These three elements also relate to the experiential. Here, fire
represents the radiation of energy, while water represents the absorp-
tion of energy. These are thesis and antithesis, giving and receiving,
which themselves are manifestations of cause and effect. Air, which
represents the transmission of energy is then the synthesis, linking
the two.

In this aspect, fire and water also represent the psychological modes of Binah and Chakhmah consciousness. As discussed earlier, "fire" is Binah consciousness, where the mind itself is constantly radiating energy. "Water," on the other hand, is Chakhmah consciousness, where the mind can absorb spiritual energy from without. "Air" is then *Ruach HaKodesh*, the medium through which such spiritual energy is transmitted.

Heaven is created from fire

This is the same as the statement made above (1:12). Our experience and depicting of the transcendental sphere must be brought into Binah consciousness.

In a physical sense, fire represents radiative energy. This usually takes place by means of the electromagnetic interaction in the form of light. "Heaven" here represents the concept of space as defined by the electromagnetic interaction, this being an important cornerstone of the principle of Relativity.

Fire represents Binah, and as discussed earlier (1:1), the word Binah comes from the root *Beyn*, meaning "between." It is from Binah that the concept of separation comes into being. Furthermore, it is only as a result of the concept of separation that space can exist. If not for Binah, all existence would be concentrated in a single point.

In the same manner, "earth is created from water." "Earth" represents the solid state, where matter exists with a minimum of space separating its molecules. This stems from Chakhmah, which tends to minimize separation and distance.

In a gas such as air, the molecules tend to fly apart and separate. Yet, at the same time, they are held together just sufficiently to give the gas substance. Gas is therefore always in a state of contained expansion. This is intermediate between the containment of solid matter and the total expansion of pure radiation.

Fire is represented by the letter Shin. Shin is the dominant letter in the word *Esh* (אש), meaning fire. It is joined with the Alef, representing air, because a fire cannot exist without air.[20]

The three heads of the Shin also suggest the flames of the fire. The hissing sound of this letter furthermore is like the hiss of a flame.

The three heads of the Shin are separated, suggesting the general concept of separation. Corresponding to the Shin is the letter Heh (ה), which is only one of the two letters in the alphabet consisting of two disconnected parts.

Water is represented by the letter Mem. Here again, Mem is the dominant letter in the word *Mayim* (מים), meaning water. Indeed, the very name of the letter Mem comes from the word *Mayim*.[21]

Mem is also a closed letter, indicating containment and unity.[22] It is also sounded with the mouth closed. It parallels the letter Yud (י), which is written as a single point.

Air is represented by Alef, since it is the initial letter of *Avir* (אויר), meaning "air." Alef is a silent letter, whose sound is as undetectable as the invisible air. In shape, it consists of an upper right and a lower left dot, representing two opposites, with a diagonal line in the middle, which both separates and connects the two.

3:5

שלש אמות אמ"ש בשנה חום קור ורויה. חום
נברא מאש קור נברא ממים ורויה מרוח
מכריע בינתים:

Three Mothers AMSh (אמש)
in the Year are
the hot
the cold
and the temperate.
The hot is created from fire
The cold is created from water
And the temperate, from Breath,
decides between them.

The year is divided into three basic parts. There is the hot summer and the cold winter, which are thesis and antithesis. The two temperate seasons, spring and autumn, are both taken together and are spoken of as the temperate season. This is the synthesis.

Here we see the concept of a cycle between opposites. This cycle, like many others, constantly swings between two opposites. At the midpoint in each swing, no matter in which direction, the cycle must pass through the intermediate midpoint.

Thus, both in going from hot to cold, and from cold to hot, the cycle must pass through a temperate season. It is out of cycles such as these that time is defined. The Sefer Yetzirah therefore states that the Cycle is the king in the domain of time (6:3).

In the annual cycle, winter is represented by Mem (מ), summer by Shin (ש), and the two temperate seasons by Alef (א). The complete cycle is then defined by the letters MAShA (מאשא). Taking their parallels, these correspond to the letters YVHV (יוהו). This is closely related, but somewhat different than the Tetragrammaton, YHVH (יהוה).

In the Tetragrammaton, the ordering of the letters is YHV (יהו). Here thesis and synthesis are seen as opposites, representing tension and equilibrium. Antithesis is then the midpoint connecting the two. The fourth letter of the Tetragrammaton, the Heh, is also a point of tension.

The temperate

The Hebrew word for "temperate," here, is *Ravayah* (רויה). This use of the word *Ravayah* is virtually unique in Hebrew literature.

The usual interpretation of *Ravayah* is abundance, as in the verse, "my cup is abundant (*ravayah*)" (Psalms 23:5). It should be recalled that it is from this verse that some Kabbalists find an allusion to the 221 Gates, discussed earlier (2:4).

One reason for the use of *Ravayah* to denote the spring and fall was because these two were the harvest seasons in the Holy Land.

The most obvious source for this usage is the verse, "We have come through fire and water, You brought us out to *Ravayah*" (Psalms 66:12). Some commentaries interpret *Ravayah* here to also mean "abundance," but from the context, "temperate" seems to be a more logical interpretation. *Ravayah* would then denote the desired meaning between "fire" and "water." The Sefer Yetzirah also uses this word in such a sense.

It is significant to note that the Talmud interprets "fire and water" in this verse to denote psychological states.[23] The Midrash likewise interprets "fire and water" in this verse as referring to two opposing kinds of purgatory.[24]

Fire is the overabundance of sensation, and it is also related to shame.[25] Water, on the other hand, denotes lack of sensation, and is related to depression. *Ravayah* is then the perfect mental state between these two extremes.

Some authorities also say that the word *Ravayah* is related to the word *Yoreh* (יורה), which denotes the early autumn rains.[26]

3:6

שלש אמות אמ"ש בנפש זכר ונקבה ראש ובטן
וגויה. ראש נברא מאש ובטן נברא ממים וגויה
מרוח מכריע בינתים:

Three Mothers AMSh (אמש)
in the Soul, male and female,
are the head, belly, and chest.
The head is created from fire,
The belly is created from water
and the chest, from breath,
decides between them.

The "soul" here also refers to the body. One reason for this is because the soul is an exact counterpart of the body. Everything found in the body is also found in the soul.

Similarly, the human body is a microcosm of the supernal "Man." See figure 42 on page 151. This is the "Man" sitting on the throne, seen by Ezekiel. The supernal "Man" represents the array of the Sefirot. The "Soul" mentioned here then also refers to the anthropomorphic representation of this array.

With respect to the Sefirot, Shin is the line between Chakhmah and Binah; Alef, between Chesed and Gevurah; and Mem, between Netzach and Hod. The top line represents the head, the center line, the chest, and the lower line, the belly.[27]

According to Rabbi Abraham Abulafia, there is also an allusion here to the two covenants mentioned above (1:3). The covenant of the tongue is in the head, while the covenant of circumcision is in the region of the belly. Between the two, in the chest, is the heart, which is king over the soul (6:3). This alludes to the Torah, which is the primary covenant.[28]

The head also represents man's creative power, which is represented by fire. The belly is man's receptive power, represented by water. The chest and lungs must both inhale and exhale, and therefore pertain to both.

In a deeper sense, the head is seen as the center of Binah consciousness. It is the head that is the seat of the conscious stream of thought. The workings of the belly, on the other hand, are almost completely subconscious. The belly therefore parallels the Mem, which denotes Chakhmah consciousness. It is for this reason that some mystics would contemplate their belly when attempting to attain Chakhmah consciousness.

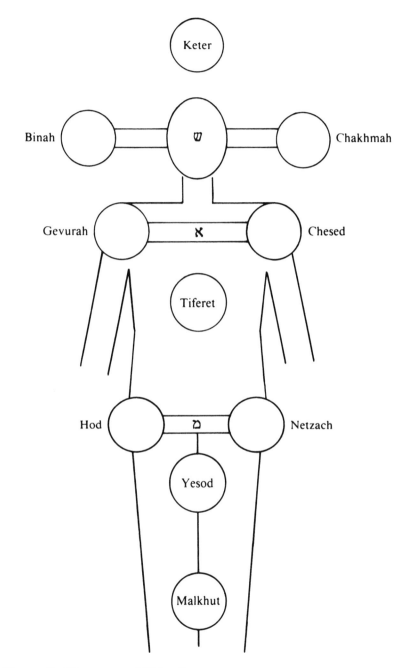

Figure 42. The supernal "Man."

Breathing borders on both the conscious and the unconscious. One usually breathes unconsciously, but one can also control one's breathing consciously. Breathing is therefore associated with both Binah and Chakhmah consciousness. It is for this reason that controlled breathing techniques are important in making the transition between these two states. Breathing is centered in the chest.

The chest

The Hebrew word for "chest" here is *Gaviyah* (גויה).[29] The use of *Gaviyah* for chest is also unique in Hebrew literature. Usually, the word refers to the body as a whole, and some commentaries here also state that it denotes the entire trunk.[30]

A possible scriptural source for this may come from Ezekiel's vision, where he said of the Chayot, "With two [wings] they covered their *Gaviyah*" (Ezekiel 1:11). The scripture may be saying that they covered their chest and heart with two of their wings.[31]

Some commentaries interpret *Gaviyah* to denote the sexual organ.[32] In the language of the Mishnah, we indeed find that the "head of the *Gaviyah*" refers to the tip of the male organ.[33] However, as the major commentaries note, only the term, "head of the *Gaviyah*" has this connotation, and not the word *Gaviyah* itself.[34]

3:7

המליך אות א׳ ברוח וקשר לו כתר
וצרפן זה בזה וצר בהם אויר בעולם ורויה בשנה
וגויה בנפש זכר באמ״ש ונקבה באש״ם:

He made the letter Alef (א) king over Breath
And He bound a crown to it
And He combined them one with another
And with them He formed
Air in the Universe
The temperate in the Year
And the chest in the Soul:
The male with AMSh (אמש)
And the female with AShM (אשם).

He made Alef king

Most simply, this means that with regard to concepts related to Breath, Alef is always the first letter in the permutation.[35]

In a deeper sense, this means that Alef was bound to the Sefirah of Malkhut (Kingship). Malkhut is said to be the "mouth," and as such, it is the Sefirah through which the power of all the other Sefirot is expressed.[36]

The first stage is therefore to make the letter "king." This means that it is brought to the "mouth," which is the Sefirah of Malkhut.[37]

Bound a crown to it

This indicates that the letters are bound to the highest of the Sefirot, Keter. As the Sefer Yetzirah states earlier (1:9), this is the direct Breath. Malkhut, on the other hand, is reflected Breath. Before a letter can be expressed through Malkhut, it must be bound to Keter. Thus, the "End is imbedded in the beginning" (1:7).

This also speaks of the physical letters, which have small "crowns" called *Taggin* on top. The Talmud thus says that when Moses ascended to heaven, he saw God "binding crowns to the letters."[38]

These crowns represent the higher spiritual nature of the letters.[39] If the letters themselves are in Assiyah, then the crowns on top bind them to Yetzirah.[40]

Air, temperate, chest

In Hebrew, air is Avir (אויר), temperate is Ravayah (רויה), and chest is Geviyah (גויה). Except for the *Resh* in *Avir*, all of these words are spelled the same:

AVYR	אויר
RVYH	רויה
GVYH	גויה

The endings of these words is consistantly VYH (ויה). This represents the hidden power of the letters Yud Heh Vav (יהו) in the three Mothers AMSh.

It is significant to note that in these words, the order of the letters is VYH (ויה). Since Vav (ו) corresponds to Alef (א), Yud (י) corresponds to Mem (מ), and Heh (ה) corresponds to Shin (ש), the letters VYH (ויה) are in the same order as AMSh (אמש).

The word *Avir* is written with a Resh (ר) instead of a Heh (ה). This is because AVYH (אויה) spells out a secret divine Name.[41]

The initial letters of *Avir*, *Ravayah* and *Geviyah* spell out *Arag* (ארג), which means "to weave." It is out of these three syntheses that the fabric of creation is woven.

Male and Female

Rabbi Eliezar Rokeach of Wormes writes that if one wishes to create a male Golem, then the sequence AMSh (אמש) must be used. If one wishes to create a female Golem, then the sequence must be AShM (אשמ). If one wishes to destroy the Golem, then the sequence is ShMA (שמא).[42]

The Hebrew word for man is Ish (איש), while that for woman is Ishah (אשה). In both cases, the letters Alef and Shin are in the same position as here.[43] We then have:

Man	AYSh איש	Woman	AShH אשה
	AMSh אמש		AShM אשמ

The only difference between the Hebrew words for man and woman and the combinations here is that Yud and Heh are substituted for the Mem. As mentioned earlier, Yud is male, while Heh is female. These letters take the place of the Mem, which is the belly, since it is here that man and woman are differentiated.[44]

Also significant is the position of the Shin, which represents fire and passion. In man, the sequence is AMSh (אמש), with the Shin exposed at the end. In woman, on the other hand, the sequence is AShM (אשמ), with the Shin concealed in the middle. This is because the sexual organ in man is external, while in woman it is internal. The Talmud thus states, "Man has his passion on the outside, while woman has hers on the inside."[45]

3:8   המליך אות מ' במים וקשר לו כתר
וצרפן זה בזה וצר בהם ארץ בעולם וקור בשנה
ובטן בנפש זכר במא"ש ונקבה במש"א:

He made Mem (מ) king over water
   And He bound a crown to it
   And He combined one with another
And with them He formed
   Earth in the Universe
   Cold in the Year
   And the belly in the Soul:
The male with MASh (מאש)
And the female with MShA (משא)

3:9

המליך אות ש' באש וקשר לו כתר
וצרפן זה בזה וצר בהם (אש) שמים בעולם וחום
בשנה וראש בנפש זכר בשא"מ ונקבה בשמ"א:

He made Shin (ש) king over fire
    And He bound a crown to it
    And He combined one with another
And with them He formed
    Heaven in the Universe
    Hot in the Year
    And the head in the Soul:
The male with ShAM (שאמ)
And the female with ShMA (שמא).[46]

CHAPTER FOUR

4:1

שבע כפולות בג״ר כפר״ת מתנהגות
בשתי לשונות ב״ב, ג״ג, ד״ד, כ״כ,
פ״פ, ר״ר, ת״ת. תבנית רך וקשה גבור וחלש:

Seven Doubles:
  Bet (ב), Gimel (ג), Dalet (ד),
  Kaf (כ), Peh (פ), Resh (ר), Tav (ת).
They direct themselves with two tongues
  Bet-Bhet, Gimel-Ghimel, Dalet-Dhalet,
  Kaf-Khaf, Peh-Pheh, Resh-Rhesh, Tav-Thav,
A structure of soft and hard,
  strong and weak

This is the set of double letters, each having two possible sounds.[1] In the Tree of Life diagram, they correspond to the seven vertical lines.

The double sound is retained by all Jews for Bet, Kaf, and Peh. The hard Bet (ב) has the sound of *b*, while the soft has the sound of *v*. The hard Kaf (כ) has the sound of *k*, the soft, the sound of *kh*, like the German *ch*, as in "*doch*." The hard Peh (פ) is pronounced like a *p*, while the soft is like an *f*.

In all these cases, the hard sound is a plosive, pronounced in an explosive puff of sound. The soft sound is a fricative.

The northern European Ashkenazic Jews pronounce the soft Tav (ת) like an *s*. Most southern European Sefardic Jews pronounce both the hard and soft Tav the same, like a *t*. Some Sefardim pronounce the soft Tav like a soft *th*, as in "thing."

The Yemenite Jews also distinguish between the soft and hard Gimel and Dalet. The soft Gimel (ג) has the sound of a *j*, or among others, like a deep gutteral fricative *g*. The soft Dalet (ד) has the sound of a hard *th*, as in "the."

As a general rule, these six letters, BGD KPT (בגד כפת), always take the hard form at the beginning of a word. This is one reason why no Biblical names are found beginning with an *f*. This would imply a Peh (פ) at the beginning of the name, and it would automatically take the hard sound, which is that of a *p*.

Table 28. Resh with a Dagesh in the Bible.

1.	HaRimah	הִרְעִמָה	1 Samuel 1:6.
2.	HaR'item	הִרְאִיתֶם	1 Samuel 10:24, 17:25, 2 Kings 6:32.
3.	Ra	רָע	Jeremiah 39:12, Proverbs 11:21, 20:22.
4.	Karat	כָּרַת	Ezekiel 16:4.
5.	Sharekh	שָׁרֵךְ	*Ibid.*
6.	Rosh	רֹאשׁ	Habakkuk 3:13.
7.	LeSharekha	לְשָׁרֶךְ	Proverbs 3:8.
8.	Marat	מָרַת	Proverbs 14:10.
9.	Rakh	רַךְ	Proverbs 15:1.
10.	SheRoshi	שֶׁרֹאשִׁי	Song of Songs 5:2.

The hard sound is distinuished by a dot, called a Dagesh, placed in the middle of the letter.

Highly significant is the fact that the Resh (ר) is here considered to be one of the Doubles. Most post-Talmudical grammarians take precisely the opposite view, and state that the Resh never takes a Dagesh. Not only is there no verbal distinction between the hard and soft Resh, but modern Hebrew grammar does not even recognize such a difference in the written form.

There are, however, ten different words, appearing in fourteen places in the Bible, which are written with a Resh containing a Dagesh.[2] See Table 28. It is obvious, however, that the usual rules applying to the letters BGD KPT (בגד כפת), do not apply to the Resh.

The present sound of the Resh is a fricative, and is therefore most probably the soft sound. The hard Resh was either lost or deliberately concealed after the destruction of the Temple. In earlier times, its use was standard, and there is evidence from their transliteration of names, that its pronunciation was known to the authors of the Septuagint.[3] By the 10th century, however, the double Resh was only used by the members of the small Mazya community in Tiberias.[4] Tiberias had been the last city in which the Sanhedrin, the great court which preserved the tradition, had flourished.[5] This was one of the mysteries that the Sanhedrin had entrusted to the community of Tiberias.

According to the Sefer Yetzirah (2:3), Resh is in the group of Dentals, ZSShRTz (זסשרצ). Along with the letters Zayin (ז), Samekh (ס), Shin (שׁ), and Tzadi (צ), it is pronounced with the teeth. According to the Long Version (2:1), it is sounded "between the teeth, with the tongue lying down, spread out." We cannot say that it is a rolled *r* sound, since this involves the tip of the tongue. It would then be closest to the *l* sound, and should be included among the Linguals, DTLNTh (דטלנת). Furthermore, the hard Resh should be a plosive, like all the other hard doubles.

There is no *r* sound in use today that meets all these criteria. Furthermore, there is no plosive sound pronounced with the teeth that could be a candidate for the hard Resh. The original pronunciation of this letter therefore remains a mystery.

Hard and Soft

The hard sound is currently indicated by a dot in the middle of the letter, known as a Dagesh.

Before printing was introduced, most manuscripts also indicated the soft sound by a line above the letter, known as a *Rafeh*. This device is used in the Damascus "Keter Torah" Pentateuch, written in the ninth century.[6] In the Firkovich collection of the Library of the Academy of Science in Leningrad, there is a codex of the Bible, dated from the year 916, that also makes use of the *Rafeh*. As late as 1480, this mark is found in handwritten Bibles and Prayer Books.[7]

The use of this mark is also mentioned by the *Tikkuney Zohar*. It states that the Rafeh above the letter is like the "firmament above the Chayot" (Ezekiel 1:22).[8]

The *Tikkuney Zohar* also states that the hard and soft sounds are related to the "Chayot running and returning" (Ezekiel 1:14). It says, "they run with the hard sound, and return with the soft."[9] According to some commentaries, this indicates that the hard plosive sound is pronounced more quickly than the soft fricative sound.[10]

However, since the Sefer Yetzirah (1:6) teaches that "running and returning" also relates to meditative techniques, it would appear that the hard and soft sounds were used for this purpose. These seven Doubles would be used to climb the vertical lines in the Tree of Life. When the initiate would use the letters to "run" and climb upward, he would use the hard sound, and when he would "return," he would use the soft sound.

The Bahir states that the letters are the body of the script, while the vowels are its soul.[11] The later Kabbalists note that the Dagesh and Rafeh are neither vowels nor letters, but intermediate between the two.[12] It is this intermediate essence that man must perfect if he is to enter the domain of Soul.

4:2   שבע כפולות בג"ד כפר"ת יסודן חכמה עושר זרע
חיים ממשלה שלום וחן:

Seven Doubles: BGD KPRT (בגד כפרת)
Their foundation is
Wisdom, Wealth, Seed,
Life, Dominance, Peace and Grace.

These are the concepts that can be controlled through the seven double letters. The methods are similar to those outlined in chapter 2.

These seven qualities parallel the seven vertical lines in the Tree
of Life diagram. They also relate to the seven times that the phrase,
"it was good," occurs in the account of creation.

4:3   שבע כפולות בג"ד כפר"ת בדבור ובתמורה
תמורת חכמה אולת תמורת עושר עוני תמורת
זרע שממה תמורת חיים מות תמורת ממשלה עבדות
תמורת שלום מלחמה תמורת חן כיעור:

Seven Doubles: BGD KPRT (בגד כפרת)
in speech and in transposition.
The transpose of Wisdom is Folly
The transpose of Wealth is Poverty
The transpose of Seed is Desolation
The transpose of Life is Death
The transpose of Dominance is Subjugation
The transpose of Peace is War
The transpose of Grace is Ugliness.

According to the *Tikkuney Zohar*, the hard sound implies harsh judgment, while the soft sound implies lenient judgment.[13] The good
qualities would then be associated with the soft sound, and the bad
qualities with the hard sound. There are, however, some authorities
who reverse this.[14]

Transpose

The word for "transpose" here is *Temurah* (תמורה). Earlier, the Sefer Yetzirah said, "He engraved them, carved them, permuted them, weighed them, and transposed them" (2:2). The word for "transposed" there was *Hemir* (המיר), which has the same root as the term used here. Earlier, we followed the commentaries who interpreted "transposed" to relate to the use of the standard ciphers. From the text here, however, it would appear that it denotes the transposition between the hard and soft sounds of the Doubles.

Peace, War

Peace and war relate both to nations and to the individual. A person can be at war with himself, or at peace with himself.[15] These letters can be used to transmit these qualities both to oneself or to another.

שבע כפולות בג״ד כפר״ת מעלה ומטה מזרח
ומערב צפון ודרום והיכל הקודש מכוון באמצע
והוא נושא את כולם:

Seven Doubles: BGD KPRT (בגד כפרת)
  Up and down
  East and west
  North and south
And the Holy Palace precisely in the center
  and it supports them all.

Up and Down

This should be compared to 1:5 and 1:13.

As discussed earlier, the six directions parallel the Six Sefirot. The order given here would then be: Netzach, Hod, Tiferet, Yesod, Chesed, Gevurah. Also see Tables 29, 30 on page 164.

The directions would indicate the direction that one must face, or the head motion that he use, when attempting to transmit the qualities mentioned in the last section.

Table 29. According to the Gra.

Bet	Wisdom	Chesed	South
Gimel	Wealth	Gevurah	North
Dalet	Seed	Tiferet	East
Kaf	Life	Netzach	Up
Peh	Dominance	Hod	Down
Resh	Peace	Yesod	West
Tav	Grace	Malkhut	Center

Table 30. According to *Sefer HaKanah*.[1]

Life	Binah
Peace	Yesod
Wisdom	Chesed
Wealth	Gevurah
Grace	Tiferet
Seed	Netzach
Dominance	Hod

[1]   *Sefer HaKanah* 86b, Raavad on 1:2 (19a).

Two of these concepts are alluded to in the Talmud: "He who wishes wisdom, let him face south; He who wishes wealth, let him face north."[16] This was reflected in the Temple, where the Menorah, which related to wisdom, was to the south, while the Table, indicating wealth, was to the north.

We see here that the letter Resh indicates peace. When there is no peace, this letter cannot be sounded correctly.

The Holy Palace

This is usually interpreted to denote Malkhut.[17] The Hebrew word for "Palace" here is *Hekhal* (היכל). This has a numerical value of 65, the same as that of *Adonoy* (אדני), the divine Name associated with Malkhut.[18]

Besides being the lowest Sefirah, Malkhut is also the end point of the Keter-Malkhut spiritual dimension. The "Holy Palace" in the center therefore not only relates to Malkhut alone, but also to its association with Keter. In channeling sustenance from Keter, the center point supports all the others.[19]

According to the Bahir, *"Hekhal HaKodesh"* here should not be read as "Holy Palace," but as "Palace of the Holy."[20] The "Holy" denotes Keter, and the "Palace of the Holy" refers to Malkhut when it is directly connected to Keter in the mystery of "Imbed their beginning in their end" (1:7).

This also represents a great mystery in creation, as explained by Rabbi Judah Liva (1525-1609), the Maharal of Prague, famed as the creator of a Golem. He states that the reason why the world was created in six days is because a three-dimensional world has six directions, as the Sefer Yetzirah states here. Each day was necessary to complete one of these six directions. The Sabbath is then the center point, which binds all together and supports them all.[21] The Sabbath thus represents Malkhut, but in the mode in which it is bound to Keter.

These seven elements also parallel the seven branches of the Menorah.[22] They are also alluded to in the verse, "Seven eyes on one stone" (Zechariah 3:9).[23] Another such allusion is the verse, "Give a portion to seven, also to eight" (Ecclesiastes 11:2).[24] As discussed earlier (1:3), the number seven denotes the perfection of creation, while eight is the entrance into the transcendental.

4:5 שבע כפולות בג"ד כפר"ת שבע ולא שש
שבע ולא שמונה בחון בהם וחקור בהם
והעמד דבר על בוריו והשב יוצר על מכונו:

Seven Doubles: BGD KPRT (בגד כפרת)
   Seven and not six
   Seven and not eight
      Examine with them
      And probe with them
   Make [each] thing stand on its essence
   And make the Creator sit on His base.

Seven and not six

This is very much like 1:4, and the two should be compared.

The seven Doubles are often associated with the seven lower Sefirot.[25] Actually, however, these seven letters represent the seven vertical lines on the Tree of Life diagram. The seven lower Sefirot are merely the lower end points of these seven vertical lines.

These letters are therefore the ladders leading upward from the seven lower Sefirot, and this is the way in which the two are associated. One of the main functions of the seven Doubles is thus to climb vertically on the ladder of the Sefirot. One rises through their hard sound, and descends with their soft sound.

The Sefer Yetzirah warned us earlier that there were Ten Sefirot, no more and no less (1:4). Here the text warns us that there are seven vertical paths, no more and no less. If an eighth vertical path were added, it would be taken as a path from Keter to the Infinite Being, and such a path cannot exist. Furthermore, if a path to Keter were omitted, one might be misled into thinking that Keter is God, and this is also erroneous.

Examine with them

This is also similar to 1:4.

One can probe and examine with these letters very much like one does with the Sefirot. In 1:4, however, the text also said, "Understand with wisdom, and be wise with Understanding," while here this is omitted. The discussion there involved the basic exercise of fluctuating between Chakhmah and Binah consciousness. Here, the exercise involves the letters themselves, rather than pure states of consciousness.

Probe with them

In 1:4 the reading was "probe *from* them," while here it is "probe *with* them."

When the text spoke of the Sefirot themselves, it could say, "probe *from* them," since it is from the Sefirot that one receives spiritual energy. Here, however, it is not the letters that provide spiritual energy, but the Sefirot to which they relate. The text therefore states, "probe *with* them," indicating that the letters are the tools through which one can probe.[26]

The upper six of these seven Sefirot represent the six directions. Malkhut is the center point, the "Holy Palace." Taken subjectively, this "center point" is the center of being of the individual reaching up to the Sefirot.

The first Sefirah that the initiate must reach is Malkhut, and he accomplishes this by meditating on the center, which is the center of his being. Only after he reaches Malkhut can he reach out to the other

Sefirot. The Bahir therefore identifies the "Holy Palace" with the very purest essence of thought.[27]

4:6

שבע כפולות בג״ד כפר״ת יסוד הקקן חצבן
צרפן שקלן והמירן וצר בהם שבעה כוכבים
בעולם שבעה ימים בשנה שבעה שערים בנפש זכר
ונקבה:

Seven Doubles: BGD KPRT (בגד כפרת) of Foundation
  He engraved them, He carved them,
  He permuted them, He weighed them,
  He transformed them,
And with them He formed,
  Seven planets in the Universe,
  Seven days in the Year,
  Seven gates in the Soul,
    male and female.

He engraved them...

The five methods mentioned here are the same as those in 2:2 and 3:3.

Seven planets

The seven vertical paths associated with the seven Doubles are manifest in the physical world as the astrological forces associated with the seven planets: Saturn, Jupiter, Mars, Sun, Venus, Mercury and Moon.

In Time, they are associated with the seven days of the week, while in man, they are the seven openings in the head. These will be enumerated in the following sections.

The Talmud also speaks of the various influences of the planets and days of the week.[28] These are closely related to their role in creation, and do not appear to follow the system of Sefer Yetzirah. See Table 31 on page 168. The seven planets are also associated with specific angels.[29]

Table 31. Planets and their angels.

	Saturn	Jupiter	Mars	Sun	Venus	Mercury	Moon
A	Michael	Barakiel	Gabriel	Raphael	Chasdiel	Tzidkiel	Anel
B	Michael	Barakiel	Gabriel	Raphael	Tzidkiel	Chasdiel	Anel
C	Kaptziel	Tzidkiel	Samael	Michael	Anel	Raphael	Gabriel
D	[Kaptziel]	Tzidkiel	Samael	Raphael	Anel	Barakiel	Gabriel
E	Kaptziel	Raphael	Samael	Michael	Anel	[Barakiel]	Gabriel
F	Kaptziel Saturday	Tzidkiel Thursday	Samael Tuesday	Raphael Sunday	Anel Friday	Michael Wednesday	Gabriel Monday

A Raziel 17b (51).
B Sodi Razi, quoted in *Kehilat Yaakov*, p. 17b.
C Rabbi Eliezar of Garmiza on *Sefer Yetzirah*, p. 12a. *Cf.* Raziel 20a (64).
D Raziel 17b (52).
E Yalkut Reuveni 16a.
F Shoshan Yesod Olam, p. 198 *ff.* The planets pertain to the first hour of the associated day, as explained below.

Table 32. The days of the week and the planets according to the Talmud, Shabbat 156a.

Sunday	One-sidedness, leadership
Monday	Anger, seclusiveness
Tuesday	Wealth, lechery
Wednesday	Intellect, memory
Thursday	Charity, generosity
Friday	Religious inclination
Saturday	Life, holiness
Sun	Independence, openness
Venus	Wealth, lechery
Mercury	Intellect, memory
Moon	Dependence, secretiveness, manic-depressiveness
Saturn	Inaction, invulnerability
Jupiter	Generosity
Mars	Blood

These angels channel the influence of the seven vertical paths through the planets. See Table 32.

Also associated with the seven planets are specific signs, as well as a system of magic squares.[30] See figures 43 and 44 on pages 170-171. The rule of seven also appears to be related to the mystical Seven Seals mentioned by the early Kabbalists.[31] See figure 45 on page 172.

In order to understand the significance of the astrological forces, we must first understand the role of angels in the chain between the Sefirot and the physical world. The Sefirot are in the Universe of Atzilut, and below this is Beriyah, the universe of the Throne, which serves to allow the Sefirot to interact with the lower worlds. Between Beriyah and Asiyah is Yetzirah, the world of the angels.

Yetzirah is known as the "world of speech." The Talmud states that "Every word emanating from God creates an angel."[32] This means that every one of God's words is actually an angel. When we speak of "God's word," we are actually speaking of His interaction with the lower worlds. The force that traverses the spiritual domain is what we call an angel.

The stars also form an important link in God's providence over the physical world.[33] Between God and man, there are many levels of interaction, the lowest being those of the angels and the stars. The Midrash thus teaches, "There is no blade of grass that does not have a constellation (*Mazal*) over it, telling it to grow."[34]

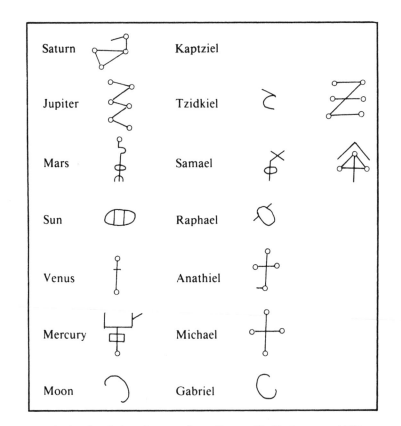

Saturn		Kaptziel		
Jupiter		Tzidkiel		
Mars		Samael		
Sun		Raphael		
Venus		Anathiel		
Mercury		Michael		
Moon		Gabriel		

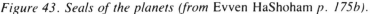

Figure 43. Seals of the planets (from Evven HaShoham *p. 175b).*

As the commentaries explain, God's providence works through the angels, but these angels, in turn, work through the stars and planets. As some authorities put it, the angels are, in a sense, like souls to the stars. Thus, for example, some sources speak of the stars as having intelligence, but the commentaries note that this is actually speaking of the angels that are associated with them.[35]

There are, however, two types of angels. We have already spoken of the teaching that there are angels created with every word of God. Elsewhere we find that angels are created every day, with a new troop being made each morning.[36] On the other hand, there are many angels who are known by name, such as Gabriel and Michael, who have permanent existence. These are obviously a second kind of angel.

This is closely related to another discussion. In the Midrash, there is a question as to when the angels were created. Some say that they were made on the second day of creation, while others maintain that they were created on the fifth day.[37]

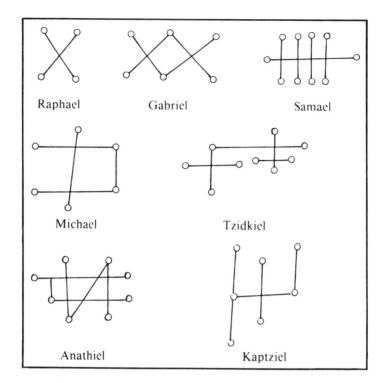

Figure 44. Seals of the planetary angels (according to Shoshan Yesod Olam *# 1727).*

In discussing this, the Kabbalists arrive at a significant conclusion. They state that there are two basic kinds of angels: permanent angels and temporary angels. The temporary angels were created on the second day, while the permanent ones, which are likened to the birds, were created on the fifth. They also state that an important difference between the permanent and temporary angels is the fact that only the permanent ones have names.[38]

One of the most important factors in astrology is the time and date of a person's birth. The Talmud thus states that there is a "Mazal of the hour."[39] The time, day, and date upon which a person is born has an important influence on his destiny.

Elsewhere the Talmud teaches that there is an angel called Laylah that oversees birth. It is this angel that proclaims if the individual will be strong or weak, wise or foolish, rich or poor.[40]

Earlier, however, we discussed the Midrashic teaching, "One angel cannot have two missions, and two angels cannot share the same mission" (1:7).[41] But if this is a general rule, how can a single

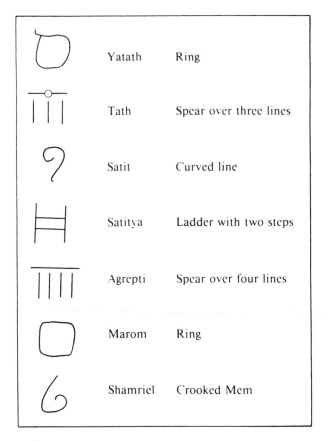

	Yatath	Ring
	Tath	Spear over three lines
	Satit	Curved line
	Satitya	Ladder with two steps
	Agrepti	Spear over four lines
	Marom	Ring
	Shamriel	Crooked Mem

Figure 45. The seven seals.

angel oversee the birth of every person who was ever to be born? Does this not mean that he has many missions?

The same question also applies to all the permanent angels who have names. These angels, which were created on the fifth day, exist forever. In the course of their existence, they must have many tasks and missions. Why does this rule not hold true with regard to them?

In answering these questions, the commentaries note that the angels are like souls to the stars.[42] A human soul is also a spiritual entity, and the same question could be asked about it. How can a single soul be involved in many tasks? But here the answer is obvious. The soul is integrated by its association with a single body. It is not differentiated into many souls by its many tasks, because its association with the body allows it to remain an integrated whole.

The same is true of the angels having names. These angels are like souls to the stars, and this also means that the stars and planets

Figure 46. The seven planets (from Maaseh Toviah, *p. 41b).*

are the "bodies" of these angels. See figure 46. As such, each star
serves as a focus for a particular angel, maintaining it as an integrated
whole, even though it may have many different tasks.

There is therefore a one-to-one relationship between the stars and
angels. Each star has its own particular angel, and each angel has its own
star. It is this relationship that allows the named angels to have many
tasks, and still not be differentiated into many angels by these tasks. Each
named angel is integrated by the star that serves as its body.

This also explains why the permanent angels have names. The
Zohar teaches that every single star in the universe has a name.[43] This
is derived from the verse, "He brings out their host by number, He
calls them all by name" (Isaiah 40:26). It is also written, "He counts
the number of the stars, He gives them each a name" (Psalms 147:4).
The Midrash indicates that the different names of the stars correspond to the names of the different angels.[44] The one-to-one relationship is therefore clearly expressed.

This also explains why the named angels were created on the fifth
day, while the unnamed, temporary angels, were created on the second
day. The named angels were associated with the stars, and could therefore not be created until after the stars. The stars were not cre-

ated until the fourth day, and the angels could therefore not be created until the fifth.

4:7
שבעה כוכבים בעולם שבתאי צדק מאדים
חמה נוגה כוכב לבנה. שבעה ימים בשנה
שבעת ימי השבוע. שבעה שערים בנפש זכר ונקבה
שתי עינים שתי אזנים שני נקבי האף והפה:

Seven planets in the Universe:
    Saturn, Jupiter, Mars,
    Sun, Venus, Mercury, Moon.
Seven days in the Year:
    The seven days of the week.
Seven gates in the Soul, male and female:
    Two eyes, two ears, two nostrils,
        and the mouth.

4:8
המליך אות ב' בחכמה וקשר לו כתר
וצרפן זה בזה וצר בהם לבנה בעולם יום ראשון
בשנה ועין ימין בנפש זכר ונקבה:

He made the letter Bet (ב) king over Wisdom
    And He bound a crown to it
    And He combined one with another
And with them He formed
    The Moon in the Universe
    Sunday in the Year
    The right eye in the Soul,
        male and female.

4:9   המליך אות ג׳ בעושר וקשר לו כתר
וצרפן זה בזה וצר בהם מאדים בעולם יום שני
בשנה ואזן ימין בנפש זכר ונקבה:

He made the letter Gimel (ג) king over Wealth
  And He bound a crown to it
  And He combined one with another
And with them He formed
  Mars in the Universe
  Monday in the Year
  The right ear in the Soul,
    male and female.

4: 10   המליך אות ד׳ בזרע וקשר לו כתר
וצרפן זה בזה וצר בהם חמה בעולם יום שלישי
בשנה ונחיר ימין בנפש זכר ונקבה:

He made the letter Dalet (ד) king over Seed
  And He bound a crown to it
  And He combined one with another
And with them He formed
  The sun in the Universe
  Tuesday in the Year
  The right nostril in the Soul,
    male and female.

4: 11   המליך אות כ׳ בחיים וקשר לו כתר
וצרפן זה בזה וצר בהם נוגה בעולם יום רביעי
בשנה ועין שמאל בנפש זכר ונקבה:

He made the letter Kaf (כ) king over Life
  And He bound a crown to it
  And He combined one with another
And with them He formed
  Venus in the Universe
  Wednesday in the Year
  The left eye in the Soul,
    male and female.

4:12 המליך אות פ׳ בממשלה וקשר לו
כתר וצרפן זה בזה וצר בהם כוכב בעולם יום
חמישי בשנה ואזן שמאל בנפש זכר ונקבה:

> He made the letter Peh (פ) king over Dominance
>> And He bound a crown to it
>> And He combined one with another
> And with them He formed
>> Mercury in the Universe
>> Thursday in the Year
>> The left ear in the Soul,
>>> male and female.

4:13 המליך אות ר׳ בשלום וקשר לו כתר
וצרפן זה בזה וצר בהם שבתאי בעולם יום
ששי בשנה ונחיר שמאל בנפש זכר ונקבה:

> He made the letter Resh (ר) king over Peace
>> And He bound a crown to it
>> And He combined one with another
> And with them He formed
>> Saturn in the Universe
>> Friday in the Year
>> The left nostril in the Soul,
>>> male and female.

4:14 המליך אות ת׳ בחן וקשר לו כתר וצרפן
זה בזה וצר בהם צדק בעולם יום שבת בשנה
ופה בנפש זכר ונקבה:

> He made the letter Tav (ת) king over Grace
>> And He bound a crown to it
>> And He combined one with another
> And with them He formed
>> Jupiter in the Universe
>> The Sabbath in the Year
>> The mouth in the Soul,
>>> male and female.

Here the Sefer Yetzirah discusses the letters in relation to the primary traits, the planets, the days of the week, and the parts of the body. There are a number of variations in these assignments, and the more important ones are given in Table 33 on pages 178-179.

Each letter can be used to influence the part of the body with which it is associated. This can be accomplished through using the array of 221 (or 231) Gates associated with that letter. These letters are used in a similar manner when creating a Golem.

Most important are the relationships between the letters, days of the week, and planets and between the seven primary traits: Wisdom, Wealth, Seed, Life, Dominance, Peace and Grace. One can use the methods of the Sefer Yetzirah to attain or enhance any one of these by using the soft pronunciation of the seven Doubles. If one wishes to transmit their opposite, one uses the hard pronunciation.

Like other stanzas, this can also be read in the imperative: "Make Bet king over Wisdom, bind a crown to it, and combine one with another, and with them form. . . ."

The meditation involves using the seven Doubles in this manner. The dominant letter is placed at the beginning, and the other six letters are then permuted. Thus, if one was seeking to transmit Wisdom, one would place Bet (ב) at the beginning, and one would then permute the remaining letters, GD KPRT (גד כפרת), in every possible manner. Similarly, if one were seeking Wealth, one would place Gimel (ג) at the beginning, and would permute the letters BD KPRT (בד כפרת) in all 720 possible ways. The permutation with which one begins is given in Table 34 on page 180.

At the same time, one should contemplate the part of the body associated with that particular trait. Thus, for Wisdom, one would concentrate on the right eye, while for Wealth, on the right ear. In a similar manner, one should also concentrate on the appropriate direction.

Also important is the day of the week associated with each trait. If one wishes to transmit a certain trait, it is best done on the specified day of the week.

In using these methods, one must also take planetary influences into account. Besides the influences given here, there are others given in Bereita of Shmuel HaKatan, which appear to be closer to those expressed in Western astrology.[45] See Table 35 on page 180.

Influence extends only from the visible members of our solar system. The distant planets such as Uranus, Neptune and Pluto, which are invisible to the unaided eye, are not considered to have any significant astrological influence. If one were to take these into account, one would also have to consider dozens of asteroids which would exert an even greater influence.

178

Table 33. The letters in relation to primary traits, planets, days of the week, and parts of the body.

	Bet ב	Gimel ג	Dalet ד	Kaf כ	Peh פ	Resh ר	Tav ת
A.	wisdom	wealth	seed	life	dominance	peace	grace
	Moon	Mars	Sun	Venus	Mercury	Saturn	Jupiter
	Sun.	Mon.	Tues.	Wed.	Thurs.	Fri.	Sat.
	R.eye	R.ear	R.nostril	L.eye	L.ear	L.nostril	mouth
B.	life	peace	wisdom	wealth	grace	seed	dominance
	Saturn	Jupiter	Mars	Sun	Venus	Mercury	Moon
	Sun.	Mon.	Tues.	Wed.	Thurs.	Fri.	Sat.
	R.eye	L.eye	R.ear	L.ear	R.nostril	L.nostril	mouth
C.	wisdom	wealth	seed	life	dominance	peace	grace
	Saturn	Jupiter	Mars	Sun	Venus	Mercury	Moon
	Sat.	Sun.	Mon.	Tues.	Wed.	Thurs.	Fri.
	mouth	R.eye	L.eye	R.nostril	L.nostril	R.ear	L.ear
D.	life	peace	wisdom	wealth	seed	grace	dominance
	Saturn	Jupiter	Mars	Sun	Venus	Mercury	Moon
	Sat.	Sun.	Mon.	Tues.	Wed.	Thurs.	Fri.
	mouth	R.eye	L.eye	R.nostril	L.nostril	R.ear	L.ear

A Gra Version.
B Short Version, Raavad.
C Long Version, *Tikkun Layl Shavout*, Yalkut Reuveni 18b. *Emek HaMelekh* 9c uses this version for body parts.
D Long Version in recap (4:14). This indicates that the Long Version was taken from two sources. This version is found in Saadia 1:3, 3:3, 5:5, 8:2. The recap may therefore have been taken from Saadia. Chakamoni is the same, except that dominance and grace are interchanged. Saadia (b) here.

Table 33. The letters in relation to primary traits, planets, days of the week, and parts of the body (continued).

	Bet ב	Gimel ג	Dalet ד	Kaf כ	Peh פ	Resh ר	Tav ת
E.	life	peace	wisdom	wealth	seed	grace	dominance
	Saturn	Jupiter	Mars	Sun	Venus	Mercury	Moon
	Sun.	Mon.	Tues.	Wed.	Thurs.	Fri.	Sat.
	R.eye	L.eye	R.nostril	L.nostril	R.ear	L.ear	mouth
F.	wisdom	wealth	dominance	life	grace	seed	peace
	Saturn	Jupiter	Mars	Sun	Venus	Mercury	Moon
	Sat.	Thurs.	Tues.	Sun.	Fri.	Wed.	Mon.
G.	life	peace	wisdom	seed	wealth	grace	dominance
	Saturn	Sun	Moon	Mars	Mercury	Jupiter	Venus
	Sat.	Sun.	Mon.	Tues.	Wed.	Thurs.	Fri.
	mouth	R.eye	L.eye	R.nostril	L.nostril	R.ear	L.ear
H.	life	peace	wisdom	grace	wealth	seed	dominance
	Saturn	Jupiter	Mars	Sun	Venus	Mercury	Moon
	Sun.	Mon.	Tues.	Wed.	Thurs.	Fri.	Sat.
I.	R.ear	L.ear	R.eye	L.eye	R.nostril	L.nostril	mouth
	Chakhmah	Binah	Netzach	Hod	Tiferet	Daat	Malkhut
J.	life	wisdom	peace	grace	wealth	seed	dominance

E Donash. Cf. Raziel 8a (17).
F Kuzari 4:25 (50b). Body parts are not given. The planet influences the first hour of the given day.
G Sheirat Yosef 10a. The days are in order, but again, the planet is that which influences the first hour of the given day.
H Otzar HaShem; Ramak, Shiur Komah 15 (29a). The same ordering of the attributes is found in Sefer HaPeliyah 39a.
I Etz Chaim, Shaar TaNTA 6. The same ordering is found in Ginat Egoz 38c.
J Raavad, p. 51b.

Table 34. Permutations of the seven Doubles
(according to Saadia B here).

Bet	ב	BGD KPRT	בגד כפרת
Gimel	ג	GBD KPRT	גבד כפרת
Dalet	ד	DGB KPRT	דגב כפרת
Kaf	כ	KPRT BGD	כפרת בגד
Peh	פ	PRT BGDK	פרת בגדכ
Resh	ר	RTBG DKP	רתבג דכפ
Tav	ת	TBG DKPR	תבג דכפר

Table 35. Influences according to Bareita of Shmuel HaKatan
(see note 45).

Saturn	Poverty, destruction, internal injury and sickness.
Mars	Blood, wickedness, strife, external injury, war, hatred, jealousy.
Jupiter	Life, peace, good, prosperity, religious feelings, joy, wealth, political advance.
Venus	Grace, love, lust, children, fruitfulness.
Mercury	Wisdom, skill, writing, language.
Sun	Light, darkness, work, accomplishment, travel, exile.
Moon	Holds keys to heaven and earth, surrogate for good and evil.

The influence of the planets in the system of Sefer Yetzirah does
not depend on their position in the sky, but on the hour of the day.
This is discussed in a number of Talmudical and Kabbalistic
sources.[46]

In order of their distance from Earth, the planets are: Saturn,
Jupiter, Mars, Sun, Venus, Mercury, Moon. Of these, Saturn is furthest from the Earth, and the Moon is closest.[47]

According to the Bible, the stars and planets were made on the
Fourth Day of creation (Genesis 1:14-19). Counting from Sunday,
the Fourth Day was Wednesday.

In Biblical reckoning, however, night always preceeds day. The
Torah therefore consistently says, "It was evening, and it was morning." Evening always preceeds morning.

The planets were placed in their positions on the eve of the
Fourth Day, that is, on Tuesday night. They were placed one at a
time, an hour apart, in order of their distance from earth. Thus, in
the first hour (6 P.M.), Saturn was placed in its position. In the second
hour (7 P.M.), Jupiter was positioned. The order of creation of the
seven planets was then as follows:

First hour	6 P.M.	Saturn
Second hour	7 P.M.	Jupiter
Third hour	8 P.M.	Mars
Fourth hour	9 P.M.	Sun
Fifth hour	10 P.M.	Venus
Sixth hour	11 P.M.	Mercury
Seventh hour	12 P.M.	Moon

This is the ordering found of the eve of Wednesday on the chart of planetary influences.

Each planet then dominated the hour in which it was positioned. After the first seven hours, their dominance began a new cycle, with the planets in the same order. This seven hour cycle continues throught the week, and it is the same every week. The entire weekly cycle is given in the tabel of planetary influences see Table 36 on page 182.

One immediately notices that the first hour of each evening is dominated by a different planet, in the following order:

Sun.	Mon.	Tues.	Wed.	Thurs.	Fri.	Sat.
Mercury	Jupiter	Venus	Saturn	Sun	Moon	Mars

The first hour of each day is dominated by the planets in the following manner:

Sun.	Mon.	Tues.	Wed.	Thurs.	Fri.	Sat.
Sun	Moon	Mars (Tew)	Mercury (Woden)	Jupiter (Thor)	Venus (Frigg)	Saturn

Note that the name of each day is associated with the planet that dominates its first hour in the morning.[48] Thus, Sunday is dominated by the Sun, Monday (moon day), by the Moon, and Saturday, by Saturn. In the English names of the other days, the Nordic or Germanic names of the planets are used.

The Romans had originally named the days after the planets dominating their first hour. This nomenclature still survives in the Romance languages. Thus, in French, Tuesday is *Mardi* (Mars' day), Wednesday is Mercredi (Mercury's day), Thursday is Jeudi (Jupiter's day), and Friday is Vendredi (Venus' day).

Saturn dominates Saturday, which is the Sabbath. In Hebrew, Sabbath is *Shabbat* (שבת), and hence, Saturn is called *Shabbatai* (שבתאי).

The planet that dominates the first hour of the day or night is said to dominate that entire period. The most auspicious times,

Table 36. Weekly cycle of planetary influences.

Hour	Wed.	Thurs.	Fri.	Sat.	Sun.	Mon.	Tues.
Night Before							
1	Saturn	Sun	Moon	Mars	Mercury	Jupiter	Venus
2	Jupiter	Venus	Saturn	Sun	Moon	Mars	Mercury
3	Mars	Mercury	Jupiter	Venus	Saturn	Sun	Moon
4	Sun	Moon	Mars	Mercury	Jupiter	Venus	Saturn
5	Venus	Saturn	Sun	Moon	Mars	Mercury	Jupiter
6	Mercury	Jupiter	Venus	Saturn	Sun	Moon	Mars
7	Moon	Mars	Mercury	Jupiter	Venus	Saturn	Sun
8	Saturn	Sun	Moon	Mars	Mercury	Jupiter	Venus
9	Jupiter	Venus	Saturn	Sun	Moon	Mars	Mercury
10	Mars	Mercury	Jupiter	Venus	Saturn	Sun	Moon
11	Sun	Moon	Mars	Mercury	Jupiter	Venus	Saturn
12	Venus	Saturn	Sun	Moon	Mars	Mercury	Jupiter
Day	Wed.	Thurs.	Fri.	Sat.	Sun.	Mon.	Tues.
1	Mercury	Jupiter	Venus	Saturn	Sun	Moon	Mars
2	Moon	Mars	Mercury	Jupiter	Venus	Saturn	Sun
3	Saturn	Sun	Moon	Mars	Mercury	Jupiter	Venus
4	Jupiter	Venus	Saturn	Sun	Moon	Mars	Mercury
5	Mars	Mercury	Jupiter	Venus	Saturn	Sun	Moon
6	Sun	Moon	Mars	Mercury	Jupiter	Venus	Saturn
7	Venus	Saturn	Sun	Moon	Mars	Mercury	Jupiter
8	Mercury	Jupiter	Venus	Saturn	Sun	Moon	Mars
9	Moon	Mars	Mercury	Jupiter	Venus	Saturn	Sun
10	Saturn	Sun	Moon	Mars	Mercury	Jupiter	Venus
11	Jupiter	Venus	Saturn	Sun	Moon	Mars	Mercury
12	Mars	Mercury	Jupiter	Venus	Saturn	Sun	Moon

Table 37. Concepts and auspicious times (according to Gra).

Wisdom
> Bet, Moon, right eye, Chesed, south, white;
> Saturday night, 7-8 P.M., 2-3 A.M.; Sunday, 9-10 A.M.,
> 4-5 P.M.

Wealth, Love
> Gimel, Mars, right ear, Gevurah, north, red;
> Sunday night, 7-8 P.M., 2-3 A.M.; Monday, 9-10 A.M.,
> 4-5 P.M.

Seed: Children and things relating to them
> Dalet, Sun, right nostril, Tiferet, east, yellow;
> Monday night, midnight-1 A.M.; Tuesday, 7-8 A.M.,
> 2-3 P.M.

Life, Health
> Kaf, Venus, left eye, Netzach, up, upper eyelid;
> Tuesday night, 10-11 P.M., 5-6 A.M.; Wednesday,
> noon-1 P.M.

Dominance, Advancement
> Peh, Mercury, left ear, Hod, down, lower eyelid;
> Wednesday night, 8-9 P.M., 3-4 A.M.; Thursday,
> 10-11 A.M., 5-6 P.M.

Peace, internal and external
> Resh, Saturn, left nostril, Yesod, west, black;
> Thursday night, 7-8 P.M., 2-3 A.M.; Friday, 9-10 A.M.,
> 4-5 P.M.

Grace, attractiveness, personality improvement
> Tav, Jupiter, mouth, Malkhut, center (self), blue;
> Friday night, midnight-1 A.M.; Saturday, 7-8 A.M.,
> 2-3 P.M.

Be careful not to violate Sabbath.

however, are those associated both with the correct day and with the correct planet. See Table 36 on page 182. Thus, for example, in our (Gra) version of Sefer Yetzirah, both Sunday and the Moon are associated with Wisdom. During the day on Sunday, the Moon is dominant in the fourth and eleventh hours, or from 9-10 A.M. and from 4-5 P.M. These are then the most auspicious times for working to attain Wisdom.[49]

There is a commandment, "There shall not be found among you. . . one who calculates times (*MeOnan*)" (Deuteronomy 18:10). In the Talmud, according to Rabbi Akiba, this specifically applies to one who calculates auspicious times, and a number of authorities accept this opinion as binding.[50] This, however, only means that one

Table 38. Days and the 42-letter name.

1	Sunday	ABG YThTz	אבג יתצ
2	Monday	KRO ShTN	קרע שטן
3	Tuesday	NGD YKSh	נגד יכש
4	Wednesday	BTR TzThG	בטר צתג
5	Thursday	ChKB TNO	חקב טנע
6	Friday	YGL PZK	יגל פזק
7	Saturday	ShKU TzYTh	שקו צית

Table 39. Days, vowels and angels.

Sunday	Semeturia, Gezeriel, Ve'enael, Lemuel	Segol
Monday	Shmaiyel, Berekhiel, Ahaniel	Sh'va
Tuesday	Chaniel, Lahadiel, Machniel	Cholam
Wednesday	Chizkiel, Rahitiel, Kidashiel	Chirak
Thursday	Shmuaiel, Ra'umiel, Kuniel	Shurek
Friday	Shimushiel, Raphael, Kidushiel	Shurek
Saturday	Tzuriel, Raziel, Yofiel	Tzerey

should not make astrology a dominant influence in one's daily life. As we see from all the commentaries on Sefer Yetzirah, when one is engaged in these mystical techniques, this prohibition is not applicable.[51] See Table 37 on page 183.

Although most versions of Sefer Yetzirah set the planets in the order in which they were created, the Gra version, which we are using, follows a different system. It is based on the ordering of the planets as found in the Zohar.[52] There, we find the following relationship between the planets, Sefirot and colors:

Moon	Mars	Sun	Saturn	Jupiter	Venus	Mercury
White	Red	Yellow	Black	Blue	upper eyelid	lower eyelid
Chesed	Gevurah	Tiferet	Yesod	Malkhut	Netzach	Hod
Sun.	Mon.	Tues.	Fri.	Sat.	Wed.	Thurs.

When the Sefirot and days are placed in their usual order, the planets appear in the order given in our version of Sefer Yetzirah. This version therefore is that which fits most closely to the teachings of the Zohar.

The association with colors is also significant, since one can also meditate on these colors when seeking to transmit the associated influence. The colors are also useful in general in meditations involving the Sefirot.[53]

Also associated with the days of the week are the letters of the 42-letter name. See Table 38. This can be used in various meditations involving these days.[54] The same is true of the angels associated with each day.[55] See Table 39.

4 : 15 שבע כפולות בג"ד כפר"ת שבהן נחקקין
שבעה עולמות, שבעה רקיעין, שבע ארצות,
שבעה ימים, שבעה נהרות, שבעה מדברות, שבעה
ימים, שבעה שבועות, שבע שנים, שבע שמיטין,
שבעה יובלות, והיכל הקדש. לפיכך חבב את
השביעיות תחת כל השמים:

Seven Doubles: BGD KPRT (בגד כפרת)
With them were engraved
Seven Universes, seven firmaments,
seven lands, seven seas,
seven rivers, seven deserts,
seven days, seven weeks,
seven years, seven sabbaticals,
seven jubilees,
and the Holy Palace.
Therefore, He made sevens beloved
under all the heavens.

Seven Universes

The later Kabbalists write that these are the Seven Chambers in the Universe of Beriyah.[56] These are given in Table 40 on page 186.

Of these, the two lowest, "Brickwork of Sapphire" and "Essence of Heaven," are mentioned in the verse, "They saw the God of Israel, and under His feet was the 'Brickwork of Sapphire,' clear like the 'Essence of Heaven'" (Exodus 24:10). These Seven Chambers parallel the seven lower Sefirot in the Universe of Atzilut. They also parallel the seven watches of angels in the Universe of Yetzirah.

Some early souces state that these Seven Universes are the seven thousand years that the world is supposed to exist.[57] The first six parallel the six weekdays, while the seventh thousand years is the "day when all will be Sabbath."[58]

Others relate the Seven Universes to the Kabbalistic doctrine of Sabbaticals. This states that there are seven distinct periods of creation, each lasting seven thousand years.[59] According to some Kabbalists, the present creation is the second, while others state that it is the sixth or seventh. In any case, there are seven cycles, each seven thousand years long. This means that the universe as we know it will last for 49,000 years.

Table 40. The seven chambers of the Universe of Beriyah.

Kodesh Kedashim	Holy of Holies
Ratzon	Desire
Ahavah	Love
Zekhut	Merit
Nogah	Luster
Etzem HaShamayim	Essence of Heaven
Livnat HaSappir	Brickwork of Sapphire

According to the master Kabbalists, Rabbi Isaac of Acco, when counting the years of these cycles, one must not use an ordinary physical year, but rather, a divine year.[60] The Midrash says that each divine day is a thousand years, basing this on the verse, "A thousand years in Your sight are as but yesterday" (Psalms 90:4).[61] Since each year contains $365\frac{1}{4}$ days, a divine year would be 365,250 years long.

According to this, each cycle of seven thousand divine years would consist of 2,556,750,000 earthly years. This figure of two-and-a-half billion years is very close to the scientific estimate as to the length of time that life has existed on earth.

If we assume that the seventh cycle began with the Biblical account of creation, then this would have occurred when the universe was 15,340,500,000 years old. This is very close to the scientific estimate that the expansion of the universe began some fifteen billion years ago.

The current Hebrew year is 5736. In this calendar, the year in which Adam was created is counted as year one. If we then count the Biblical genealogies from the time of Adam, we find that 5736 years have elapsed since the time he was formed. However, the Kabbalists clearly say that other human beings existed before Adam, and this is even supported in scripture.[62]

Actually, there are two accounts of creation in the Book of Genesis. The first chapter of Genesis speaks of the initial creation of the universe, while the second chapter speaks of the creation of Adam. During the six days of creation described in the first chapter, God did not actually create the world, but rather, created the ingredients which would allow the world to develop. It thus refers to the creation of all matter, along with space and time.[63] It was during these six days that God brought the universe into being from absolute nothingness.[64]

After these six days of creation, God allowed the universe to develop by itself, renewing His creation each seven thousand divine years or 2.5 billion earthly years. All the laws of nature and the prop-

Table 41. Firmaments, earths, and attributes (from *Otzar HaShem*).

1	Vilon	Eretz	Chesed	Life
2	Rakia	Adamah	Gevurah	Peace
3	Shachakim	Arka	Tiferet	Wisdom
4	Zevul	Charba	Netzach	Grace
5	Ma'on	Yabashah	Hod	Wealth
6	Makhon	Tevel	Yesod	Seed
7	Aravot	Chalad	Malkhut	Dominance

erties of matter had been fixed for all time, as it is written, "He has established them forever; He has made a decree which shall not be transgressed" (Psalms 148:6).[65] It is similarly written, "Whatever God decrees shall be forever; nothing shall be added to it, and nothing shall be taken away" (Ecclesiastes 3:14).[66]

Each of the six cycles of creation brought something new into the world. The fifth cycle was the one that brought forth life, and this took place around two and a half billion years ago. Around 974 generations before Adam, or some 25,000 years ago, man developed all the physical and mental capabilities that we possess today.[67] This man had evolved from "the dust of the earth" (Genesis 2:7), but he still lacked the divine soul that would make him a spiritual being. God then created Adam, the first true human being with a soul, "and He blew in his nostrils a soul of life" (Genesis 2:7).[68] According to tradition, the creation of Adam took place on Rosh HaShanah, the Hebrew New Year, which occurred on September 9, 3761 B.C.E.[69]

Seven Firmaments

These are listed in the Long Version (4:13) as being: Vilon, Rakia, Shechakim, Zevul, Ma'on, Makhon, Aravot. These are also mentioned in the Talmud.[70] See Table 41.

According to the Ari, these parallel the seven lower Sefirot of the Universe of Asiyah.[71]

Seven Earths

The Long Version (4:13) lists these as: Adamah, Tevel, Nashiyah, Tzaya, Chalad, Eretz, Chalad. Another source gives them as: Eretz, Adamah, Arkah, Gey, Tzaya, Nasya, Tevel.[72] Still another ancient source lists them: Eretz, Adamah, Arka, Chariva, Yabasha, Tevel, Chalad.[73]

According to many authorities, these refer to the seven continents: North America, South America, Europe, Africa, Asia, Australia, Antarctica.[74] There is no continent on the north pole, and hence, the north is said to be "open."[75]

Both the seven firmaments and the seven earths are said to parallel the Sefirot in the lower world. They also parallel the seven attributes under discussion here.

Seven Seas

Many commentaries state that these are the seven lakes and seas in the Holy Land.[76]

In modern terminology, the seven seas represent the seven oceans: the North Atlantic, South Atlantic, North Pacific, South Pacific, Indian Ocean, Arctic Ocean, Antarctic Ocean. The seas in the Holy Land represent a microcosm of these oceans.

Seven Rivers

These are the seven rivers associated with the Holy Land: The Jordan, Yarmoch, Kirmyon, Poga, Pishon, Gichon, Chidekel.[77] The Euphrates is not counted because it includes them all.[78] These parallel the great rivers of the world.

Seven Deserts

These are the seven deserts through which the Israelites passed during the Exodus from Egypt: Eitan, Shur, Sin, Sinai, Paran, Tzin, Kadmut.[79]

Seven Days

These are the seven days of the week. They are also the seven days of the major festivals, Pesach (Passover) and Succot (Tabernacles).

Seven Weeks

These are the seven weeks between Pesach and Shavuot. The Torah thus says, "You shall count from the day after the holiday, . . . seven complete weeks" (Leviticus 23:15).

Seven Years

These are the seven years in the Sabbatical cycle. The Torah pre-scribes that on the seventh year the land should lie fallow and not be worked: "Six years shall you sow your field. . .but the seventh year shall be a Sabbath of solomn rest for the land" (Leviticus 25:3-4).

Seven Sabbaticals

At the end of seven Sabbatical cycles, the Jubilee year was cele-brated. All slaves would then be freed, and real property would be returned to its hereditary owner. The Torah states, "You shall num-ber seven Sabbaticals, seven times seven years . . . making forty-nine years . . . And you shall sanctify the fiftieth year, and proclaim liberty throughout the land . . . it shall be a jubilee to you" (Leviticus 25:8,10).

Seven Jubilees

This is seven times 49 (or 50) years, a total of 343 (or 350) years. The First Temple stood for 410 years, and during this period, Israel observed seven jubilees.[80]

This also relates to the concept of Sabbaticals of creation, where each jubilee period consists of 49,000 years. There will be seven such jubilee periods, and the universe will therefore last a total of 343,000 years. These are divine years, each one consisting of 365,250 earthly years. Thus, the total time between the initial expansion and final collapse of the universe will be 125,287,500,000 years. This figure of 125 billion years is very close to the scientific calculation. After this period the universe will become completely spiritual.

One of the aspects of the future world will be extreme longevity on the part of mankind. Regarding this period, it is foretold, "As a child one shall die at a hundred years old" (Isaiah 65:20).[81] According to Rabbi Isaac of Acco, the lifespan will have become so extended that one who dies at the age of a hundred will be considered like a child currently dying at the age of 3. Thus, the normal lifespan will be approximately 33 times its present value, or around 2,000 years.[82] Isaac of Acco furthermore states that these will be divine years, so the human lifespan will eventually be extended to the order of eighty million years![83]

The Holy Palace

The is the seventh point, the center of the other six, as explained above (4:4).

He made sevens beloved

According to Rabbi Abraham Abulafia, there are seven levels in creation: Form, matter, combination, mineral, vegetable, animal, and man. Man is thus the seventh level, and is most beloved by God.[84]

4 : 16
שתי אבנים בונות שני בתים, שלש אבנים
בונות ששה בתים, ארבע אבנים בונות
ארבעה ועשרים בתים, חמש אבנים בונות מאה
ועשרים בתים, שש אבנים בונות שבע מאות
ועשרים בתים, שבע אבנים בונות חמשת אלפים
וארבעים בתים, מכאן ואילך צא וחשוב מה שאין
הפה יכול לדבר ואין האוזן יכולה לשמוע:

Two stones build 2 houses
Three stones build 6 houses
Four stones build 24 houses
Five stones build 120 houses
Six stones build 620 houses
Seven stones build 5040 houses
From here on go out and calculate
that which the mouth cannot speak
and the ear cannot hear.

Two stones

Here the letters of the alphabet are called "stones." The Kabbalists say that they are "stones quarried from the great Name of God."[85]

The text here is discussing the number of permutations possible with a given number of letters. If one has 2 letters, AB, one can permute them in 2 ways: AB and BA. These are the "2 stones" that "build 2 houses."

If one has 3 letters, one can make 6 permutations: ABC, ACB, BAC, BCA, CAB, CBA. Use has already been made of this above (1:13, 3:6-8). In a similar manner, 4 letters can be permuted in 24 ways, and 5 in 120.

The numbers are not difficult to obtain. If one starts with one letter X, a second letter can be placed either to its right or to its left. This gives 2 permutations: AX and XA.

Now if we take each combination XY, we can place a third letter in three possible positions: AXY, XAY, XYA. Since the letters XY themselves could be permuted in 2 ways, the total number of permutations is 2×3, or 6.

Similarly, if we have 3 letters XYZ, a fourth letter can be placed in one of 4 places: AXYZ, XAYZ, XYAZ, XYZA. Since the 3 letters XYZ can be permuted in 6 different ways, the total number of permutations is 6×4, or 24.

If we then take 4 letters WXYZ, a fifth letter can be inserted on one of 5 places: AWXYZ, WAXYZ, WXAYZ, WXYAZ, WXYZA. Since WXYZ can be permuted in 24 ways, the total number of permutations is 5×24, or 120.

We therefore see, that for a given number of letters, the number of permutations is given by

$$1 \times 2 \times 3 \times \ldots \times N.$$

This is known as N factorial, and is usually written $n!$ The number of permutations for all numbers of letters up to 22 is given in Tables 42 and 43 on page 192.

In general, letter permutations played an important role in the practices of the meditative Kabbalists. These permutations were often chanted very much like a mantra in order to bring about a desired state of consciousness.[86] A number of such texts contain extensive tables of such permutations.[87]

That which the mouth cannot speak

This expression is also found in the Talmud.[88]

Assume that a person wished to pronounce all 5040 possible permutations of seven letters. He would therefore have to pronounce a total of 5040×7, or 35,280 letters. Assuming that he could pronounce three letters a second, it would take over three hours to recite them all. Difficult, but not impossible.

Table 42. Permutations for 7 letters.

Number of Letters	Permutations		
1	1	=	1
2	1 × 2	=	2
3	1 × 2 × 3	=	6
4	1 × 2 × 3 × 4	=	24
5	1 × 2 × 3 × 4 × 5	=	120
6	1 × 2 × 3 × 4 × 5 × 6	=	720
7	1 × 2 × 3 × 4 × 5 × 6 × 7	=	5040

Table 43. Permutations for 22 letters.

Number of Letters	Permutations	N
1	1	1!
2	2	2!
3	6	3!
4	24	4!
5	120	5!
6	720	6!
7	5,040	7!
8	40,320	8!
9	362,880	9!
10	3,628,800	10!
11	39,916,800	11!
12	479,001,600	12!
13	6,227,020,800	13!
14	87,178,291,200	14!
15	1,307,674,368,000	15!
16	20,922,789,888,000	16!
17	355,687,428,096,000	17!
18	6,402,373,705,728,000	18!
19	121,645,100,408,832,000	19!
20	2,432,902,008,176,640,000	20!
21	51,090,942,171,709,440,000	21!
22	1,124,000,727,777,607,680,000	22!

If one wished to pronounce all possible permutations of eight letters, he would have to recite a total of 40,320 × 8, or 322,560 letters.
At the same rate, this would take approximately thirty hours. For all
practical purposes, this is outside the realm of normal human capa-
bility. The text therefore states that this is something that "the mouth
cannot speak, and the ear cannot hear."

The Sefer Yetzirah includes it here, since it is possible to pronounce all the permutations of the seven Doubles, and apparently,
this was done in some techniques.[89] In the next chapter, the text will
be speaking of the twelve Elementals, which can be permuted almost
a half billion ways. At the same rate as above, it would take 63 years
to pronounce all these permutations.

From Table 43, we see that there are about a sextillion (10^{21}) possible permutations of all 22 letters of the Hebrew alphabet. This is
very close to the total number of stars in the observable universe.
This universe contains around a hundred billion (10^{11}) galaxies, each
one with approximately ten billion (10^{10}) stars. A very similar figure
is also found in the Talmud.[90] Thus, from the permutations of the
alphabet, a name can be formed for every star in the universe. This
is in accordance with the teaching that every star has an individual
name.[91]

CHAPTER FIVE

5:1 שתים עשרה פשוטות ה' ו' ז', ח'
ט' י', ל' נ' ס', ע' צ' ק', יסודן
שיחה הרהור הלוך, ראיה שמיעה מעשה, תשמיש
ריח שינה, רוגז לעיטה שחוק:

Twelve Elementals:
  Heh (ה), Vav (ו), Zayin (ז),
  Chet (ח), Tet (ט), Yud (י),
  Lamed (ל), Nun (נ), Samekh (ס),
  Eyin (ע), Tzadi (צ), Kuf (ק).
Their foundation is
  speech, thought, motion,
  sight, hearing, action,
  coition, smell, sleep,
  anger, taste, laughter.

Anger

This can also be interpreted as temper or agressiveness.

Taste

The Hebrew word here, *L'eitah*, literally means swallowing. Many commentaries, however, interpret it to mean taste.[1]

These attributes do not have opposites. They can either be present or absent, but their absence is not the opposite of their presence. They are therefore represented by the twelve Elementals, which only have a single sound.

As we shall see, these qualities parallel the twelve months, as well as the twelve signs of the zodiac. They also have a parallel in the twelve tribes of Israel.

There are two ways of ordering the twelve tribes. The first is that which occurs in the beginning of the Book of Exodus (1:2-5): Reuben, Simeon, Levi, Judah, Issachar, Zebulun, Benjamin, Dan, Naftali, Gad, Asher, Joseph.[2]

The first six here are Reuben, Simeon, Levi, Judah, Issachar, and Zebulun. These are the six sons of Leah in order of their birth.[3] Then

Table 44. The twelve tribes.

Letter	Month	Sign	Permutation	Exodus	Numbers	House
ה	Nissan	Aries	YHVH	Reuben	Judah	Life
ו	Iyar	Taurus	YHHV	Simeon	Issachar	Property
ז	Sivan	Gemini	YVHH	Levi	Zebulun	Attraction
ח	Tamuz	Cancer	HVHY	Judah	Reuben	Ancestors
ט	Av	Leo	HVYH	Issachar	Simeon	Descendents
י	Elul	Virgo	HHVY	Zebulun	Gad	Health
ל	Tishrei	Libra	VHYH	Benjamin	Ephraim	Coition
נ	Cheshvan	Scorpio	VHHY	Dan	Manasseh	Death
ס	Kislev	Sagittarius	VYHH	Naftali	Benjamin	Travel
ע	Tevet	Capricorn	HYHV	Gad	Dan	Government
צ	Shevat	Aquarius	HYVH	Asher	Asher	Friends
ק	Adar	Pisces	HHYV	Joseph	Naftali	Enemies

comes Benjamin, the son of Rachel. Joseph, the other son of Rachel, was in Egypt, and is therefore not mentioned until the end. Following these are Dan and Naftali, the sons of Bilhah, Rachel's handmaid. Then comes Gad and Asher, the sons of Leah's handmaid, Zilpah, who were born after the sons of Bilhah.

A number of authorities list the twelve tribes in this order.[4] According to this, Joseph's sign comes out to be Pisces (Dagim), and this is also reflected in Talmudic teachings[5] (see Table 44).

Other authorities list the tribes in the order of their camps in the desert.[6] See figure 47 on page 200. This order is: Judah, Issachar, Zebulun; Reuben, Simeon, Gad; Ephraim, Manasseh, Benjamin; Dan, Asher, Naftali.[7] On the eastern camp was Judah, Issachar and Zebulun; on the south, Reuben, Simeon, and Gad; on the west, Ephraim, Manasseh, and Benjamin, and on the north, Dan, Asher, and Naftali. According to some authorities, this was also the order of the stones on the Urim and Thumim.[8]

This change of order occured after Levi was given the priesthood and removed from the order of the tribes. To complete the twelve, Joseph was divided into two tribes, Ephraim and Manasseh. This was in accordance to Jacob's blessing, "Ephraim and Manasseh shall be like Reuben and Simeon to me" (Genesis 48:5).

When the traits are in the order given in our (Gra) version, the tribes must be matched up with them in the order of the camps.[9] The division of Joseph, however, is not considered, and therefore, Joseph is in the place of Ephraim, and Levi in the place of Manasseh. See Table 45.

Table 45. The Gra version.

Month	Quality	Tribe	
Nissan	Speech	Judah	
Iyar	Thought	Issachar	
Sivan	Action	Zebulun	
Tamuz	Sight	Reuben	
Av	Hearing	Simeon	
Elul	Action	Gad	
Tishrei	Coition	Ephraim	(Joseph)
Cheshvan	Smell	Manasseh	(Levi)
Kislev	Sleep	Benjamin	
Tevet	Anger	Dan	
Shevat	Taste	Asher	
Adar	Laughter	Naftali	

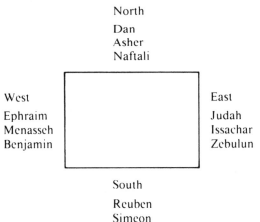

North

Dan
Asher
Naftali

West   East

Ephraim   Judah
Menasseh   Issachar
Benjamin   Zebulun

South

Reuben
Simeon
Gad

Figure 47. The tribes in the desert.

These twelve attributes also parallel the twelve permutations of
the Tetragrammaton. Even though four letters can normally be permuted 24 different ways, since two letters are the same here, this
number is halved.[10] See figure 48.

One begins with the name YHVH. Retaining the Y at the beginning, the V is first placed at the end (YHHV), and then immediately
after the Y (YVHH). See figure 49 on page 202.

The Y is then placed at the end, setting the first H in the beginning (HVHY). As before, the middle letter, which is now the final H,
is first placed at the end (HVYH). It is then placed after the initial
letter (HHVY).

The H in the initial permutation in this triad (HVHY) is then
placed at the end, leaving the V at the beginning (VHYH). Again, the
middle letter, the Y, is first placed at the end (VHHY), and then after
the first letter (VYHH).

The V is then placed at the end, leaving the final H in the beginning (HYHV). The middle H is then moved to the end (HYVH), and
then to the second position (HHYV).

According to most authorities, this is the order of permutations
of the Tetragrammaton paralleling the months of the year.[11] There
are certain verses that also pertain to these, where the letters of the
permutations appear as either the initial or final letters of the
words.[12]

Also associated with these are the Twelve Houses, which are the twelve angular divisions of the sky. See Table 45 on page 199. The positioning of the constellations and planets in these determine their astrological influence.[13] This division is also used in western astrology.

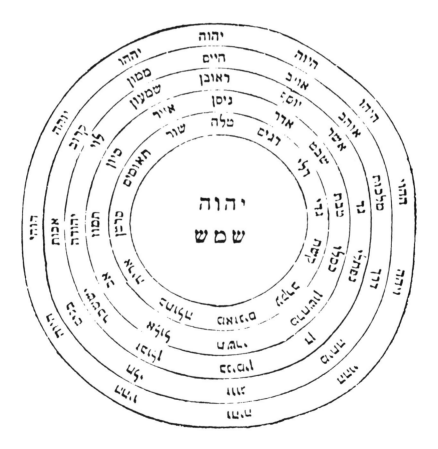

Figure 48. Circle of permutations, houses, tribes, months, and signs (according to Raavad 5a).

ניסן חסד: גולגלתא דנוקבא	יְהֹוָה אֲהִיָה יִשְׂמְחוּ הַשָּׁמַיִם וְתָגֵל הָאָרֶץ:
אייר גבורה: אוז ימין דנוק'	יְהַוֻ אֲהַהִי יִתְהַלֵּל הַמִּתְהַלֵּל הַשְׂכֵּל וְיָדוֹעַ:
סיון תפארת: אוז שמא' דנוק'	יּוְהַה אִיהַה יְרוּתִיי וְגִלְצֵלַע הַמִּשְׁכָּן הַשֵּׁנִית:
תמוז נצח : עין יסין דניק'	הֲוְהִי הֶיהָא זֶה אֵינֶנּוּ שׁוֶה לִי:
אב הוד : עין שמאל דנוק'	הַוְיַה הַיָּאה הַסֻּכָּה נִשְׁמַע יִשְׂרָאֵל הַיּוֹם:
אלול יסוד : חוטמא דניק'	הִהְיֶי הִתְיָא וּצְדָקָה תִּהְיֶה לָּנוּ כִּי:
תשרי חסד : גלגלתא דרא	וְהָיָה יָהָאָב וַיִּרְאוּ אוֹתָהּ שָׂרֵי פַרְעֹה:
חשון גב רה: אוז יסין דז"א	וְהַחֵי יֹהַהָא וְרָגַשׁ הַיּוֹם הַזֶּה יְהוָה:
כסלו תפאר":אוז שמא'דז"א	וַיְהָה יָאהָה וַיִּרְא יוֹשֵׁב הָאָרֶץ הַכְּנַעֲנִי:
טבת נצח : עין יסין דז"א	הָיְהוּ הָאֵהִי לַיהוה אַתִּי וּגְרוּסָתָהּ שְׂמֹן:
שבט הוד :עין שמאל דז"א	הַוֻיֶה הַאִיהָי הָסֵר יְסִירֵנוּ וְהָיָה הִיא:
אדר יסוד : חוטמא דז"א	הַהְיֻו הַהָאִי עִירֹה וְלַשּׂוֹרֵקָה בְּנִי אֲתֹנוֹ:

Figure 49. Permutations of YHVH and EHYH according to Or HaLevanah, p. 86. Elul and Adar are interchanged according to the older Kabbalists. Also included are the verses from which the permutations are derived, the Sefirot, and organs of Partzufim.

5:2

שתים עשרה פשוטות ה' ו' ז', ח' ט' י', ל' נ' ס',
ע' צ' ק', יסודן שנים עשר גבולי אלכסון, גבול
מזרחית רומית גבול מזרחית צפונית גבול מזרחית
תחתית, גבול דרומית רומית גבול דרומית מזרחית
גבול דרומית תחתית, גבול מערבית רומית גבול
מערבית דרומית גבול מערבית תחתית, גבול צפונית
רומית גבול צפונית מערבית גבול צפונית תחתית,
ומתרחבין והולכין עד עדי עד והן הן גבולות עולם:

Twelve Elementals
   HVZ ChTY LNS OTzQ (הוז חטי לנס עצק)
Their foundation is the twelve diagonal boundaries:
   The east upper boundary
   The east northern boundary
   The east lower boundary
      The south upper boundary
      The south eastern boundary
      The south lower boundary
   The west upper boundary
   The west southern boundary
   The west lower boundary
      The north upper boundary
      The north western boundary
      The north lower boundary
They extend continually until eternity of eternities
And it is they that are the boundaries of the Universe.

The twelve Elementals are said to relate to the twelve diagonal boundaries. See Table 46 on page 204. These correspond to the twelve edges of a cube. When a person uses these letters in any meditation, he must also concentrate on the appropriate direction.

The ordering here begins on the east, and then goes through the four primary directions: east, south, west, north. This corresponds to the teaching, "Whenever you turn, turn toward the right."[14]

The ordering of directions is also the same as that of the four camps in the desert.[15] The twelve diagonal boundaries thus correspond to the twelve tribes. It is for this reason that our (Gra) version gives three boundaries for each of the four sides. These correspond to the three tribes in each of the four camps.[16]

In each of these four directions, one first takes the upward boundary, then the right boundary, and then the lower boundary. In

Table 46. Two versions of the diagonal boundaries.

Letter	Gra, Long Version	Short Version	Permutation	Tribe
ה	east upper	east north	YHVH	Judah
ו	east north	east south	YHHV	Issachar
ז	east lower	east upper	YVHH	Zebulun
ח	south upper	east lower	HVHY	Reuben
ט	south east	north upper	HVYH	Simeon
י	south lower	north lower	HHVY	Gad
ל	west upper	west south	VHYH	Joseph
נ	west south	west north	VHHY	Levi
ס	west lower	west upper	VYHH	Benjamin
ע	north upper	west lower	HYHV	Dan
צ	north west	south upper	HYVH	Asher
ק	north lower	south lower	HHYV	Naftali

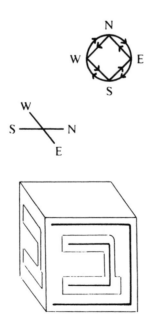

Figure 50. The letter Bet formed by the path of tracing the boundaries.

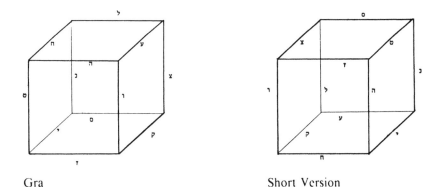

Gra   Short Version

Figure 51. The position of the Elementals according to both main versions.

this manner, one describes the letter Bet (ב) on each side. This corresponds to the teaching that the world was created with a Bet, this being the first letter of the Torah.[17] See figure 50.

A number of other versions give the twelve boundaries like they are here.[18] Other versions, however, use a different system. They give all the eastern boundaries first, then the two remaining northern ones, then all the western boundaries, and finally the two remaining southern edges.[19] See figure 51.

The Bahir relates these twelve diagonals to the Tree of Life.[20] There is a one-to-one relationship between the diagonal boundaries and the diagonal lines in the Tree of Life diagram.

These twelve boundaries also correspond to the twelve permutations of the Tetragrammaton. The permutations beginning with Y corresponding to the east; those beginning with the first H, to the south; the V, to the west, and the final H, to the north.[21]

They extend to eternity of eternities

The term, "eternity of eternities," which in Hebrew is *Adey Ad*, has already been discussed (1:5) as denoting a realm beyond space and time. The use of the term here would imply that the diagonal boundaries actually extend beyond the realm of space and time.

Earlier, when the Sefer Yetzirah (4:4) spoke of the six primary directions, it did not call them boundaries. The reason why they are called "boundaries" (*gevulim*) here is because they are used in method of meditating on the "boundaries" of space. The initiate meditates on the four letters Bet which seal the universe on four sides, setting the limits of thought.[22] He also meditates on the twelve permutations of the Tetragrammaton, which correspond to the twelve diagonals. In this manner, he can reach the level where they extend to "eternity of eternities," beyond the realm of space and time.

In discussing the twelve diagonals, the Bahir says, "On the inside of them is the Tree."[23] This is the Tree of Life, the array of the Ten Sefirot, connected by the 22 letters. The Tree is not inside the twelve boundaries from an earthly point of view, since it is external to the physical universe. It is only inside these boundaries when viewed from the point at infinity, that has been discussed earlier (1:7). It is at this point that all the boundaries are unified.

When a person meditates on the infinity of the diagonal boundaries, he is also able to move along the diagonal paths in the Tree of Life. This is important, since it is much easier to ascend along the diagonals than along the vertical paths.

Boundaries of the Universe

These boundaries parallel the boundaries of the twelve tribes mentioned in Ezekiel 48. Each of these diagonal boundaries relates to one of the twelve tribes.

According to the Talmud, these boundaries correspond to the twelve pillars upon which the universe rests.[24] This is based on the verse, "He stood up the boundaries of the nations, according to the number of the children of Israel" (Deuteronomy 32:8). The Talmud also relates these to the "arms of the universe."

Instead of "boundaries of the Universe," the Short Version reads, "arms of the Universe."[25] The obvious allusion is to the verse (Deuteronomy 33:26-27):

> There is none like the God of Jeshurun
> The Rider of the heavens is your Helper
> His pride is in the skies (*shekhakim*).
>> A dwelling is the God of eternity
>> And below are the Arms of the Universe
>> He drives the enemy from before you
>> And He said, "Destroy!"

This verse occurs after the blessing of the tribes, where Moses blesses the entire nation of Israel.[26] Although the verse is speaking of

God helping the Israelites in a mundane sense, it also has mystical overtones.

Moses begins by calling God, "the Rider of the heavens." The word "rider," *rokhev* (רוכב), is closely related to *markava* (מרכבה), the mystical "chariot" that is the essence of the mystical experience. The concept of "riding" involves traveling and leaving one's natural place.[27] When Moses says that God "rides" the heavens, it means that He leaves His natural state where He is absolutely unknowable and inconceivable, and allows Himself to be visualized in a mystical vision.

As the verse continues, this takes place through the skies known as *Shekhakim*. This term always refers to the two Sefirot, Netzach and Hod, which are the Sefirot involved in prophecy and inspiration.[28]

It then says, "A dwelling (*me'onah*) is the God of eternity." As discussed earlier (1:5), the word *ma'on* (and *me'onah*) indicate a level above space and time, the "place of the universe."[29]

The word for "eternal" here is Kedem, which usually indicates Keter.[30] The Hebrew word for Crown, Keter (כתר) also comes from the root *Katar* (כתר), meaning to "surround."[31] It is through the attribute of Keter or Kedem (eternity) that God encompasses all space and time.

It is below this that there exist the "Arms of the Universe." These are the infinities involving the twelve diagonal boundaries.

On the highest level, we conceive of God as being totally divorced from all space and time. This conception involves a state of consciousness that pertains neither to perception nor to nonperception. On a lower level, we see Him as the one who defines space and time, as the "Place of the Universe." This involves a state of consciousness perceiving Nothingness. On a still lower level, we see God as being beyond the boundaries of the universe.

Thus, if a person wishes to experience God, he must begin at the lower level and work his way upward. He therefore begins with the "arms of the Universe," contemplating the infinity of space in the twelve diagonal boundaries. Only after this can he reach the level of "a Dwelling is the God of eternity," where he conceives God as the "Place of the Universe." Finally, however, he must attain a conception of God as being totally divorced from space and time. He then sees Him as the "Rider of the heavens," who merely uses all depictions as a means through which He can be conceptualized.

A very important element in attaining the mystical experience is the negation of the self. When a person sees himself as nothing, then his self becomes transparent to the Divine. Commenting on the verse, "from under the Arms of the Universe," the Talmud states that a person must "make himself like he does not exist."[32] Through contemplating the infinities of the universe, one can nullify the ego.

In another very significant teaching, the Talmud states that, "The spirit (*ruach*) depends on the stormwind (*sa'arah*) . . . and the stormwind hangs from the *arms* of God."[33] This is also based on the verse, "From under the Arms of the Universe." The stormwind (*sa'arah*), however, was the first manifestion of Ezekiel's vision, as he says, "I looked, and behold, a stormwind coming out of the north" (Ezekiel 1:4).[34] The stormwind relates to the stormy state of consciousness that precedes the true mystical experience, which is called "Spirit" (*Ruach*).

The Talmud states that the state of *Sa'arah*, which is the gateway to the mystical experience, depends on the Arms of the Universe. One attains this state when one meditates on the infinities of the diagonal boundaries and the permutations of the Tetragrammaton associated with them.

In the text here, we see that the ordering of the twelve diagonal boundaries begins with the east and ends with the north. Since the last direction upon which one meditates is the north, Ezekiel saw the "stormwind coming from the north."

The state of "stormwind," as well as the "great cloud, and flashing fire" seen by Ezekiel are the forces of the evil Husks (*Klipah*), which must be breached before one can enter into the mysteries.[35] The passage in Deuteronomy therefore concludes, "He drives the enemy from before you." Since after contemplating the "Arms of the Universe," one encounters the enemy—the *Klipah*—Moses had to promise that God would drive this force away and allow one to enter unharmed.[36]

In the Long Version, the reading here in Sefer Yetzirah is "Heights of the Universe." Some commentaries state that these "Heights" are the "Arms of the Universe."[37]

The term, "Heights of the Universe," occurs three times in scripture. In Jacob's blessing to Joseph, he grants him, "the desire of the Heights of the Universe" (Genesis 49:26). Moses likewise blessed the tribe of Joseph with, "the treasure of the Heights of the Universe" (Deuteronomy 33:15).[38]

The Zohar states that these Heights are related to the feminine principle in creation, especially to the Sefirah of Malkhut.[39] It is through meditation on the twelve infinite lines of the universe that one can enter into Malkhut and begin the climb up the Tree of Life.

The twelve diagonal boundaries are therefore like transmission lines, through which creative energy flows into the universe from the twelve diagonal paths in the Tree of Life. As such, these infinities are the interface between the physical and the transcendental.

5:3 שתים עשרה פשוטות ה' ו' ז', ח' ט' י', ל' נ' ס',
ע' צ' ק', יסודן חקקן חצבן צרפן שקלן והמירן
וצר בהם שנים עשר מזלות בעולם שנים עשר חדשים
בשנה שנים עשר מנהיגים בנפש זכר ונקבה:

Twelve Elementals
   HVZ ChTY LNS OTzQ (הוז חטי לנס עצק)
Their foundation is [that]
He engraved them, carved them, permuted them,
   weighed them, and transformed them,
And with them He formed
   twelve constellations in the Universe
   twelve months in the Year
   and twelve directors in the Soul,
     male and female.

5:4 שנים עשר מזלות בעולם טלה שור תאומים
סרטן אריה בתולה מאזנים עקרב קשת גדי
דלי דגים:

Twelve constellations in the Universe:
   Aries (T'leh, the Ram)
   Taurus (Shor, the Bull)
   Gemini (Teumim, the Twins)
     Cancer (Sartan, the Crab)
     Leo (Ari, the Lion)
     Virgo (Betulah, the Virgin)
   Libra (Maznayim, the Scales)
   Scorpio (Akrav, the Scorpion)
   Sagittarius (Keshet, the Archer)
     Capricorn (Gedi, the Kid)
     Aquarius (Deli, the Water Drawer)
   Pisces (Dagin, the Fish).

Table 47. Hebrew lunar months and their correspondences.

Month	Equivalent	A	B	Sign	Angel*
Nissan	March-Apr.	Samael	Uriel	Aries	Uriel
Iyar	Apr.-May	Aniel	Imriel	Taurus	Lahatiel
Sivan	May-June	Gansharish	Tzafaniel	Gemini	Paniel
Tamuz	June-July	Cadniel	Tariel	Cancer	Zuriel
Av	July-Aug.	Tzidkiel	Barakiel	Leo	Barakiel
Elul	Aug.-Sept.	Akhniel	Paniel	Virgo	Chaniel
Tishrei	Sept.-Oct.	Barakiel	Tzuriel	Libra	Tzuriel
Cheshvan	Oct.-Nov.	Ismariel	Kabriel	Scorpio	Gabriel
Kislev	Nov.-Dec.	Gabriel	Adniel	Sagittarius	Maduniel
Tevet	Dec.-Jan.	Gabriel	Tzafiel	Capricorn	Shaniel
Shevat	Jan.-Feb.	Uriel	Yariel	Aquarius	Gabriel
Adar	Feb.-March	Berakhiel	Sumiel	Pisces	Rumiel

*According to Raziel 416, 141.

5:5   שנים עשר חדשים בשנה ניסן אייר סיון תמוז
אב אלול תשרי חשון כסלו טבת שבט אדר:

Twelve months in the year
Nissan, Iyar, Sivan,
Tamuz, Av, Elul,
Tishrei, Cheshvan, Kislev,
Tevet, Shevat, Adar.

The references to the zodiac are shown in Table 47 on page 210.
Figure 52 shows the zodiac as it appeared in the 1720 edition of
Tzurat HaAretz.

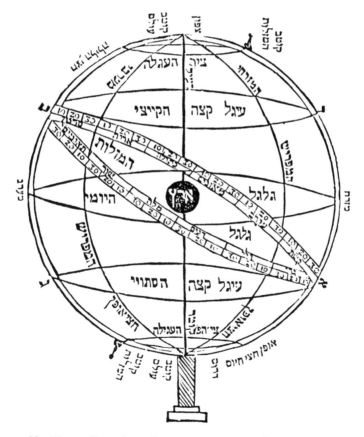

Figure 52. The zodiac (from Tzurat HaAretz, *p. 59a).*

5:6   שנים עשר מנהיגים בנפש זכר ונקבה שתי ידים
שתי רגלים שתי כליות מרה דקין כבד קורקבן
קבה טחול:

> Twelve directors in the soul
>   male and female,
> The two hands, the two feet,
>   the two kidneys,
>   the gall bladder, the intestines,
>   the liver, the korkeban,
>   the kivah, the spleen.

The intestines

In Hebrew, the word here is *Dakkin*. This usually denotes the
small intestine, but it can also include the large intestine or colon.

In other versions, instead of *Dakkin*, the Sefer Yetzirah uses the
term *Massas* or *Hemsess*. Ordinarily in Hebraic literature, this does
not denote a human organ. The term usually refers to the Omasum
or manyplies, the third stomach in ruminating (cud-chewing) animals
such as cattle.[40] See figure 53 on page 213. This organ is also called
the psalterium, since its longitudinal folds are arranged like the leaves
in a book.

According to a number of commentaries, the *Massas* denotes the
stomach in man.[41] In a number of places, the midrash implies that
the function of the *Massas* is to "grind" food.[42]

According to the substitution in the Gra Version here, it would
appear that the analogue of the *Massas* in man is the small intestine.
This is also supported by a number of authorities.[43] This would be
in agreement with the Kabbalists, since according to them, the stomach is the *Korkeban*.

The Korkeban

The term *Korkeban* is most often used to denote the gizzard in
fowl.[44] In the Talmud and Midrash, however, this term is occasionally if rarely used to denote a human organ, usually identified with
the "grinding of food."[45]

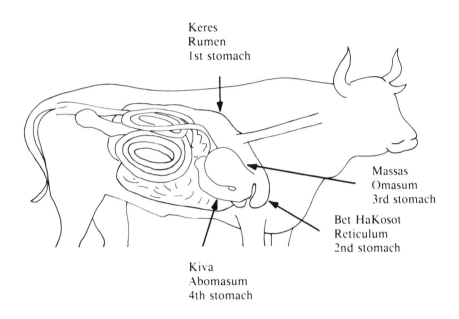

Figure 53. The four stomachs in a ruminant.

The Zohar clearly identifies the *Korkeban* as the stomach, and this opinion is shared almost universally by all later Kabbalists.[46]

Other commentaries identify the *Korkeban* with various different internal organs. Some say that it is the esophagus.[47] Others say that it is the small intestine.[48] Still another opinion has that it is the colon.[49] Some even say that it is the appendix.[50]

The Kivah

The *Kivah* is also an organ usually associated with animals. In ruminants, it is the fourth stomach, known as the maw or abomasum. In calves, it is also known as the rennet bag, since it contains the rennet making glands.[51] According to some commentaries, the *Kiva* is the stomach.[52] Others identify it with the intestine.[53] Another opinion has that it is the colon.[54]

In animals, the *Kiva* was part of the offering given to priests, as the Torah states, "They shall give to the priest the shoulder, the two cheeks, and the *Kiva*" (Deuteronomy 18:3). Maimonides states that the reason for this is because the *Kivah* is the first among the digestive organs, and this opinion is echoed by the Kabbalists.[55] According to this, the analogue in man would be the esophagus.

The Talmud and Zohar, however, apparently teach that the main function of the Ivah in man is to induce sleep.[56] This is also reflected in Sefer Yetzirah (5:9). This would indicate an organ of glandular nature, possibly the pancreas. Significantly, an early Midrash attributes to the *Kiva*, a "sleep of sweetness."[57]

One reason why the *Kiva* might be associated with sleep is because in animals it is the organ that digests milk. The human analogue may also be associated with milk, and milk is known to induce sleep.[58] The Talmud also states that in general, eating brings on sleep.[59]

It is also possible that the *Korkeban* and *Kiva* are not human organs at all. This would mean that use is made of them only when the Sefer Yetzirah is used with relation to animals and birds. By making use of these organs, one may create an animal or bird rather than a human. This might have been the technique that the Talmudic sages used to create a prime calf.

5:7

המליך אות ה' בשיחה וקשר
לו כתר וצרפן זה בזה וצר בהם טלה בעולם
וניסן בשנה ורגל ימין בנפש זכר ונקבה:
המליך אות ו' בהרהור וקשר לו כתר
וצרפן זה בזה וצר בהם שור בעולם ואייר בשנה
וכוליא ימנית בנפש זכר ונקבה:
המליך אות ז' בהלוך וקשר לו כתר וצרפן זה בזה
וצר בהם תאומים בעולם וסיון בשנה ורגל שמאל
בנפש זכר ונקבה:

He made the letter Heh (ה) king over speech
and He bound a crown to it
And He combined one with another
And with them He formed
Aries in the Universe
Nissan in the Year
And the right foot in the Soul
male and female.

He made the letter Vav (ו) king over thought
And He bound a crown to it
And He combined one with another
And with them He formed
Taurus in the Universe
Iyar in the Year
And the right kidney in the Soul
male and female

He made the letter Zayin (ז) king over motion
And He bound a crown to it
And He combined one with another
And with them He formed
Gemini in the Universe
Sivan in the Year
And the left foot in the Soul
male and female.

5:8

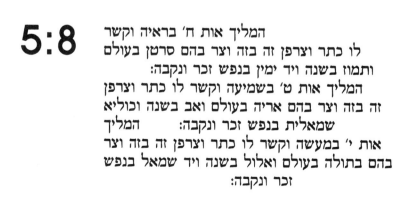

המליך אות ח' בראיה וקשר
לו כתר וצרפן זה בזה וצר בהם סרטן בעולם
ותמוז בשנה ויד ימין בנפש זכר ונקבה:
המליך אות ט' בשמיעה וקשר לו כתר וצרפן
זה בזה וצר בהם אריה בעולם ואב בשנה וכוליא
שמאלית בנפש זכר ונקבה: המליך
אות י' במעשה וקשר לו כתר וצרפן זה בזה וצר
בהם בתולה בעולם ואלול בשנה ויד שמאל בנפש
זכר ונקבה:

He made the letter Chet (ח) king over sight
  And He bound a crown to it
  And He combined one with another
And with them He formed
    Cancer in the Universe
    Tamuz in the Year
    And the right hand in the Soul
        male and female.

He made the letter Tet (ט) king over hearing
  And He bound a crown to it
  And He combined one with another
And with them He formed
    Leo in the Universe
    Av in the Year
    And the left kidney in the Soul
        male and female

He made the letter Yud (י) king over action
  And He bound a crown to it
  And He combined one with another
And with them He formed
    Virgo in the Universe
    Elul in the Year
    And the left hand in the Soul
        male and female.

5:9

המליך אות ל' בתשמיש וקשר
לו כתר וצרפן זה בזה וצר בהם מאזנים בעולם
ותשרי בשנה ומרה בנפש זכר ונקבה:
המליך אות נ' בריח וקשר לו כתר וצרפן
זה בזה וצר בהם עקרב בעולם וחשון בשנה ודקין
בנפש זכר ונקבה: המליך אות
ס' בשינה וקשר לו כתר וצרפן זה בזה וצר בהם קשת
בעולם וכסלו בשנה וקבה בנפש זכר ונקבה:

He made the letter Lamed (ל) king over coition
> *And He bound a crown to it*
> *And He combined one with another*

And with them He formed
>> *Libra in the Universe*
>> *Tishrei in the Year*
>> *And the gall bladder in the soul*
>>> *male and female.*

He made the letter Nun (נ) king over smell
> *And He bound a crown to it*
> *And He combined one with another*

And with them He formed
>> *Scorpio in the Universe*
>> *Cheshvan in the Year*
>> *And the intestine in the Soul*
>>> *male and female.*

He made the letter Samekh (ס) king over sleep,
> *And He bound a crown to it*
> *And He combined one with another*

And with them He formed
>> *Sagittarius in the Universe*
>> *Kislev in the Year*
>> *And the Kivah in the Soul*
>>> *male and female.*

5:10

המליך אות ע' ברוגז וקשר
לו כתר וצרפן זה בזה וצר בהם גדי בעולם
וטבת בשנה וכבד בנפש זכר ונקבה:
המליך אות צ' בלעיטה וקשר לו כתר וצרפן
זה בזה וצר בהם דלי בעולם ושבט בשנה וקורקבן
בנפש זכר ונקבה: המליך אות
ק' בשחוק וקשר לו כתר וצרפן זה בזה וצר בהם דגים
בעולם ואדר בשנה וטחול בנפש זכר ונקבה. עשאן
כמין עריבה סידרן כמין חומה ערכן כמין מלחמה:

He made the letter Eyin (ע) king over anger
  And He bound a crown to it
  And He combined one with another
And with them He formed
    Capricorn in the Universe
    Tevet in the Year
    And the liver in the Soul
      male and female.

He made the letter Tzdi (צ) king over taste
  And He bound a crown to it
  and He combined one with another
And with them He formed
    Aquarius in the Universe
    Shevat in the Year
    And the Korkeban in the Soul
      male and female.

He made the letter Kuf (ק) king over laughter
  And He bound a crown to it
  And He combined one with another
And with them He formed
    Pisces in the Universe
    Adar in the Year
    And the spleen in the Soul
      male and female.

He made them like a trough
He arranged them like a wall
He set them up like a battle.

There are several variant readings found in the different versions and commentaries. The major ones are given in Table 48 on page 219.

In this version, the *Kivah* is associated with sleep, the liver with anger, and the spleen with laughter. The same association is found in the Talmud.[60]

Here we see that the signs of the zodiac are associated with the twelve Hebrew lunar months, rather than with the position of the Sun, as in Western astrology. The assignment here approximates that of Western astrology, but is more accurate from a Kabbalistc viewpoint.

If one wishes to attain a deep understanding of the significance of the astrological signs, one must contemplate the patterns of stars that form each one. As one gazes at these stellar arrays, not only does

Table 48. Various versions of the meaning of the signs.

		Gra	Short[1]	Long[2]	Saadia[3]	Ramak[4]
ה	Nissan	speech	[sight]	speech	sight	sight
	Aries	R. foot	R. hand	liver	liver	R. hand
ו	Iyar	thought	[hearing]	thought	hearing	hearing
	Taurus	R. kidney	L. hand	gall	gall	L. hand
ז	Sivan	motion	[smell]	motion	smell	speech
	Gemini	L. foot	R. foot	spleen	spleen	R. foot
ח	Tamuz	sight	[speech]	sight	speech	taste
	Cancer	R. hand	L. foot	massas	massas	L. foot
ט	Av	hearing	[taste]	hearing	taste	anger
	Leo	L. kidney	R. kidney	R. kidney	R. kidney	R. kidney
י	Elul	action	[coition]	action	action	motion
	Virgo	L. hand	L. kidney	L. kidney	L. kidney	L. kidney
ל	Tishrei	coition	[action]	coition	coition	laughter
	Libra	gall	liver	korkeban	korkeban	liver
נ	Cheshvan	smell	[motion]	smell	motion	thought
	Scorpio	intestine	spleen	kivah	kivah	spleen
ס	Kislev	sleep	[anger]	sleep	anger	coition
	Sagittarius	kivah	gall	R. hand	R. hand	gall
ע	Tevet	anger	[laughter]	anger	laughter	sleep
	Capricorn	liver	massas	L. hand	L. hand	massas
צ	Shevat	taste	[thought]	taste	thought	smell
	Aquarius	korkeban	kivah	R. foot	R. foot	kivah
ק	Adar	laughter	[sleep]	laughter	sleep	action
	Pisces	spleen	korkeban	L. foot	L. foot	korkeban

[1] The traits are not listed explicitly in the Short Version, but are given by the Raavad. This ordering, however, is found in 5:1. Donash has a similar ordering, but he interchanges liver and spleen, sight and hearing, coition and taste. *Kuzari* 4:25 also uses this ordering, but instead of "anger, laughter, thought," he has, "thought, anger, laughter."

[2] This ordering is also used by Ramak in *Pardes Rimonim* 21:16.

[3] Saadia 8:3. Also see 1:3, 6:5-15; Saadia B, here. This same ordering is found in the Long Version in the recap, 5:21, indicating that it was added from Saadia. This ordering was also used by Chakamoni 73a, Rabbi Eliezer Rokeach 10b, and by Rabbi Yosef Tzayach in *Sheirit Yosef* 10a, 11a, and *Tzaror HaChaim* 34b.

[4] *Shiur Komah* 15 (Adam), pp. 29a, b.

Table 49. Signs and planets of the zodiac.

Zodiac Influences		Planetary Influences	
Remainder	Sign	Remainder	Planet
0	Cancer	0	Mercury
1	Leo	1	Moon
2	Virgo	2	Saturn
3	Aries	3	Jupiter
4	Taurus	4	Mars
5	Gemini	5	Sun
6	Libra	6	Venus
7	Scorpio		
8	Sagittarius		
9	Capricorn		
10	Aquarius		
11	Pisces		

the picture of the sign emerge, but one also gains insight into its inner essence.

In general, it was forbidden to actually draw pictures of the figures represented by the astrological signs.[61] In ancient times, the making of such pictures actually led to the worship of these signs as gods.[62] To draw the stars alone, or even to connect them with lines so as to make their patterns recognizable, however, is permitted.[63]

For the purpose of contemplation, the pictures and diagrams found in most astrological texts are next to useless. Instead, we must turn to the writings of the ancients. One of the best descriptions of the constellations, dating from the second century, is found in Ptolemy's *Almagest*, and this is quoted in ancient Hebrew manuscripts.[64] I have used Ptolemy's tables in constructing the diagrams of the constellations.

He made them like a trough

The constellations are said to be like a trough because they channel spiritual sustenance down to the physical world. The months are like a wall. The parts of the body are involved in a constant state of war, as discussed later (6:3).[65]

Besides his time of birth, a person's name also plays an important role in determining astrological signs. In order to determine this influence, one must write the person's name and the name of his mother in Hebrew characters. The letters must then be added up, so as to determine the numerical value of both names.[66]

To determine the sign of the zodiac, one must cast off twelves, and take the remainder. That is, one must divide the above sum by twelve, and determine the remainder. This is used to determine the sign of the zodiac.[67]

To determine the planetary influence, one must cast off sevens. Like before, one must divide by seven, and retain only the remainder. This is used to determine the appropriate planet. Note that in the table, the order of the planets is that of Saturday night. In Hebrew reckoning, this is the beginning of the first day of the week, and hence, the first period of creation.

This method can more easily be understood if we take an example. Assume that a person's name is Abraham (אברהם) and his mother's name is Sarah (שרה). Making use of the numerical value for each letter, we see that Abraham has a numerical value of 248, while that for Sarah is 505. Adding the two together, the final sum is 753.

To determine the sign of the zodiac, we must divide by twelve, yielding 62, with a remainder of nine. Consulting Table 49 on page 220, we find that the appropriate sign is Capricorn.

Similarly, to determine the planet, we divide 753 by seven. The quotient is 107, with a remainder of four. We thus find that Mars will exert a strong influence on a person named Abraham, who is the son of Sarah.

Also important are the 28 "camps" of the Divine Presence, corresponding to the 28 days of the lunar month.[68] The length of the lunar month is 29 days, 12 hours, 2643 seconds (29.53059 days).[69] This is the period during which the Moon goes through all of its phases.

Besides this, there is also the sidereal month, the time during which the Moon passes through all twelve signs of the zodiac. This period is 27 days, 6 hours, 780 seconds (27.25902 days). This is the period during which the Moon revolves around the earth, and returns to its original position with regard to a fixed star.

The lunar month is longer than the sidereal month. The reason for this is because, in order to complete a lunar month, the Moon must not only pass through the twelve signs of the zodiac, but it must also occupy its previous position in relation to the Sun. During this month, however, the Sun itself has advanced through the zodiac. The lunar month is therefore longer than the sidereal month by a factor of one twelfth. The Moon therefore passes through each of the twelve signs of the zodiac in 2 days, 6 hours, 1865 seconds (2.271585 days).

Table 50. The 28 times of Ecclesiastes (3:2–8).

A time to be born	and a time to die.
A time to plant	and a time to uproot.
A time to kill	and a time to heal.
A time to wreck	and a time to build.
A time to weep	and a time to laugh.
A time of mourning	and a time of dancing.
A time to throw stones	and a time to hoard stones.
A time to embrace	and a time to shun.
A time to seek	and a time to lose.
A time to safeguard	and a time to discard.
A time to tear	and a time to sew.
A time to be still	and a time to speak.
A time to love	and a time to hate.
A time of war	and a time of peace.

Table 51. The 28 times and their associated qualities.

1. A time to be born (seed)	2. a time to die (desolation)
3. A time to plant (seed)	4. a time to uproot (desolation)
5. A time to kill (death)	6. a time to heal (life)
7. A time to wreck (death)	8. a time to build (life)
9. A time to throw stones (poverty)	10. a time to hoard stones (wealth)
11. A time to lose (poverty)	12. a time to seek (wealth)
13. A time to embrace (grace)	14. a time to shun (ugliness)
15. A time to safeguard (grace)	16. a time to discard (ugliness)
17. A time to be still (wisdom)	18. a time to speak (foolishness)
19. A time to sew (wisdom)	20. a time to tear (foolishness)
21. A time of war (war)	22. a time of peace (peace)
23. A time to hate (war)	24. a time to love (peace)
25. A time of mourning (subjugation)	26. a time of dancing (dominance)
27. A time to weep (subjugation)	28. a time to laugh (dominance)

Besides the 28 lunar days, the sidereal month can also be divided into 28 equal parts. Each one of these parts is one of the Moon's "camps." The moon passes through each of its camps in 23 hours, 1310 seconds.

The 28 camps parallel the 28 "times" mentioned in Ecclesiastes.[70] See Tables 50 and 51 on page 222. These are related to the seven qualities corresponding to the seven Doubles, as discussed above (4:2-3). See Table 52 on page 224.

The 28 camps are associated with the twelve signs of the zodiac through the 42 Letter Name, given above (4:14). See Table 53 on page 224. This name is combined with the letters of the Tetragrammaton in the manner shown in figure 54 on page 225. This yields a total of 168 letters, or six for each of the 28 camps.

The 168 letters can also be divided into twelve groups, each consisting of 14 letters. Each of these groups then corresponds to a specific sign of the zodiac, as given in Table 54 on page 225. It is these letters that are dominant as the Moon passes through each of the twelve signs.

Also associated with each of the twelve signs is a permutation of the names YHVH and Adonoy (אדני). By meditating on these combinations, as well as the derivatives of the 42 Letter Name, one can gain knowledge of things that will happen in the designated times. See figure 55 on page 226.

The 28 "times" of Ecclesiastes can be divided into two groups of 14. One group consists of the good times, while the other consists of the evil times. The 14 good times are said to come from the 14 letters of YHVH Elohenu YHVH:

YHVH ELHYNU YHVH   יהוה אלהינו יהוה

One then takes the letter, which in the alphabet comes after each of these 14. This yields the letters[71]

KUZU BMUKSZ KUZU   כוזו במוכסז כוזו

The 14 evil times are said to originate from these 14 letters. These 28 letters can therefore be used to transmit the appropriate concepts.

There is another system that also provides insight into each hour of the day. As discussed earlier (2:5), when various letters are combined with the Tetragrammaton, five vowels are used. When one wishes to make such a combination relating to the hours of the day, however, one must add a sixth vowel, the Shva (:).[72] The array associated with each letter of the Tetragrammaton then consists of 36 elements.

Table 52. The 28 times and the 14 letters of the three names.
YHVH Elohenu YHVH.

Seed	י	Y to be born	כ	K to die
	ה	H to plant	ו	U to uproot
Life	ו	V to heal	ז	Z to kill
	ה	H to build	ו	U to wreck
Wealth	א	E to hoard stones	ב	B to throw stones
	ל	L to seek	מ	M to lose
Grace	ה	H to embrace	ו	U to shun
	י	Y to safeguard	כ	K to discard
Wisdom	נ	N to be still	ס	S to speak
	ו	U to sew	ז	Z to tear
Peace	י	Y of peace	כ	K of war
	ה	H to love	ו	U to hate
Dominance	ו	V of dancing	ז	Z of mourning
	ה	H to laugh	ו	U to weep

Table 53. The 28 camps of the divine presence (The 42 letter name combined with the letters YHV).

1.	Y A HV Y B	2.	HV Y G HV	הו י ג הו	י א הו י ב
3.	Y Y HV Y T	4.	HV Y Tz HV	וה ט צ הו	י י הו י ת
5.	Y K HV Y R	6.	HV Y O HV	הו י ע הו	י ק הו י ר
7.	Y Sh HV Y T	8.	HV Y N HV	הו י נ הו	י ש הו י ט
9.	Y N HV Y G	10.	HV Y D HV	הו י ד הו	י נ הו י ג
11.	Y Y HV Y Kh	12.	HV Y Sh HV	הו י ש הו	י י הו י כ
13.	Y B HV Y T	14.	HV Y R HV	הו י ר הו	י ב הו י ט
15.	Y Tz HV Y Th	16.	HV Y G HV	הו י ג הו	י צ הו י ת
17.	Y Ch HV Y K	18.	HV Y B HV	הו י ב הו	י ח הו י ק
19.	Y T HV Y N	20.	HV Y O HV	הו י ע הו	י ט הו י נ
21.	Y Y HV Y G	22.	HV Y L HV	הו י ל הו	י י הו י ג
23.	Y P HV Y Z	24.	HV Y K HV	הו י ק הו	י פ הו י ז
25.	Y Sh HV Y K	26.	HV Y V HV	הו י ו הו	י ש הו י ק
27.	Y Tz HV Y Y	28.	HV Y Th HV	הו י ת הו	י צ הו י י

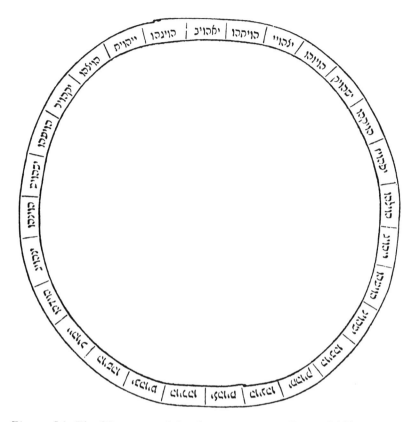

Figure 54. The 28 camps of the divine presence (Raavad 19b).

Table 54. The 28 camps divided among the 12 constellations.

Aries	Y A HV Y B HY Y G HV Y Y	י א הו י ב הו י ג הו י י
Taurus	HV Y TH HV Y TZ HV Y K HV	הו י ת הו י צ הו י ק הו
Gemini	Y R HV Y E HV Y SH HV Y T	י ר הו י ע הו י ש הו י ט
Cancer	HV Y N HV Y N HV Y G HV	הו י נ הו י נ הו י ג הו
Leo	Y D HV Y Y HV Y KH HV Y SH	י ד הו י י הו י כ הו י ש
Virgo	HV Y B HV Y T HV Y R HV	הו י ב הו י ט הו י ר הו
Libra	Y TZ HV Y TH HV Y G HV Y CH	י צ הו י ת הו י ג הו י ח
Scorpio	HV Y K HV Y B HV Y T HV	הו י ק הו י ב הו י ט הו
Sagittarius	Y N HV Y O HV Y Y HV Y G	י נ הו י ע הו י י הו י ג
Capricorn	HV Y L HV Y P HV Y Z HV	הו י ל הו י פ הו י ז הו
Aquarius	Y K HV Y SH HV Y K HV Y V	י ק הו י ש הו י ק הו י ו
Pisces	HV Y TZ HV Y Y HV Y TH HV	הו י צ הו י י הו י ת הו

ירהוי"ע הוי"ש הוי"ט מיד"נ מיג"ד יוה"ה תאומים	הוי"ה הוי"נ הויקה"ן אמי"ד מנד"י יהה"ן שור	יההו"י בההו"י נההו"י מהג"י אהדי"א יהו"ה טלה
הוי"ב הוי"ע הויכ"הו דהג"י דמהי"ג הוה"י בתולה	ידהו"י יההו"כ הוי"ש דימ"ג דינ"א היו"ה אריה	הוי"נ הוי"נ הוינה"ן הני"א דנמה"י היה"ן סרטן
ינההו"ע הוי"י הוי"נ נימ"ד נימד"א והה"י קשת	הוי"ק הוי"ב הויטה"ן גדי"א נדמה"י ויה"ה עקרב	יההוי"ח הוי"נ הוי"ה מהה"י נמהי"ד והי"ה מאזנים
הוי"נ הוי"י הוי"ח ה"ן ינמ"ד ינד"א ההו"י דגים	י"ק הוי"ש הוי"ק הוי"ן ידנ"א ידמה"ג היו"ה דלי	הוי"ל הוי"פ הויזה"ן יהד"ג ימהנ"ד הוי"ה גדי

Figure 55. The 28 camps divided among the twelve constellations. Includes permutations of YHVH and Adny (From Raavad, p. 20b).

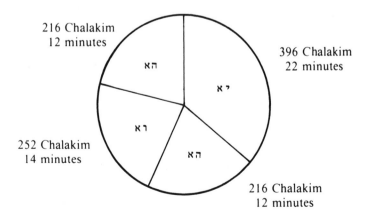

Figure 56. The Chalakim in an hour when they pertain to night hours.

הא   יוד

אהֲ   אה   אהֲ   אֲהֶ   אָהֲ   אֲהֶ   אִי   אִי   אֲי   אֲי   אִי   אִי
אֱהֶ   אֱהֶ   אֱהֶ   אֱהֶ   אֲהֶ   אֲהֶ   אֲהֶ   אִי   אִי   אִי   אִי   אִי   אִי
אֵהֲ   אֵה   אֵהֲ   אֵהֶ   אָהֲ   אֵהֲ   אִי   אִי   אִי   אִי   אִי   אִי
אֹהֲ   אֹה   אֹהֲ   אֹהֶ   אֹה   אֹה   אִי   אִי   אִי   אִי   אִי   אִי
אֹה   אֹה   אֹהֶ   אָהֶ   הָא   הַא   אִי   אִי   אִי   אִי   אִי   אִי
אֻהֲ   אֻה   אֻהֶ   אֻהֶ   אֻהֶ   אֻהֶ   אִי   אִי   אִי   אִי   אִי   אִי

Each Element = 6   Each Element = 11

Total = 216   Total = 396

הא   ואו

אהֲ   אה   אהֲ   אֲהֶ   אָהֲ   אֲהֶ   או   או   אֲו   אֲו   או   או
אֱהֶ   אֱהֶ   אֱהֶ   אֱהֶ   אֲהֶ   אֲהֶ   או   או   או   או   או   או
אֵהֲ   אֵה   אֵהֲ   אֵהֶ   אָהֲ   אֵהֲ   או   או   או   או   או   או
אֹהֲ   אֹה   אֹהֲ   אֹהֶ   אֹה   אֹה   או   או   או   או   או   או
אֹה   אֹה   אֹהֶ   אָהֶ   הָא   הַא   או   או   או   או   או   או
אֻהֲ   אֻה   אֻהֶ   אֻהֶ   אֻהֶ   אֻהֶ   או   או   או   או   או   או

Each Element = 6   Each Element = 7

Total = 216   Total = 252

Figure 57. Alef combined with the letters of the Tetragrammaton through six vowels.

Both in the Talmud and in Kabbalah, the normative division of the hour is into *Chalakim*, with 1080 *Chalakim* making an hour. Thus, there are 18 *Chalakim* to a minute.

The duration of each letter, expressed in *Chalakim*, is taken as being equal to its numerical value. Thus, Alef (א) is one *Chelek*, Yud (י) is ten, Heh (ה) is five, and Vav (ו) is six.

In the array, the Yud and Alef together add up to eleven. Since there are 36 elements in the array, its total numerical value is 36 × 11, or 396. Proceeding in the same manner with each of the four squares, the values obtained are 396, 216, 252, and 216. The total of all these is 1080. This is exactly the number of *Chalakim* in an hour. See figure 56 on page 226. Each of these combinations therefore pertains to a precise period in the hour. See figure 57.

There are, however, twelve permutations of the Tetragrammaton. These can either pertain to the twelve hours of the day, or to the twelve hours of the night.

When the Alef precedes the letters of the Name, as in figure 56, these permutations pertain to the twelve hours of the night. When the letters of the Name precede the Alef, they represent the twelve hours of the day.

CHAPTER SIX

6:1

אלו הם שלש אמות אמ״ש ויצאו
מהם שלשה אבות והם אויר מים
אש ומאבות תולדות, שלשה אבות ותולדותיהם
ושבעה כוכבים וצבאותיהם ושנים עשר גבולי
אלכסון. ראיה לדבר עדים נאמנים בעולם שנה נפש
ושנים עשר חק ושבעה ושלשה פקדן בתלי וגלגל
ולב:

These are the Three Mothers AMSh (אמש).
And from them emanated Three Fathers,
   and they are air, water, and fire.
      and from the Fathers, descendents.
Three Fathers and their descendents.
   And seven planets and their hosts,
   And twelve diagonal boundaries
A proof of this
   true witnesses in the Universe, Year, Soul
   and a rule of twelve
      and seven and three:
He set them in the Teli, the Cycle, and the Heart.

From them emanated three Fathers

This is the same as 3:2, except that here the Fathers "emanate," while above, they were "born."

From the Mothers, AMSh, emanated the concept of thesis, antithesis, and synthesis, as discussed earlier. These are the Fathers, represented by fire, water, and air. From this triad comes the three columns of the Sefirot, and from them, all the rest of creation.

The Teli

This is one of the most mysterious words in the Sefer Yetzirah. The term occurs neither in the Bible nor in the Talmud, and there is considerable discussion as to its meaning.[1]

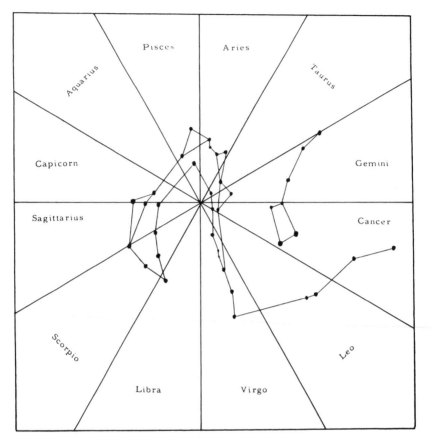

Figure 58. The constellations of Draco and Ursa Minor (according to Ptolemy).

The only place where we find a similar word is in a single reference to a weapon, where Jacob told Esau, "Take your instruments, your *Teli* and your bow" (Genesis 27:3). Some commentaries interpret the *Teli* here to be a kind of sword, and it is given this name because it hangs (*talah*) from one's side.[2] Others say that it is a quiver, in which the arrows are piled (*talal*).[3]

The term, however, appears more suggestive of a kind of bola. This is a line with a ball at the end, used to ensnare animals. It would be called a *Teli* because the ball hangs (*talah*) from the line. This is also supported by the fact that the scripture clearly states that Esau was to trap (*tzad*) an animal.

According to many Kabbalists, the Teli mentioned here in Sefer Yetzirah is the imaginary axis around which the heavens rotate.[4] It is seen as an imaginary line from which the celestial sphere hangs,

Figure 59. Draco. (Based on a 14th century Hebraic manuscript).

very much like a bola from its line. According to this, the word *Teli* (תלי) comes from the root *Talah* (תלה), meaning "to hang."[5]

Many authorities identify the *Teli* with the "Pole Serpent" (*Nachash Bare'ach*), mentioned in the verse, "By His spirit, the heavens were calmed, His hand has pierced the Pole Serpent" (Job 26:13).[6] It is also mentioned in the verse, "On that day, with His great, harsh sword, God will visit and overcome the Leviathan, the Pole Serpent, and the Leviathan, the Coiled Serpent, and He will kill the dragon of the sea" (Isaiah 27:1).

This Pole Serpent, which is identified with the Leviathan, may then be seen as an imaginary creature from which the earth hangs. Thus, in an ancient mystical Midrash, we find that the world "hangs from a fin of the Leviathan."[7]

The Pole Serpent is often associated with the constellation of Draco.[8] This is not surprising, since Draco is very close to the North Pole. Indeed, around 4500 years ago, Thuban, a star in Draco's tail, was the pole star.

There are, however, two imaginary poles in the sky. The first is the celestial pole, which is directly above the earth's north pole. The second is known as the ecliptic pole. This is the pole of the sphere of which the ecliptic is the equator.

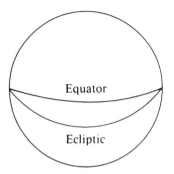

Figure 60. The Teli *as the obliquity between equator and ecliptic.*

The ecliptic is the great circle of the celestial sphere traced by the plane of the earth's orbit around the sun. If we view the sun and stars as revolving around the earth, we will notice that in the course of the year, at a given time each day, the sun will occupy a slightly different position in relation to the constellations and other stars. In this perspective, the ecliptic is the annual path of the sun moving from west to east through the heavens.[9]

In describing the positions of the stars, the ancients made use of the ecliptic pole, rather than the celestial pole. In this system, we find that the constellation of Draco actually surrounds the ecliptic pole. It also has stars in the sections of all the signs of the zodiac.[10] It is therefore literally the Pole Serpent, since it is the serpent that surrounds the ecliptic pole. See figures 58 and 59 on pages 232 and 233.

Since the Pole Serpent has stars in all the houses of the zodiac, it is also seen as supporting them all.[11] It is as if Draco was at the top of the celestial sphere, and all the other stars were hanging from it. As such, Draco is seen as the overseer and director of all the other stars. Draco is therefore associated with the Teli, which, as the Sefer Yetzirah states (6:3), is "over the Universe like a king on his throne." It is called the Teli because all the other constellations hang (*talah*) from it.

In ancient times, *the Teli*, in the form of Draco, was worshipped as an idolatrous deity.[12] Rabbi Isaac of Acco also identifies it with the idol Baal, mentioned in the Bible.[13]

Many philosophical commentaries on Sefer Yetzirah, as well as astronomical texts, interpret the *Teli* as being the inclination between two celestial planes.[14] In modern astronomy, this is usually called the obliquity, and it usually denotes the inclination separating the ecliptic and the celestial equator, which is the imaginary circle above the earth's equator, as shown in figure 60. In this sense, the *Teli* is also

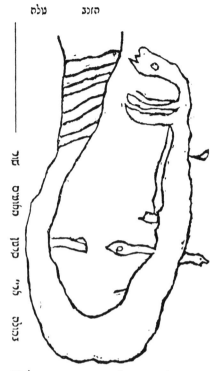

עולה הזנב

זוקפו ירך גדל עמוד גיד

ראש החלי דגים דלי גדי קשת עקרב מאזנים

Figure 61. The Teli *as it appears in Commentary of Rabbi Eliezer Rokeach of Wormes, p. 12b.*

often referred to as a dragon or fish. See figure 61. This is because it has the shape of a fish, wide in the center, and coming to a point at both ends.[15]

Hebrew astronomers also used the term *Teli* to denote the inclination of the orbit of a planet from the ecliptic, particularly in the case of the moon.[16]

There are two points where the orbit of a planet intersect the plane of the ecliptic. The point through which the planet passes from the south of the ecliptic plane to the north is called the ascending node, while the other point is known as the descending node. In medieval astronomy, the ascending node was often called the "dragon's head," while the descending node was referred to as the "dragon's tail." With regard to the intersection points of the equator and the ecliptic, these are the two equinoxes. See figure 62 on page 236. The vernal (spring) equinox is the head, while the autumnal equinox is the tail of the dragon.

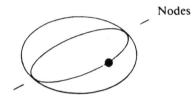

Figure 62. The Teli *as the inclination of the orbit of a planet from the ecliptic.*

The "dragon," whose head and tail form the two nodes, is then identified as the Teli. Most early Hebrew writers refer to it by its Arabic name, *Al Jaz'har.*[17] *Juz'har* is a Persian word, meaning "knot" or "node."

Rabbi Abraham Abulafia also identifies the Teli with the celestial "knots" (*Kesharim*).[18] He writes that the head of the Teli denotes merit, while its tail signifies liability.[19]

Especially important are the lunar nodes, since it is only at these points that an eclipse, either of the sun or the moon, can occur.[20] The Teli can then be seen as the imaginary dragon swallowing the sun or moon.

Although the obliquity is often referred to as the Teli, it is questionable if this is the Teli mentioned here by the Sefer Yetzirah.

There is also a tradition that there are two Telis or dragons, one male and the other female. These are identified as the two Leviathans, and are mentioned in the account of creation, "God created the great dragons" (Genesis 1:21).[21] According to the Talmud, the Pole Serpent mentioned by Isaiah is the male dragon, while the Coiled Serpent (*Nachash Akalkalon*) is the female.[22] Some Kabbalists state that the constellation of Draco is the male Pole Serpent, while the inclination of the ecliptic is the female Coiled Serpent.[23] The female therefore encompasses the male, this being the mystery of, "a female shall surround a male" (Jeremiah 31:22).[24]

Other commentaries identify the Teli with the Milky Way, and say that this is the Pole Serpent.[25] According to this, the Teli would be the axis of the galaxy, rather than that of the celestial sphere. In the *Book of Raziel*, however, it appears that the Milky Way is called the River Dinur, mentioned in Daniel, and not the Teli.[26]

Another important opinion is that of the practical Kabbalists. They write that Teli is actually a place under the firmament of Vilon, and that it is inhabited by humanoid beings, which deport themselves in holiness and purity like angels. The divine mysteries are revealed to these beings, and they have the authority to reveal these things to mortal humans. Methods are also given whereby these beings can be contacted.[27]

While adhering to the view that the Teli is the segment between the ascending and descending nodes, Rabbi Judah HaLevi (1068-1118) also writes that the Teli alludes to the spiritual world, and to hidden mysteries which cannot be grasped.[28] Rabbi Abraham Abulafia similarly writes that the "knots" of the Teli are "knots" of love and mystical union.[29]

The nodes of the Teli are the points where two divergent orbits meet. The physical and spiritual worlds can also be looked upon as

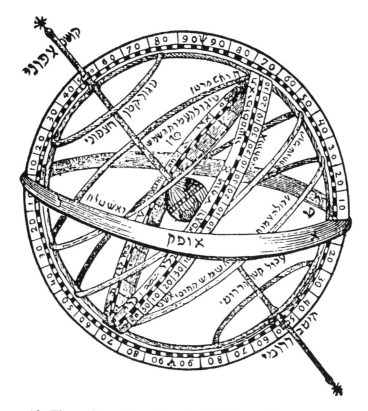

Figure 63. The zodiac. (from Maaseh Toviah*, p. 40a).*

two divergent orbits. The Teli would then represent the nodes where the physical and spiritual meet.

This picture is clarified through a Talmudic example. The Talmud presents a picture where, "the stormwind hangs (*talah*) between the two arms of God like an amulet."[30] This "hanging" can be identified with the Teli. As discussed earlier, the "stormwind" (*sa'arah*) refers to the initiation into the prophetic or mystical experience.[31] The two nodes of the Teli are the spiritual points from which this "amulet" hangs. The Talmud furthermore states that the "arms" from which it hangs are the "arms of the universe." As discussed earlier, the "arms of the universe" denotes the twelve diagonal boundaries (5:2).

One of the most significant interpretations is that of the Bahir. The Bahir states: "What is the Teli? It is the likeness before the Blessed Holy One. It is thus written, 'His locks are hanging (*taltalim*)' (Song of Songs 5:11)."[32]

The link with this biblical verse is highly significant. In its entirety, the verse reads, "His head is a treasure of fine gold, His locks are hanging, black like a raven."

In both Talmudic and Kabbalistic traditions, this verse has two interpretations. First, it relates to a vision of God, indicating that when He is visualized in battle, He is seen a young man with black hair.[33] The Kabbalists say that this is *Zer Anpin* (Small Face, Microprosopus), the personification of the six Sefirot from Chesed to Yesod.[34]

The second interpretation relates this verse to the Torah. The Talmud states that the hanging (or piled) hair relates to the fact that every letter of the Torah contains "piles and piles" (*teli tela'im*) of wisdom.[35] Besides this, the hanging hairs are said to relate to the lines upon which the letters of the Torah are written.[36]

The Torah which is spoken of here is not the ordinary written Torah, but the primeval Torah, which was written "with black fire on white fire."[37] According to many Kabbalists, this primeval Torah in itself is identified with *Zer Anpin*.

In this picture, each letter of the Torah is seen as a hair in the beard of Zer Anpin. These are not seen as simple hairs, but as channels, through which God's wisdom emanates from His "head." The "head" is the concealed wisdom of God, while the letters are its outward revelation.[38] The portion of God's wisdom that we can comprehend bears the same relationship to His true wisdom that the hair does to the brain. The brain is the center of all thought, while the hair is essentially dead. There is a world of difference between the two, yet all that we can comprehend is the "hair."

The verse says, "His head is a treasure of fine gold." This refers to the unknowable divine Intellect. Since all that we can comprehend is a "hair," the verse continues, "His locks are hanging (piled), black like a raven." Even these hairs contain "piles and piles" (*teli tela'im*) of wisdom. Still, it is "black like a raven." Even these "hairs" are black and incomprehensible. Each of these hairs corresponds to a "point" in the letters of the Torah.[39] Each letter contains "piles and piles" of wisdom.

These *taltalim*, which mean "hangings" or "piles," thus refer to the divine wisdom that is revealed. According to the Midrash, however, they do not refer to the letters themselves, but to the lines (*sirtut*) upon which they are written. When one writes a physical Torah, one must first draw lines upon which to write the letters. These lines are not actually drawn with ink, but are merely impressed into the parchment with a sharp instrument. These almost invisible lines represent the "hanging" of the hair, the link between the letter and its spiritual root.

From each hair in the divine beard of *Zer Anpin*, there hangs a universe. Each of these universes is also related to a letter in the Torah.[40] According to this, the Teli denotes the "hair" in the divine beard from which our universe "hangs." This is the axis around which the universe revolves.

The Teli also relates to the meditation on a letter. In this meditation, one pictures the letters as written with black fire on white fire. One contemplates the letter, concentrating on the near invisible line upon which it is drawn. This line is seen as a hair in the divine beard, from which the universe hangs.

The scripture calls the "hangings" of the divine beard *Taltalim*. The Zohar relates this to the word *Talpiot*, which, as the Talmud teaches, is the "hill (*tell*) to which all mouths (*piot*) turn."[41] This "hill" is the mount upon which the Temple was built, which Jacob called the "gate of heaven" (Genesis 28:17).[42] This *Talpiot* is the tangible link between the physical and the spiritual. According to the Kabbalists, the same holds true of the Teli.[43]

The Cycle

The Hebrew word for cycle here is *Galgal*. In a number of places in the Talmud, this word is also used to denote the cycle of events in the world.[44] Later (6:3), the *Galgal* is depicted as the king over time. This is because all time is defined by cyclic motion. The word *Galgal* also means sphere or circle. In some places in the Talmud the word is used to denote the sphere of the zodiac.[45]

The Sefer Yetzirah (2:4) earlier stated that the 22 letters had to be fixed in the *Galgal* to produce the 231 Gates. The word *Galgal* therefore also denotes the mystical array of the 22 letters.

In this respect, the *Teli* denotes the almost invisible lines upon which the letters are written. The *Galgal* is the circle in which they are drawn.

The Sefer Yetzirah also associated the mystical experience with the whirlwind known as a *Sufah* (1:6). It is significant that the prophet Isaiah associates such a whirlwind with the *Galgal*, saying, "Like a sphere (*galgal*) before the whirlwind (*sufah*)" (Isaiah 17:13). It is also associated with God's voice, as in the verse, "The voice of Your thunder was in the sphere (*galgal*)" (Psalms 77:19).[46]

Most significantly, the *Galgal* is also seen as being below the feet of the Cherubim. God thus told an angel, "Come to the innards of the Galgal, beneath the Cherub" (Ezekiel 10:2). This Cherub is explicitly identified with the Chayot seen in Ezekiel's initial vision, as he says, "And the Cherubim went up, this is the Chayah that I saw on the river Chebar" (Ezekiel 10:15). Earlier (1:3), we have also discussed how the Cherubim serve as the focus of the mystical experience. The *Galgal* is therefore a cycle that lifts one up to the level of the Chayot, which are in the Universe of Yetzirah.

The Bahir states that the *Galgal* is the Womb.[47] In one sense, this is speaking of the *Galgal* as the cycle of time. The present is the womb in which the future is born. As we have seen earlier (1:5), the dimension of time is seen as extending between Chakhmah and Binah. Chakhmah is the past, while Binah is the future. The present is the interface between these two Sefirot. Binah is the Mother, and the *Galgal* is Her womb.

An important cycle that we have discussed earlier (1:4) is the oscillation between Chakhmah and Binah consciousness. The first initiation into the spiritual domain comes through this exercise, and hence, as a *Galgal*, it is the entrance into the mysteries. In this sense, the *Galgal* is the womb from which one is reborn into a spiritual plane.

The Heart

The heart is seen as king over the soul (6:3). Of all parts in the body, it is the dominant one. The soul relates to the spiritual dimension. Thus, when the Sefer Yetzirah speaks of the mystical experience, it describes it as a "running of the heart" (1:8).

The Hebrew word for heart is Lev (לב), and as mentioned earlier (1:1), this is also the number 32 in Hebrew. As the Bahir states, the heart represents the 32 Paths of Wisdom.[48] It is through these 32 paths that one ascends into the spiritual dimension. The *Book of Raziel* similarly states, "Breath (*Ruach*) emanates from the heart, just like the Holy Spirit (*Ruach HaKodesh*) emanates from the Throne [of Glory]."[49]

The Bahir also states that this Heart is the scriptural "Heart of heaven."

The one place where this is mentioned is in the account of the revelation at Sinai: "You came close, and you stood under the mountain, and the mountain burned in fire, until the heart of heaven — darkness, cloud, and gloom. And God spoke to you from out of the fire" (Deuteronomy 4:11,12).[50]

From the context, we see that the fire that reached to "the heart of heaven" was the fire associated with revelation, from which God spoke. Such fire is the third step in the initiation of revelation, as we find in the case of Ezekiel's vision, which was initiated with "a stormwind . . . a great cloud, and flashing fire" (Ezekiel 1:4). It was only in the fire that he visualized the Chashmal. Similarly, in Elijah's vision, the three steps were, "wind . . . sound . . . and fire" (1 Kings 19:11-12). In one place, the Midrash also relates this fire to the ladder in Jacob's dream.[51] This ladder is also the vehicle through which one climbs into the transcendental.

The three steps mentioned by Ezekiel also appear parallel those taught by the Sefer Yetzirah (1:10-12). First comes Breath (*Ruach*), which can also be translated as wind, which is the "stormwind" of Ezekiel. Then comes "water from Breath," which can be associated with the raincloud that he saw. The opaqueness of this cloud is similar to the "mire and clay" mentioned in Sefer Yetzirah.

The third step is "fire from water." This is the "flashing fire" seen by Ezekiel. The Sefer Yetzirah says that out of this fire one depicts, "The throne of Glory, Serafim, Ophanim, and holy Chayot" (1:12). Similarly, after experiencing the fire, Ezekiel was able to visualize the Chayot and the Throne of Glory.

It is this fire of revelation that is said to reach "to the heart of heaven." The heart is the king over the dimension of spirit, and one travels through this dimension by means of fire. This fire therefore reaches the "heart." The Heart represents the 32 paths on the Tree of Life.

In this verse, the scripture states that God spoke "out of the fire." Elsewhere, however, it says, "You heard His voice out of the midst of the darkness" (Deuteronomy 5:20). But as the Zohar states, the "fire" mentioned here is the fire of darkness.[52] It is the burning longing that comes from the total nullification of thought. This is also associated with the "black fire" with which the primeval Torah was written.[53]

In the Kabbalah, the word "heaven" is usually associated with *Zer Anpin*. The "heart of heaven" is therefore the heart of *Zer Anpin*.[54]

It is significant that the Bahir relates the *Teli* to the hair on the head, while the *Galgal* is related to the womb or belly. The Heart is naturally associated with the chest. Thus, from these three, we have the head, belly and chest, the three parts of the body associated with the Three Mothers, AMSh.

The *Teli*, associated with the head, would then relate to the Shin. The *Galgal*, associated with the belly, would relate to the Mem, and the Heart, to the Alef. Out of the Three Mothers, we derive the kings over the Universe, Year and Soul. This results in the five-dimensional continuum being divided into space, time, and the spiritual.

In another sense, the *Teli* is the axis, representing the longitudinal angle. The *Galgal* is the sphere, representing the azimuthal angle or latitude. The Heart is the radius or altitude. Thus, these three kings represent the three-dimensional in spherical coordinates. The five-dimensional continuum can likewise be represented in hyperspherical coordinates.

The Kabbalists note that the initial letters of *Teli* (תלי), *Galgal* (גלגל) and *Lev* (לב) spell out *TaGeL* (תגל). This is in the verse, "My soul will rejoice (*TaGel*) in my God" (Isaiah 61:10).[55] It is through meditation on these three elements that the soul can attain mystical ecstasy.

This word also occurs in the verse, "God is king, let the earth rejoice (*TaGel*)" (Psalms 97:1). This can be interpreted to say, "God is King, Teli Galgal Lev is the earth," indicating that these are the three kings over His creation, as the Sefer Yetzirah later states (6:3). These are the deep mystery, as it is written, "The mystery of another do not reveal (*T'GaL*)" (Proverbs 25:9).

6:2 שלש אמות אמ״ש אויר מים אש אש למעלה
ומים למטה ואויר רוח חק מכריע בינתים וסימן
לדבר האש נושא את המים, מ׳ דוממת ש׳ שורקת א׳
אויר רוח חק מכריע בינתים:

Three Mothers: AMSh (אמש)
Air, water, and fire.
Fire is above, water is below,
and air of Breath is the rule
that decides between them.
And a sign of this thing
is that fire supports water.
Mem hums, Shin hisses,
and Alef is the breath of air
that decides between them.

This is essentially a repetition of 3:4 and 2:1.

Water and Mem represent Chakhmah, while fire and Shin denote Binah. Since Chakhmah is usually considered to be above Binah, it is somewhat difficult to understand why fire is seen as being above water.[56]

The reason behind this, however, is related to the penetration of Chakhmah and Binah into *Zer Anpin* (Microprosopus). The Kabbalists teach that Yesod of Chakhmah penetrates down to Yesod of *Zer Anpin*, while Yesod of Binah only penetrates as far as the heart (Tiferet) of *Zer Anpin*. Since Binah ends in the heart, it is often identified with this organ. Chakhmah is clothed in Binah, and since Binah ends in the heart, it is there that Chakhmah is first revealed. The 32 Paths are thus identified with the heart (*LeV*), which is Binah, but they are also identified with Chakhmah.[57]

Thus, even though "fire is above and water is below," still, "fire supports water." Wisdom may penetrate creation to a greater degree than Understanding, and may be found in lower levels, but still, Binah "supports" Chakhmah, and is below it. This is reflected in the sounds of the Mem and Shin, which represent these as states of consciousness.

As discussed earlier, on the basis of the Bahir, the *Teli* is identified with the head, the *Galgal* with the belly, and the Heart with the chest. Thus, the *Teli* relates to Shin and fire, the *Galgal*, to Mem and water, and the Heart to Alef and air. What we therefore discover is that space is related to fire, time to water, and spirit to air.

6:3 תלי בעולם כמלך על כסאו גלגל בשנה כמלך
במדינה לב בנפש כמלך במלחמה:

The Teli in the Universe is like a king on his throne.
The Cycle in the Year is like a king in the province.
The Heart in the Soul is like a king in war.

The Teli in the Universe

The word "king" always alludes to the Sefirah of Malkhut (Kingship). It denotes the interaction between a ruler and his subjects. When we speak of an entity as a king, it is an indication that it is interacting with something that is below it.

The *Teli* is the king over the Universe, that is, over the domain of space. It is seen as a "king on his throne." Although the *Teli* interacts with space, it does not become part of it.

We can see this in two ways. First of all, we can take the view that the *Teli* is the axis around which the universe revolves. In circular motion around an axis, everything moves but the axis itself. The axis is the focus of the motion, but does not partake in it. Similarly, the *Teli* is king over space, but does not become part of it.

The same is true if we view the *Teli* as the link between the spiritual and the physical. In this respect also, the spiritual does not enter into the physical.[58]

As discussed earlier, (1:4,12), a "Throne" always involves a concept of lowering and concern. The *Teli* thus represents the spiritual being lowered so as to interact with the physical.

Even though a king sitting on his throne may not come between his subjects, he is still highly affected by them. The spiritual is similarly affected by the physical.

The Cycle in the Year

Unlike the axis, the cycle not only defines time, but also becomes part of time. The cycle cannot stand still in time, but must include itself within the flow of time. Hence, it is like a "king in the province."

That which defines space can remain aloof from space. That which defines time, on the other hand, cannot remain apart from it.

In human terms, it is the mind that provides a perception of both space and time. You can stand in one place and perceive a large portion of space. Like the *Teli*, you can perceive large areas of space, and still remain aloof from them. You do not actually have to be in a portion of space in order to perceive it.

This is not true of time. You can only perceive the time in which you exist. You may perceive the past in memory, or the future in the imagination, but direct perception only exists in the present. You can perceive space at a distance, but time only when in proximity to it.

Since no one can perceive the future, you cannot know what you will do later. It is due to this fact that you can have free will in the present. Thus, it is this basic difference between space and time that allows freedom of action.

The Heart in the Soul

The different spacial points, as well as past and future, involve end points in their respective continua. Still, they do not represent opposites. In the spiritual dimension, on the other hand, the two end points are good and evil, and these are diametrical opposites.

Since the heart is the midpoint between these opposites, it is seen as the site of battle between good and evil. The Talmud therefore identifies the heart as the scene of the battle between the Good Urge (*Yetzer Tov*) and the Evil Urge (*Yetzer HaRa*).[59]

6:4 גם את זה לעומת זה עשה אלהים טוב לעומת רע רע לעומת טוב טוב מטוב רע מרע הטוב מבחין את הרע והרע מבחין את הטוב טובה שמורה לטובים ורעה שמורה לרעים:

"Also God made one opposite the other" (Ecclesiastes 7:14).
Good opposite evil,
   Evil opposite good.
Good from good
   Evil from evil.
Good defines evil
   And evil defines good.
Good is kept for the good ones
   And evil is kept for the evil ones.

One opposite the other

This speaks of the heart, which is like a "king in battle." The two extremes on the spiritual axis—good and evil—are actual opposites. Like light and darkness, the two cannot coexist.

Good from good

As discussed earlier (1:5), good is the point on this axis that is closest to God. Evil is the side that is furthest from Him. All good comes from the side of good, while all evil comes from the other side.

Good defines evil

The Zohar explains that light can only be recognized because of the existence of darkness.[60] If there were no darkness, light would be an integral part of the environment, and such an integral part cannot be sensed. Thus, for example, we cannot sense the air, since it is an integral part of our normal environment. Since air is always present, there is no need for us to have senses to detect its presence or absence.

Similarly, if light were always present, without being divided into shades and colors, we could not see anything with it. Every shade or color involves some absorbtion of light, and hence, a degree of darkness.

In a similar manner, good can only be recognized because of the existence of evil. If evil did not exist, then we would not have any free choice whatever. We would be like mere puppets or robots. It is only because of the existence of good and evil that free will can exist, where we can choose between them. Conversely, it is only as a result of free will that good and evil can be recognized and defined.

Good is kept for the good ones

The dimension of good and evil not only serves to define these concepts, but also serves to reward them. It is taught that God created the world in order to bestow good to the world.[61] But what good does He offer?

First of all, we must realize that any good that God gives must be the ultimate good that His creation can accept. The Psalmist said "How great is Your good, stored up for those who fear You" (Psalms 31:20). Our sages interpret this to say that God bestows good in the greatest possible abundance.[62] In another place, they teach us that this verse means that God is telling us, "You according to your strength, and Me according to Mine."[63] In other words, God gives us the greatest good that we can possibly accept.

But what is this ultimate good? What is the greatest possible good that God can bestow?

If we think about it, the answer is really quite simple. The greatest possible good is God Himself.[64] There is no other ultimate true good. The Psalmist thus said, "I have no good but You" (Psalms 16:2). In the Talmud, Rabbi Acha interprets this to mean that no true good exists in the world, except that of God Himself.[65]

The ultimate good is therefore to partake of God, and it is this good that He planned to give the world. He would create a world where creatures ultimately could partake of His essence. The Psalmist sings of this, "Taste and see that God is good, happy is the man who finds refuge in Him" (Psalms 34:9).

God therefore created the world in such a way that we could draw close to Him and partake of His essence. Of course, we are not speaking of physical closeness, but of spiritual closeness. Such closeness involves the knowledge and understanding of God, as well as resembling Him to the greatest degree possible.

Here again, we hear this in the words of the Psalmist, "But for me, the nearness of God is good. I have made God my refuge, that I may tell of His works" (Psalms 73:28). The Psalmist is teaching us that his ultimate good is nearness to God. This nearness involves "telling of His works"—that is, a deep knowledge and perception of the Divine.[66]

The ultimate good that God offers is therefore the opportunity to perceive Him. In one place, our sages thus teach us that God created the world in order that men may know Him.[67] This is not a separate reason, but the way in which He bestows His good upon us.[68] God thus told us through His prophet, "I am your God, I teach you for your good" (Isaiah 48:17). The Psalmist expresses the same idea when he says, "You are good, and You do good, teach me Your decrees" (Psalms 119:68).

To know God and understand Him in any way is to have a deep awe and dread of His Majesty. All true wisdom is that of God. But such wisdom and knowledge imply the fear and reverence of God. The Psalmist thus said, "The beginning of Wisdom is the fear of God" (Psalms 111:10). Solomon expressed the same idea when he said, "The fear of God is the beginning of Knowledge" (Proverbs 1:7).[69]

We can therefore say that the ultimate goal of creation is that we should come close to God, and therefore both know and fear Him. Again we hear the words of Solomon, "Whatever God does shall be forever . . . God has made it so that man should fear Him" (Ecclesiastes 3:14). The Talmud comments on this, saying that the world was created for the fear of God.[70] This is man's true purpose in the world, as we find again, "The sum of the matter, when all has been heard: Fear God and keep His commandments, for this is all of man" (Ecclesiastes 12:13). In the Talmud, Rabbi Elazar comments on this and says, "Solomon is teaching us that all the world was created for the fear of God."[71]

When our sages say that the world was created for the fear of God, they are not contradicting the teaching that it was created as a vehicle for His good. What they are doing is expressing what this good ultimately is. It is a knowledge of God that is most perfectly expressed by the reverence and awe that we call the "fear of God."

The ultimate place where we will be worthy of this vision and perception will be in what we call *Olam HaBah*—The Future World or the World to Come. It is a world of absolute life and goodness. It is of the vision of the World to Come that the Psalmist is speaking of when he says, "I believe that I will gaze upon God in the land of the living" (Psalms 27:13). This "land of the living" is the Future World.[72]

It is this future world that is the goal of all creation. Our sages thus teach us, "This world is like an antechamber before the World to Come. Prepare yourself in the antechamber before you enter the palace."[73]

Since this Future World is the ultimate goal of creation, it is also the place of ultimate good. In the language of the Talmud, it is called, "the World where all is good."[74] It is a good that surpasses anything that this world may possibly have to offer. This is what our sages mean when they say, "One moment of delight in the Future World is more than all the good of this world."[75]

We can obtain some idea of what this Future World will be like from a common saying of Rav, quoted in the Talmud.[76] He said, "In the Future World, there will be no eating, drinking, childbearing or business. Neither will there be jealousy, hatred or strife. The righteous will sit with their crowns on their heads, delighting in the radiance of the Divine Presence."

Our sages teach us that this "radiance of the Divine Presence" is a perception of the Divine.[77] In the Future World, we will perceive and comprehend God in the greatest degree possible.

This perception of God in the Future World is totally beyond our present grasp. That of the least of us will pale the achievements of the greatest sages in this world. Still, of course, it will be impossible to perceive God in His entirety. This is impossible for any being other than God Himself. Although incomparable to anything in this life, our perception will still be less than a drop in an infinite ocean. Nevertheless, it will far exceed anything possible in this world.[78]

In order that we may approach Him, God created a dimension of nearness to His being. By moving through this dimension, we are able to come closer and closer to God, even though we can never actually reach Him. This dimension is what we call the spiritual world. Our sages call the highest spiritual world *Atzilut*—the World of Nearness. All the spiritual worlds were created as vehicles through which we may draw near to God. In a sense, they serve as a filter, allowing us to draw near, and still not be obliterated by His infinite Light.[79]

In a number of places, our sages speak of these worlds as the Celestial Treasuries. Thus, Israel sings to God, "The King will bring me into His chamber" (Song of Songs 1:4). The sages comment that God will bring the righteous into His celestial chambers and allow them to probe the treasuries on high.[80]

This is also the meaning of the light that was made on the first day of creation. Our sages teach us that it was not mere physical light, but a wonderous light with which one could see "from one end of the universe to the other."[81] This was the light of *perception*, shining in all the spiritual worlds, with which one could experience this vision of God. Our sages thus continue, "God set this light aside for the righteous in the World to Come."[82]

This is the light of perception with which we will partake of the Divine—the "radiance of the Divine Presence." Elihu was speaking of this when he told Job that God will "turn back his soul from destruction, and illuminate him in the light of life" (Job 33:30). Solomon informs us that this light is the source of eternal life, when he says, "In the light of the King's face is life" (Proverbs 16:15).[83]

God's ultimate goal in creation was therefore the World to Come, where man could perceive a vision of God. Not God Himself, of course, but a vision. Perhaps through many filters, but still, a vision of God. The Psalmist sings of this vision, "In righteousness, I will see Your face, when I awake, I will be satiated with a vision of You" (Psalms 17:15). The Psalmist is speaking of the time when he will awake to the delights of the Future World. Our sages comment on this verse, "God will satisfy the righteous with a vision of the Divine Presence."[84]

The bliss of the Future World will be endless. In His endless goodness, God will give us a world of good without end. The Psalmist is speaking of this when he exclaims, "In Your presence is fullness of joy, in Your right hand is bliss forever" (Psalms 16:11).[85]

Of course, everything about this Future World is totally beyond our powers of description. Even the visions of the greatest prophets will pale in comparison. It is something that no human mind can possibly imagine in this life. It cannot come through human understanding, but only as a gift from God, and when He gives it, we will understand. The prophet therefore says when speaking of the World to Come: "Never has the ear heard it—no eye has seen it—other than God: That which He will do for those who hope in Him" (Isaiah 64:3).[86]

This good is not given as a reward, but as a direct result of a person's binding himself to good. A person attains that to which he attaches himself.[87]

6:5

שלשה כל אחד לבדו עומד אחד מזכה ואחד
מחייב ואחד מכריע בינתים. שבעה שלשה
מול שלשה ואחד חק מכריע בינתים. ושנים עשר
עומדין במלחמה שלשה אוהבים שלשה שונאים
שלשה מחיים ושלשה ממיתים. שלשה אוהבים הלב
והאזנים שלשה שונאים הכבד והמרה והלשון שלשה
מחיים שני נקבי האף והטחול ושלשה ממיתים שני
הפה ואל מלך נאמן מושל בכולם ממעון קדשו
הנקבים

עד עדי עד. אחד על גבי שלשה, שלשה על גבי
שבעה על גבי שנים עשר וכלם אדוקים זה בזה:
שבעה,

Three:
> *Each one stands alone*
>> *one acts as advocate*
>> *one acts as accuser*
>>> *and one decides between them.*

Seven:
> *Three opposite three*
>> *and one is the rule deciding between them.*

Twelve stand in war:
> *Three love,*
> *three hate,*
>> *three give life*
>> *and three kill*

Three love: the heart and the ears.
Three hate: the liver, the gall, and the tongue.
Three give life: the two nostrils and the spleen.
Three kill: the two orifices and the mouth.
And God faithful King rules over them all
> *from His holy habitation*
>> *until eternity of eternities.*

One on three
> *three on seven*
> *seven on twelve,*
And all are bound, one to another.

One acts as an advocate

See 2:1 and 3:1.

Seven: three opposite three

The sequence three, seven, twelve, can be defined in a number
of ways. One, which we have discussed earlier (1:2), involved the
lines connecting the Sefirot. However, there is another important
sequence that also yields these numbers.

This second sequence can also be expressed in a number of ways.
The most obvious involves the first three regular polygons. The simplest polygon, the triangle has three points. When inscribed in a
square, one then has seven points. Finally, when both are inscribed
in a pentagon, there are a total of twelve points. See figure 64 on page
252. On a more sophisticated level, this sequence can be represented
by a triangle, a tetrahedron, and a hypertetrahedron.

Another significant sequence that yields exactly the same result
is that of truncated triangles. See figure 65 on page 252.

Section A (figure 65) consists of three points. Here, the one to
the right is the advocate, the one to the left is the accuser, and the
middle point is the deciding one. This is the concept of thesis, antithesis, and synthesis, discussed earlier (2:1).

Figure 66 (on page 253) consists of seven points in a truncated
triangle. This can be divided into two triangles, each representing the
original triad, and a center point in the middle. In the top section of
figure 66, we can clearly see seven distinct steps from right to left.

We also have twelve points in a truncated triangle shown in both
figures 65 and 66. Here there are no longer seven distinct steps, since
three are duplicated in the top and bottom lines. The three on top
are the ones that give life, while the three on the bottom are the three
that kill. The triangle to the right represents love, while that to the
left are the three who hate. (See section B in figure 66).

Hate can also be represented in this diagram by a large inverted
triangle. It is hate because the three points are separated. The smaller,
inner triangle, where the points are not separated, then represents
love. The two triangles to the right and left (in figure 66) are then life
and death.

And God faithful King

The expression here is exactly the same used in 1:5. The Hebrew
word *Ma'on* for habitation has also been explained there.

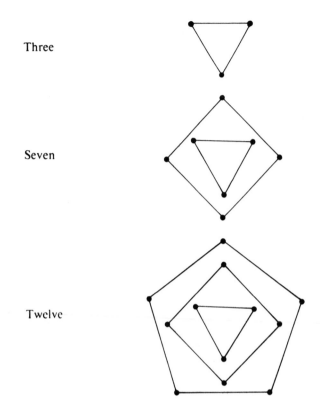

Three

Seven

Twelve

Figure 64. The sequence of polygons.

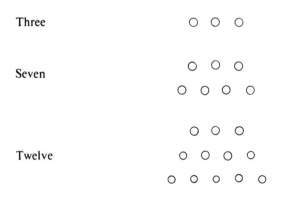

Three

Seven

Twelve

General formula: n (n + 5)/2

Figure 65. The sequence of truncated triangles.

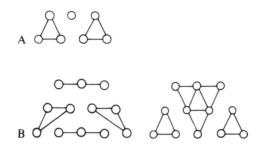

Figure 66. A) Three opposite three, and one is the rule deciding between them. B) Twelve stand in war: Three love, three hate, three give life, and three kill.

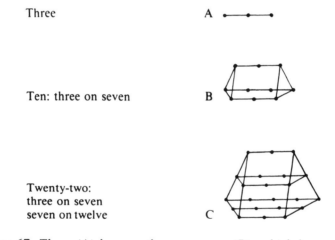

Three   A

Ten: three on seven   B

Twenty-two:
three on seven
seven on twelve   C

Figure 67. Three (A) become three on seven (B), which becomes seven on twelve (C). The general formula here is n(n+1) (n+8)/6.

One on three

The One is the ineffable, which is not counted in the sequence.

Three on seven

When the truncated triangle of three is placed on that of seven, one has a truncated pyramid containing ten points. These represent the Ten Sefirot. See figure 67.

When this, in turn, is placed on the truncated triangle containing twelve points, this yields a truncated pyramid with 22 points. These represent the 22 letters of the alphabet.

6:6

אלו הם עשרים ושתים אותיות שבהן חקק אהי"ה
י"ה יהו"ה אלהים אלהים יהו"ה יהו"ה צבאות
אלהים צבאות אל שדי יהו"ה אדני ועשה מהם שלשה
ספרים וברא מהם את כל עולמו וצר בהם את כל
היצור ואת כל העתיד ליצור:

These are the twenty-two letters
  with which engraved
  Ehyeh, Yah, YHVH Elohim, YHVH,
  YHVH Tzavaot, Elohim Tzavaot, El Shaddai,
  YHVH Adonoy,
And with them He made three Books,
  and with them He created His Universe,
  and He formed with them all that was ever formed,
  and all that ever will be formed.

This is very similar to 1:1. The ten divine names here represent the Ten Sefirot in descending order. See Table 55.

Table 55. The ten divine names.

Sefirah	Name
Keter	Ehyeh (I Will Be)
Chakhmah	Yah
Binah	YHVH (pronounced Elohim)
Chesed	El
Gevurah	Elohim
Tiferet	YHVH
Netzach	YHVH Tzavaot (Lord of Hosts)
Hod	Elohim Tzavaot (God of Hosts)
Yesod	El Shaddai (Almighty God)
Malkhut	YHVH Adonoy

6:7

כשבא אברהם אבינו ע"ה הביט וראה והבין
וחקר וחקק וחצב ועלתה בידו הבריאה שנאמר
ואת הנפש אשר עשו בחרן מיד נגלה עליו אדון הכל
יתברך שמו לעד והושיבו בחיקו ונשקו על ראשו
וקראו אברהם אוהבי וכרת ברית לו ולזרעו עד עולם
שנאמר והאמין בה' ויחשבה לו צדקה. וכרת לו ברית
בין עשר אצבעות ידיו והוא ברית הלשון ובין עשר
אצבעות רגליו והוא ברית המילה. וקשר עשרים
ושתים אותיות התורה בלשונו וגילה לו את סודו
משכן במים דלקן באש רעשן ברוח בערן בשבעה
נהגן בשנים עשר מזלות:

And when Abraham our father, may he rest in peace,
    looked, saw, understood, probed,
        engraved and carved,
He was successful in creation,
    as it is written,
        "And the souls that they made in Haran" (Genesis
12:5).
Immediately there was revealed to him the Master of all,
    may His name be blessed forever,
He placed him in His bosom, and kissed him on his head,
    and He called him,
    "Abraham my beloved" (Isaiah 41:8).
He made a covenant with him
    and with his children after him forever,
        as it is written,
    "And he believed in God, and He considered
        and He considered it righteousness" (Genesis 15:6).
He made with him a covenant
    between the ten fingers of his hands —
        this is the covenant of the tongue,
    and between the ten toes of his feet —
        this is the covenant of circumcision,
And He bound the 22 letters of the Torah to his tongue
    and He revealed to him His mystery
He drew them in water,
    He flamed them with fire,
    He agitated them with Breath,
    He burned them with the seven [planets]
    He directed them with the twelve constellations.

And when Abraham our father...

It is from here that a tradition is derived linking Abraham to the Sefer Yetzirah.

Engraved and carved

Here we clearly see that "engraving" and "carving" involve meditative techniques.[88] This has already been discussed previously (1:14).

Before one can engage in these techniques, however, one must, "look, see, understand, and probe." These techniques have also been discussed (1:4).

And he was successful

The complete verse quoted here relates to Abraham's leaving Haran at God's command, and it states, "So Abram went, as God had told him ... and Abram took his wife Sarai, and his nephew Lot, and all the substance that they had gathered, and the souls that they had made in Haran" (Genesis 12:5). This implies that before God had spoken to him and told him to leave his land, Abraham had already mastered the mysteries of Sefer Yetzirah.

The Kabbalists note that the verse says, "the souls that *they* made," in the plural. This indicates that one attempting to make a Golem should not work alone, but should do so in partnership with others.

He made a covenant

See 1:3.

He drew them in water

This indicates that the symbolism of water and fire, discussed earlier (1:11,12), also relate to meditative techniques.

APPENDIX 1
Other Versions of the Sefer Yetzirah

THE SHORT VERSION

(In order to show how it can be done, this has been translated in the imperative. The bracketed portions are those omitted by Donash.)

Chapter 1

1. With 32 wondrous paths of Wisdom engrave Yah, the Lord of Hosts, [God of Israel, the Living God, King of the universe, Almighty God, merciful and gracious, High and Exalted, dwelling in eternity, whose name is Holy, and create His universe] with three books, with text (*Sepher*), with number (*Sephar*), and with communication (*Sippur*).

2. Ten Sefirot of Nothingness plus twenty-two [foundation] letters: Three Mothers, Seven Doubles, and Twelve Elementals.

3. Ten Sefirot of Nothingness: The number of the ten fingers, five opposite five, with a single covenant precisely in the middle, like the circumcision of the tongue and the circumcision of the membrum.

4. Ten Sefirot of Nothingness: Ten and not nine; ten and not eleven. Understand with Wisdom, and be wise with Understanding. Examine with them and probe from them, make a thing stand on its essence, and make the Creator sit on His base.

5. Ten Sefirot of Nothingness: Their measure is ten which have no end. A depth of beginning, a depth of end; a depth of good, a depth of evil; a depth above, a depth below; a depth east, a depth west; a depth north, a depth south. The singular Master, God faithful King, dominates them all from His holy dwelling until eternity of eternities.

6. Ten Sefirot of Nothingness: Their vision is like the "appearance of lightning," their limit has no end. His Word in them is "running and returning." They rush to His saying like a whirlwind, and before His throne they prostrate themselves.

7. Ten Sefirot of Nothingness: Their end is imbedded in their beginning, and their beginning in their end, like a flame in a burning coal. For the Master is singular, He has no second. And before One, what do you count?

8. Ten Sefirot of Nothingness: Bridle your mouth from speaking and your heart from thinking. And if your heart runs, return to the place, as it is written, "The Chayot running and returning" (Ezekiel 1:14). Regarding this a covenant was made.

9. Ten Sefirot of Nothingness: One is the Breath of the Living God, blessed and benedicted be the Name of the Life of worlds. Voice, Breath and Speech. This is the Holy Breath (*Ruach HaKodesh*).

10. Two: Breath from Breath. With it engrave and carve twenty-two foundation letters—three Mothers, seven Doubles, and twelve Elementals—and one Breath is from them.

11. Three: Water from Breath. With it engrave and carve chaos and void, mire and clay. Engrave them like a garden plot, carve them like a wall, cover them like a ceiling.

12. Four: Fire from water. With it engrave and carve the Throne of Glory, Seraphim, Ophanim, holy Chayot, and Ministering Angels. From the three establish His dwelling, as it is written, "He makes His angels of breaths, His ministers from flaming fire" (Psalms 104:4).

13. Five: With three of the simple letters seal "above." Choose three and place them in His great Name: YHV. With them seal the six extremities. Face upward and seal it with YHV.

Six: Seal "below." Face downward and seal it with YVH.

Seven: Seal "east." Face straight ahead and seal it with HYV.

Eight: Seal "west." Face backward and seal it with HVY.

Nine: Seal "south." Face to the right and seal it with VYH.

Ten: Seal "north." Face to the left and seal it with VHY.

14. These are the Ten Sefirot of Nothingness. One is the Breath of the Living God. Breath [from Breath], Water [from Breath], Fire [from water, and the extremities], up, down, east, west, north and south.

Chapter 2

1. Twenty-two foundation letters: three Mothers, seven Doubles, and twelve Elementals. The three Mothers, AMSh, their foundation is the pan of merit, the pan of liability, and the tongue of decree deciding between them.

2. Twenty-two letters: Engrave them, carve them, weigh them, permute them, and transform them, and with them depict the soul of all that was formed and all that will be formed in the future.

3. Twenty-two [foundation] letters: They are engraved with voice, carved with breath, and placed in the mouth in five places: AChHO, BVMP, GYKQ, DTLNTh, ZSShRTz.

4. Twenty-two foundation letters: They are set in a circle as 231 Gates. The circle rotates back and forth. And this is a sign: There is

no good higher than delight (*ONG*), and there is no evil lower than plague (*NGO*).

5. How? Weigh them and transpose them, Alef with each one, and each one with Alef; Bet with each one, and each one with Bet. They repeat in a cycle. Therefore, everything formed and everything spoken emanates in one name.

6. Form substance out of chaos and make nonexistence into existence. Carve great pillars out of air that cannot be grasped. This is the sign: One foresees, transposes, and makes all creation and all words with one Name. And a sign of this: Twenty-two objects in a single body.

Chapter 3

1. Three Mothers, AMSh: Their foundation is the pan of liability, the pan of merit, and the tongue of decree deciding between them.

2. Three mothers, AMSh: A great, mystical, concealed secret, sealed with six rings. And from it emanate fire and water, separating themselves as male and female. Three Mothers, AMSh, are their foundation, and from them are born the Fathers, from which everything was created.

3. Three Mothers, AMSh, in the Universe are air, water, and fire. Heaven was created from fire, earth was created from water, and the air decides between the fire and the water.

4. Three mothers, AMSh, in the Year are fire, water, and breath. The hot is created from fire, the cold is created from water, and the temperate from breath decides between them.
   Three Mothers, AMSh, in the Soul are fire, water, and breath. The head is created from fire, the belly is created from water, and the chest, created from breath, decides between them.

5. Three Mother, AMSh: Engrave them, carve them, permute them, and with them seal three Mothers in the Universe, three Mothers in the Year, and three Mothers in the Soul, male and female.

6. Make Alef king over breath, bind a crown to it, and combine one with another. And with them seal air in the Universe, the temperate in the Year, and the chest in the Soul, the male with AMSh, and the female with AShM.

7. Make Mem king over water, bind a crown to it, and combine one with another. And with them seal earth in the Universe, the cold in

the Year, and the belly in the Soul, the male with MASh, and the female with MShA.

8. Make Shin king over fire, bind a crown to it, and combine one with another. And with them seal heaven in the Universe, the hot in the Year, and the head in the soul, the male [with ShAM], and the female [with ShMA].

Chapter 4

1. Seven Doubles, BGD KPRT: Their foundation is life, peace, wisdom, wealth, grace, seed, dominance. Each has two sounds: B-Bh, G-Gh, D-Dh, K-Kh, P-Ph, R-Rh, T-Th. [A structure of] soft and hard, [a structure of] strong and weak, double because they are transposes. The transpose of life is death, the transpose of peace is evil, the transpose of wisdom is folly, the transpose of wealth is poverty, the transpose of grace is ugliness, the transpose of seed is desolation, the transpose of dominance is subjugation.

2. [Seven Doubles, BGD KPRT: Seven and not six, seven and not eight. Examine with them and probe from them, make each thing stand on its essence, and make the Creator sit on His base.]

3. Seven Doubles, BGD KPRT, parallel the seven extremities. These are the six extremities: up, down, east, west, north, south. And the Holy Palace precisely in the middle upholds them all.

4. Seven Doubles, BGD KPRT: Engrave them, carve them, combine them, as planets in the Universe, days in the Year, and gates in the Soul. From them engrave seven firmaments, seven earths, seven weeks. Seven is therefore beloved under all the heavens.

5. [How? Make Bet king over life, bind a crown to it, and with it depict Saturn in the Universe, Sunday in the Year, and the right eye in the Soul.

6. [Make Gimel king, bind a crown to it, and with it depict Jupiter in the Universe, Monday in the Year, and the left eye in the Soul.

7. [Make Dalet king, bind a crown to it, and with it depict Mars in the Universe, Tuesday in the Year, and the right ear in the Soul.

8. [Make Kaf king, bind a crown to it, and with it depict the Sun in the Universe, Wednesday in the Year, and the left ear in the Soul.

9. [Make Peh king, bind a crown to it, and with it depict Venus in the Universe, Thursday in the Year, and the right nostril in the Soul.

10. [Make Resh king, bind a crown to it, and with it depict Mercury in the Universe, Friday in the Year, and the left nostril in the Soul.

11. [Make Tav king, bind a crown to it, and with it depict the Moon in the Universe, the Sabbath in the Year, and the mouth in the Soul.]

12. The Seven Doubles, how does one permute them? Two stones build two houses, three build six houses, four build 24 houses, five build 120 houses, six build 720 houses, and seven build 5040 houses. From there on go out and calculate that which the mouth cannot speak and the ear cannot hear.

These are the seven planets in the Universe: The Sun, Venus, Mercury, the Moon, Saturn, Jupiter, Mars.[1] These are the seven days in the Year: The seven days of creation. And the Seven gates in the Soul are the two eyes, the two ears, the two nostrils, and the mouth. And with them were engraved the seven firmaments, the seven earths, the seven hours. Seven is therefore beloved for every desire under heaven.[2]

Chapter 5

1. Twelve Elementals: HV ZCh TY LN SO TzQ. Their foundation is sight, hearing, smell, speech, taste, coition, action, motion, anger, laughter, thought, and sleep. Their measure is the twelve diagonal boundaries: the north-east boundary, the south-east boundary, the upper-east boundary, the lower-east boundary, the upper-north boundary, the lower-north boundary, the south-west boundary, the north-west boundary, the upper-west boundary, the lower-west boundary, the upper-south boundary, the lower-south boundary. They continually spread for ever and ever. They are the Arms of the Universe.

2. Twelve Elementals: HV ZCh TY LN SO TzQ. Engrave them, carve them, weigh them, permute them, transpose them, and with them depict the twelve constellations in the Univese: Aries, Taurus, Gemini, Cancer, Leo, Virgo, Libra, Scorpio, Sagittarius, Capricorn, Aquarius, and Pisces; the twelve months in the Year: Nissan, Iyar, Sivan, Tamuz, Av, Elul, Tishrei, Mar-cheshvan, Kislev, Tevet, Shevat, Adar; and the twelve directors in the Soul: two hands, two feet,

two kidneys, the spleen, the liver, the gall bladder, the *hemsess*, the *kiva*, and the *korkeban*.

[How does one permute them? Make Heh king, bind a crown to it, and with it depict Aries in the Univese, Nissan in the Year, and the right hand in the soul, male and female.

[Make Vav king, bind a crown to it, and with it depict Taurus in the Universe, Iyar in the Year, and the left hand in the Soul.

[Make Zayin king, bind a crown to it, and with it depict Gemini in the Universe, Sivan in the Year, and the right foot in the Soul.

[Make Chet king, bind a crown to it, and with it depict Cancer in the Universe, Tamuz in the Year, and the left foot in the Soul.

[Make Tet king, bind a crown to it, and with it depict Leo in the Universe, Av in the Year and the right kidney in the soul.

[Make Yud king, bind a crown to it, and with it depict Virgo in the Universe, Elul in the Year, and the left kidney in the Soul.

[Make Lamed king, bind a crown to it, and with it depict Libra in the Universe, Tishrei in the Year, and the liver in the Soul.

[Make Nun king, bind a crown to it, and with it depict Scorpio in the Universe, Mar-cheshvan in the Year, and the spleen in the Soul.

[Make Samekh king, bind a crown to it, and with it depict Sagittarius in the Universe, Kislev in the Year, and the gall bladder in the Soul.

[Make Eyin king, bind a crown to it, and with it depict Capricorn in the Universe, Tevet in the Year, and the *hemsess* in the Soul.

[Make Tzadi king, bind a crown to it, and with it depict Aquarius in the Universe, Shevat in the Year, and the *kivah* in the Soul.

[Make Kuf king, bind a crown to it, and with it depict Pisces in the Universe, Adar in the Year, and the *korkeban* in the Soul.]

3. Three Mothers which are three Fathers, from which emanate fire, breath and water. Three Mothers, seven Doubles, and Twelve Elementals.

4. These are the twenty-two letters which were founded by the Blessed Holy One [Yah, YHVH of Hosts, God of Israel, the Living God, high and exalted] dwelling in eternity, whose name is Holy, [exalted and holy is He].

Chapter 6

1. Three are the Fathers and their offspring, seven are the planets and their host, and twelve are the diagonal boundaries. And the proof of this, true witnesses, are the Universe, the Year, and the Soul. He

decreed Twelve, (Ten), Seven and Three, and He appointed them in the Teli, the Cycle, and the Heart. The three are fire, water, and breath; fire above, water below, and breath, the decree that decides between them. A sign of this is that fire upholds water.

Mem hums, Shin hisses, and Alef is the decree that decides between them.

2. The Teli in the Universe is like a king on his throne, the Cycle in the Year is like a king in the province, the Heart in the Soul is like a king in battle.

"Also every desire, one opposite the other was made by God" (Ecclesiastes 7:14). Good opposite evil, good from good, evil from evil. Good makes evil recognizable, and evil makes good recognizable. Good makes evil recognizable, and evil makes good recognizable. Good is kept for the good, and evil is kept for the wicked.

3. Three: each one stands alone. Seven are divided, three opposite three, with a decree deciding between them. Twelve stand in war: three who love, three who hate, three who give life, and three who kill. The three who love are the heart, the ears and the mouth; the three who hate are the liver, the gall bladder, and the tongue. And God, the faithful King dominates them all. One over three, three over seven, seven over twelve, and all of them are bound, one to another.

4. And when Abraham our father gazed, he looked, saw, delved, understood, engraved, carved, permuted and depicted, and he was successful. And the Master of all, Blessed be He, revealed Himself to him, and took him in His bosom, [kissed him on the head, and called him, "My beloved"]. He made a covenant with him between the ten toes of his feet—this is the covenant of circumcision—and between the ten fingers of his hands—this is the covenant of the tongue. He bound the twenty-two letters to his tongue and revealed their foundation. He drew them in water, burned them in fire, agitated them with breath. He ignited them with the seven (planets), and directed them with the twelve constellations.

THE LONG VERSION

Chapter 1

1. With thirty-two mystical paths of Wisdom engraved Yah, YHVH of Hosts, God of Israel, the Living God, God Almighty, high and exalted, dwelling in eternity on high, and His name is Holy, and He created His universe with three books, with text, with number, and with communication. [They are] Ten Sefirot of Nothingness and twenty-two foundation letters.

2. Ten Sefirot like the number of ten fingers, five opposite five. The singular covenant is directly in the middle, like the circumcision of the tongue in the mouth, and like the circumcision of the membrum.

3. Ten Sefirot of Nothingness: Ten and not nine, ten and not eleven. Understand with Wisdom, and probe with Understanding. Discern with them and probe from them. Make a thing stand on its essence, and make the Creator sit on His base, for He alone is the Former and Creator, and there is none besides Him. And His measure is ten and they have no end.

4. Ten Sefirot of Nothingness: Bridle your heart from thinking, bridle your mouth from speaking. And if your heart runs, return to the place, as it is written, "And the Chayot running and returning." Regarding this a covenant has been made.

5. Ten Sefirot of Nothingness: Their end is imbedded in their beginning, and their beginning in their end, like a flame bound to a burning coal. Know, think and depict that the Master is unitary, and the Creator is One, and He has no second. And before One, what do you count?

6. Ten Sefirot of Nothingness: Their measure is ten which have no end: A depth of beginning and a depth of end; a depth of good and a depth of evil; a depth of above and a depth of below; a depth of east and a depth of west, a depth of north and a depth of south. The unique Master, God faithful King, dominates them all from His holy dwelling until eternity of eternities.

7. Ten Sefirot of Nothingness: Their vision is like the appearance of lightning, and their limit has no end. They speak of them as "running and returning," they pursue His word like a whirlwind, and before His throne they prostrate themselves.

8. Ten Sefirot of Nothingness and twenty-two foundation letters: Three Mothers, seven Doubles, and twelve Elementals, and Breath is in each of them.

9. Ten Sefirot of Nothingness: One is the Breath of the Living God, His throne is established from eternity,[3] blessed be the name of the Life of Worlds constantly, forever and ever: Voice, Breath and Speech. Speech is the Holy Breath (*Ruach HaKodesh*). Its inception has no beginning, and its termination has no end.

10. Ten Sefirot of Nothingness: One is the Breath of the Living God, two is breath from breath, three is water from breath, four is fire from water, and up and down, east and west, north and south.

11. Two is breath from Breath. With them He engraved and carved the four direction-breaths (*ruchot*) of heaven: east and west, north and south. And breath (*ruach*) is in each one of them.

12. Three is water from breath. With them he engraved and carved chaos and void, clay and mire. He made them like a garden bed, he carved them like a wall, and he covered them like a ceiling, and he poured snow over them, and dust was made. It is thus written, "For to snow he said, become earth" (Job 37:6).

Chaos is an azure[4] line that surrounds all the world. Void consists of the spongy[5] rocks that are imbedded in the abyss, from between which water emanates.[6]

13. Four is fire from water. With it He engraved and carved the Throne of Glory, Serafim, Ophanim, holy Chayot, and ministering angels. And from these three He founded His abode, as it is written, "He makes his angels of breaths, His ministers from flaming fire" (Psalms 104:4).

14. Five: He sealed "above." He selected three letters from among the Elementals and fixed them in His great Name: YHV. With them He sealed the six directions. He faced upward and sealed it with YHV.

Six: He sealed "below," faced downward, and sealed it with YVH.

Seven: He sealed east, faced forward, and sealed it with VYH.

Eight: He sealed west, faced backward, and sealed it with VHY.

Nine: He sealed south, faced to His right, and sealed it with YVH.

Ten: He sealed north, faced to His left, and sealed it with HVY.

These are Ten Sefirot of Nothingness: One is the Breath of the Living God, two is breath from Breath, three is water from breath, four is fire from water; above and below, east and west, north and south.

Chapter 2

1. Twenty-two foundation letters: three Mothers, seven Doubles, and twelve Elementals. And all of them are engraved with voice, carved with breath, and set in the mouth in five places: the letters AChHO, GYKQ, DTLNTh, ZSTzRSh, BVMPh. They are bound to the tongue like a flame bound to a burning coal. AChHO is pronounced with the base of the tongue and the throat. BVMPh is pronounced between the lips and with the tip of the tongue. GYKQ is pronounced with the (back) third of the tongue. DTLNTh is pronounced with the tip of the tongue, together with the voice. ZSTzRSh is pronounced between the teeth, with the tongue lying flat and spread out.

2. Twenty-two foundation letters: They are set in the Cycle in 231 Gates. The cycle oscillates back and forth. And a sign for this, if in good, there is nothing higher than delight (ONG), and if in evil, there is nothing lower than the plague (NGO).

3. Twenty-two foundation letters: He engraved them, carved them, weighed them, and transposed them, Alef with them all. And He permuted them, and with them He formed the soul of all that was ever formed, and the soul of all that ever will be formed.

4. How? He weighed them and transposed them, Alef with them all, and all of them with Alef, Bet with them all, and all of them with Bet, [continuing] likewise with all the [letters]. And all of them oscillate cyclically. Thus, they emerge through 231 Gates, and everything formed and everything said emanates from one Name.

5. From Chaos He formed substance, and He made that which was not into that which is. He carved great stones out of air that cannot be grasped.

Chapter 3

1. Three Mothers, AMSh: Their foundation is the pan of merit, the pan of liability, and the tongue of decree deciding between them.

2. Three Mothers, AMSh: A great, concealed, mystical secret, covered with six rings. From them emanate fire, water and breath. They are divided as male and female. Know, think and contemplate that fire supports water.

3. Three Mothers, AMSh: The progeny of the heavens is fire, the progeny of the air is breath, and the progeny of the earth is water.

Fire is above and water is below, and breath is the decree deciding between them. From them were born Fathers, and from them all things were created.

4. Three Mothers, AMSh, in the Universe are breath, water and fire. The heavens were created from fire, the earth was created from water, and the air from breath decides between them.

5. Three Mothers, AMSh, in the Year are the hot, the cold, and the temperate. The hot was created from fire, the cold from water, and the temperate from breath decides between them.

6. Three Mothers, AMSh, in the Soul are the head, the belly and the chest. The head was created from fire, the belly was created from water, and the chest from breath decides between them.

7. Three Mothers, AMSh: He engraved them, carved them, permuted them, and sealed with them three Mothers, AMSh, in the Universe, three Mothers, AMSh, in the Year, and three Mothers, AMSh, in the Soul, male and female.

8. He made the letter Alef king over breath, bound a crown to it, permuted one with another, and with them formed air in the Universe, the temperate in the Year, and the chest in the Soul, male and female.

He made the letter Mem king over water, bound a crown to it, permuted one with another, and with them formed the earth in the Universe, the cold in the Year, and the belly in the Soul, male and female.

He made the letter Shin king over fire, bound a crown to it, permuted one with another, and with them formed the heavens in the Universe, the hot in the Year, and the head in the Soul, male and female.

9. How did He form them? AMSh AShM, MASh MShA, ShAM ShMA. The heaven is fire, the air is breath, and the earth is water. Man's head is fire, his belly is water, and his heart is breath.

10. Three Mothers AMSh. With Alef He formed breath, air, the temperate, the chest, the tongue of decree between them.
With Mem: water, earth, the cold, the belly, the pan of merit.
With Shin: fire, heaven, the hot, the head, the pan of liability.
This is AMSh.

Chapter 4

1. Seven Doubles, BGD KPRT: Their foundation is life, peace, wisdom, wealth, seed, grace, and dominance. They function with two

tongues, the doubling of opposites: B Bh, G Gh, D Dh, K Kh, P Ph, R Rh, T Th. A structure of soft and hard, strong and weak.

These are the opposites: The opposite of wisdom is foolishness, the opposite of wealth is poverty, the opposite of seed is desolation, the opposite of life is death, the opposite of dominance is subjugation, the opposite of peace is war, the opposite of grace is ugliness.

2. Seven Doubles, BGD KPRT: Seven and not six, seven and not eight. They parallel the six ribs and the six orders, and the Holy Palace is precisely in the center. "Blessed be the glory of God from His Place" (Ezekiel 3:12). He is the place of the universe, and the universe is not His place.[7] And He supports them all.

3. Seven Doubles, BGD KPRT of foundation: He engraved them, carved them, permuted them, weighed them, transformed them, and with them He formed seven planets in the Universe, seven days in the Year, and seven gates in the Soul, seven and seven.

4. How did He permute them? Two stones build two houses, three stones build six houses, four stones build 24 houses, five stones build 120 houses, six stones build 720 houses, seven stones build 5040 houses. From there on go out and calculate that which the mouth cannot speak and the ear cannot hear.

5. He made the letter Bet king over wisdom, bound a crown to it, permuted one with another, and with them He formed Saturn in the Universe, the Sabbath in the Year, and the mouth in the Soul, male and female.

6. He made the letter Gimel king over wealth, bound a crown to it, permuted one with another, and with them He formed Jupiter in the Universe, Sunday in the Year, and the right eye in the Soul, male and female.

7. He made the letter Dalet king over seed, bound a crown to it, permuted one with another, and with them He formed Mars in the Universe, Monday in the Year, and the left eye in the Soul, male and female.

8. He made the letter Kaf king over life, bound a crown to it, permuted one with another, and with them He formed the Sun in the Universe, Tuesday in the Year, and the right nostril in the Soul, male and female.

9. He made the letter Peh king over dominance, bound a crown to it, permuted one with another, and with them He formed Venus in the Universe, Wednesday in the Year, and the left nostril in the Soul, male and female.

10. He made the letter Resh king over peace, bound a crown to it, permuted one with another, and with them He formed Mercury in the Universe, Thursday in the Year, and the right ear in the Soul, male and female.

11. He made the letter Tav king over grace, bound a crown to it, permuted one with another, and with them He formed the Moon in the Universe, Friday in the Year, and the left ear in the Soul, male and female.

And with them He engraved seven firmaments, seven earths, seven seas, seven rivers, seven deserts, seven days, seven weeks, seven years, seven sabbaticals, seven jubilees, and the Holy Palace. He therefore engraved the seventh for every desire under the heavens.

12. Seven planets in the Universe are: Saturn, Jupiter, Mars, Sun, Venus, Mercury, Moon.

Seven days in the Year are the seven days of the week.

Seven gates in the Soul, male and female, are the two eyes, two ears, two nostrils, and the mouth.

13. Seven firmaments are Vilon, Rakia, Shechakim, Zevul, Ma'on, Machon, and Aravot.

Seven earths are Adamah, Tevel, Neshiyah, Tziyah, Chalad, Eretz, Gai.

And He made each one stand alone: The Universe alone, the Soul alone, and the Year alone.

14. Seven Doubles BGD KPRT:

With Bet He formed Saturn, the Sabbath, the mouth, life and death.

With Gimel He formed Jupiter, Sunday, the right eye, peace and evil.[8]

With Dalet He formed Mars, Monday, the left eye, wisdom and foolishness.

With Kaf He formed the Sun, Tuesday, the right nostril, wealth and poverty.

With Peh He formed Venus, Wednesday, the left nostril, seed and desolation.

With Resh He formed Mercury, Thursday, the right ear, grace and ugliness.

With Tav He formed the Moon, Friday, the left ear, dominance and subjugation.

These are BGD KPRT.

Chapter 5

1. Twelve Elementals, HV ZCh TY LN SO TzQ: Their foundation is sight, hearing, smell, speech, taste, coition, motion, anger, laughter, thought, joy, and sleep.

2. Twelve Elementals, HV ZCh TY LN SO TzQ: Their foundation is twelve and not eleven, twelve and not thirteen. The twelve diagonal boundaries peel off as six orders divided between each direction: the eastern upper boundary, the eastern northern boundary, the eastern lower boundary; the southern upper boundary, the southern eastern boundary, the southern lower boundary; the western upper boundary, the western southern boundary, the western lower boundary; the northern upper boundary, the northern western boundary, the northern lower boundary. They continuously spread until eternity of eternities, and it is they that are the Heights of the Universe.

4. Twelve Elementals, HV ZCh TY LN SO TzQ: He engraved them, carved them, permuted them, weighed them, transposed them, and with them He formed twelve constellations in the Universe, twelve months in the Year, and twelve directors in the Soul, male and female. Two rejoice (*OLZ*), two slander (*LOZ*), two advise (*YOTz*), two rejoice (*OLTz*). And they are the *korkeban*, the teeth, the two hands and the two feet. He made them like a controversy, he arranged them like a war, one opposite the other.

5. Seven: Three opposite three, and one deciding between them.
   And twelve stand in war: Three allies, three enemies, three lifegivers, and three killers.
   Three allies are the heart, the ears and the eyes. Three enemies are the liver, the gall, and the tongue. Three lifegivers are the two nostrils and the spleen. Three killers are the two orifices and the mouth. And God faithful King dominates them all from His holy Dwelling until eternity of eternities.

6. One over three, three over seven, seven over twelve. All of them are attached, one to the other. And a sign for this is the twenty-two objects and one body.

7. And these are the twelve directors: two hands, two feet, two kidneys, the liver, the gall, the spleen, the *hemsess*, the *korkeban*, and the *kivah*.

8. He made the letter Heh king over speech, bound a crown to it, permuted them one with another, and with them He formed Aries in the Universe, Nissan in the Year, and the liver in the Soul, male and female.

9. He made the letter Vav king over thought, bound a crown to it, permuted them one with another, and with them He formed Taurus in the Universe, Iyar in the Year, and the gall bladder in the Soul, male and female.

10. He made the letter Zayin king over motion, bound a crown to it, permuted them one with another, and with them He formed Gemini in the Universe, Sivan in the Year, and the spleen in the Soul, male and female.

11. He made the letter Chet king over sight, bound a crown to it, permuted them one with another, and with them He formed Cancer in the Universe, Tamuz in the Year, and the *hemsess* in the Soul, male and female.

12. He made the letter Tet king over hearing, bound a crown to it, permuted them one with another, and with them He formed Leo in the Universe, Av in the Year, and the right kidney in the Soul, male and female.

13. He made the letter Yud king over action, bound a crown to it, permuted them one with another, and with them He formed Virgo in the Universe, Elul in the Year, and the left kidney in the Soul, male and female.

14. He made the letter Lamed king over coition, bound a crown to it, permuted them one with another, and with them He formed Libra in the Universe, Tishrei in the Year, and the *korkeban* in the Soul, male and female.

15. He made the letter Nun king over smell, bound a crown to it, permuted them one with another, and with them He formed Scorpio in the Universe, Cheshvan in the Year, and the *kivah* in the Soul, male and female.

16. He made the letter Samekh king over sleep, bound a crown to it, permuted them one with another, and with them He formed Sagittarius in the Universe, Kislev in the Year, and the right hand in the Soul, male and female.

17. He made the letter Eyin king over anger, bound a crown to it, permuted them one with another, and with them He formed Capricorn in the Universe, Tevet in the Year, and the left hand in the Soul, male and female.

18. He made the letter Tzadi king over taste, bound a crown to it, permuted them one with another, and with them He formed Aquarius in the Universe, Shevat in the Year, and the right foot in the Soul, male and female.

19. He made the letter Kuf king over laughter, bound a crown to it, permuted them one with another, and with them He formed Pisces in the Universe, Adar in the Year, and the left foot in the Soul, male and female.

20. He divided the witnesses and made each one stand alone: the Universe alone, the Year alone, and the Soul alone.

21. Twelve Elementals: HV ZCh TY LN SO TzQ:
   With Heh He formed Aries, Nissan, the liver, sight and blindness.
   With Vav He formed Taurus, Iyar, the gall, hearing and deafness.
   With Zayin He formed Gemini, Sivan, the spleen, smell and the inability to smell.
   With Chet He formed Cancer, Tamuz, the *hemsess*, speech and dumbness.
   With Tet He formed Leo, Av, the right kidney, taste and hunger.
   With Yud He formed Virgo, Elul, the left kidney, action and paralysis.
   With Lamed He formed Libra, Tishrei, the *korkeban*, coition and impotence.
   With Nun He formed Scorpio, Mar-cheshvan, the *kiva*, motion and lameness.
   With Samekh He formed Sagittarius, Kislev, the right hand, anger and lack of liver.
   With Eyin He formed Capricorn, Tevet, the left hand, laughter and the lack of spleen.
   With Tzadi He formed Aquarius, Shevat, the right foot, thought and the lack of heart.
   With Kuf He formed Pisces, Adar, the left foot, sleep and insomnia.
   These are the twelve Elementals, HV ZCh TY LN SO TzQ. And all of them are attached to the Teli, the Cycle, and the Heart.

Chapter 6

1. Three Mothers, AMSh; seven Doubles, BGD KPRT; twelve Elementals, HV ZCh TY LN SO TzQ. These are the twenty-two letters with which formed YH YHVH of Hosts, God of Israel, the Living God, El Shaddai, high and exalted, dwelling in eternity, and His name is Holy.

"YH YHVH"—two (divine) Names.

"Of Hosts" (*Tzava'ot*)—Because He is a sign (*ot*) in His host (*Tzava*).[9]

"God of Israel" (*YSREL*)—A prince (*SaR*) before God (*EL*).

"The Living God"—Three are called "living": the Living God, living waters, and the tree of life.

"El"—is harsh.

"Shaddai"—Because (He decreed): Until here is enough (*dai*).[10]

"High"—Because He sits in the height of the universe, and is high above all the high.

"Exalted" (*Nisa*)—because He supports (*nasa*) and sustains those on high and below. All that support are on the bottom, with their burden below them, but He is on top, and His burden is below him. He supports and sustains the entire Universe.

"He dwells in eternity"—Because His kingdom exists for eternity of eternities, without interruption.

"Holy is His Name"—Because He is holy, His ministers are holy, and to Him they say, "Holy, holy, holy" (Isaiah 6:3).

2. Twelve below, seven over them, and three over seven. From the three He founded His abode. And all of them hang from One and stand on it. And a sign of One, He has no second.[11] He rules alone in His universe, for He is One, and His name is One.[12]

3. Three Fathers and their progeny, seven subduers and their host, twelve diagonal boundaries. A proof of this, trusted witnesses, are the Universe, the Year, and the Soul.

4. The Sefirot of the Universe are ten and twelve: fire, breath, water, seven planets, and twelve constellations.

The Sefirot of the Year are ten and twelve: cold, hot, temperate, seven days, and twelve months.

The Sefirot of the Soul are ten and twelve: the head, chest, belly, seven gates, and twelve directors.

5. A rule of ten, three, seven and twelve, and He appointed them in the Teli, the Cycle, and the Heart. The Teli in the universe is like a king on his throne, the Cycle in the Year is like a king in the province, and the Heart in the Soul is like a king in battle.

6. The general rule is this: Some of these combine with others, and some are the transpose of others. Some are opposite of others, and others are the opposite of these. If some exist, others do not, and if others exist, these do not. And all of them are attached to the Teli, the Cycle and the Heart.

7. Also every desire, "God made one opposite the other" (Ecclesiastes 7:14). Good opposite evil, and evil opposite good. Good from good,

and evil from evil. Good discerns evil, and evil discerns good. Good is stored away for the good, and evil is stored away for the wicked.

8. And when Abraham our father, of blessed memory, came, he looked, saw, probed, understood, engraved, carved, permuted, formed, and thought, and he was successful. The Lord of all, may His name be blessed for eternity, revealed Himself to him, kissed him on the head, and called him, "Abraham My friend" (Isaiah 41:8). He made a covenant with him and his seed forever. "And he believed in God, and He considered it righteousness" (Genesis 15:6). The Glory of God was decreed upon him, as it is written, "Before I formed you in the womb, I knew you" (Jeremiah 1:5). He made a covenant between the ten fingers of his hands, and this is the Holy Tongue (the Hebrew language). He bound the twenty-two letters on his tongue, and the Blessed Holy One revealed to him their mystery. He drew them in water, ignited them with fire, agitated them with breath, burned them with the seven planets, and directed them with the twelve constellations.

9. Heaven fire heat head. Air breath temperate chest. Earth water cold belly. This is AMSh.

10. Saturn Sabbath mouth. Jupiter Sunday right eye. Mars Monday left eye. Sun Tuesday right nostril. Venus Wednesday left nostil. Mercury Thursday right ear. Moon Friday left ear. This is BGD KPRT.

11. And these are the twelve constellations: Aries Nissan liver sight blindness. Taurus Iyar gall hearing deafness. Gemini Sivan spleen, smell inability to smell. Cancer Tamuz *hemsess* speech dumbness. Leo Av right kidney taste hunger. Virgo Elul left kidney action paralysis. Libra Tishrei *korkeban* coition impotence. Scorpio Marcheshvan *kivah* motion lameness. Sagittarius Kislev right hand anger lack of liver. Capricorn Tevet left hand laughter lack of spleen. Aquarius Shevat right foot thought lack of heart. Pisces Adar left foot sleep insomnia. This is HV ZCh TY LN SO TzQ.

12. Three enemies are the tongue, the liver, the gall. Three allies are the eyes, the ears, the heart. Three lifegivers are the teeth, the nose, and the spleen. Three killers are the two lower orifices and the mouth.

13. Three not in one's control are his eyes, his ears and his nose. Three good sounds to the ear are a blessing, good news, praise. Three bad sights to the eye are an adultress, and evil eye, a roving eye.[13] Three good sights are humility, a good eye, a true eye. Three evil to the tongue are slander, talebearing, saying one thing with the mouth and another in the heart. Three good for the tongue are silence, watching the tongue, and true speech.

SAADIA VERSION

Chapter 1

1. With thirty-two mystical Paths of Wisdom engraved YH, YHVH of Hosts, God of Israel, the Living God, El Shadai, high and exalted, dwelling in eternity and Holy is His name. He created His universe with three books, with script, number and telling. Ten Sefirot of Nothingness, twenty-two letters: three Basics,[14] seven Doubles, twelve Elementals.

2. Ten Sefirot of Nothingness, like the number of ten fingers, five opposite five, with a unitary covenant directly in the middle, as the circumcision of the tongue and mouth. Their measure is ten which have no end: A depth of beginning and a depth of end, a depth of good and a depth of evil, a depth of above and a depth below, a depth east and a depth west, a depth north and a depth south. And the unitary Master, God faithful King, dominates them all from His holy abode, until eternity of eternities.

3. Twenty-two letters, a foundation of three Basics, seven Doubles, and twelve Elementals.

The three Basics are AMSh. Their foundation is a pan of merit, a pan of liability, and the tongue of decree deciding between them.

The seven Doubles are BGD KPRT. Their foundation is life and peace, wisdom and wealth, seed, grace and dominance.

The twelve Elementals are HVZChTYLNSOTzQ. Their foundation is sight, hearing, smell, speech, taste, coition, action and motion, haughtiness, laughter, thought, and sleep.

4. Through them YH, YHVH of Hosts, God of Israel, the Living God, El Shadai, High and Exalted, dwelling on high and Holy is His name, engraved three Fathers and their progeny, seven directors and their host, and twelve diagonal boundaries. A proof of this, true witnesses are the Universe, Year and Soul, a rule of ten, three, seven and twelve. He appointed them in the Teli, Cycle and Heart.

Chapter 2

1. Ten Sefirot of Nothingness: ten and not nine, ten and not eleven. Understand with Wisdom, and be wise with Understanding. Discern with them, probe from them, and know, think and depict. Stand a thing on its essence, and make the Creator sit on His basis. And their measure is ten which have no end. Their vision is like an appearance

of lightning, and their limit has no end. His word in them "runs and returns," they pursue His saying like a whirlwind, and before His throne they prostrate themselves.

2. Twenty-two letters are a foundation of three Basics, seven Doubles, and twelve Elementals. The three Basics, AMSh, are a great, concealed, mystical, exalted secret, from which emanates fire, breath and water, from which everything was created. The seven Doubles function with two tongues: Bei Bhei,[15] Gimel Ghimel, Dalet Dhalet, Kaf Khaf, Peh Pheh, Resh Rhesh, Tav Thav. Hard and soft, they are strong and weak structures. They are doubles because they are opposites. The opposite of life is death, the opposite of peace is evil, the opposite of wisdom is foolishness, the opposite of wealth is poverty, the opposite of seed is desolation, the opposite of grace is ugliness, the opposite of dominance is subjugation.

3. Seven Doubles, BGD KPRT: Seven and not six, seven and not eight. Six ribs for six orders, with the Holy Palace precisely in the center. Blessed by God from His place. His is the place of the universe, and the universe is not His place.

4. Twelve Elementals: Twelve and not eleven, twelve and not thirteen. The twelve diagonals peel off to six orders, separating between one direction and another: an east north boundary, an east upper boundary, and east lower boundary; a north west boundary, a north upper boundary, a north lower boundary; a west south boundary, a west upper boundary, a west lower boundary; a south east boundary, a south upper boundary, a south lower boundary.

5. With them YH, YHVH of Hosts, God of Israel, the Living God, El Shadai, High and Exalted, dwelling on high and Holy is His name, engraved twenty-two letters and set them in the Sphere. He oscillated the Sphere back and forth, and the Sphere (continues to) oscillate back and forth. As a sign of this, there is nothing higher than delight (*ONG*), and there is nothing more evil than plague (*NGO*).

6. Proof of this, trustworthy witnesses, are the Universe, Year and Soul. The Sefirot of the Universe are ten; three are fire, breath and water; seven are the seven planets; twelve are the twelve constellations. The Sefirot of the Year are ten; three are the cold, the hot and the temperate; seven are the seven days of creation; twelve are the twelve lunar months. The Sefirot of the Soul are ten; three are the head, chest and belly; seven are the seven gates, twelve are the twelve directors.

Chapter 3

1. Ten Sefirot of Nothingness: Bridle your mouth from speaking; bridle your heart from thinking. And if your heart runs, return to the place, for it is written, "running and returning." Regarding this a covenant was made. And their measure is ten which have no end. Their end is imbedded in their beginning, and their beginning in their end, like a flame attached to a burning coal. Know, think and depict that the Creator is One, there is no other, and before One what do you count?

2. The twenty-two letters are a foundation of three Basics, seven Doubles, and twelve Elementals. The three Basics, AMSh, are fire, breath and water. The offspring of heaven is fire, the offspring of air is breath, and the offspring of earth is water. Fire is above, water is below, and breath is the decree that decides between them. Mem hums, Shin hisses, and Alef is the decree deciding between them. AMSh is sealed with six rings and cocooned[16] in male and female. Know, think and depict that fire upholds water.

3. The seven Doubles, BGD KPRT, function with two tongues: Bei Bhei, Gimel Ghimel, Dalet Dhalet, Kaf Khaf, Peh Pheh, Resh Rhesh, Tav Thav. They are soft and hard, a structure that is strong and weak. They are doubled because they are opposites. The opposite of life is death, the opposite of peace is evil, the opposite of wisdom is folly, the opposite of wealth is poverty, the opposite of seed is desolation, the opposite of grace is ugliness, and the opposite of dominance is subjugation.

4. The twelve Elementals are HVZChTYLNSOTzQ. He engraved them, carved them, permuted them, weighed them and transformed them. How did He permute them? Two stones build two houses, three build six houses, four build 24 houses, five build 120 houses, six build 720 houses, seven build 5040 houses. From there on go out and calculate that which the mouth cannot speak and the ear cannot hear.

5. With these Yah, YHVH of Hosts, God of Israel, the Living God, El Shaddai, High and Exalted, dwelling in eternity on high and holy is His name, engraved.

YaH: is two names.

YHVH is four names.

Hosts: (Tzavaot) means that He is a sign (*ot*) in His host (*tzava*).

Israel: He is a prince (*sar*) before God (*El*).

El Shaddai: El is hard. Shaddai indicates that until here it is enough (*dai*).

High: because He sits in the height of the universe, and is high above all the high.

Exalted: because He upholds and sustains those on high and below. All others who carry something are on the bottom and their burden is above them, but He is on top, and His burden is below Him. He upholds and sustains the entire universe.

Dwelling in Eternity: because His kingdom exists for eternity of eternities without interruption.

And Holy is His Name: Because He is holy, his ministers are holy, and to Him they proclaim, "Holy, holy, holy."

6. Proof of this, trustworthy witnesses, are the Universe, Year and Soul. Twelve are below, seven are above them, and three are above the seven. From these three He founded His abode, and all of them depend on One. As a sign, this is a One that has no second. He is a singular King in His universe, where He is One and His name is One.

Chapter 4

1. Ten Sefirot of Nothingness: One is the Breath of the Living God, Life of worlds, His throne is established from eternity, blessed and benedicted is His name, constantly, forever and ever. This is the Holy Breath (*Ruach HaKodesh*).

2. Two: Breath from Breath. With it He engraved and carved four directions (breaths) of heaven: east, west, north, and south. And there is a breath in each one of them.

3. The twenty-two letters are a foundation consisting of three Basics, seven Doubles, and twelve Elementals. The letters are carved with Breath, engraved with voice, and set in the mouth in five places: AHChO, BVMP, GYKQ, DTLNTh, ZSTzRSh. AHChO is pronounced with the base of the tongue and the throat. BVMP is pronounced between the lips and with the tip of the tongue. GYKQ utilizes the first third of the tongue. DTLNTh is pronounced with half the tongue and the voice. ZSTzRSh is pronounced between the teeth with the tongue sleeping.

4. The twenty-two letters: He engraved them, carved them, permuted them, weighed them, transformed them, and from them He formed all that was ever formed and all that would ever be formed. How did He permute them? Alef with them all and all of them with Alef; Bet

with them all, and all of them with Bet; Gimel with them all, and all of them with Gimel. All of them oscillate cyclically, and emerge through 231 Gates. As a result, everything spoken and everything formed emerges as one Name.

5. He formed substance from chaos, and made that which was not into that which is. He carved great pillars from air that cannot be grasped.

6. Three: water from breath. With it He engraved and carved chaos and void, clay and mire. He made them like a garden plot, He carved them like a wall, and He decked them like a ceiling. He poured water on them, and it became dust, as it is written, "For to snow He said, become earth" (Job 37:6). Chaos is the azure line that surrounds the universe. Void consists of the split stones imbedded in the abyss, from between which water emerges. It is thus written, "He spread over it a line of Chaos and stones of Void" (Isaiah 34:11).

7. Four: fire from water. With it He engraved and carved the Throne of Glory and all the host on high. It is thus written, "He makes His angels of breaths, and His ministers of flaming fire" (Psalms 104:4).

8. He chose three Elementals, and set them in His great name. And with them He sealed the six directions.
He sealed "above," faced upward, and sealed it with YHV.
Six: He sealed "below," faced downward, and sealed it with YVH.
Seven: He sealed east, faced forward, and sealed it with HVY.
Eight: He sealed west, faced backward, and sealed it with HYV.
Nine: He sealed south, faced to His right, and sealed it with VYH.
Ten: He sealed north, faced to His left, and sealed it with VHY.
These are the Ten Sefirot of Nothingness. One is the Breath of the Living God, two is breath from Breath, three is water from breath, four is fire from water; above and below, east and west, north and south.

Chapter 5

1. He made Alef king over breath, bound a crown to it, permuted one with another, and with it He formed air in the Universe, the tem-

perate in the Year, and the chest in the Soul, male and female. The
male with AMSh, and the female with AShM.

2. He made Mem king over water, bound a crown to it, permuted
one with another, and with it He formed earth in the Universe, the
cold in the Year, and the belly in the Soul.

3. He made Shin king over fire, bound a crown to it, permuted one
with another, and with it He formed heaven in Universe, the hot in
the Year, and the head in the soul.

    As male and female, how did He permute them? AMSh AShM,
MShA MASh, ShAM ShMA. Heaven is fire, air is breath, earth is
water. Man's head is fire, his heart is breath, and his belly is water.

4. The seven Doubles are BGD KPRT. He engraved them, carved
them, permuted them, weighed them, and transformed them. With
them He formed planets, days and gates.

5. He made Bet king, bound a crown to it, permuted them one with
another, and with it He formed Saturn in the Universe, the Sabbath
in the Year, and the mouth in the Soul.

6. He made Gimel king, bound a crown to it, permuted them one
with another, and with it He formed Jupiter in the Universe, Sunday
in the Year, and the right eye in the Soul.

7. He made Dalet king, bound a crown to it, permuted them one with
another, and with it He formed Mars in the Universe, Monday in the
Year, and the left eye in the Soul.

8. He made Kaf king, bound a crown to it, permuted them one with
another, and with it He formed the Sun in the Universe, Tuesday in
the Year, and the right nostril in the Soul.

9. He made Peh king, bound a crown to it, permuted them one with
another, and with it He formed Venus in the Universe, Wednesday
in the Year, and the left nostril in the Soul.

10. He made Resh king, bound a crown to it, permuted them one
with another, and with it He formed the Star of the Sun (Mercury)[17]
in the Universe, Thursday in the Year, and the right ear in the
Soul.

11. He made Tav king, bound a crown to it, permuted them one with
another, and with it He formed Moon in the Universe, Friday in the
Year, and the left ear in the Soul.

12. He separated the witnesses and stood them alone, one by one: the
Universe alone, the Year alone, and the Soul alone.

Chapter 6

1. The twelve Elementals are HVZChTYLNSOTzQ. He engraved them, carved them, permuted them, weighed them and transformed them, and with them He formed constellations, months and directors. Two are extreme, two stabilize, two advise, and two rejoice. They are the *korkebans*[18] the two hands, and the two feet. He made them like a dispute, and arranged them like a battle. "And God made one opposite another" (Ecclesiastes 7:14).

2. Three: each one is alone. Seven are divided, three against three, with one as the decree deciding between them. Twelve: twelve stand in war, three allies, three enemies, three killers, and three lifegivers. All of them are attached, one to another. A sign of this is twenty-two objects and one body.

3. How did He permute them? HV VH, ZCh ChZ, TY YT, LN NL, SO OS, TzQ QTz.

4. He made Heh king, bound a crown to it, permuted one with another, and with it He formed Aries in the Universe, Nissan in the Year, and the liver in the Soul.

5. He made Vav king, bound a crown to it, permuted one with another, and with it He formed Taurus in the Universe, Iyar in the Year, and the gall bladder in the Soul.

6. He made Zayin king, bound a crown to it, permuted one with another, and with it He formed Gemini in the Universe, Sivan in the Year, and the spleen in the Soul.

7. He made Chet king, bound a crown to it, permuted one with another, and with it He formed Cancer in the Universe, Tamuz in the Year, and the *mesess* in the Soul.

8. He made Tet king, bound a crown to it, permuted one with another, and with it He formed Leo in the Universe, Av in the Year, and the right kidney in the Soul.

9. He made Yud king, bound a crown to it, permuted one with another, and with it He formed Virgo in the Universe, Elul in the Year, and the left kidney in the Soul.

10. He made Lamed king, bound a crown to it, permuted one with another, and with it He formed Libra in the Universe, Tisrei in the Year, and the *korkeban* in the Soul.

11. He made Nun king, bound a crown to it, permuted one with another, and with it He formed Scorpio in the Universe, Cheshvan in the Year, and the *kivah* in the Soul.

12. He made Samekh king, bound a crown to it, permuted one with another, and with it He formed Sagittarius in the Universe, Kislev in the Year, and the right hand in the Soul.

13. He made Eyin king, bound a crown to it, permuted one with another, and with it He formed Capricorn in the Universe, Tevet in the Year, and the left hand in the Soul.

14. He made Tzadi king, bound a crown to it, permuted one with another, and with it He formed Aquarius in the Universe, Shevat in the Year, and the right foot in the Soul.

15. He made Kuf king, bound a crown to it, permuted one with another, and with it He formed Pisces in the Universe, Adar in the Year, and the left foot in the Soul.

16. He separated the witnesses and stood each one alone: the Universe alone, the Year alone, and the Soul alone.

Chapter 7

1. Air, temperate, chest. Earth, cold, belly. Heaven, hot, head. And this is AMSh.

2. Saturn, Sabbath, mouth. Jupiter, Sunday, right eye. Mars, Monday, left eye. Sun, Tuesday, right nostril. Venus, Wednesday, left nostril. Sun Star (Mercury), Thursday, right ear. Moon, Friday, left ear. And this is BGD KPRT.

3. Aries, Nissan, liver. Taurus, Iyar, gall bladder. Gemini, Sivan, spleen. Cancer, Tamuz, *mesess*. Leo, Av, right kidney. Virgo, Elul, left kidney. Libra, Tishrei, *korkeban*. Scorpio, Mar-cheshvan, *kivah*. Sagittarius, Kislev, right hand. Capricorn, Tevet, left hand. Aquarius, Shevat, right foot. Pisces, Adar, left foot. And these are H V Z Ch T Y L N S O Tz Q.

Chapter 8

1. With Alef He formed these: breath, air, temperate, chest, and the tongue of decree. With Mem He formed these: water, earth, cold,

belly, and the pan of liability. With Shin He formed these: fire, heaven, hot, head, and the pan of merit.

2. With Bet He formed these: Saturn, Sabbath, mouth, life and death. With Gimel He formed these: Jupiter, Sunday, right eye, peace and evil. With Dalet He formed these: Mars, Monday, left eye, wisdom and foolishness. With Kaf He formed these: Sun, Tuesday, right nostril, wealth and poverty. With Peh He formed these: Venus, Wednesday, left nostril, seed and desolation. With Resh He formed these: Sun Star (Mercury), Thursday, right ear, grace and ugliness. With Tav He formed these: Moon, Friday, left ear, dominance and subjugation.

3. With Heh He formed these: Aries, Nissan, liver, sight and blindness. With Vav He formed these: Taurus, Iyar, gall bladder, hearing and deafness. With Zayin He formed these: Gemini, Sivan, spleen, smell and inability to smell. With Chet He formed these: Cancer, Tamuz, *mesess*, speech and dumbness. With Tet He formed these: Leo, Av, right kidney, taste and hunger. With Yud He formed these: Virgo, Elul, left kidney, coition and castration. With Lamed He formed these: Libra, Tishrei, *korkeban*, action and paralysis. With Nun He formed these: Scorpio, Cheshvan, *kivah*, motion and lameness. With Samekh He formed these: Sagittarius, Kislev, right hand, anger and lack of liver. With Eyin He formed these: Capricorn, Tevet, left hand, laughter and lack of spleen. With Tzadi He formed these: Aquarius, Shevat, right foot, thought and lack of heart, where it is not. With Kuf He formed these: Pisces, Adar, left foot, sleep, dead and gone.

4. And all of them are attached to the Teli, Cycle and Heart. Teli in the Universe is like on a throne, Cycle in the Year is like a king in the province, Heart in the body is like a king in battle. The general rule is this. Some permute with others, and others permute with these. Some are with others, and others are with these. Some are the opposite of others, and others are the opposite of these. Some are the parallel of others, and others are the parallel of these. If not some, then not others; and if not others, then not these. And all of them are attached to the Teli, the Cycle, and the Heart.

5. And When Abraham our father understood, formed, permuted, probed, thought and was successful, the Blessed Holy One revealed Himself to him, declaring to him, "Before I formed you in the womb, I knew you, and before and emerged from the womb, I sanctified you. I have made you a prophet for the nations" (Jeremiah 1:5). He made him His friend, and made a covenent with him and his children forever and until eternity.

APPENDIX II
The Thirty-Two Paths
of Wisdom

The Thirty-Two Paths of Wisdom are presented as different states of consciousness. This presentation most probably dates from the Gaonic period (7th-10th centuries), and is found in a number of Kabbalistic texts.[1] These states are also related to the 32 times where God's name appears in the first chapter of Genesis.

The Thirty-Two Paths of Wisdom

1. Mystical Consciousness (*Sekhel Mufla*). This is the Light that was originally conceived, and it is the First Glory.[2] No creature can attain its excellence.

2. Radiant Consciousness (*Sekhel Maz'hir*). This is the Crown of creation and the radiance of the homogeneous unity that "exalts itself above all as the Head."[3] The masters of Kabbalah call it the Second Glory.

3. Sanctified Consciousness (*Sekhel MeKudash*). This is the foundation of the Original Wisdom, and it is called "Faithful Faith."[4] Its roots are AMeN. It is the father of faith, and from its power faith emerges.

4. Settled Consciousness (*Sekhel Kavua*). It is called this because all the spiritual powers emanate from it as the [most] ethereal of emanations. One emanates from the other through the power of the original Emanator, may He be blessed.[5]

5. Rooted Consciousness (*Sekhel Nishrash*). It is called this because it is the essence of the homogeneous Unity. It is unified in the essence of Understanding, which emanates from the domain of the Original Wisdom.

6. Transcendental Influx Consciousness (*Sekhel Shefa Nivdal*). It is called this because through it the influx of Emanation (*Atzilut*) increases itself. It bestows this influx on all blessings, which unify themselves in its essence.

7. Hidden Consciousness (*Sekhel Nistar*). It is called this because it is the radiance that illuminates the transcendental powers that are seen with the mind's eye and with the reverie of Faith.[6]

8. Perfect Consciousness (*Sekhel Shalem*). It is called this because it is the Original Arrangement. There is no root through which it can be pondered, except through the chambers of Greatness, which emanate from the essence of its permanence.

9. Pure Consciousness (*Sekhel Tahor*). It is called this because it purifies the Sefirot. It tests the decree of their structure and the inner essence of their unity, making it glow. They are then unified without any cutoff or separation.

10. Scintillating Consciousness (*Sekhel MitNotzetz*). It is called this because it elevates itself and sits on the throne of Understanding. It

shines with the radiance of all the luminaries, and it bestows an influx of increase to the Prince of the Face.[7]

11. Glaring Consciousness (*Sekhel MeTzuchtzach*). It is called this because it is the essence of the Veil which is ordered in the arrangement of the system. It indicates the relationship of the Paths (*netivot*) whereby one can stand before the Cause of Causes.

12. Glowing Consciousness (*Sekhel Bahir*). It is called this because it is the essence of the Ophan-wheel of Greatness.[8] It is called the Visualizer (*Chazchazit*), the place which gives rise to the vision that the Seers perceive in an apparition.[9]

13. Unity Directing Consciousness (*Sekhel Manhig HaAchdut*). It is called this because it is the essence of the Glory.[10] It represents the completion of the true essence of the unified spiritual beings.

14. Illuminating Consciousness (*Sekhel Meir*). It is called this because it is the essence of the Speaking Silence (*Chashmal*).[11] It gives instruction regarding the mysteries of the holy secrets and their structure.

15. Stabilizing Consciousness (*Sekhel Ma'amid*). It is called this because it stabilizes the essence of creation in the "Glooms of Purity."[12] The masters of theory said that this is the Gloom [at Sinai].[13] This is the meaning of, "Gloom is its cocoon" (Job 35:9).[14]

16. Enduring Consciousness (*Sekhel Nitzchi*). It is called this because it is the Delight (*Eden*) of the Glory. As it is, there is no Glory lower than it. It is called the Garden of Eden, which is prepared for the [reward of the] saints.

17. Consciousness of the Senses (*Sekhel HaHergesh*). This is prepared for the faithful saints so that they should be able to clothe themselves in the spirit of holiness. In the arrangement of the supernal Entities, it is called the Foundation of Beauty (*Yesod HaTiferet*).

18. Consciousness of the House of Influx (*Sekhel Bet HaShefa*). By probing with it, a secret mystery (*raz*) and an allusion are transmitted to those who "dwell in its shadow"[15] and bind themselves to probing its substance from the Cause of Causes.[16]

19. Consciousness of the Mystery of all Spiritual Activities (*Sekhel Sod HaPaulot HaRuchniot Kulam*). It is called this because of the influx that permeates it from the highest blessing and the supreme Glory.

20. Consciousness of Will (*Sekhel HaRatzon*). It is called this because it is the structure of all that is formed. Through this state of consciousness one can know the essence of the Original Wisdom.[17]

21. Desired and Sought Consciousness (*Sekhel HaChafutz VeHaMevukash*). It is called this because it receives the divine Influx so as to bestow its blessing to all things that exist.

22. Faithful Consciousness (*Sekhel Ne'eman*). It is called this because spiritual powers are increased through it, so that they can be close to all who "dwell in their shadow."[19]

23. Sustaining Consciousness (*Sekhel Kayam*). It is called this because it is the sustaining power for all the Sefirot.

24. Apparitive Consciousness (*Sekhel Dimyoni*). It is called this because it provides an appearance for all created apparitions, in a form fitting their stature.

25. Testing Consciousness (*Sekhel Nisyoni*). It is called this because it is the original temptation through which God tests all of His saints.

26. Renewing Consciousness (*Sekhel MeChudash*). It is called this because it is the means through which the Blessed Holy One brings about all new things which are brought into being in His creation.

27. Palpable Consciousness (*Sekhel Murgash*). It is called this because the consciousness of all things created under the entire upper sphere, as well as all their sensations, were created through it.

28. Natural Consciousness (*Sekhel Mutba*). It is called this because the nature of all that exist under the sphere of the sun was completed through it.

29. Physical Consciousness (*Sekhel Mugsham*). It is called this because it depicts the growth of everything that becomes physical under the system of all the spheres.

30. General Consciousness (*Sekhel Kelali*). It is called this because it is the means through which the "generalizers of the heavens" collect their rules regarding the stars and constellations, forming the theory that comprises their knowledge of the Ophan-wheels of the spheres.

31. Continuous Consciousness (*Sekhel Tamidi*). Why is it called this? Because it directs the path of the sun and moon according to their laws of nature, each one in its proper orbit.

32. Worshiped Consciousness (*Sekhel Ne'evad*). It is called this because it is prepared so as to destroy all who engage in the worship of the seven planets.

APPENDIX III
THE GATES

The 221 Gates of Rabbi Eliezar
Rokeach of Wormes

The tables on pages 304-309 are presented here exactly as they are printed in the Przemysl edition, (1889), of the commentary on Sefer Yetzirah. In order to derive the proper arrays from these tables, lines containing only eleven letters must be doubled. The other lines, which contain twenty-two letters, are left as they are. All the letters are then paired into groups of two. One can see how this is done by comparing the table for Alef with the array given in chaper 2:4.

These are the 221 Gates that Rabbi Eliezar prescribes for use in creating a Golem. They can also be used from less advanced meditative exercises. When utilizing any letter, the appropriate array must be used.

304

Array for Alef	For Bet
אב גד הו זח טי כלמנסעפצקרשת	בג דה וזחטיכלם נסעף צקרש תא
אג הז טכ מס פק ש	בד וחיל נעצרת
אד זי מע קת גוטלסצשבהחכנפר	בה חכנפראדזי מעקת גוטלס צש
אח טמ פש גז כסק	בו ינצת דח לער
או כע שדטנקבזלפת היסר גחמצ	בז לפת היס רגח מצא וכעש דטנק
אז מק גטס שהכף	בח נר דיע תולצ
אח סת זנ שומר הלק דכך גיף נטע	בט עא חסתנזנש ומר הלק דכך גיף
אט פג כק המש זס	בי צד לר ונת חע
אי קוסבכר זע גלש חף דמת טיהנ	בכ רז ע גלש חף דמ תטיקה נאיקוס
אכ שטק זף הס גמ	בל תי רח צו עד נ
אל	**במ**
אמ גס הפז קט שכ	בנ דע וצח ריתל
אנ צט תמדרפח של געזר כבסוקי	בס וקיא נהצט תמדף חשלגעזרכ
אס זש מה קכג פט	בע חתנור לדצי
אע טב פיגכזד קלהרמו שנזתסח	בפ יג צכדקלה רמו שנזת סחא עט
אפ כה שס טג קמז	בצ לות עי דר נח
אצ מח גרסיה תפלז בקנט דשעכו	בק נטדשעכו אצ מח גרסיהתפלז
אק סכז גש פמטה	בר על חדת צניי
ארפנכח הבש צסל טוג תקע מיזד	בש צסלטוג תקע מיזד ארף נכחה
אש קפס מכט זהג	בת רצ ע נ ל י ח ו ד
את שרק צפעס נמלך יתחז והדגב	בא תש רק צפעס נמלך יתחז וה דג
For Gimel	For Dalet
גד הו זח טי כלמנסעפצקרשת אב	דה וז חט יכ למנס עפצק רשתאבג
גה הז כם ספ קש א	דו מי לנ עצ רת ב
גו טלסצ שבתחב נפראדזי מעקת	דז ימעקת גוטלס צש בההחכנפר א
גז כס קא ה ט מפש	דח לערב וינצת
גח מצא וכעשדטנקב זלפת היסר	דט נקב זלפת היסר גח מצא וכעש
גט סשה כפא זמק	די עתו לצב חנר
גי פבטע אחש תזגנשומר הלק דכך	דכ צגיף בטע אחסתנזנשומר הלק
גכ קהמ שזס אטפ	דל רונת חע ביצ
גל שחף דמת טצהנאיקוס בכר זע	דמ תלה נאיקוס בכר זע גלש חף
גמ אכשטק זף הס	דן בלתי רח צו עד
גן	**דס**
גס הפז קט שכ אמ	דע ולחרית לבנ
גע זר כב סו קיאנהצטתמדפחשל	דף משלג עזר כבסוקי אנה צטתם
גף טאס זשם הקכ	דצ יב עח תנורל
גצ כד קל הר מושנזתסחאעטבפי	דק להרמו שנזת סחא עט בפיגצכ
גק מז אפ כה שס ט	דר נח בצלות עי
גר סיה תפלז בקנטדשעכו אצמח	דש עכואצינח גרסיה תפלז בקנט
גש פם טה אק סכ ז	דת צניי ברע לח
גת קע מי זדארפנ כמה בשצס לטו	דא רפנ כמה בשצס לטוג תקע מיז
גא שק פסם כט זה	דב ת רצע נליחו
גב אתשרק צפעס כמלך יתחז והד	דג בא תשרקצפעס נמלך יתחזוה

For Heh	For Vav
הו זח עי כל מנ סע פצ קר שת	וו חט יכלמנסעפפצקרשתא בג דה
הז טכ מס פק שאג	וח יל נעצרת בד
הח כנפר אדזי מעקת גוטלס צשב	וט לסצש בהה כנפר אדזי מעקתג
הט מפש גז כסקא	וי נצת דחל ערב
הי סר גח מצא וכעשדטנגכבזולפת	וכ עש דט נקבזולפת היסרגחמצא
הכ פא זמק גטשש	ול צבח נרדי עת
הל קדכץ גיפ בטעאהס תזנשומר	ומ רהלק דכץ גיפ בטעאהס תזנש
המשזמ אטפ גכק	ונ תחע ביצד לר
הנ איקוסבכרזועגלש חפ דמת טץ	וס בכר זע גלש חפדמתטהנאיק
הס גמא כש טק זפ	וע ד נבלתי רחז

הע	ופ
הפ זק טש כא מג ס	ול חרית לבנדע
הצ טת מדפא שלג עזר כבסו קיאן	וק יאנה צטת מדפח שלגעזרכבס
הק כג פט אס זש מ	ור לד ציבע חתנ
הר מוש נזת סחאעטבטבפיגצכדקל	וש נזת סחאעטבטבפיגצכד קלה רמ
מש סט גקמז אפכ	ות עיד רנח בצל
התפלז בקנט דשעכו אצמא גרסי	וא צמח גרסיה תפלז בקנט דשעכ
הא קס כז גש פמט	וב רעל חדת צני
הב שצסל טוג תקעמיזד ארפנ כה	וג תקע מיזדארפנכחהבשצס לט
הג א שק פסמ כטז	וד בתר צע נליח
הד גבא תשרק צפעס נמלך יטחזו	וה דג בא תשרקצפעס נמלך יטחז

For Zayin	For Chet
זח טיכלמנסעפפצקרשת אב גד הו	חט יכלמנסעפפצקרשתא בגדהוז
זט כמ ספק שאגה	חי ל נעצרת בדו
זי מעקת גוטלסצשבהה כנ פר אד	חכ נפר אדזי מעקת גוטלסצשבה
זכ סק אהט מפ שג	חל טכג וינצתד
זל פת היסרגחמצט וכעשד טנקב	חמ לא וכעשד טנקבזולפת היסרג
זמ קג טס שה כפא	חנ ר דיעת ולצב
זנ שומר הלקדכיגכיפ בטע אהסת	חס תז נש ומר הלק דכיגכיפבטעא
זס א טפג כק המש	חע ביצד לרונת
זע גלש חפדמדהטצהנאיק וס בכר	חפ דמח טצהנאיקוסבכרזוע גלש
זפ הס גמא כשטק	חצ ו עד נבלתיר

זץ	חק
זק טשכ אמג סהפ	חר יתל בנ דע וץ
זר כבסוקי אנה צטת מדפח שלגע	חש לג עזר כבסוקי אנהצטת מדפ
זש מה כקגפטא ס	חת נור לד ליבע
זת סחא עטבפיג צכד קלתרמושנ	חא עטב פיג צכדקלהרמו שנזתס
זא פנה שסט גקמ	חב צלות עידר נ
זב קנט דשעכואצמח גרסיה תפל	חג רסיה תפלז בקנט דשעכואצמ
זג שפינטה אקסכ	מד תצניו ברעל
זד ארפנ כההנשצס לטוג תקעמי	חה בשצס לטוג תקע מיזד ארפנכ
זה גאש קפס מכט	חו ד בתר צעלני
זו הדג בא תשרק צפעסנמלךדיטח	חז והדג בא תשרק צפעסנמלך יט

For Tet	For Yud
טי כלמנסעפפצקרשת אבגדהוזח	יכ למנסעפפצ קרשת אבגדהו זחט
טכ מס פק שא גה ז	יל נעצרת בדוח
טל סצשבה חכנפר אדזי מעקת גו	ים עקת גוטלס צשבהח כנפר אדז
טם פשגזכסקאה	ין צת דחל ערבו
טן קב זלפת היסר גח מצאוכעשד	יס רג חמצא וכעשד טנקב זלפתה
טס שה כפאז מקג	יע תול צבח נרד
טע אחס תזנש ומרהלקדכץ גיפב	יפ בטע אחס תזנש ומרהלק דכצג
טפ ג כק המש זסא	ילד לרונת חענ
טצ ה נאיקוס בכרז עגלשחפדמת	יק וס בכרזגעגל שחף דמת טצ הנא
טקזפה סג מא כש	ירח לו עד נבלת

טר	יש
טש כא מג סה פזק	יתל בנד עוצחר
טת מדפח שלג עזר כבסוקי אנהל	יא נה צטת מדפח שלג עזר כנסוק
טא סז שמה ככג פ	יב עח תנור לדץ
טב פיגץ כדקל הרמושנזת סחאע	יג צכד קלה רמו שנזת סחא עטנף
טג קמז אפכה שס	יד רנח בצ לו תע
טד שעכו אצמח גרסיה תפלז בקן	יה תפלז בקנט דשעכו אלמח גרס
טה ק קסכ זג שפם	יו בר על חדת צן
טו ג תקע מיזד ארפנכחה בשצסל	יז ד ארפנכחה בשצס לטוג תקעם
טז ה גא שקף סמכ	יחוד בתר צענל
טח ז והדג בא השרק צפעס נמלרי	יט חז והדג בא תשרק צפעס נמלך

For Kaf	For Lamed
כל מן סע פץ קר שת אבגדהוזחטי	לם נסעפצקרשתא בג דה וזחטיכ
כם ספק שאג הזט	לן עצרת בדוחי
כן פרא דזימעקת גיטלס צשב הח	לס צש בתח כנפר ארזי מעקתגוע
כס קאהטמפשגז	לע רב וינצת דח
כע שד טנקב זלפת היסר גח מצאו	לפ תהיסר גח מצא וכעשדטנקבז
כף א זמק גטס שה	לצ בח נרדי עתו
כצ גיף בטעאמס תזנש ומרה לקד	לק דכץ גיף בטע אחסתזנשו מרה
כק ה משזס אט פג	לר ונת חע בילד
כרז עגלשחפדמת טץ הנאיק וסב	לש חף דמתמצה נאיק וסבכר זעג
כשטק זפה קגמא	לת יר חצו עד נב

כת	לא
כא מגס הפזק טש	לב נד עו צחרית
כב סוקיא נה צטת מדפח שלגעזר	לג עזרכבסו קיא נהצטת מדפחש
כג פט אסז שמהק	לד ציבעחתנור
כד קל הרמוש נתז סחא עטב פיגץ	לה רמו שנזתסח אעטבפיג צכדק
כה שסטגק מז אפ	לו תעידרנח בץ
כו אצמח גרסיה תפלז בקנטד שע	לז בקנט דשעכ ואצמח גרסיהתפ
כז ג שפמטה אקס	לח דת צניוברע
כח הבשצס לטיגת קעמיזד ארפנ	לט וגתקע מיז דארפנכח הבשצס
כט זה גא שק פס מ	לי חודבת רצענ
כי טחז והדגבא תשרקצפעס נמל	לכ יטחז והדגבא תשרק צפעס נמל

307

For Mem	For Nun
מן סעפצקרשת אב גדהוזח טיכל	נס עפצקרשת אבגדהוזחטי כל מ
מס פק שאגהזטכ	נע צרת בד וחיל
מע קת גוטל סצשבהחכנ פראדזי	נפ ראדזימעקת גוטלסצשב הח כ
מף שגזכסקאהט	נצ תד חל ערבוי
מצ א וכעשד תנקבזלף תהיסרגח	נק בזולפת היסר גחמצאו כעשדט
מק גטסשהכפאז	נר דיעתולצבח
מר הלק דכץ גיפבטע אחסתז נשו	נש ומרהלק דכצגי פבטע אחסתז
מש זסאטפגכקה	נת מעביצדצרו
מת טצהנאיק וסבכ רזעגל שחפד	נא יקוסבכרזעגלשחפדמטמצה
מא כשטקזפהסג	נב לתיריחציעד
מב	**נג**
מג סהפזקטשכא	נד עו צחריתלב
מד פחשלג עזרכב סוקיא נהצטט	נה צטתמדפ חשלג עזרכב סוקיא
מה קכגפטאסזש	נו רלדזיבעחת
מו שנזותסח אעט בפיגצ כדקלהר	נז תסח אעטבכפי גצכדקל הרמוש
מז אפכהשסטסגק	נח בצלו תעידר
מח גרסי התפלז בקנטד שעכואצ	נט דשעכו אלמח גרסיהתף לזבק
מט האקסכזגשפ	ני וברעלחדתצ
מי זדארפנ כחהבשצס לטוג תקע	נכ חהבס צסלטו גתקעם יזדארפ
מכ טזהגאשקפס	נל יחודבתרעצ
מל כיטחזוהדג בא תשרק צפעסנ	נם לך יטחז והדג בא תשרקצקפעס

For Samekh	For Eyin
סע פצקרשת אבגדהו זחטיכל מן	עפצקרשת אבגדה וזחטי כל מנס
סף קשאאגהזטכמ	עץ רתבדוחילן
סצ שבהחכנ פראדזי מעקת גוטל	עק תגוטלסצ שבהחכנ פרא דזים
סק אה טממפשגזכ	ער בוינצתדחל
סר גחמצאו כעשדטנק בזלף תהי	עש דטנקבזולפת היסרגח מצאו כ
סש הכפאזמקגט	עת ולצבחנרדי
סת זנשו מרהלק דכצגיפ בטעאח	עא חסתזנשומרה לקד כצגי פבט
סא טפגכקהמשז	עב יצדלרונתח
סב כרזעגל שחפד מתטצה נאיקן	עג לשחפדמת טצהנאיק וסב כרז
סג מאכשטקזפה	עד נבלתיריחצו
סד	**עה**
סה פזקטשכאמג	עו צחריתלבנד
סו קיא נהצטת מדפחשלג עזרכב	עז רכב סוקי אן הצטתמדפחשלג
סז שמה קכגפטא	עח תנור לדציב
סח א עטבפיגצכד קלהרם ושנזת	עט בפיגצכדקלהרמו שנזת סח א
סט גקמזאפכהש	עי דרנחבצלות
סי התפלז בקנטד עכוא צמחגר	עכ ואצמח גרסיהת פלז בקנטש
סכ זגשפפמטהאק	על חדתצניוב
סל טוגתק עמיזדא רפנכחהב שץ	עם יזדארפנכ חהבשצ סלטו גתק
סמ כטזהגאשקפ	ען ליחודבתרצ
סן מלכיטחזו והדג באתשרק צפע	עס נמלכיטחזוה דגבא תשרק צפ

308

For Peh	For Tzadi
פצקרשת אבגדהו זחטי כלמנ סע	צק רשתאב גדהוזחזחטי כל מנסעפ
פק שא גהזטכמס	צרת בדוחילנע
פר אדזי מעקת גוטלסצשב החכנ	צש בההחכנפר אדזימ עקת גוטלס
פש גזכסקא הטמ	צת דחלערבוינ
פת היסרגח מצא וכעשד טנקבזל	צא וכעשדט נקבזלפת היסרגח מ
פא זמק גטסשהכ	צב חנרדיעתול
פב טעא חסתזנס ומרהלק דכצגי	צג יפבטעאחסת זנשומרת לק דכ
פג כקהמשסזסאט	צד לרונתחעבי
פד מתטצ הנאיקן סבכרזע גלשח	צה נאיקוסבכר זעגל שחפד מתט
פה סגמאכשטקז	צו עדנבלתירח

פו	צז
פז קטשכא מגסה	צח ריתלבנדעו
פח שלגעזרכב סוקיא נהצט תמד	צט המדפח שלגעזר כבסוקיא נה
פט אסזשמהקבכג	צי בעחתנו רלד
פי גצכדקל הרמוש נזתסחא עטב	צך דקלהרמו שנזת סחא עטבפיג
פכ השסטגסקמזא	צל ותעידרנחב
פל זבכנט דשעכוא צמהג רסיהת	צם חגרסי התפלז בקנטדש עכוא
פם טהאקסכזגש	צן יוברעלחדת
פנ כההבשסצס לטוגת קע מיזדאר	צס לטוגתק עמיזדא רפנכח הבש
פס מכטזהגא שק	צע נליחודבתר
פע סנמלכי טחהזוהרדגבא תשרק צ	צף עסנמ לכיטחז והרדגבא תשרק

For Kuf	For Resh
קר שת אבגדהו זחטי כלמנסעפצ	רש תאבגדהוזחטיכלמנסעפפצק
קש אגהזטכמספ	רת בדוחיל נעץ
קת גוטל סצשבה חכנפר אדזימע	רא ד זימעקתגוטלסצשבהבהחכנפ
קא הטמפשגזכס	רב וינצת דחלע
קב זלפת היסר גחמצאו כעשדטנ	רג ח מצא וכעשדטנקבזלפת היס
קג ט סשה כפא זם	רד יעת ולצ בחנ
קד כץ גיפבטע אחסתזנשומר הל	רה לק דכצ גיפבטעאחס תזנשום
קה מש זס אט פג כ	רו נתח עבי צדל
קו סבכר זעגלש חפ דמתטצהזהנאי	רז עגלש חפ דמתטצהזהנאיקוס בכ
קז פה סגמא כשט	רח צו עד נבלתי

קח	רט
קט שכאם גסה פז	רי ת לב נדע וצח
קי אנה צטת מדפחשלגעזר בכסו	רך בסוקי אנהצטתמדפח שלגעז
קכ ג פט אס זשמה	רל ד ציבע חתנו
קל הרמוש נזתסחאעטב פיג צכד	רם וש נמתסחאעטב פיגצכד קלה
קם זאפכה שס טג	רן ח בצלות עיד
קן ט דש עכו אצמחגרסיהתפלזב	רס יה תפלז בקנטדשעכו אצמחג
קס כ זג שפפטהא	רע ל חדת צניוב
קע מיזד ארפנכחה בשצס לטוגת	רף נ כההבשסצס לטוגתקעמיז דא
קף ס מכט זהג אש	רץ ע נליחוד כת
קץ פעסנמלכיטחז והדג בא תשר	רק צפעס נמלכ יטחזוהרדגבא תש

For Shin	For Tav
שת אבגדהוזחטיכלמנסעפצקר	תא בגדהוזחטיכלמנסעפצקרש
שא גה זט כמספק	תב דוה יל נעצר
שב החכנפר אדזי מעקת גוטל סצ	תג וטלס צשבהח כנפר אדזימעק
שג ז כסק אהט מפ	תד חל ערב וינצ
שד ט נקב זלפת היסרגחמצצאוכע	תה יסר גחמצא וכעשדטנקב זלפ
שה כפאז מקגטס	תו ליצב חנרדיע
שו מר הלקדרכצגיפבטע אחס תזנ	תז נש ומרהלקדרכצגיפ בטע אחס
שז סא טפג כקהמ	תח ע ביצד לרונ
שח פ רמת טצה נאץ וסבכר זעגל	תט צה נאיק וסבכרזעגל שדפחמ
שטק זפה סגמאכ	תי רח צו עד נבל
שׁי	תכ
שכ א מגס הפזקט	תל ב נדעו צחרי
של געזר כבסוקי אנהצטת מדפח	תמ ד פחשלגעזורכנסוקי אנה צט
שמ ה קכג פטא סז	תנ ור לדצי בעח
שנ זתסחאעטבטבפיג צכד קלה רמר	תס ח אעטבבפילגצכדקלה רמו שנז
שס טג קמז אפ כה	תע ידר נח בצלו
שע כו אצמחגרסיה תפלז בקנטד	תפ לז בקנט דש עכואצצמאגרסיה
שפ מט הא קס כזג	תצ ני וברע לחד
שצ סלטגותקע מיזד ארפנ כחהב	תקע מיזד ארפנכחה בשצס לטוג
שק פס מכט זה גא	תר צע נליחוד ב
שר קצפעס נמליטחז והדג באת	תש רק צפעס נמלך יטחזוהדגבא

The 231 Gates According to the Later Kabbalists

These tables appear in *Emek HaMelekh* (Amsterdam, 1563), pages 4 to 6.

According to the later Kabbalists, they can be used for creating a Golem and for similar meditations.

Alef: Partzuf of Keter		Bet: Partzuf of Chakhmah	

Alef: Partzuf of Keter

אב גד הו זח טי כל מן סע עף צק רש שת	י
אג דה הו זח טי יך למ נס עף צק רש שת תב	ו
אד הו זח טי כל מן סע עף צק רש שת תב בג	ד
אה וז חט טי כל מן סע עף צק רש שת תב גד	ה
או זח טי כל מן סע עף צק רש שת תב בג דה	י
אז חט יך למ נס עף צק רש שת תב בג גד הו	ו
אח טי יך למ נס עף צק רש שת תב בג דה הו וז	י
אט יך למ נס עף צק רש שת תב גד דה הו וז זח	ו
אי כל מן סע עף פץ קר שת בג דה וז חט	ה
אך למ נס עף צק רש שת תב בג גד הו וז חט טי	י
אל מן סע עף פץ קר שת בג דה וז חט טי יך כל	יה
אמ נס עף צק רש שת תב גד הו וז חט טי יך כל	י
אן סע עף פץ קר שת בג דה הו וז חט טי יך למ	ו
אס עף צק רש שת תב גד דה הו וז חט טי יך כל מן	ד
אע פץ קר שת בג דה הו וז חט טי יך למ נס	ה
אף צק רש שת תב גד הו וז חט טי יך למ נס סע	י
אץ קר שת בג דה הו וז חט טי יך למ נס עף	ו
אק רש שת תב גד הו וז חט טי כל מן סע עף פץ	א
אר שת בג דה הו וז חט טי כל מן סע עף צק	ו
אש תב גד הו וז חט טי כל מן סע עף פץ קר	ה
את בג דה הו וז חט טי כל מן סע עף צק רש	י

Bet: Partzuf of Chakhmah

בג דה הו זח טי יך למ נס עף צק רש שת תא	י
בד הו זח טי כל מן סע עף צק רש שת תא אג	ו
בה וז חט טי יך למ נס עף צק רש שת תא אג גד	ד
בו זח טי כל מן סע עף צק רש שת תא אג גד דה	ה
בז חט יך למ נס עף צק רש שת תא אג גד הו	י
בח טי כל מן סע עף צק רש שת תא אג דה הו וז	ו
בט יך למ נס עף צק רש שת תא גד דה הו וז זח	י
בי כל מן סע עף צק רש שת תא אג דה הו וז חט	ו
בך למ נס עף צק רש שת תא גד הו וז חט טי	ה
בל מן סע עף פץ קר שת אג דה הו וז חט טי יך	י
ב"ם נס עף צק רש תא גד הו וז חט טי כל ליה	יה
בן סע עף צק רש שת אג דה וז חט טי יך למ	י
בס עף צק רש שת תא גד הו וז חט טי יך כל מן	ו
בע פץ קר שת תא גד הו וז חט טי יך למ נס	ו
בף צק רש שת אג דה הו וז חט טי יך למ נס סע	ד
בץ קר שת אג דה הו וז חט טי יך למ נס עף	ה
בק רש שת תא גד דה הו וז חט טי יך למ נס עף צק	ו
בר שת אג דה הו וז חט טי כל מן סע עף פץ קר	א
בש תא גד דה הו וז חט טי כל מן סע עף פץ קר	ו
בת אג דה וז חט טי יך למ נס עף פץ קר רש	ה
בא גד הו זח טי כל מן סע עף פץ קר שת	י

Gimel: Partzuf of Binah		Dalet: Partzuf of Daat	

Gimel: Partzuf of Binah

גד הו זח טי כל מן סע עף צק רש שת אב	י
גה הו זח טי כל מן סע עף צק רש שת תא בד	ו
גו זח טי כל מן סע עף צק רש שת אב דה	ד
גז חט טי כל מן סע עף צק רש הא בד הו	ה
גה טי כל מן סע עף צק רש שת אב דה וז	ה
גט יך למ נס עף צק רש שת אב בד הו וז	י
גי כל מן סע עף צק רש שת אב דה וז חט	י
גך למ נס עף צק רש שת אב בד הו זח טי	ו
גל מן סע עף צק רש שת אב דה וז חט טי יך	ה
גמ נס עף צק רש תא גד הו וז חט טי יך כל	י
גן סע עף צק רש שת אב דה הו וז חט טי יך כל מן	יה
גס עף צק רש שת אב בד תא הו זח טי יך כל מן	י
גע פץ קר שת אב דה הו וז חט טי יך למ נס	ו
גף צק רש תא בד הו זח טי כל מן סע	ד
גץ קר שת אב בד דה הו וז חט טי למ נס עף	ה
גק רש תא בד הו זח טי כל מן סע עף פץ	י
גר שת אב דה הו וז חט טי יך למ נס עף צק	ו
גש תא בד הו וז חט טי כל מן סע עף פץ קר	א
גת בד דה הו וז חט טי כל מן סע עף פץ קר רש	ו
גא בד הו וז חט טי כל מן סע עף פץ קר שת	ה
גב דה הו זח טי כל מן סע עף צק רש שת תא	י

Dalet: Partzuf of Daat

דה וז חט יך למ נס עף צק רש שת תא בג	י
דו זח טי כל מן סע עף צק רש שת תא אב גה	ו
דז חט יך למ נס עף צק רש שת תא בג גה הו	ד
דח טי כל מן סע עף צק רש שת תא אב גה וז	ה
דט יך למ נס עף צק רש שת תא בג הו זח	י
די כל מן סע עף צק רש שת תא בג גה הו וז חט	ו
דך למ נס עף צק רש שת אב גה הו וז חט טי	י
דל מן סע עף צק רש שת אב בג גה הו וז חט טי יך	ו
דמ נס עף צק רש תא בג גה הו וז חט טי כל	ה
דן סע עף פץ קר שת אב גה הו וז חט טי יך כל לם	י
דס עף צק רש תא בג גה הו וז חט טי כל מן	יה
דע פץ קר שת אב גה וז חט טי יך למ נס	ו
דף צק רש תא בג גה הו וז חט טי כל מן סע	ו
דץ קר שת אב גה הו וז חט טי כל מן סע עף	ד
דק רש תא בג גה הו וז חט טי כל מן סע עף פץ	ה
דר שת אב גה הו וז חט טי כל מן סע עף צק	י
דש תא בג גה הו וז חט טי כל מן סע עף פץ קר	ו
דת אב גה הו וז חט טי כל מן סע עף פץ קר רש	א
דא בג גה הו זח טי כל מג סע עף פץ קר שת	ו
דב גה הו זח טי כל מן סע עף צק רש שת תא	ה
דג הו זח טי כל מן סע עף צק רש שת תא אב	י

Heh: Partzuf of Chesed		Vav: Partzuf of Gevurah	

Heh: Partzuf of Chesed

י	הו זח טי כל מן סע פץ קר שת אב גד
ו	הז חט יך כל מן סע עף צק רש תא בג דו
ד	הח טי כל מן סע פץ קר שת אב גד וז
ה	הט יך כל מן סע עף צק רש תא בג דו וז
י	הי כל מן סע פץ קר שת אב גד וז חט
ו	הך למ סע פץ קר רש תא בג דו וז חט טי
י	הל מן סע עף צק רש תא אב גד וז חט טי
ו	המ נס עף צק רש תא בג דו זח טי כל
ה	הן סע פץ קר שת אב גד וז חט יך כל למ
י	הס עף צק רש תא בג דו וז חט טי כל מן
יה	הע פץ קר שת אב גד וז חט יך כל מן נס
י	הף צק רש תא בג דו זח טי כל מן סע
ו	הץ קר שת אב גד וז חט יך כל מן סע עף
ד	הק רש תא בג דו זח טי כל מן סע פץ
ה	הר שת תא בג דו וז חט יך למ נס עף צק
י	הש תא בג דו וז חט טי כל מן נס עף צק קר
ו	הת אב גד דו וז חט יך כל מן סע עף צק קר רש
א	הא בג דו וז חט טי כל מן סע עף פץ קר שת
ו	הב גד וז חט יך כל מן סע עף צק רש תא
ה	הג דו וז חט טי כל מן סע עף צק רש תא אב
י	הד וז חט יך למ נס עף צק רש תא אב בג

Vav: Partzuf of Gevurah

י	וו חט יך למ נס עף צק רש תא בג דה
ו	וח טי כל מן סע עף צק רש תא אב גד הז
ד	וט יכ למ סע עף צק רש תא בג דה זח זח
ה	וי כל מן סע פץ קר שת אב גד הז הז חט
י	וך למ סע עף צק רש תא בג דה הז זח טי
ו	ול מן סע עף פץ קר שת אב גד הז חט יך
י	ומ נס עף צק רש תא בג דה זח טי כל
ו	ון סע פץ קר שת אב גד הז חט טי יך למ
ה	וס עף צק רש תא בג דה זח טי כל מן
י	וע פץ קר שת אב גד הז חט טי כל למ נס
יה	וף צק רש תא בג דה זח טי כל מן נס עף
י	וץ קר שת אב גד הז זח טי כל מן סע עף
ו	וק רש תא בג דה זח טי כל מן סע עף פץ
ד	ור שת אב גד הז זח טי כל מן סע עף צק
ה	וש תא בג דה זח טי כל מן סע עף פץ קר
י	ות אב גד הז זח טי כל מן סע עף פץ קר רש
ו	וא בג דה זח טי כל מן סע עף צק רש תא
א	וב גד הז זח טי כל מן סע עף צק רש תא
ו	וג דה חט טי כל מן סע עף צק רש תא בג
ה	וד הז חט יכ למ סע עף צק רש תא בג דג
י	וה זח טי כל מן סע עף פץ קר שת אב גד

Zayin: Partzuf of Tiferet		Chet: Partzuf of Netzach	

Zayin: Partzuf of Tiferet

י	זח טי כל מן סע פץ קר שת אב גד הו
ו	זט יכ למ סע עף צק רש תא בג דה וח
ד	זי כל מן סע פץ קר שת אב גד הו וח חט
ה	זך למ סע פץ קר שת אב גד הו וח טי
י	זל מן סע עף צק רש תא בג דה וח חט יך
ו	זמ נס עף צק רש תא בג דה וח טי כל
י	זן סע פץ קר רש תא בג גד הו וח חט טי כל למ
ו	זס עף צק רש תא בג דה וח חט טי כל למ
ה	זע פץ קר שת אב גד הו וח חט יך למ נס
י	זף צק רש תא בג דה וח חט יך למ סע
יה	זק רש תא בג דה וח חט יכ למ סע עף פץ
י	זר שת אב גד הו וח חט יך כל מן סע עף צק
ו	זש תא בג דה וח חט טי כל מן סע פץ קר
ד	זת אב גד הו וח חט יך למ נס עף צק רש
ה	זא בג דה וח חט טי כל מן סע עף צק רש שת
י	זב גד הו וח חט יך כל מן סע עף צק רש תא
ו	זג דה וח חט טי כל מן סע פץ קר שת תא אב
א	זד הו וח חט יך כל מן סע עף פץ קר שת אב בג
ו	זה וח חט יך למ נס עף צק רש תא בג
ה	זו חט יכ למ נס עף צק רש תא אב גד
י	זז חט יך כל מן סע עף צק רש תא גד דה

Chet: Partzuf of Netzach

י	חט יך למ נס עף צק רש תא בג דה וז
ו	חי כל מן סע עף פץ קר שת אב גד הו וז זט
ד	חך למ סע עף צק רש תא בג דה וז זט טי
ה	חל מן סע עף צק רש תא בג דה וז זט יך
י	חמ נס עף צק רש תא בג דה וז חט טי כל
ו	חן סע פץ קר שת אב גד הו וח טי יך כל למ
י	חס עף צק רש תא בג דה וח טי יך כל מן
ו	חע פץ קר שת אב גד הו וז זט יך כל מן סע
ה	חף צק רש תא בג דה וז חט יך למ נס עף
יה	חק רש תא בג דה וז זט יך כל מן סע פץ
י	חר שת אב גד הו וז זט יך למ נס עף צק
ו	חש תא בג דה וז זט יך כל מן סע עף פץ קר
ר	חת אב גד הו וז זט יך למ נס עף צק רש
ה	חא בג דה וז זט יך כל מן סע עף פץ קר שת
י	חב גד הו וז יך למ נס עף צק רש תא
ו	חג דה וז חט יך כל מן סע עף פץ קר שת אב
א	חד וז חט יך כל מן סע עף צק רש תא בג
ו	חה וז חט יך למ נס עף צק רש תא בג דה
ה	חו זט יך למ נס עף צק רש תא בג דה
י	חז טי כל מן סע עף פץ קר שת אב גד הו

Tet: Partzuf of Hod		Yud: Partzuf of Yesod	

Tet: Partzuf of Hod

טי כל מן סע פץ קר שת אב גד הו זח	י
טך למ נס עף צק רש תא בג דה וז חי	ו
טל מן סע פץ קר שת אב גד הו זח חי	ד
טמ סע פץ קר שת אב גד דה וז חי כל	ה
טן סע פץ קר שת אב גד הו זח יד למ	י
טס עף צק רש תא בג דה וז חי כל מן	ו
טע פץ קר שת אב גד הו זח יד למ נס	י
טף צק רש תא בג דה וז חי כל מן סע	ו
טץ קר שת אב גד הו זח יד למ נס עף	ה
טק רש תא בג דה וז חי כל מן סע עף	י
טר שת אב גד הו זח יד למ נס עף צק יה	יה
טש תא בג דה וז חי כל מן סע עף פץ קר	י
טת אב גד הו זח יד למ נס עף פץ קר	ו
טא בג דה וז יח כל מן סע פץ קר שת	ד
טב גד הו זח יד למ נס עף פץ קר שת אב	ה
טג דה וז חי כל מן סע עף פץ קר שת אב	י
טד הו זח יד למ נס עף פץ קר שת אב בג	ו
טה הו חי כל מן סע עף פץ קר שת אב גד	א
טו זח יכ לן סע פצק קר שת אב גד הו	ו
טז חי כל מן סע עף פץ קר שת אב גד הו	ה
טח יך כל מן סע עף צק רש תא בג דה וז	י

Yud: Partzuf of Yesod

יך למ נס עף צק רש תא בג דה וז חט	י
יל מן סע פץ קר שת אב גד הו זח טך	ו
ים נס עף צק רש תא בג דה וז חט כל	ד
ין סע עף צק רש תא בג דה וז חט טך למ	ה
יס עף צק רש תא בג דה וז חט כל מן	י
יע פץ קר שת אב גד הו זח יד למ נס	ו
יפ צק רש תא בג דה וז חט כל מן סע	י
יץ קר שת אב גד הו זח טך למ נס עף	ו
יק רש תא בג דה וז חט כל מן סע עף	ה
יר שת אב גד הו זח טך למ נס עף צק	י
יש תא בג דה וז חט כל מן סע עף פץ קר	יה
ית אב גד הו זח טך למ נס עף פץ קר רש	י
יא בג דה וז חט כל מן סע עף פץ קר שת	ו
יב גד הו זח טך למ נס עף פץ קר שת תא	ד
יג דה וז חט כל מן סע עף פץ קר שת אב	ה
יד הו זח טך למ נס עף פץ קר שת אב בג	י
יה וז חט כל מן סע עף פץ קר שת אב גד	ו
יו זח טך למ נס עף פץ קר שת אב גד גד	א
יז חט כל מן סע עף פץ קר שת אב גד הו	ו
יח טך למ נס עף צק רש תא בג דה וז	ה
יט כל מן סע עף פץ קר שת אב גד הו זח	י

Kaf: Partzuf of Malkhut

כל מן סע פץ קר שת אב גד הו זח טי	י
כמ נס עף צק רש תא בג דה וז חט טי יל	ו
כן סע פץ קר שת אב גד הו זח טי יל	ו
כס עף פץ קר שת אב גד דה וז חט טי יל מן	ד
כע פץ קר שת אב גד הו זח טי יל מן נס	ה
כף צק רש תא בג דה וז חט טי יל מן סע	י
כץ קר שת אב גד הו זח טי יל למ נס עף	ו
כק רש תא בג דה וז חט טי יל מן סע עף	י
כר שת אב גד הו זח טי יל מן סע פץ	ד
כש תא בג דה וז חט טי יל מן סע עף פץ קר	ה
כת אב גד הו זח טי יל למ נס עף פץ צק רש יה	יה
כא בג דה וז חט טי יל מן סע פץ קר שת	י
כב גד הו זח טי יל מן סע עף פץ קר שת תא	ו
כג דה וז חט טי יל למ נס עף פץ קר שת אב	ד
כד הו זח טי יל מן סע עף פץ קר שת אב	ה
כה וז חט טי יל מן סע עף פץ קר שת אב בג	ה
כו זח טי יל מן סע עף פץ קר שת אב גד דה	י
כז חט טי יל מן סע עף פץ קר שת אב גד הו	א
כח טי יל מן סע עף צק רש תא בג דה וז	ו
כט יל מן סע עף פץ קר שת אב גד הו זח	ה
כי למ נס עף פץ קר שת אב גד הו זח חט	י

Lamed: Back of Keter

למ נס עף צק רש תא בג דה וז חט טי יך	י
לן סע עף צק רש תא בג דה וז חט טי יך כמ	ו
לס עף צק רש תא בג דה וז חט טי יך מן	ד
לע פץ קר שת אב גד הו זח טי יך כמ נס	ה
לף צק רש תא בג דה וז חט טי יך מן סע	א
לק רש תא בג דה וז חט טי יך כמ נס עף	ו
לר שת אב גד הו זח טי יך כמ נס עף פץ	א
לש תא בג דה וז חט טי יך מן סע עף צק	ו
לת אב גד הו זח טי יך כמ נס עף פץ קר	ה
לא בג דה וז חט טי יך מן סע עף פץ קר רש	א
לב גד הו זח טי יך כמ נס עף פץ קר שת תא	וה
לג דה וז חט טי יך מן סע עף פץ קר שת אב	י
לד הו זח טי יך כמ נס עף פץ קר שת אב בג	ו
לה וז חט טי יך מן סע עף פץ קר שת אב גד	ד
לו חט טי יך מן סע עף פץ קר שת אב גד דה	ה
לז חט טי יך כמ נס עף פץ קר שת אב גד הו	ה
לח טי יך כמ נס עף פץ קר שת אב גד הו	ו
לט יך כמ נס עף פץ קר שת אב גד הו זח	ו
לי כמ נס עף פץ קר שת אב גד הו זח חט	ה
לך מן סע עף פץ קר שת אב גד הו זח טי	י

Mem: Back of Chakhmah		Nun: Back of Binah	
מן סע פץ קר שת אב גד הו זח טי כל	י	נס עף צק רש תא בג דה וז חט טי כל לם	י
מס עף צק רש שת אב גד הו זח הט יך לן	ו	נע פץ קר שת אב גד הו זח טי כל מס	ו
מע פץ קר שת אב גד דה וז חט טי כל נס	ד	נף צק רש תא בג דה וז חט טי כל לם סע	ד
מף צק רש שת אב גד דה וז חט טי כל נס עף	ה	נץ קר שת אב גד הו זח טי כל מס עף	ה
מץ קר שת אב גד הו זח טי כל נס עף	א	נק רש תא בג דה וז חט טי כל לם סע פץ	א
מר שת אב גד הו זח טי כל נס עף פץ	ו	נר שת אב גד הו זח טי כל מס צק	ו
מש תא אב גד הו זח טי כל לן סע עף פץ קר	א	נש תא בג דה וז חט טי כל לם סע פץ קר	א
מת תא בג גד דה וה זח טי כל נס עף פץ קר רש	ה	נת אב גד הו זח טי כל מס עף פץ צק קר רש	ו
מא בג דה וז חט טי כל לן סע עף פץ צק רש שת	א	נא בג דה וז חט טי כל לם סע פץ קר שת	ה
מב גד דה וז חט טי כל נס עף צק רש שת תא	וה	נב גד דה וז חט טי כל מס עף פץ קר רש תא	א
מג דה הו חט טי כל לן סע עף פץ קר שת אב	י	נג דה וז חט טי כל מס עף פץ קר רש תא בג	וה
מד הו זח טי כל נס עף פץ צק רש תא בג	ו	נד הו זח טי כל נס עף פץ קר רש תא בג	י
מה וז חט טי כל לן סע עף פץ קר רש הא בג גד	ד	נה וז חט טי כל לם סע פץ קר שת אב גד	ו
מו זח טי כל נס עף פץ צק רש הא בג גד דה	ה	נו זח טי כל מס עף פץ קר שת אב גד דה	ד
מז חט טי כל לן סע עף פץ קר רש שת אב בג גד הז	ה	נז חט טי כל לם סע פץ קר שת אב גד דה הו	ה
מח טי כל נס עף פץ צק רש תא בג גד דה וז	ו	נח טי כל מס עף פץ קר שת אב גד דה וז	ה
מט יך לן סע עף פץ קר שת אב תא בג גד הו וז	ו	נט יך לם סע פץ קר שת אב גד דה וז זח	ו
מי כל נס עף פץ צק רש שת אב גד הו זח	ה	ני כל מס עף פץ קר שת אב גד הו זח זח	ו
מך לן סע עף פץ קר שת אב גד דה וז זח טי	ה	נך לם סע עף פץ קר שת אב גד הו זח חט	ה
מל נס עף פץ צק רש תא בג גד דה וז חט טי יך		נל מס עף צק רש שת אב גד הו זח טי כל	ה
		נם סע עף צק רש תא בג דה וז חט טי כל	

Samekh: Back of Daat		Eyin: Back of Chesed	
סע פץ קר שת אב גד הו זח טי כל מן	י	עף צק רש תא בג דה וז חט טי כל לם נס	י
סף צק רש תא בג דה וז חט טי כל מן נע	ו	עץ קר שת אב גד הו זח טי כל מן סף	ו
סץ קר שת אב גד הו זח טי כל מן עף	ד	עק רש תא בג דה וז חט טי כל לם נס פץ	ד
סק רש תא בג דה וז חט טי כל מן נע עף	ה	ער שת אב גד הו זח טי כל מן סף צק	ה
סר שת אב גד הו זח טי כל מן עף צק	א	עש תא בג דה וז חט טי כל לם נס פץ קר	א
סש תא בג דה וז חט טי כל מן עף צק	ו	עת אב גד הו זח טי כל מן סף צק קר רש	ו
סת אב גד הו זח טי כל מן עף צק רש	א	עא בג דה וז חט טי כל לם נס פץ קר שת	א
סא בג דה וז חט טי ךלמ נע פץ קר שת	ו	עב גד הו זח טי כל מן סף צק רש שת תא	ה
סב גד הו זח טי כל מן נע פץ צק קר שת תא	ה	עג דה וז חט טי כל לם נס פץ קר שת אב בג	א
סג דה וז חט טי כל מן נע פץ קר שת אב	א	עד הו זח טי כל מן סף צק רש שת אב גד	וה
סד הו זח טי כל מן עף פץ קר שת אב בג וה	וה	עה וז חט טי כל מן ספף צק רש תא בג גד	י
סה וז חט טי כל מן נע פץ קר שת אב בג גד	י	עו זח טי כל מן נס ספף צק רש תא בג דה	ו
סו זח טי כל מן עף פץ צק רש תא בג דה	ו	עז חט טי כל מן נס פץ קר שת אב גד דה הו	ד
סז חט טי כל מן נע פץ קר שת אב גד דה	ד	עח טי כל מן סף צק רש שת אב גד דה וז	ה
סח טי כל מן נע פץ קר שת אב גד דה וז	ה	עט יך לם נס פץ קר שת אב גד דה וז זח	ה
סט יך לם נע פץ קר שת אב גד דה וז	ה	עי כל מן נס ספף צק רש תא בג דה וז חט	ו
סי כל מן עף פץ צק רש תא בג דה וז חט	ו	עך לם נס ספף קר שת אב גד הו זח טי	ו
סך לם נע פץ קר שת אב גד הו זח טי	ו	על מן סף פץ קר שת אב גד הו זח טי יך	ה
סל מן עף פץ צק רש תא בג דה וז חט טי יך	ה	עם נס פץ קר שת אב גד הו זח טי כל	ה
סמ נע פץ קר שת אב גד הו זח טי כל	ה	ען סף צק רש תא בג דה וז חט טי יך לם	
סן עף פץ קר שת אב גד הו זח טי כל לם		עס פץ קר שת אב גד הו זח טי כל מן	

Peh: Back of Gevurah		Tzadi: Back of Tiferet	
פק קר שת אב גד הו זח טי כל מן סע	י	צק רש תא בג דה הו זח יכ למ נס עף	י
פק רש תא בג דה הו זח טי למ נס עץ	ו	צר שת אב גד הו זח טי כל מן סע פק	ו
פר שת אב גד הו זח טי יך למ נס עץ צק	ד	צש תא בג דה וז חט טי למ נס עף קר	ד
פש תא בג דה וז חט טי כל מן סע עץ קר	ה	צת אב גד הו זח טי כל מן סע עף פק קר רש	ה
פת אב גד הו זח טי כל מן סע צק קר רש	א	צא בג דה וז חט טי למ נס עף קר שת	א
פא בג דה וז חט טי למ נס עץ קר שת	ו	צב גד הו זח טי כל מן סע פק קר רש שת תא	ו
פב גד הו זח טי כל מן סע צק קר שת תא	א	צג דה וז חט טי למ נס עף קר שת תא אב	א
פג דה וז חט טי למ נס עין קר רש שת אב	ו	צד הו זח טי כל מן סע פק רש שת תא בג	ו
פד הו זח טי כל מן סע צק רש שת אב בג	ה	צה וז חט טי למ נס עף קר שת תא בג גד	ה
פה וז חט יכ למ נס עץ קר שת אב גד	א	צו זח טי כל מן סע פק רש תא בג גד דה	א
פו זח טי יך כל מן סע צק רש שת אב גד דה	וה	צז חט טי למ נס עף קר שת תא בג גד דה הו	וה
פז חט יך כל מן סע עץ קר שת אב גד הו	י	צח טי כל מן סע פק רש שת אב בג גד דה הו וז	י
פח טי כל מן סע צק רש תא בג דה וז	ו	צט יכ למ נס עף קר שת תא אב בג גד דה הו וז זח	ו
פט יך למ נס עץ קר שת אב בג גד הו זח	ד	צי כל מן סע עף קר שת אב גד דה הו וז חט	ד
פי כל מן סע צק רש שת אב גד דה וז חט	ה	צך למ נס עף קר שת תא בג דה הו וז חט טי	ה
פך למ נס עץ קר שת אב בג דה וז חט טי	ה	צל מן סע פק רש תא בג גד הו וז חט טי כל	ה
פל מן סע צק רש שת אב גד הו זח טי יך	ו	צמ נס עף רש תא בג דה וז חט טי כל	ו
פמ נס עץ קר שת אב בג דה וז חט טי כל	ו	צן סע פק רש תא בג דה וז חט טי למ	ו
פן סע צק רש שת אב גד הו זח טי כל	ה	צס עף קר שת תא בג גד הו זח טי כל מן	ה
פס עץ קר שת אב גד הו זח טי יך למ	ה	צע פק רש תא בג דה וז חט טי כל מן נפ	ה
פע צק רש תא בג דה וז חט טי כל מן סע		צף קר שת אב גד הו זח טי כל מן סע	

Kuf: Back of Netzach		Resh: Back of Hod	
קר שת אב גד הו זח טי כל מן סע פץ	י	רש תא בג דה וז חט טי יך למ נס עף צק	י
קש תא בג דה וז חט טי כל מן סע עף צר	ו	רת אב גד הו זח טי כל מן סע עף פץ קש	ו
קת אב גד הו זח טי כל מן סע פץ צר רש	ד	רא בג דה וז חט טי למ נס עף צק קש שת	ד
קא בג דה וז חט טי כל מן סע עף רץ שת	ה	רב גד הו זח טי כל מן סע פץ קש שת תא	ה
קב גד הו זח טי כל מן סע פץ צר שת תא	א	רג דה וז חט טי למ נס עף צק קש שת תא אב	א
קג דה וז חט טי למ נס עף צר שת אב	ו	רד הו זח טי כל מן סע עף צק קש תא בג	ו
קד הו זח טי כל מן סע פץ רש תא בג	א	רה וז חט טי למ נס עף צק קש שת אב בג גד	א
קה וז חט טי למ נס עף צר שת אב בג גד	ו	רו זח טי כל מן סע עף צק קש שת אב גד דה	ו
קו זח טי כל מן סע פץ רש תא בג דה	ה	רז חט טי למ נס עף צק קש תא בג גד הו	ה
קז חט טי למ נס עף צר שת אב בג גד דה	א	רח טי כל מן סע עף צק קש תא בג דה וז	א
קח טי כל מן סע פץ רש תא בג דה וז	וה	רט יך למ נס עף צק קש שת אב בג דה וז זח	וה
קט יך למ נס עף צר שת אב בג דה וז זח	י	רי כל מן סע עף צק קש תא בג דה וז חט	י
קי כל מן סע פץ רש תא בג דה וז חט	ו	רך למ נס עף צק קש שת אב גד הו זח טי	ו
קך למ נס עף צר שת אב גד הו זח טי	ד	רל מן סע עף צק קש תא בג דה הו זח טי יך	ד
קל מן סע פץ רש תא בג דה הו זח טי יך	ה	רם נס עף צק קש שת אב גד הו זח טי כל	ה
קמ נס עף צר שת אב בג דה וז חט טי כל	ה	רן סע עף צק קש תא בג דה וז חט טי כל מן	ה
קן סע פץ רש תא בג דה וז חט טי כל מן	ו	רס עף צק קש שת אב גד הו זח טי כל מן	ו
קס עף צר שת אב גד הו זח טי כל מן	ו	רע פץ צק קש תא בג דה וז חט טי כל מן נס	ו
קע פץ רש תא בג דה וז חט טי כל מן סע	ה	רף צק קש תא בג דה וז חט טי כל מן סע	ה
קף צר שת אב גד הו זח טי כל מן סע	ה	רץ קש תא בג דה וז חט טי כל מן סע עף	ה
קץ רש תא בג דה וז חט טי כל מן סע עף		רק שת אב גד הו זח טי כל מן סע פץ	

Shin: Back of Yesod		Tav: Back of Malkhut	
שת אב גד הו זח טי כל מן סע פץ קר	י	תא בג דה וז חט יך לם נס עף צק קר רש	י
שא בג דה וז חט יך לם נס עף צק רת	ו	תב גד הו זח טי כל מן סע פץ קר רש שא	ו
שב גד הו זח טי כל מן סע פץ קר תא	ד	תג דה וז חט יך לם נס עף צק קר רש אב	ד
שג דה וז חט יך לם נס עף צק רת אב	ה	תד הו זח טי כל מן סע פץ קר רש שא בג	ה
שד הו זח טי כל מן סע פץ קר תא בג	א	תה וז חט יך לם נס עף צק קר רש שא אב גד	א
שה וז חט יך לם נס עף צק רת אב גד	ו	תו זח טי כל מן סע פץ קר רש שא בג דה	ו
שו זח טי כל מן סע פץ קר תא בג דה	א	תז חט יך לם נס עף צק רש אב גד הו	א
שז חט יך לם נס עף צק רת אב גד הו	ו	תח טי כל מן סע פץ קר רש שא בג דה וז	ו
שח טי כל מן סע פץ קר תא בג דה וז	ה	תט יך לם נס עף צק רש אב גד הו זח	ה
שט יך לם נס עף צק רת אב גד הו זח	א	תי כל מן סע פץ קר רש שא בג דה וז חט	א
שי כל מן סע פץ קר תא בג דה וז חט	וה	תך לם נס עף צק רש אב גד הו זח טי וה	וה
שך לם נס עף צק רת אב גד הו זח טי	י	תל מן סע פץ קר שא בג דה וז חט יך	י
של מן סע פץ קר תא בג דה וז חט יך	ו	תמ נס עף צק רש אב גד הו זח טי כל	ו
שמ נס עף צק רת אב גד הו זח טי כל	ד	תן סע פץ קר שא בג דה וז חט יך לם	ד
שן סע פץ קר תא בג דה וז חט יך לם	ה	תס עף צק רש אב גד הו זח טי כל מן	ה
שס עף צק רת אב גד הו זח טי כל מן	ה	תע פץ קר שא בג דה וז חט טי כל מן נס	ה
שע פץ קר תא בג דה וז חט טי כל מן נס	ו	תף צק רש אב גד הו זח טי כל מן סע	ו
שף צק רת אב גד הו זח טי כל מן סע	ו	תץ קר שא בג דה וז חט יך לם נס עף	י
שץ קר תא בג דה וז חט טי כל מן סע עף	ה	תק רש אב גד הו זח טי כל מן סע עף פץ	ה
שק רת אב גד הו זח טי כל מן סע פץ	ה	תר שא בג דה וז חט יך לם נס עף צק	ה
שר תא בג דה וז חט יך לם נס עף פץ צק		תש אב גד הו זח טי כל מן סע פץ קר	

APPENDIX IV
EDITIONS AND
COMMENTARIES

Printed Editions

Mantua 1562, 4° 108 *ff.* First Edition. Includes commentaries of Raavad, Ramban B, Moshe Botril, Saadia B, Eliezer of Wormes B. Major text is the Short Version, but also includes the Long Version as an appendix (*ff.* 102-108). Published by Yaakov ben Naftali Gazolo.

Lemberg, 1680. Contains six versions of the text.[1]

Amsterdam, 1713, 12° 48*ff.* Also includes the *Zoharic Sifra DeTzeniuta* and parts of the Talmudic tract of *Tamid.* With introduction by R. Moshe (ben Yaakov) Hagiz.[2]

Constantinople, 1719, 8° 28 *ff.* Includes abridged commentaries of Raavad, Ramban B, and the Ari. Published by Yonah ben Yaakov and Yeshiah Ashkenazi.

Constantinople, 1724, 4°. Same as 1719 edition.

Zolkiev, 1745, 4°. Contains all commentaries in Mantua edition, as well as that of the Ari. Also contains Long Version.

Koretz, 1779, 4° 36 *ff.* Includes commentary *Otzar HaShem*, attributed to R. Moshe ben Yitzchak of Kiev (q.v.).

Grodno, 1797, 8°. Includes commentary *Pri Yitzchak*, by R. Yitzchak Isaac ben Yekutiel of Mohelov (q.v.).

Grodno, 1806, 4° 86 *ff.* With vocalized text and all commentaries in Mantua edition. Also includes commentary of Ari and R. Eliahu Gaon of Vilna (Gra). Edited by Menachem Mendel of Sklav.

Dyhrenfurth, 1812.[3]

Vilna-Grodno 1820, 4°. Contains all commentaries as in Mantua edition, as well as that of Gra.

Salonica, 1831.[4]

Cracow, 18—.[5]

Prague, no date, 4°. Contains commentaries as in Mantua edition.

Lvov, 1860, 4° 176 *ff.* Contains commentaries as in Mantua edition, as well as *Otzar HaShem, Pri Yitzchak*, and commentaries of Ari and Gra. Published by Benjamin Bischko.

Jerusalem, 1874-85, three volumes, 186 *ff.* Contains commentary of Gra, edited by his disciple R. Moshe Shlomo of Tulchin. Also includes supercommentary on Gra, *Toldot Yitzchak*, by R. Yitzchak ben Yehudah Leib Kahanah (q.v.).

Warsaw, 1884, 4° 106 *ff.* The standard edition in current use. Consists of two sections. The first section contains all commentaries as in Mantua edition, as well as *Otzar HaShem*. The commentary *Chakamoni*, by R. Shabbatai Donello, is printed separately at the end of this section. Second section contains *Pri Yitzchak* and commentary of Gra, with commentary of Ari at the end. Also contains Long Version at end. This edition contains many typographical errors in the commentaries.

London, 1902, 8° 79 pp. With commentary by Donash ibn Tamim (q.v.)

Jerusalem, 1962. Reprint of Warsaw edition.

Jerusalem, 1965, 204 pp. Long Version, with commentary, *Yotzer Or*, by Bentzion Moshe Yair Weinstock.

Israel, 1970. Reprint of London 1902 edition.

Jerusalem, 1972, 143 pp. Critical edition of first chapter, based on all printed editions, commentaries and manuscripts, by Yisrael Weinstock. *"LeBirur HaNusach shel Sefer Yetzirah," Temirin* 1:9-61.

Other Books Containing The Sefer Yetzirah

Chemed Elohim, by R. Benyamin HaLevi. Kabbalistic prayers and readings for the entire year. Contains vocalized text of Ari (Gra) Version. In later editions (1772), the text is from a manuscript from the library of R. Benyamin HaLevi, owned by his father, and edited by the Kabbalist, R. Shuliman ibn Ochna, one of the main disciples of the Ari.[6]

Ismir, 1738.
Venice, 1756, 122 *ff.*
Venice, 1766.
Venice, 1772, 122 *ff.*
Venice, 1787, 108 *ff.*
Livorno, 1793.
Venice, 1793.
Livorno, 1797.
Salonica, 1800.

Livorno, 1801.
Livorno, 1803.
Livorno, 1810.
Livorno, 1820.
Livorno, 1827.
Livorno, 1837.
Belgrad, 1841, 12° 127*ff.* Edited by R. Chaim ben David Chaim.
Livorno, 1842.
Livorno, 1862.
Venice, 1866.

[Seder] Kiryat Moed. Kabbalistic and other readings for the nights of the Seventh of Passover, Shavuot, Hoshanah Rabbah, and the Seventh of Adar (anniversary of Moses' death).

Constantinople, 1736.
Livorno, 1743.
Constantinople, 1754.
Venice, 1756.
Pisa, 1786.
Livorno, 1795.
Vienna, 1801.
Livorno, 1805.
Vienna, 1822.
Livorno, 1830.
Livorno, 1841.
Livorno, 1865.
Vienna, 1870.
Livorno, 1892, 8⁰ 259 *ff.*

Likutey Tzvi, Kol Bo, Warsaw (Levin-Epstein), no date, p. 105. First and last stanzas, as part of Shavuot night service.

Mishnayot (vocalized), Venice, 1704.

Same, but in a somewhat different version, Venice, 1737.

Ne'edar BaKodesh. Contains Ari (Gra) Version, together with *Idra Rabba, Idra Zuta,* and *Sifra DeTzniuta,* as recited on Shavuot night. Introduction by R. Moshe Hagiz.[7]

Amsterdam, 1723, 56 *ff.*
Ismir, 1738.
Ismir, 1746.
Ismir, 1755, 8° 70 *ff.* From manuscript in library of R. Benyamin HaLevi, edited by R. Shuliman ibn Ochna (see *Chemed Elohim*).

Shaarey Tzion, edited by R. Nathan Noteh ben Moshe Hanover. Prayers and readings for various occasions based on the teachings of the Ari. Prague, 1662.

With additions: Tikkun Seuday, Kaddish, by R. Yermiyah of
   Vertish.
       Amsterdam, 1672, 54 *ff.*
       Prague, 1682.
       Prague, 1688, 52 *ff.*
       Wilhelmsdorf, 1690.
       Prague, 1692.
       Dessau, 1698.
       Venice, 1701.
With additions by R. Mordecai Markil ben Yisrael Nissan
       Diherenfurth, 1705.
       Amsterdam, 1706.
       Venice, 1707.
       Wilhelmsdorf, 1712.
       Amsterdam, 1718.
       Amsterdam, 1720, 131 *ff.*
       Constantinople, 1732.
       Amsterdam, 1736. A somewhat different version.
       Venice, 1736, 187 *ff.*
       Sulzbach, 1747.
       Amsterdam, 1751.
       Venice, 1751.
       Venice, 1753, 187 *ff.*
       Amsterdam, 1760.
       Amsterdam, 1764.
       Amsterdam, 1766, 123 *ff.*
       Amsterdam, 1770.
       Amsterdam, 1774.
       Amsterdam, 1779, 123 *ff.*
       Sulzbach, 1782, 142 *ff.*
       Amsterdam, 1784.
       Novydwor, 1788.
       Poritzk, 1794.
       Livorno, 1795.
       Vienna, 1795.
       Dihernfurth, 1798.
       Pisa, 1799.
       Dihernfurth, 1804.
       Vienna, 1804.
       Vienna, 1809.
       Minkovitz, 1812.
       Amsterdam, 1817.
       Gorodno, 1819.
       Medzyboz, 1823.

Dihernfurth, 1828.
Ostrog, 1828, 188 *ff.*
Venice, 1836.
Josefov, 1839.
Josefov, 1841.
With Yiddish Translation
Iassi, 1843.
Zitamar, 1849.
Livorno, 1861.
Vienna, 1864, 142 pp.
Lvov, 1863.
Lvov, 1871.
Przemysl, 1917, 12° 196 *ff.* With commentaries, *Poteach Shaarim, Shaarey Orah, Maasim Tovim,* as well as *Tikkun HaKelali,* by R. Nachman of Breslov.
New York, 1974. Reprint of the above.
Tikkun Layl Shavuot. Readings for Shavuot night according to the order arranged by R. Shlomo AlKabatz. Contains first and last stanzas of the Long Version.
Venice, 1648.
Venice, 1654.
Venice, 1655.
Venice, 1659.
Amsterdam, 1700.
Amsterdam, 1708.
Furth, 1723, 8° 70 *ff.*
Furth, 1728, 12° 188 *ff.*
Venice, 1730.
Venice, 1739.
Furth, 1739, 96 *ff.*
Venice, 1743, 97 *ff.*
Frankfort am Mein, 1751.
Sulzbach, 1754.
Venice, 1766, 142 *ff.*
Vienna, 1794, 8° 141 *ff.*
Vienna, 1803.
Livorno, 1805.
Blizorka, 1808.
Sklav, 1814.
Ostrog, 1814.
Ostrog, 1823.
Blilovka, 1824.
Livorno, 1831.

Slavita, 1836, 4^0 165 *ff.*
Sudylkov, no date.
Zitamar, 1867, 168 *ff.*
Vienna, 1861.
Vienna, 1864.
Josefov, 1865, 140 *ff.*
Brody, 1876, 8^0 128 *ff.*
And many others.

Manuscripts

Ari (Gra) Version

Jewish Theological Seminary, Ms. Adler 1327. 16th century.

Short Version

British Museum, Ms. 736, *ff.* 40a-43b. 13 century. Earliest and best text of this version.
Paris, Ms. 763, *ff.* 1a-3a. 13th century.
Parma, Ms. 1390, *ff.* 36b-38b. 14th century.
Paris, Ms. 802, *ff.* 57b-59b. 14th century.
Hebrew Union College, Cincinatti, Ms. 523. 14th century.
British Museum, Ms. Gaster 415, *ff.* 29a-32a. 14th century.
Vatican, Ms. 441, *ff.* 118a-122a. 16th century.
Oxford, Ms. 2455, *ff.* 3a-8b. 16th century.
Cambridge, Ms. Add 647, *ff.* 7b-9b. 16th century.

Long Version

Vatican, Ms. 299, *ff.* 66a-71b. Very old, probably from the 10th or 11th century. This is the earliest and best complete manuscript of Sefer Yetzirah. Is also contains an introduction by an early anonymous writer, published by Yisrael Weinstock, *Tarbitz* 32:157 (1963), *Sinai* 54:255-56 (1964). The text in this manuscript is often referred to in R. Yehudah Barceloni's commentary on Sefer Yetzira.

Oxford, Ms. 1531, *ff.* 1b-12a. 13th century.
British Museum, Ms. 752, *ff.* 79a-81a. 14th century. Contains same
    text as Vatican 299, with some errors.
British Museum, Ms. 737, *ff.* 379b-387a. 16th century.

Saadia Version

Geniza Fragment, Taylor Schechter 32.5. 11th century. This manu-
    script apparently contained the entire Sefer Yetzirah on a sin-
    gle page. Published by A.M. Habermann, *Sinai* 10 (1947).
Geniza Fragment, Cambridge-Westminster, Talmud 23-25.
British Museum, Ms. 754, *ff.* 212a-216a. 14th century.
Paris, Ms. 770, *ff.* 41a-45a. 15th century.

Commentaries

Aaron (ben Yosef) Sargado, 890-960. Portions of this commentary
    are cited by R. Moshe Botril (q.v.).
Abraham (ben Shmuel) Abulafia, 1240-1296. *Gan Naul.* Written in
    Sicily in 1289. Munich, Ms. 58. Printed in part in *Sefer
    HaPeliyah (Sefer HaKanah)*, Koretz, 1784, pp. 50c-56c.
——. *Otzar Eden HaGanuz.* Also contains important autobiographi-
    cal material, including a list of thirteen earlier commentaries
    on Sefer Yetzirah used by Abulafia. Written in Sicily in 1285.
    Oxford, Ms. Or 606.
Abraham ben David, *"The Raavad."* Commentary printed in the
    Manuta, 1562 edition, as well as together with Rittangel's
    Latin translation (Amsterdam, 1642), and included in most
    major subsequent editions. Although the Raavad is usually
    identified as R. Abraham ben David of Posquieres
    (1120-1198), one of the early Kabbalists, the accepted opinion,
    both among Kabbalists and historians, is that he was not the
    author of this commentary.[8] From internal evidence, it was
    written in 1430. Many authorities attribute this commentary
    to R. Yosef HaArukh (q.v.) or R. Yosef (ben Shalom) Ashke-
    nazi (q.v.).[9] This commentary appears to follow the system of
    R. Yitzchak Bardashi (q.v.).[10]
Abraham ibn Ezra, 1092-1167. This commentary is mentioned by R.
    Abraham Abulafia, where it is described as combining philoso-
    phy and Kabbalah.[11] In a letter to his brother, Ibn Ezra himself

also apparently refers to this commentary.[12] No known copy
of this commentary is existent.

Abu Shal Donash ibn Tamim. See Donash.

Anonymous Commentaries

Jerusalem, Ms. 8° 330:26, 29, 30.

Leiden, Ms. 24:6-10.

Oxford, Mss. 632.2

1557:7,9
1594:5,6
1623:5
1794:10
1947:1
2280:3

Paris, Mss. 680:6,7,8
763:2,3,4,5,6,8
766:3,5,6
770:5
774:3
799:2
843:2
1048:3
1092:10

Ari. See Yitzchak Luria.

Azriel (ben Shlomo) of Gerona, 1160-1238, master of the Ramban in
Kabbalah. Commentary mentioned by R. Abraham Abulafia.
Parma, Ms. 1390, 14th century. According to some scholars,
the printed commentary attributed to the Ramban was actually written by R. Azriel.[13] See Moshe ben Nachman, Ramban B.

Barceloni. See Yehudah Barceloni.

Barukh (ben Barukh) Torgami, 13th century, *Maftechot HaKabbalah*.
Torgami was the master of R. Abraham Abulafia, and the latter also mentions his commentary, which consists largely of
gematriot and other word manipulations. Paris, Ms. 770:1,
with fragments in Oxford, Ms. 1598:3. Published in G.
Scholem, *HaKabbalah Shel Sefer HaTemunah VeShel Abraham
Abulafia*, Jerusalem, 1965, pp. 229-239.

Bentzion Moshe Yair Weinstock, contemporary, *Yotzer Or*. Commentary on the Long Version anthologizing earlier sources. Jerusalem, 1965, 204 pp.

Birkat Yosef. See Yosef Edles Ashkanazi.

Chaim of Vidzy, 18th century, *Gan Yah*. Commentary on Gra Version, following teachings of Ari and Gra. Written around 1800.
Breslau, 1831, 4° 42 *ff.*

Chakamoni. See Shabbatai Donnolo.

David Chabilo, 1588-1661. Existent in manuscript belonging to the late Warsaw community.

Donash (or Adonim) Ibn Tamim, 10th century.[14] Written in Kairwan, Tunisia, in 955, based on the lectures of Donash's master, R. Yitzchak Israeli. Originally written in Arabic, but translated in several versions into Hebrew. Mentioned by Abraham Abulafia. First commentary on Short Version. Existent in manuscripts Berlin Or 8° 243:4, Paris 1048:2, fragments of which were published by Georges Vajda.[15] A translation by R. Nachum HaMaarabi is in Munich, Ms. 47, and parts of it were published by Yehudah Leib Dukes, in his introduction to *Kuntres HaMesoret*, Tubingen, 1846. The complete text was published by Menasheh Grossberg on the basis of Oxford, Ms. 2250:2, London, 1902, 8° 79 pp. Reprinted, Israel, 1970.

Eliezer Ashkenazi. This commentary is mentioned by Abraham Abulafia, who says that it is deeply Kabbalistic. No known copy existent.[16]

Eliezer Ha-Darshan Ashkenazi. Mentioned by Abraham Abulafia, who states that he did not see it. Extant in manuscript, Munich Leipzig 30. Some identify this with commentary of R. Eliezer Rokeach of Wormes.[17]

Eliezer Ha-Kalir, around sixth century. Concepts found in Sefer Yetzirah are woven into some of his poetry.[18] Some authorities place R. Eliezer HaKalir as early as the second century, identifying him with R. Eliezer, son of R. Shimon bar Yochai, author of the Zohar.[19]

Eliezer (ben Yehudah) Rokeach of Wormes (Garmiza), 1160-1237. His treatment to the first three chapters is highly mystical, but the astrological concepts in the later chapters is taken largely from *Chakamoni*. He is unique in utilizing 221 Gates, rather than 231. British Museum, Ms. 737, 16th century. Edited by R. Tzvi Elimelekh Shapiro of Dinov, and published by his grandson, Moshe Shapiro, as *Perush HaRA MeGarmiza*, Przemysl, 1888, 22 *ff.*

––––– . Abridgement of the above, first published in the Mantua, 1562, edition.[20]

Elchanan Yitzchak (ben Yakir) of London, middle 13th century. Based on lectures of R. Yitzchak of Dampierre.[21] Fulda Landesbibliothek, Ms. 4, published by Georges Vajda, *Kobetz al Yad* 16:145-197 (1966).

Eliahu ben Menachem Ha-Zeken, around 1000. Often cited in commentary of R. Moseh Botril.

Eliahu (ben Shlomo), Gaon of Vilna, "The Gra," 1720-1797. Consid-

ered one of the greatest geniuses of all time. Purely Kabbalistic
commentary on the Gra Version, which he edited. First published in Grodno, 1806, and contained in subsequent editions,
most notably that of Warsaw, 1884. An edition edited by his
disciple R. Moshe Shlomo of Tulchin, and also containing a
supercommentary, *Toldot Yitzchak*, by R. Yitzchak ben
Yehudah Leib Kahanah (q.v.) was published in Jerusalem,
1874, 186 pp.

Ezra, 1157-1238. Disciple of Isaac the Blind, and master of Ramban
in Kabbalah. His commentary on Sefer Yetzirah is mentioned
by R. Abraham Abulafia. Some identify this with Ramban B
(see Moshe ben Nachman).

Gan Yah. See Chaim of Vidzy.

Gan Naul. See Abraham Abulafia.

Ginat Egoz. See Yosef Gikatalia.

Gra. See Eliahu, Gaon of Vilna.

Hadrey Kodesh. See Meir Kornik.

Hai (ben Sherira) Gaon, 969-1038. Fragments of his commentary are
quoted by R. Moshe Botril. Jellinec assembed these fragments
and printed them together, *Litteraturblatt des Orients* (OLB)
1851, pp. 546-556.

_____ . *Sheelot U'Tshuvot al Sefer Yetzirah*. Questions and answers
regarding the Sefer Yetzirah. Vatican, Ms. 181. Quoted in
Bachya, commentary on Exodus 34:6, *Pardes Rimonim* 11:1.

Isaac. See Yitzchak.

Isaac of Acco. See Yitzchak DeMin Acco.

Isaac the Blind. See Yitzchak Sagi Nahor.

Jacob. See Yaakov.

Joseph. See Yosef.

Judah. See Yehudah.

Kuzari. See Yehudah HaLevi.

Luria. See Yitzchak Luria.

Meir Aristola. The existence of this commentary is mentioned by R.
Shlomo AlKabatz (1505-1584) in his *Aperion Shlomo*, chapter
3.[22]

Meir (ben Moshe) Kornik, 1752-1826, *Hadrey Kodesh*. Commentary
on first and last stanzas of Long Version, as found in Tikkun
Layl Shavuot (q.v.). Dihrenfurth, 1812, 16 *ff.*

Meir (ben Shlomo) Ibn Sahula. Only known commentary written on
Saadia Version, other than that of Saadia himself. Written in
1331. Rome, Angelica Library, Ms. Or. 45, 14th century.

Menachem Epstein, *Yetzirah*, Odessa, 1913, 30 pp. A discussion
regarding the creation of a Golem through Sefer Yetzirah,
based on the Talmud and later sources. Also includes an analy-

sis of *Niflaot Maharal MiPrague,* Pieterkov 1909.

Moshe Botril, early 15th century. Written in 1409, and quotes many earlier sources no longer in existence.[23] Vatican, Ms. 441, 15th century. First printed in Mantua, 1562, and in most subsequent editions.

Moshe Cordevero, "The Ramak," 1522-1570. Dean of the Safed School of Kabbalah. Existent in manuscript, Jerusalem 8° 2646.[24] The Sefer Yetzirah is also discussed extensively in the Ramak's other works.

Moshe (ben Maimon) Maimonides, "The Rambam," 1135-1204. The existence of such a commentary is mentioned by R. Yechiel Heilpern in *Seder HaDorot (Sefarim, Sefer Yetzirah).* No copy is known to exist, and in general, the Rambam's philosophy appears to oppose the approach of the Sefer Yetzirah.

Moshe ben Nachman, Nachmanides, "The Ramban," 1194-1267. One of the leading Talmudists and Kabbalists in his time. Commentary is mentioned by Abraham Abulafia, Jerusalem, Ms. 8° 330:28, *ff.* 259a-261b, published by Gershom Scholem, *Kiryat Sefer* 6:385-410 (1930).

———. Ramban B. Commentary first printed in Mantua, 1562, and in many subsequent editions. Does not coincide with many quoted exerpts from Ramban's commentary cited in early sources, as does previous text.[25] According to most authorities, this is commentary of Ezra or Azariah of Gerona (q.v.).[26]

Moshe ben Yaakov of Kiev, 1449-1530, *Otzar HaShem.* First published in Koretz, 1779, and included in many later editions. R. Moshe of Kiev is also known as author of *Shoshan Sodot* (Koretz, 1784).

Moshe (ben Yaakov) ibn Shoshan. Written in 1511. Munich, Ms. 104.[27]

Moshe ben Yosef of Alisai. See Saadia.

Nachum HaMaarabi. See Donash ibn Tamim, Yitzchak Yisraeli.

Otot U'Moadim. See Yehoshua Eisenbach.

Otzar Eden HaGanuz. See Abraham Abulafia.

Otzar HaShem. See Moshe of Kiev.

Peretz (ben Yitzchak) Ha-Cohen, 13th century. In his noted work, *Maarekhet Elokut,* Mantua, 1558, he mentions that he wrote a commentary on Sefer Yetzirah.[28]

Pri Yitzchak. See Yitzchak Isaac of Mohalov.

Raavad. See Abraham ben David, Yosef HaArukh, Yosef Ashkenazi.

Ramak. See Moshe Cordevero.

Ramban. See Moshe ben Nachman, Azrial, Ezra.

Rambam. See Moshe Maimonides.

Raziel, also known as Raziel HaMalakh and Raziel HaGadol. An ancient anonymous magical and Kabbalistic text. Actually consists of three books, *Raziel HaMalakh* (or Sefer HaMalbush, pp. 2b-7a), *Raziel HaGadol* (pp. 7b-33b), and *Sefer Raziel* (or Ma'ayin HaChakhmah, pp. 34a-48b). The second book, *Raziel HaGadol*, contains many important comments on Sefer Yetzirah. Some attribute this section to Abraham Abulafia.[29] First published in Amsterdam, 1701, 4° 46 *ff.* Other editions include:

Gorodna, 1793.
Minkowitz, 1803.
Lvov, 1804, 42 *ff.*
Medzyboz, 1818, 49 *ff.*
Kapust, 1820.
Lvov, 1821.
Ostrog, 1821, 40 *ff.*
Medzyboz, 1824.
Minkowitz, 1827.
Ostrog, 1827.
Ostrog, no date, 4°.
Lvov, 1835.
Salonica, 1840.
Calcutta, 1845, 8° 134 *ff.*
Warsaw, no date, 40 *ff.*

Edited by R. Yisrael (ben Shabatai Shapiro) Maggid of Koznitz:

Warsaw, 1812.
Lvov, 1842.
Lvov, 1840, 40 *ff.*
Lvov, 1863.
Lvov, 1865, 64 pp.
Lvov, 1869.
Josefov, 1873, 72 pp.
Vilna, 1881, 4°.
Warsaw, 1881.
Lvov, 1882.
New York (Naftali Zvi Margolies), no date, 155 pp.

Saadia (ben Yosef) Gaon, 891-941, *Tzafsor Ktaav AlMabadi*, written in Arabic in 931. Oxford, Ms. 1533, 13th century. Published with French translation by Meyer Lambert, under the title, *Commentaire sur le Sefer Yetzirah; our Livre Creation par le Gaon Saadja d Fayyoum*, Paris 1891. Also published with Hebrew translation by Yosef ben David Kapach, Jerusalem, 1972, 143 pp.

―――. Translated into Hebrew by anonymous author in the 11th cen-
    tury. Vatican, Ms. 236, 16th century. This is the text quoted
    in commentary of Yehudah Barceloni (q.v.).
―――. Translated into Hebrew by R. Moshe ben Yosef of Alisna.
    Parma, Ms. 769, 14th century. Exerpts of this translation were
    published by A. Jellinek, *Litteraturblatt des Orients* (OLB),
    1851, p. 224.
―――. Saadia B. First published in Mantua, 1562, and in many later
    editions. On Long Version, cannot be attributed in its entirety
    to Saadia Gaon, since it mentions many later sages, such as
    Abraham ibn Ezra and R. Yaakov Tam. Most probably written
    by a 13th century Ashkenazic scholar, possibly named Saadia.
    A more complete version, including an introduction not in
    printed editions is existent in manuscript, Munich 40, Jerusa-
    lem 8° 1136, 15th century.[30] Introduction was published by M.
    Steinschneider. *Magazin für die Wissenschaft des Judentums*,
    1892, p. 83.
Shabbatai (ben Avraham) Donnelo, 9-3-982, *Chakomoni* or
    Tachkamoni. Written in 946, and mentioned both by Rashi,[31]
    and by Abraham Abulafia. Parma, Ms. 417, 15th century, and
    Munich, Ms. 36:2.[32] First published by David Castelli, as *Il
    Commento di Sabbathai Donnolo sur Libro della Creazione*,
    Firenze, 1880, 8°. Also included in Warsaw, 1884, edition, pp.
    62a-74b. Published together with *Kitzur Chovot HaLevavot*,
    Jerusalem, 1945.[33]
Shlomo ibn Gabriel, 1021-1050. In a number of his poems, he elabo-
    rates on the doctrines of Sefer Yetzirah. See Shirey Shlomo ibn
    Gabriel, edited by Bialik and Rawnitzki, Berlin-Tel Aviv,
    1924-29, Vol. 2, No. 58.
Shlomo (ben Shimon) Toriel, 16th century. Oxford, Ms. 2455:1.
Shmuel (ben Saadia) ibn Motot, 15th century, *Meshovev Netivot*. Vat-
    ican, Ms. 225, 15th century, Paris, Mss. 769:1, 824:9, 842:2.
Shmuel (ben Elisha) Porteleone. London, Ms. Jews College.
Tachkamoni. See Shabbatai Donnelo.
Toldot Yitzchak. See Yitzchak Kahanah.
Tzahallel (ben Netanel) Gaon. Some of his poems expound upon the
    teachings of Sefer Yetzirah. Published by Davidson, *Hebrew
    Union College Annual* 3:225-55 (1926), with additions by E.
    Baneth, *Monatsschrift für Geschichte und Wissenschaft des
    Judentums* (MGWJ) 71:426-42 (1927).
Yaakov ben Nisim of Kairwan, 908-976. Philosophical commentary
    based on teachings of Yitzchak Yisraeli, and much like com-
    mentary of Donash. Munich, Ms. 92:20. Published by
    Yehudah Leib Dukes, *Kuntres HaMesoret*, Tubingen, 1846.[34]

Yaakov of Sagovia. His commentary is mentioned by Abraham
Abulafia, who states that it is completely Kabbalistic. No
known copy in existence.[35]

Yehoshua Eisenbach, *Otot U'Moadim*, Bartfeld, 1904, 4° 35 *ff.*

Yehudah (ben Barzilai) Barceloni, 1082-1148. An extensive, mostly
philosophical and Talmudical commentary, quoting numerous
early sources, most notably Saadia Gaon. A most important
source book regarding early Jewish theology. Published by
Shlomo Zalman Chaim Halberstam, Berlin, 1885, 30, 354 pp.
Reprinted, Jerusalem, 1971.

Yehudah (ben Shmuel) Ha-Chasid of Regensburg, 1145-1217. Mentioned by Abraham Abulafia, who notes that it follows
Chakamoni of Shabbatai Donnelo (q.v.). *Cf.* Leipzig, Ms. 30.
(The commentary of R. Eliezer Rokeach of Wormes, a disciple
of R. Yehudah HaChasid, often quotes his master, and this
commentary also often follows *Chakamoni.*) No known copy
in existence.[36]

Yehudah Ha-Levi, 1068-1118. In his famed *Kuzari* 4:25, he provides
a highly insightful philosophical commentary on Saadia Version. *Kuzari* was written in Arabic, translated into Hebrew by
Yehudah ibn Tebon (1120-1193), and first published in Fano,
1506, 62 *ff.* There have been over twenty-six subsequent editions, including numerous translations and commentaries on
this important classic.

Yehudah (ben Nisim) ibn Malka, 14th century. Written in Arabic,
and quoted in commentary of R. Moshe Botril, as well as in
Megillat Setarim (Venice, 1554), a commentary by R. Shmuel
ibn Motot (q.v.) on Pentateuch commentary of Abraham ibn
Ezra (q.v.).[37] Paris, Ms. 764:3, an excerpt of which is in
Hirschfeld, Arabic Chrestomathy, London, 1892, pp. 19-31. A
Hebrew translation of this commentary is in Oxford, Ms.
1536. See George Vajda, *Juda ben Nissim ibn Malka:
Philosphe juif Marocain*, Paris, 1954.

Yetzirah. See Menachem Ekstein.

Yitzchak Bardashi, 12th century.[38] Mentioned by Abraham Abulafia,
who makes special note of his arrangement of the 231 Gates.[39]
Here, his system is almost exactly the same as that found in
Raavad (see Abraham ben David).

Yitzchak (ben Leib) Kahanah, 1824-1900, *Toldot Yitzchak.* Super-
commentary on commentary of R. Eliahu, Gaon of Vilna
(Gra). First published in Jerusalem, 1874, and with additions,
Jerusalem, 1879.

Yitzchak De-Min Acco (Isaac of Acco), 1250-1340. Disciple of
Ramban. Commentary draws heavily on that of Yitzchak Sagi

Nahor. Jerusalem, Ms. 8° 404, published by Gershom Scholem, *Kiryat Sefer* 31:379-396 (1957).

Yitzchak Luria, "The Ari," 1534-1572. Leading luminary of the Safed school, and the most influential of all Kabbalists. Commentary weaves teachings of Sefer Yetzirah into the Ari's general scheme. First published in Constantinople, 1719, Zolkiev, 1745, and in other editions. Included at end of Warsaw, 1884, edition. A discussion of the Thirty-two Paths of Wisdom by the Ari is found in *Likutey Shas*, 1783, *ff.* 27a, b, and also at end of Warsaw edition.[40]

Yitzchak Sagi Nahor (Isaac the Blind), 1160-1236. Son of R. Abraham ben David of Posqueres, and master of Azriel and Ezra of Gerona (q.v.). Considered one of the greatest of all Kabbalists. His is one of the few commentaries to openly discuss the meditative aspects of Sefer Yetzirah. Rome, Angelica Library, Ms. 46, 15th century; Oxford, Ms. 2456:12; Leyden, Ms. 24:16.[41] Published by Gershom Scholem, at end of *HaKabbalah BeProvence*, Jerusalem, 1966.[42]

Yitzchak Isaac (ben Yekutiel Zalman) of Mohalov, 1728-1806, *Pri Yitzchak*. Kabbalistic commentary based on Zohar and teachings of the Ari. First published in Grodno, 1797, 8° (also including additions to his *Beer Yitzchak*, his commentary on *Tikuney Zohar*, first published in Zolkiev, 1778). Also included in Lvov, 1860, edition, and in second part of Warsaw, 1884, edition.

Yitzchak (ben Shlomo) Yisraeli, 830-932. One of the greatest sages of his time. According to his disciple, Donash ibn Tamim (q.v.), Saadia Gaon (q.v.) would often consult him with regard to scientific matters. Philosophical and astronomical commentary, much like that of Donash ibn Tamim (q.v.), originally written in Arabic. Existent in manuscript, Biblioteque National, Paris, and in translation by Nachum HaMaarabi.[43] A fragment of this translation was published by Yehudah Leib Dukes, *Kuntres HaMaesoret*, Tubingen, 1846, pp. 5-10.

Yosef (ben Shalom) Ashkenazi, 14th century. According to most scholars, he is the author of the commentary printed under the name of Abraham ben David (Raavad, q.v.). Possibly identified with Yosef HaArukh. Existent in manuscript, British Museum, Gaster 415, 14th century.[44]

Yosef Edels (Ashkenazi), *Birkat Yosef*. Kabbalistic commentary on Gra Version, based on teachings of the Ari. Salonica, 1831, 32 *ff.*

Yosef Ha-Arukh (Joseph the Tall), 14th century. See Yosef Ashkenazi, Abraham ben David. R. Moshe Cordevero cites the commentary on the Thirty-Two Paths of Wisdom, appearing in commentary of Abraham ben David (Raavad, q.v.), and attributes them to Yosef HaArukh.[45] However, in a number of places, R. Moshe Botril cites a commentary by R. Yosef HaArukh on Sefer Yetzirah, and it does not coincide with Raavad.[46.]

Yosef Gikatalia, 1248-1323. One of the greates Kabbalists, best known for his *Shaarey Orah*, first published in Riva di Trento, 1561, a year before the first edition of Sefer Yetzirah. The second chapter of his *Ginat Egoz* is essentially a commentary of Sefer Yetzirah. Printed in Hannau, 1615, 2° 75 *ff.*; Zolkiev, 1773, Mohelov, 1798, 4°; Hannau edition reprinted anonymously around 1970.

Yosef of Saporta. A fragment of his commentary is quoted by R. Moshe Botril (1:12).

Yosef Sar Shalom, 15th century. His commentary is mentioned by R. Aaron AlRabi in his supercommentary to Rashi.[47]

Yosef ben Uziel, said to be a disciple of the prophet Jeremiah. See Introduction, notes 42, 43.

Yosef Or. See Bentzion Moshe Yair Weinstock.

Translations

Arabic

Saadia Gaon, 891-941. In *Siddur of Saadia Gaon*, Oxford, Ms. David Oppenheim 1010.[48]

Czech

Otakar Griese, 1921.

English

Akiva ben Joseph (pseudonym), *The Book of Formation*, 1970.
M. Doreal, *Sepher Yetzirah*. Translation and analysis. Denver, 1941, 48 pp.

Alfred Edersheim, 1825-1889, in his book, *The Life and Times of Jesus*, London, 1884 (and other editions), Vol. 2, pp. 692-698.

Irving Friedman, *The Book of Creation*. Translation and comments. Samuel Weiser, York Beach, ME, 1977.

Isidor Kalish, "Sepher Yezira, a Book on Creation or the Jewish Metaphysics of Remote Antiquity." With preface, explanatory notes and glossary. In *A Sketch of the Talmud*, New York, 1877, 8° 57 pp.

Phineas Mordel, *Sefer Yetzirah*. Hebrew text and translation in a new version deduced logically by the author, but not accepted in kabbalistic or scholarly circles. Philadelphia, 1894, 2, 10 pp.

_____ . *The Origin of Letters and Numerals according to the Sefer Yetzirah*. Same as above, but introduction contains important historical data and quotes significant manuscripts. Originally published in Jewish Quarterly Review, New Series 2:557-583 (1912), 3:517-544 (1913). Published separately, Philadelphia, 1914. Reprinted by Samuel Weiser, York Beach, ME, 1975.

Saul Raskin, in *Kabbalah in Word and Image*. Hebrew text with English and Yiddish translation. New York, 1952, 80 pp. Illustrated.

Knut Senring. *The Book of Formation (Sepher Yetzirah)*. With introduction by Arthur Edward Waite. New York, 1923, 62 pp. Reprinted by Ktav, New York, 1970.

William Wynn Westcott, *Sepher Yetzirah, the Book of Formation*. Based on text of Rittangel (q.v.). London, 1887. Reprinted with additional notes as a volume of *Collectanes Hermatica*, London, 1893, 43 pp. Printed separately, London, 1911, 49 pp. The 1893 edition was reprinted by Samuel Weiser, York Beach, ME, 1975.

French

Comtesse Calomira de Cimara, *Sepher Yetzirah*, Paris, 1913, 4° 27 pp.

Gerard Encausese (Papus), *Sefer Yetzira*, Paris, 1888.

Karppe, *Etude sur les Origines . . . du Zohar*, Paris, 1901, pp. 139-158.

Meyer Lambert, *Commentaire sur le Sefer Yesirah: Our Livre Creation par le Gaon Saadja de Fayyoum*, Paris, 1891, pp. 1-11.

German

E. Bischof, 1913.

Lazarus (Eliezer) Goldschmidt, *Das Buch der Schöpfung (Sepher Jeṣirah)*. With introduction, bibliography and notes. Hebrew texts compare all printed editions. A valuable reference work.[49] Frankfort am Mein, 1894, 92 pp.

Yohann Freidrich von Meyer, *Das Buch Yezirah: die Älster Kabbalistischen Urunded der Hebräer*. Hebrew text and German translation. Leipzig, 1830, 4° 36 pp.

Frieherr Albert von Thimus, *Die Harmonikale Shmbolik des Alterthums*. Analysis of Sefer Yetzirah. Köln, 1868-76, Vol. 2.

Hungarian

Bela Tennen, *A Teremtés Könyr*, Budapest, 1931, 62 pp.

Italian

S. Savini, 1923.

Latin

Athanasius Kirscher, *Werke Oedipus Aegyptacus* 2:1, Rome, 1653.[50]

Johannes Pistorius (John Pistor), 1546-1608, *"Liber de Creations Cabalistinis, Hebraice Sepher Jezira*; Authore Abrahamo," in his *Artis Cabalisticae hoc est Reconditae Theologiae et Philosophiae Scriporum*. Some scholars attribute this translation to Johann Reuchlin, or to Paul Ricci (an apostate Jew who also translated Yosef Gikatalia's *Shaarey Orah* into Latin).[51] At the end of British Museum Ms. 740, there is a note that it was written in 1488 by a Jew, Yitzchak of Rome. Basille, 1587, Vol. 1, pp. 869-872.

Gulelmus Postellus (William Postell), 1510-1581, *Abrahami Patriarchæ Liber Jezirah sive Formationis Mundi, Patribus quidem Abrahami tempora prædentibus revalatus*. First translation of Sefer Yetzirah. This translation is based on the Short Version, but in a somewhat different form than that published in the Mantua, 1562 edition. A similar version is found in some earlier manuscripts. This translation was published ten years before the first Hebrew edition. Paris, 1552, 16° 84 pp.

Joanne Stephano Rittangelio (John Stephan Rittangel), 1606-1652, *Liber Jezirah, qui Abrahamos Patriarchæ Adscribitur, unacum Commentario Rabi Abraham F.D. super 32 semitis Sapientiæ, a quibus Liber Jezirah incipit.* Contains Hebrew text, commentary of R. Abraham ben David (Raavad, q.v.), and the Thirty-Two Paths of Wisdom. Notes and Illustrations. Amsterdam, 1642, 4° 208, 8 pp.

Yiddish

Saul Raskin, *Kabbalah in Word and Image.* Contains Hebrew text with English and Yiddish translations. New York, 1952, 80 pp.

NOTES

Introduction

1. This is discussed at length in my *Meditation and Kabbalah*, and *Meditation and the Bible* (York Beach, ME: Samuel Weiser).
2. *Kuzari* 4:27.
3. Barceloni, p. 100. This is in the British Museum, Ms. 600. See M. Marguliot, *Catalogue of Hebrew and Samaritan Manuscripts in the British Museum*, Vol. 2, p. 197. Also in the Vatican, Ms. 299, and the British Museum, Ms. 752. Another account also states that Rava and Rav Zeira gazed (*tzafah*) in the *Sefer Yetzirah* for three years (Barceloni, p. 268).
4. Thus, in a number of places in the text, the word *Tzar* is used instead of *Yatzar*. This is more easily read in the imperative than in the third person past.
5. *Sanhedrin* 67b, Barceloni, *loc. cit.* Also see *Shulchan Arukh, Yoreh Deah* 179:15, *Sifsey Cohen* 179:18; *Tshuvot Radbaz* 3:405.
6. Yehudah ben Nissim ibn Malka, *Commentary on Sefer Yetzirah* (Oxford, Ms. 1536), quoted in George Vajda, *Juda ben Nissim ibn Malka, Philosophe juif Marocain*, (Paris, 1954), p. 171; Gershom Scholem, *Kabbalah and its Symbolism*, (New York, 1969), p. 177. There is some question as to whether this Raziel is the same as the published edition. Abraham Abulafia also mentions having studied this book, see *Sheva Netivot HaChakhmah*, in A. Jellinek, *Philosophie und Kabbalah*, (Leipzig, 1854), p. 21.
7. A.M. Habermann, *Sinai* 10:3b (1974) with regard to Geniza fragment Taylor-Schechter 32:5. This is the Saadia Version, which is the longest.
8. Yisrael Weinstock, "LeBirur HaNusach shel Sefer Yetzirah," *Temirin* 1:20, note 41, 1:16, note 31.
9. See *Ne'edar BaKodesh, Shaarey Tzion*.
10. Barceloni, p. 105. In the Pistoris translation, chapters five and six are combined, as well as in many manuscripts. See Weinstock, *loc. cit.*, note 33. The divisions in *Donash* and *Chakamoni* were put in by the printer, and do not exist in the original manuscripts.
11. Saadia Gaon, *Commentary on Sefer Yetzirah*, translated into Hebrew by Yosef Kapach (Jerusalem, 1972), p. 34.
12. See Introduction to *Raziel; Shimushey Tehillim* in *Tshuvot Rashba* 413; R. Moshe Cordevero, Commentary on *Zohar Shir*

HaShirim(Jerusalem, Ms. 4° 74), in G. Scholem, *Kitvey Yad BaKabbalah*, p. 233-4.

13. See *Bahir*, Ed. Reuven Margolios (Jerusalem 1951), Nos. 95, 101, 106.
14. Saadia Gaon, pp. 17, 33.
15. Hai Gaon, quoted in Bachya on Exodus 34:6, *Pardes Rimonim* 11:1, *Kerem Chemed* 8:57; *Donash*, pp. 16,26, *Chakamoni* (in Warsaw, 1884 edtion), p. 66a, *Kuzari* 4:25 (Warsaw, 1880), 42a; *Or HaShem* 4:10 (Vienna, 1860), 90b, Tzioni on Genesis 12:5; Nissim ben Yaakov, introduction to his commentary on Sefer Yetzirah, quoted in Goldschmidt, *Das Buch der Schöpfung* (Frankfort am Mein, 1894), p. 31, note 2. Rabbi Abraham Abulafia, however, apparently was not certain as to the authorship, and writes, "let it be whoever it is." *Or HaSekhel* 4:2 (Vatican, Ms. 233), p. 48b, quoted in Landauer, *Litteraturblatt des Orients* (OLB) 1846, Goldschmidt, p. 8, note 4.
16. *Zohar* (Tosefta) 2:275b end, *Zohar Chadash* 37c; *Raziel* (Amsterdam, 1701), 8b, [New York, Margolies, no date, p. 17].
17. See note 3. Cf. Barceloni, p. 268.
18. Saadia, p. 33.
19. Barceloni, p. 100.
20. *Zohar* 1:37b.
21. Tzioni *ad loc.*, Raavad on Sefer Yetzirah 6:4.
22. Abraham left Haran at God's command when he was 75 years old (Genesis 12:4). According to most authorities, Abraham made the covenant with God mentioned in Genesis 15 when he was 70 years old, before he left Haran. See *Seder Olam Rabbah* 1, Mekhilta on Exodus 12:40, Ramban, *Sifsei Chachamim, ibid.*; Rashi, *Sanhedrin* 92b, "*U'Ta'u*," Tosefot, *Shabbat* 10b, "*VeShel*," *Avodah Zarah* 9a, "*U'Gemiri*," Rosh, *Yebamot* 6:12. This covenant may have been related to the system of Sefer Yetzirah, see below, chapter 1, note 70. See R. Eliezer of Wormes, Commentary on Sefer Yetzirah, p. 1a.
23. See note 95. Also see *Zohar* 1:79a, 2:198a.
24. Barceloni, p. 266. *Cf.* Botril on 1:1; Saadia B (Munich, Ms. 40), p. 77a, quoted in Scholem, *Kabbalah and its Symbolism*, p. 171. Also see Saadia, p. 141, Barceloni, p. 99.
25. *Pesikta Chadata*, in A. Jellinek, *Bet HaMidrash* (Leipzig, 1853), 6:36, quoted in Barceloni, p. 268, *Sefer Rokeach* (Jerusalem, 1967), p. 19, and in translation, in Scholem, *Kabbalah and its Symbolism*, p. 178. See chapter 2, note 61.
26. Genesis 14:18, Rashi, Targum J. *ad loc.* Psalm 110:4, *Nedarim* 32b, Ran *ad loc.* "*U'Malki Tzedek*"; Radak, Ralbag, on Joshua 10:1.

27. *Pirkey Rabbi Eliezer* 48 (Warsaw, 1852), 116a. It is also taught that Moses studied the letters on Mount Sinai, *Ibid.* 46 (110b).
28. *Bava Batra* 16b. Abraham was considered a leading figure in his time, *Kiddushin* 32b, Ramban of Genesis 40:14.
29. *Pirkey Rabbi Eliezer* 8 (18b), Ran, *loc. cit.*
30. *Shabbat* 156a.
31. *Avodah Zarah* 14b. *Cf.* Barceloni, p. 100.
32. *Sanhedrin* 91b, *Be'er Shava, ad loc., Zohar* 1:99b, 1:133b, 1:233a, Barceloni, p. 159.
33. *Shnei Luchot HaBrit, Torah SheBeK'tav, VaYeshev* (Lvov, 1860), 3:65a; *Pitchey Tshuvah, Yorah Deah* 62:2. See *Yerushalmi Peah* 1:1, Rashi on Genesis 37:2.
34. *Berakhot* 55a. *Cf.* Barceloni, p. 102, Raavad on 6:4, *Metzaref LeChakhmah* (Jerusalem, n.d.), 28a. Also see Ramban on Exodus 31:3. According to Rashi, the "knowledge" mentioned in this verse refers to *Ruach HaKodesh.*
35. *Tanchuma, Pekudey* 2, *Zohar* 2:162b.
36. *Pesikta Chadata*, in *Bet HaMidrash* 6:37. A similar tradition is attributed to R. Yehudah ben Batirah in his *Sefer Bitachon*, said to be quoted by R. Chamai Gaon in his *Sefer HaYichud* (this book is quoted in *Pardes Rimonim* 11:4), cited in *Avodat HaKodesh* 3:17 (Warsaw, 1894), 80a Chelkak MeChokak on *Evven HaEzer* 1:8. This is also found in Jewish Theological Seminary, Ms. Halberstam 444, p. 200, and in Latin in Johanne Reuchlin, *De Arte Cabalistica* (1603), col. 759. Also see *Peliyah* (Koretz, 1784), 36a, *Yalkut Reuveni* (Warsaw, 1884), 20b; R. Yehudah HaChasid, *Sefer HaGematria*, quoted by Abraham Epstein, *Beiträge zur Jüdischen Altertumskunde* (Vienna, 1887), pp. 122-3; Saadia B, introduction to Sefer Yetzirah, published by M. Steinschneider, *Magazin fur die Wissenschaft das Judentums*, 1892, p. 83. Also see *Rav Pa'alim* (Warsaw, 1894), p. 41. For English translation, see Scholem, *Kabbalah and its Symbolism*, pp. 178-180; Phineas Mordell, *The Origin of Letters & Numerals According to the Sefer Yetzirah* (New York, 1975), pp. 51, 52.
37. *Alfa Beta deBen Sirah*, in *Otzar Midrashim*, p. 43. *Cf.* Chelkat Mechokek on *Evven HaEzer* 1:8, Mishnah LaMelekh on *Yad, Ishut* 15:4. See Rahi, *Chagigah* 15a, *"BeAmbati."*
38. *Sefer Maharil*, beginning of *Likutim* at end of book (Jerusalem, 1969), 85a.
39. *Bet Chadash*, on *Tur Yoreh Deah* 195 *"VeLo"* (77b); *Turey Zahav, Yoreh Deah* 95:7; *Bet Shmuel, Evven HaEzer* 1:10, *Birkey Yosef, Evven HaEzer* 1:14, *Tshuvot R. Yaakov Emdin* 2:97, *Tshuvot*

Tashbatz 3:263; *Pachad Yitzchak, "Ben Bito"* (30a). According
to some sources, Rav Zeira and Rav Pappa were born in the
same manner, see *Alfa Beta DeBen Sirah, Otzar Midrashim* p.
43, *Yuchsin* (Jerusalem 1962), 39c, *Tzemach David* (Warsaw,
1878), p. 26, *Seder HaDorot, Tanaim VeAmoraim*, R. Zeira 3
(Warsaw, 1882), Vol. 2, p. 59c.

40. Yosef ben Uziel is mentioned at the beginning of *Alfa Beta DeBen
Sirah* (Ed. Steinschneider, Berlin, 1858), in *Otzar Midrashim* p. 35.
There is also a dispute between Uziel, son of Ben Sirah, and Yosef
ben Uziel, *Ibid.* p. 36. Also see pp. 37, 39. There is also a treatise
called *Bareita of Yosef ben Uziel*, which is said to be based on teachings that Jeremiah revealed to him, see Leipzig, Ms. 30, p. 12, A.
Epstein, *HaChoker*, Cracow-Vienna, 1893-95, 2:41; Mordell, p. 48.
This *Bareita* is apparently quoted in Recanti on Genesis 3:24 (15c).
This Yosef ben Uziel may be identified as the great-grandfather of
Judith. She is described as "Judith, daughter of Merari, son of Ox,
son of Joseph, son of Oziel, son of Helkias" (Apocrypha, Judith
8:1). Helkias or Chilkiah of course, is the father of Jeremiah (1:1),
and the generations of Jeremiah and Ben Sirah may have been
eliminated from the text, perhaps due to the sensitivity regarding
the birth of the latter. In another source, Judith is identified as a
"daughter of the prophets," see Nissim ben Yaakov, *Chibur Yafeh*
(Amsterdam, 1746), 22a, *Bet HaMidrash* 1:130, *Otzar Midrashim*
p. 104. *Cf.* Ran, *Shabbat* (on Rif 10a, top), *Kol Bo* 44, *Shulchan
Arukh, Orach Chaim* 670:2 in *Hagah*. See further, *Yotzer* for second
Sabbath of Chanukah, end.

41. Paris, Ms. 762, British Museum Ms. 15299, quoted by J.L.
Barges in *Sefer Tagin* (ed. Schneur Zaks, Paris 1866), and also
quoted by Mordell, p. 49.

42. *Rav Pa'alim*, p. 66, *Seder HaDorot, Sefarim, Sefer Yetzirah;
Otzar Sefarim, Yud* 386. There is a manuscript that concludes,
"Thus ends the Mishnah of Abraham and the Mishnah of Yosef
ben Uziel," Oxford, Ms. 1947:3, described in Neubauer, Cata-
logue of the Manuscripts in the Bodleian Library (Oxford,
1886-1906), 1947:3; Goldsmidt, p. 11, note 2. Also see Oxford,
Ms. David Oppenheim 965. This is discussed at length in
Mordell, pp. 47-50. See chapter 5, note 38.

43. *Bava Batra* 15a. *Maaseh Bereshit* was also revealed to Daniel,
see *Seder Olam Rabbah* 29 (Jerusalem, 1971), p. 102; *Tanna
DeBei Eliahu Rabbah* 17 (Jerusalem, 1963), 79b, from Daniel
2:19. Regarding a similar revelation to Ezra, see Apocrypha, 2
Esdras 14:44.

44. *Berakhot* 33a. These were not put in writing, and were therefore forgotten, see *Megillah* 18a.

45. *Yerushalmi, Sanhedrin* 7:13 (41a), according to reading in Frank, *La Cabbalah*, p. 77.
46. *Avot* 2:8, *Succah* 28a, *Bava Batra* 134a.
47. *Chagigah* 14b, *Tosefta* 2. He was also expert in magic, see *Sanhedrin* 68a. See Yosef Tzayach, *Tzaror HaChaim*, Jews College, London, Ms. 318, p. 32a.
48. *Sefer HaTaggin* (Paris, 1866), in *Otzar Midrashim* p. 564, also quoted in *Machzor Vitri* (Berlin, 1889), p. 674. See chapter 3, note 38.
49. *Avot* 2:8.
50. *Chagigah* 14b, *Tosefta* 2; *Zohar Chadash* 7a. See Radal, introduction to *Pirkey Rabbi Eliezer* 6b.
51. We thus find that he went to the river Dismas, see *Shabbat* 147a, Rashi, *ad loc., Avot Rabbi Nathan* 14:6. In another source, however, we find that he went to Emmaus where his wife was, *Kohelet Rabbah* on 7:7. See Neubauer, *Geographie du Talmud (Paris, 1868), p. 100; Otzar Yisrael* 2:79.
52. *Midrash Tanaim* on Deuteronomy 26:13 (Ed. David Tzvi Hoffman, Berlin, 1908), p. 175. See my introduction to *The Bahir*, note 37. Also see below, chapter 4, note 5. Emmaus was a town near Tiberias.
53. *Bava Batra* 10b; *Hekhelot Rabbatai* 16:3 *(Batey Midrashot* 1:92).
54. *Chagigah* 2:2 (16a). See discussions in *Bavli* and *Yerushalmi, ad loc.*
55. *Antiquities* 15:10:5 (Tr. William Whiston; New York, n.d.), p. 471. See *Yuchsin* 9d, *Shalshelet HaKabbalah* (Jerusalem, 1962), p. 57, *Seder HaDorot, Tanaim, VeAmoraim,* "Menachem." Samius mentioned in *Antiquities* 14:10:4 is most probably Shammai.
56. *Wars* 2:8:7, 12.
57. *Antiquities* 15:10:4, p. 471.
58. *Minachot* 29b. A text on the subject is also ascribed to him, see *Batey Midrashot* 2:471. See chapter 3, note 38.
59. *Chagigah* 14b. He also learned the magical spells involving cucumbers from Rabbi Yehoshua, *Sanhedrin* 68a.
60. He was thus the only one of the four who entered Paradise who "emerged in peace," *Chagigah* 14b. He was able to describe synesthesia, a common experience of the mystical state, see Mekhilta on Exodus 20:15. It was he who also taught that God cannot be seen in even the most abstract vision, see Mekhilta on Exodus 20:4, Barceloni, p. 14.
61. *Pardes Rimonim* 1:1; R. Yitzchak de Lattes, responsum at beginning of *Zohar; Shalshelet HaKabbalah*, p. 63. *Pardes*

Rimonim was completed in 1548, and first published in Salonica, 1584. The responsum of R. Yitzchak de Lattes was written in 1558. *Shalshelet HaKabbalah* was first published in Venice, 1587. This, then, appears to be the time that this tradition was in circulation.

62. It is thus taught that an anonymous *Mishnah* is Rabbi Meir, *Tosefta* is Rabbi Nehemiah, *Sifra* is Rabbi Yehudah, *Sifri* is Rabbi Shimon (bar Yochai), and all follow Rabbi Akiba, *Sanhedrin* 86a, *Iggeret Sherirah Gaon* (Jerusalem, 1972), p. 27. Also see *Gittin* 67a, Rashi, *ad loc. "Otzar," Avot Rabbi Nathan* 18:1, *Tosefta, Zavim* 1:2. A mishnah of Rabbi Akiba is mentioned in *Sanhedrin* 3:4 (27b), *Tosefta, Maaser Sheni* 2:13; *Shir HaShirim Rabbah* 8:1, *Kohelet Rabbah* 6:2. This is apparently related to the "first *Mishnah*," which we find in *Eduyot* 7:2, *Gittin* 5:6 (55b), *Nazir* 6:1 (34b). See Maharitz Chayot, *Yoma* 53b.

63. *Berakhot* 47a, *Shabbat* 15a, *Bekhorot* 5a, *Eduyot* 1:3. See Rambam, introduction to *Mishnah*, introduction to *Yad*. See Maharitz Chayot, *Shabbat* 6b.

64. See note 62.

65. Rambam, introduction to *Mishnah*, introduction to *Yad*; *Tshuvat Sherirah Gaon, Cf. Yebamot* 49a, *Sanhedrin* 57b, *Minachot* 70a, *Chulin* 60b, *Yerushalmi, Berakhot* 9:5 (68a), Maharitz Chayot, *Shabbat* 6b. See Saadia, p. 33, that *Sefer Yetzirah* was likewise preserved.

66. Rashi, *Shabbat* 6b, *"Megillat."*

67. Introduction to *Yad*.

68. Chayot, *Sotah* 20a, from *Bereshit Rabbah* 9:5, 20:29, *Yerushalmi, Taanit* 1:1 (3a). See *Sefer Chasidim* 282, as well as *Eruvin* 21b, 54b, *Shnei Luchot HaBrit* 3:231a.

69. Rashi, *loc. cit., Bava Metzia* 92a, *"Megillat."*

70. *Chagigah* 2:1 (11b).

71. See my *Meditation and Kabbalah*, chapter 2:1.

72. *Hekhalot Rabatai* 1:1, *Tshuvat Hai Gaon*, in *Sheelot U'Tshuvot HaGaonim* (Lyck, 1864), (#99), quoted in *HaKotev* on *Eyin Yaakov, Chagigah* 14b (#11); *Otzar HaGaonim, Chelek HaTshuvot, Chagigah*, p. 14; R. Chananel on *Chagigah* 14b, *Arukh, "Avney Shayish."* For philosopher's opinion, see *Yad, Yesodey HaTorah* 2:12, 4:13; Rambam on *Chagigah* 2:1, *Moreh Nevuchim*, introduction to part 3; *Or HaShem* 4:10 (90a, b).

73. Rashi (in *Eyin Yaakov*), *Chagigah* 11b, *"Ain Dorshin" (Cf.* Rashi, *Chagigah* 13a, *"Sitrey Torah,"* where he also includes *Sefer Yetzirah*), *Kuzari* 4:25 (53a), see *Kol Yehudah, ad loc.; Or HaShem* 4:10 (90b), *Metzaref LeChakhmah* 6 (23a, b).

74. We thus find that a disciple of Rabbi Yehudah the Prince expounded upon the Markava before him, *Yerushalmi, Chagigah* 2:1 (9a top).

75. So in *Tosefot, Gittin* 56a *"Agla," Bekhorot* 19a *"DeHach." Cf.* Rashi, *Sanhedrin* 65b, *Shabbat* 11a, *Eruvin* 63a, *Pesachim* 68a, *Arukh, "Tilta,"* Targum J. Ibn Ezra on Genesis 15:9, where other interpretations are found. Some say that it indicates a "three year old calf," while others, "a calf a third the size of its mother."

76. *Sanhedrin* 65b. *Cf. Pesikta Chadata, Bet HaMidrash,* 6:36, which states that they are the tongue for the Saturday night meal.

77. *Sanhedrin* 67b.

78. We thus find the term, "rules of medicine" (*hilkhot rafua*), *Yerushalmi, Yevamot* 8:2 (47a), *Sifri* (247) on Deuteronomy 23:2. We also find an expression, "It is a rule (*halakhah*) that Esau hates Jacob," Sifri on Numbers 9:10, Rashi on Genesis 33:4.

79. Barceloni, p. 268. Vatican, Ms. 299, 66a.

80. Barceloni, p. 103. *Cf. Yad Ramah, Sanhedrin* 65b.

81. *Ner Elohim,* quoted in G. Scholem, *HaKabbalah shel Sefer Hetemunah VeSehl Abraham Abulafia* (Jerusalem, 1965), p. 217.

82. *Tshuvot Rashba* 413.

83. *Sanhedrin* 17b. Pumpadita was founded in the year 255, and stood for some 800 years.

84. *Chagigah* 13a, *Cf.* Maharsha, *ad loc.* Note that on the bottom of this folio, Rav Yehudah explains the Chashmal.

85. See Rashash, *ad loc.*

86. See note 34.

87. *Shabbat* 156a. See note 30. See chapter 3, note 38.

88. *Kiddushin* 71a. Some say that this Name is the essence of *Maaseh Bereshit, Tosefot, Chagigah* 11b *"Ain Dorshin."* The 42 letter name is actually derived from the first verses of Genesis, see *Zohar* 1:30a, *Tikuney Zohar* 13a, *Peliyah* 37b, *Sefer HaKanah* (Cracow, 1894), 88a, *Pardes Rimonim* 21:13. It is significant to note that the initial letters of *Maaseh Bereshit,* Mem Bet, spell out the number 42.

89. *Shabbat* 41a.

90. *Ibid.* 12a, *Sotah* 33a.

91. *Chagigah* 13a.

92. Rashi states that the text of *Hakhalot Rabatai* was the essence of *Maaseh Markava,* Rashi (in Eyin Yaakov) on *Chagigah* 11b. See note 72.

93. See note 16. Also see *Reyah Mehemna, Zohar* 2:187b; *Tikuney Zohar* 70 (132b end). It is significant that most commentators on *Sefer Yetzirah*, even those as late as R. Moshe Botril, who lived over a century after the *Zohar* was published, do not quote the *Zohar*.
94. *Chagigah* 13a.
95. *Yerushalmi, Sanhedrin* 7:13 (41a), *Bereshit Rabbah* 39:14, 84:4, *Tanchuma, Lech Lecha* 12. This is also stated anonymously in Sifri (32) to Deuteronomy 6:5, *Avot Rabbi Nathan 12:7. Rabbi Elazar said many things in the name of R. Yosi ben Zimra, cf. Berakhot* 32b.
96. *Midrash Tehillim* 3:2 (17a). Bracketed portion is not in all editions. There is also a teaching that God placed the *Sefer Yetzirah* in the Torah, see *Bet HaMidrash* 6:36.
97. *Sanhedrin* 65b.
98. *Chulin* 122a end.
99. *Bava Metzia* 85b. See below, chapter 3, note 11. R. Zeira also had his throat slit and was miraculously resurrected, *Megillah* 7b.
100. Barceloni, p. 268. *Cf. Bet HaMidrash* 6:36.
101. *Sanhedrin* 65b. Rashi says that they accomplished this using the *Sefer Yetzirah*, also see Raavad on 6:4, *Metzaref LeChakhmah* 27a, b. There is a question as to whether this was an actual creation or an illusion, *cf. Yad Ramah, ad loc.,* Barceloni, pp. 102, 103, *Tshuvot Radbaz* 3:405, *Bet Yosef on Yoreh Deah* 179, *Tshuvot Maharshal* 98. Some authorities here read Rabbah instead of Rava, see Yaakov Emdin, *ad loc.,* Margolios on *Bahir* 196.
102. *Bahir* 196. *Cf. Avodat HaKodesh* 3:9; Hillel of Verona, *Tagmuley HaNefesh* (Lyck, 1874), 9b, Ramban on Genesis 2:7.
103. *Cf. Tshuvot Chacham Tzvi* 93.
104. *Peliyah* 2c: "He reversed his name (*RBA*) and created (*BRA*)."
105. Targum J. on Genesis 1:27. The sum 612 is also the numerical value of *Brit*, meaning covenant. See below 1:3, 1:8.
106. It is significant that, when written this way, Abracadabra contains the word BRA (*Bara*), meaning to create, while the remaining letters add up to 26, the numerical value of the Tetragrammaton. Abracadabra is usually written in descending order, and similar devices are found, see Rashi, *Avodah Zarah* 12b, Raziel 40b (139), Gra on *Sefer Yetzirah* 2:4.
107. Barceloni, p. 102.
108. Quoted in Barceloni, p. 104. Also see note 72.
109. Sasoon Ms. 218, p. 22, described in *Ohel Dawid* (Oxford, 1932), p. 271. Also see L. Zunz, *Literaturgeschichte* (Berlin, 1865), p.

32, Nehemiah Aloni, *HaShitah HaAnogramit shel HaMilonut BeSefer Yetzirah, Temirin* 1:69 (Jerusalem, 1972). *Cf.* A. Mirski, *Sinai* 65:184 (1929); *Idem., Yalkut HaPiutim* (Tel Aviv, 1958), pp. 17-23.

110. See *Bareita DeShmuel HaKatan*, beginning of chapter 5.

111. *BaMidbar Rabbah* 14:12. All the sevens in *Sefer Yetzirah* are also mentioned in another early Midrash, Pirkey Rabbi Eliezer 18 (43b, 44a), see below 4:7.

112. *Temirin*, p. 21.

113. Donash ibn Tamim, *Commentary on Sefer Yetzirah* (London, 1902), p. 65; Barceloni, p. 138. See above, note 68.

114. Yaakov ben Nissan, *Commentary on Sefer Yetzirah*, Munich, Ms. 92:20, quoted in Goldschmidt, p. 30, note 4.

115. See *Revue des Edudes Juives* (REJ) 105:133-136, 140; *Temirin*, p. 11.

116. *Otzar Eden HaGanuz* (Oxford, Ms. Or 606), p. 78b.

117. Saadia, p. 34.

118. Barceloni, pp. 105, 116, 211; Donash, p. 49.

119. Ramak, *Commentary on Sefer Yetzirah* 1:13 (Jerusalem, Ms. 8° 2646:2), p. 10b. *Cf.* G. Scholem, *Kitvey Yad BaKabbalah* (Jerusalem, 1930), p. 93. Also see *Pardes Rimonim* 21:16.

120. Introduction to *Perush HaGra* on *Sefer DeTzeniuta* (Vilna, 1843), p. iv. The Gra used ten versions, choosing that of the Ari, but correcting certain errors in the printed editions.

Chapter One

1. *Kuzari* 4:25 (43a-44a).

2. Raavad, *ad loc., Tikuney Zohar Chadash* 112c, *Peliyah* 213a, *Pardes Rimonim* 12:1, *Mavo Shaarim* 5:2:6, *Etz Chaim, Shaar HaTzelem* 2.

3. *Avot* 5:1.

4. *BaMidbar Rabbah* 14:12.

5. *Rosh HaShanah* 32a, *Megillah* 21a, *Zohar* 1:15a, 1:16b, *Tikuney Zohar* 12 (27a). See note 185.

6. Raavad, *ad loc., Peliyah* 49c.

7. *Bahir* 106, Barceloni, p. 106, *Tikuney Zohar* 30 (75a).

8. See chapter 6, note 57. *Cf.* Isaac of Acco, *ad loc.*, p. 381/1.

9. Barceloni, p. 107, Isaac of Acco, *Otzar Chaim* (Moscow, Ms. Guenzburg 775), p. 111b. *Cf. Bahir* 147. There is thus a tradi-

tion that God placed the *Sefer Yetzirah* in the Torah, see *Bet HaSefer* 6:36, *Chakamoni* (in Warsaw, 1884 edition), 66a. Also see *Otiot DeRabbi Akiba*, end of Bet.

10. *Peliyah* 2d, Recanti (Lvov, 1880), 18c, *Iggeret HaTiyul, Chelek HaSod* 2.

11. See R. Yosef Tzayyach, *Evven HaShoham* (Jerusalem, Ms. 8° 416), p. 24a. The general formula for the array discussed below, 1:2, is 11n—1, and 32 is one of the only powers of two that fulfills this when *n* is an integer.

12. *Zohar* 2:31a bottom. See *Chotem Takhnit* (Amsterdam, 1865), p. 101, Hirsch on Psalms 119:35. Also see Ramban on *Sefer Yetzirah* (Jerusalem, Ms. 8° 330:28, published by G. Scholem, *Kiryat Sefer*, Vol. 6, 1930), p. 402/2, Isaac of Acco on *Sefer Yetzirah* 283/3.

13. See Raavad, Saadia, Ramban, *ad loc.* Also see Genesis 18:14, Exodus 15:11, 8:18, Leviticus 22:21, Deuteronomy 17:8, Judges 13:18, Psalms 139:6, and commentaries *ad loc.*, especially Hirsch.

14. *Zohar* 3:193b.

15. *Ibid., Peliyah* 30a.

16. *Bahir* 141, *Maarekhet Elohut* (Mantua, 1558), p. 83b, *Tikuney Zohar* 52 (87a), 19 (41b).

17. *Bahir* 141. See *Chagigah* 13a, Ecclesiasticus 3:21. Note that this is attributed to Ben Sirah, who, according to tradition, was involved with the Sefer Yetzirah. Regarding quoting from Ben Sirah, see Ritva (in *Eyin Yaakov*), *Bava Batra* 98b.

18. *Shaarey Orah* 10. Also see *Tikuney Zohar* 42 (81b).

19. *Raziel* 9b (22).

20. See Ramban, p. 402.

21. *Avot* 4:1, Ari, *ad loc., Shaar Maamarey Chazal* (Tel Aviv, 1961), p. 32a, 68a. *Cf.* Rashi on Exodus 31:3.

22. *Toldot Yaakov Yosef, Pekudey* (Warsaw, 1881), p. 78b, quoted in *Sefer Baal Shem Tov, Ki Tetze*, note 1.

23. *Tamid* 32a. See note 37.

24. Ibn Ezra on Exodus 31:3, Hirsch on Genesis 41:33.

25. *Shaarey Orah* 8. Also see *Tur, Orach Chaim* 5.

26. *Pardes Rimonim* 27:27. See note 65.

27. *Berakhot* 61a, *Tikuney Zohar* 13b, 14b, 17a. See note 8.

28. See chapter 6, note 57. Also see *Zohar* 2:201a. When the word *Chakhmah* is spelled out, it adds up to 613, *Raziel* 12a. The letters of the word *Chakhmah* also spell out *Koach Mah*, "the strength of What," *Zohar* 3:28a, 3:235b, *Tikuney Zohar* 69 (102b). The word *Koach*, however, has a numerical value of 28. When the final letters are counted, there are 27 letters in the

Hebrew alphabet. The number 28, then, represents the level above this, which cannot be expressed with letters, *Peliyah* 2b.

29. See Hirsch on Genesis 26:5, 47:22, Exodus 15:25.
30. Thus, writing by erasing is called *Chak Tokhot, Gittin* 20a. *Shulchan Arukh, Orakh Chaim* 32:18. Also see *Otzar Chaim* 202b, *Maarekhet Elohut* 196b, Gra on 1:10.
31. *Cf.* Isaiah 10:1, etc.
32. *Zohar* 1:15a, *Zohar HaRakia, Mikdash Melekh, ad loc., Shefa Tal* 6 (Hanau, 1612), p. 45b ff., *Emek HaMelekh* (Amsterdam, 1653), 6b, *Likutey Torah* (R. Shneur Zalman of Liadi), *BeChukotai*, 46b. Also see *Razial* 11a (27), R. Chananel on *Chagigah* 13a. *Cf. Likutey Moharan* 64. Also see chapter 2, note 48.
33. See *Bahir* 2, Ramban on Genesis 1:2.
34. Yitzchak Sagi Nahor, Yitzchak DeMin Acco (301/27), Ramban A, a 1, R. Yehudah Chayit, *Minchat Yehudah*, on *Maarekhet Elohut*, 196b.
35. *Peliyah* 2c.
36. *Sanhedrin* 65b. See Introduction, note 97.
37. See note 23.
38. Baal Shem Tov, quoted by R. Yesachar Ber of Zlotchov, *Mevaser Tzedek, Bereshit* (Dubno, 1798); quoted in *Sefer Baal Shem Tov, Re'eh* 8.
39. See *Bereshit Rabbah* 12:9, *Midrash Tehillim* 114:3, Ramban on Genesis 43:20, *Tosefot Yom Tov* on *Succah* 4:5, HaGra, *Yoreh Deah* 276:19. Also see Rashi on Genesis 2:4, Psalms 68:5, *Midrash Tehillim* 113:3, *Eruvin* 18b, Ibn Ezra on Exodus 15:2, Rashi on Exodus 17:16, Radak on Isaiah 26:4, Minchat Shai on Psalms 94:7, 118:5, *Kuzari* 4:3 (9a), *Moreh Nevuchim* 1:63.
40. Eliezer of Wormes A, Ramban B, *ad loc.,* from *Sidra Rabba DeBereshit* 1, in *Batey Midrashot* 1:19.
41. *Zohar* 2:104b, 2:169b, 2:257b, 3:35a, *Tikuney Zohar* 2a; *Shaarey Orah* (Warsaw, 1883), pp. 33a, 35b.
42. Ramban A, ad loc.
43. *Berakhot* 31b. *Cf.* 1 Samuel 1:3.
44. See *Shaarey Orah* 2. Also see *Peliyah* 2d, that this is Chakhmah and Binah. Actually, however, it is through the union of the two, which is through Yesod.
45. *Bahir* 171, *Pardes Rimonim* 15. See Radbaz, Magen David, Dalet.
46. *Etz Chaim, Shaar Arikh Anpin* 9; *Cf. Zohar* 2:4b, 3:131b. For various other opinions, see Rashi, Ibn Ezra, Ramban, *Baaley Tosefot, ad loc.,* Tosefot, Rosh HaShanah 17b, "Shalosh," *Sefer Chasidim* 250.

47. *Shaarey Gan Eden* (Cracow, 1881), 2b.
48. *Tosefot, Kiddushin* 3b *"DeAssar," Kuzari* 4:3. Also see Leviticus 19:2, 21:8, Isaiah 6:3, commentaries *ad loc., VaYikra Rabbah* 24:9.
49. *Kuzari* 4:25 (43b, 46b, 47a).
50. *Otiot DeRabbi Yitzchak* (Zalkiev, 1801), p. 3b, 4a. *Cf. Ginat Egoz* (Hanau, 1615), 34a.
51. *Tshuvot Rivash* 157, *Elemah Rabatai, Eyin Kol* 1:2; Radbaz, *Metzudot David* 2, *Shomer Emunim (HaKadmon)* 2:64, 65, *Kisey Melekh* on *Tikuney Zohar* 22 (64b) (Lublin, 1927), 94b #50.
52. See *Etz Chaim, Shaar Mochin DeTzelem* 5,8, *Shaar Drushey HaTzelem* 6, *Shaar Kisey HaKavod* 5; *Nahar Shalom* (in *Etz Chaim*, Tel Aviv, 1960, Vol. 3), p. 170ff.; Gra on 1:1 (3a). See chapter 2, note 45.
53. *Zohar 1:31a.*
54. *Shiur Komah* 15 (Warsaw, 1883), 28a. According to this, one could interpret *Belimah*, "without anything," to indicate that the vowels are written without letters. Just like the Sefer Yetzirah later writes, "Three Mothers, AMSh," and "Seven Doubles, BGD KPRT," here it writes, "Ten Sefirot, without anything." In the time of the Sefer Yetzirah, there was no way of writing the vowels (see below, chapter 2:5). Regarding the assignment of the vowels to the Sefirot, see *Tikuney Zohar* 70 (126a), *Pardes Rimonim* 19:4, 32:2. For other systems, see *Ginat Egoz* 66a *ff., Shoshan Sodot* (Koretz, 1784), 74b; *Perush HaNikkud* (Paris, Ms. 774), p. 38b *ff.*
55. Rashi, Ibn Ezra, Ralbag, *ad loc.,* R. Avraham ben Chiyah, *Hegyon HaNefesh* (Leipzig, 1860), 3a, Chayit 28a.
56. *Chulin* 89a, Radak, *Sherashim, "BLM," Raziel* 8b, *Pardes Rimonim* 3:4. Ibn Janach, *Sherashim, "BLM,"* actually quotes Sefer Yetzirah 1:8. Also see Appendix 1, note 5.
57. *Cf.* Bachya on Deuteronomy 33:27.
58. Yitzchak DiMin Acco, *ad loc.,* 385/1.
59. Eliezer of Wormes B on 2:1, Raavad on 1:10, Ramban B on 1:10. Also see Abraham Abulafia, *Mafteach HaRayyon* (Vatican, Ms. 291), p. 30a. *Cf. Chakamoni* 66c.
60. Berakhot 55a, Raavad on 1:10. See Introduction, notes 34, 86.
61. See *Midrash Tehillim* 119:36. *Cf.* R. Schneur Zalman, *Likutey Amarim, Shaar HaYichud VeHeEmunah* 1.
62. *Etz Chaim, Shaar HaKlipot* 2; *Likutey Amarim, Sefer Shel Benonim* 3.
63. *Shabbat* 55a, *Bereshit Rabbah* 81:2, *Yerushalmi Sanhedrin* 1:1, from Jeremiah 10:10. See Rashi on Job 28:27, who quotes this

in the name of Sefer Yetzirah. One reason why these letters are called Mothers may be because in Hebrew, mother is *Em*, spelled Alef Mem, the first two of these three fundamental letters. Saadia substitutes *Umot*, see Appendix 1, note 14.

64. See *Minchat Shai, ad loc.* Also see *Berakhot* 57a, *BaMidbar Rabbah* 10:4, *Bahir* 104, *Zohar* 3:290b, *Tikuney Zohar* 69 (106b).

65. Raavad on 1:10, 2:1, *Pardes Rimonim* 27:27; Yitzchak Sagi Nahor 287, Ytzchak DiMin Acco 383/5; *Maarekhet Elohut* 53b. For reason why they are not called "fathers," see *Or HaGanuz* on *Bahir* 95, *Shaar Gan Eden* 10d.

66. Yitzchak Sagi Nahor, line 13.

67. *Pardes Rimonim* 1:1.

68. See *Bahir* 124, 138, 188, 193. See Exodus 9:33, 17:11, Leviticus 9:22, 16:21, Numbers 27:23, Deuteronomy 34:9, 1 Kings 8:22, 8:38, 2 Chronicles 6:12.

69. Barceloni, p. 141, *Pardes Rimonim* 1:1.

70. *Cf.* Rashi on Genesis 15:10.

71. See Long Version 6:8.

72. Abraham Abulafia, *Otzar Eden HaGanuz* 4b, *Mafteach HaRayyon* 25b. See note 9.

73. See *Sotah* 7:6, *Bahir* 109, 123, *Shaar HaKavanot* (Tel Aviv, 1962), Vol. 2, p. 263. *Cf. Maarekhet Elohut* 147b. The tongue and palate are also male and female, see *Etz Chaim, Shaar MaN U'MaD* 13, p. 259, *Shaar Rashbi* (Tel Aviv, 1961), p. 296. The five and five also allude to the five phonetic families and the five primary vowels, see *Perush HaNikkud* 39b. See below 2:3.

74. Abraham Abulafia, *Sefer HaCheshek* (Jewish Theological Seminary, Ms. 1801), p. 9a. This is quoted in *Shaarey Kedushah,* Part Four (British Muesum, Ms. 749), p. 12a.

75. Ramban on Exodus 30:19. It is for a very similar reason that the hands are washed before prayer, see *Berakhot* 60b, *Tshuvot Rashba* 191.

76. See *Derashot HaRan* #8 (Jerusalem, 1974), p. 128; *Avodat HaKodesh* 4:25. *Cf. Bereshit Rabbah* 70:8. Also see Numbers 7:89.

77. Abarbanel on 1 Samuel 3:3. This may be the reason why God was said to "dwell among the Cherubs," 1 Samuel 4:4, 2 Samuel 6:2. He is also said to "ride a Cherub," Psalms 18:11, *Cf.* Targum, *ad loc.* See *Maarekhet Elohut* 163b.

78. *Avodat HaKodesh* 4:25. *Cf.* Yoma 9b.

79. *Tikuney Zohar Chadash* 112b, quoted in *Pardes Rimonim* 23:20 *"Keruvim."* See Yoma 54a.

80. *Cf.* Genesis 17:12.

81. Maharal, *Tiferet Yisrael* 2. *Cf.* Ramban, *Torat HaAdam* (in *Kitvey Ramban*, Jerusalem, 1964), Vol. 2, pp. 302, 303.
82. The toes represent the Universe of Beriyah, *Pardes Rimonim* 1:1. Beriyah, however, is the level of Neshamah.
83. See *Shavuot* 18a, *Yad, Issurey Biyah* 4:11, *Yoreh Deah* 185:4; *Tikkuney Zohar* 69 (110a), *Sefer Chasidim* 173.
84. *Shavuot* 18b; *Zohar* 1:90b, 1:112a, 1:155a, 3:43a, 3:56a, 3:246a, *Zohar Chadash* 11a.
85. See R. Yitzchak Santar, *Sefat Emet* (Berlin, 1787), p. 44b. Also see *VaYikra Rabbah* 31:4. Abraham Abulafia also writes that the covenant of circumcision must precede that of the tongue, which is the Torah, see sources in note 72.
86. Barceloni, p. 141, Ramban B on 1:10, *Pardes Rimonim* 1:1. See below, 2:6.
87. Ramban A, Ytzchak Sagi Nahor, *ad loc., Maarkekhet Elohut* 36a, 82b, Chayit 41a, 47a, 113a (*Paz*), *Pardes Rimonim* 1:5.
88. *Pardes Rimonim* 3:1.
89. See Yitzchak Sagi Nahor, *Yitzchak DiMin Acco* (387), Ramban A, *ad loc.,* Recanti on Exodus 31:3 (15c), *Pardes Rimonim* 1:6. Abraham Abulafia states that this is related to the teaching that the Markavah can only be taught to one who is "wise, understanding with his knowledge," *Otzar Eden HaGanuz* 7a.
90. *Chotem Takhnit*, p. 80, Hirsch on Psalms 7:10, *Bet HaOtzar* p. 186. *Cf.* Ramban A, *ad loc.*
91. Examples of this include *Shaarey Orah; Pardes Rimonim, Shaar Arkhey HaKinuyim; Kehillat Yaakov.* One can also use the different divine names associated with the Sefirot, see below 6:6. One can also use the Tetragrammaton with the vowels associated with the Sefirot, see note 54. This is discussed at length in my *Meditation and Kabbalah.*
92. See *Chotem Takhnit*, p. 104. Both words, *Bachan* and *Chakar*, occur in Jeremiah 17:10.
93. Yitzchak Sagi Nahor, line 70.
94. A similar expression is found in *Gittin* 89b. Regarding the meaning of the word *Bori*, see Rashi, *ad loc. "VeHeEmidu."*
95. 1 Kings 8:13, Isaiah 4:5, Daniel 8:11. *Cf.* Psalms 33:14.
96. See *Sodey Razya* (Bilgorey, 1936), p. 32.
97. *Cf. Bahir* 24.
98. *Zohar* 2:37a, *Avodat HaKodesh* 3:42, *Shiur Komah* 21. *Cf. Moreh Nevuchim* 1:11.
99. Ramban A, *ad loc.* (407/7). See chapter 2, note 76.
100. This is based on Exodus 15:17, where the word *Makhon* is read as *Mekuvan*. See Rashi, *ad loc., Yerushalmi, Berakhot* 4:5. This teaches that the Temple on high parallels the Temple (*Bet*

HaMikdash) below. The Temple is also called *Makhon*, see note
95. *Makhon* is also one of the seven heavens, see chapter 4, note
70.

101. Radac, *ad loc.* Also see *Nefesh HaChaim* 1:13, in *Hagah
     "U'LeFi."*
102. See *Mesechta Atzilut 5, Pardes Rimonim* 16.
103. The Universe of Yetzirah parallels the six Sefirot: Chesed,
     Gevurah, Tiferet, Netzach, Hod, Yesod, *Makhon* is the sixth of
     the seven heavens, and hence, parallels Yesod.
104. Gra, *ad loc.* See *Kehilat Yaakov* (Lvov, 1870), Vol. 2, p. 22a.
     Also see *Tikuney Zohar* 15a, b. Also see note 109.
105. This is obvious in the Saadia Version 2:1.
106. *Cf.* Psalms 111:10, *Bahir* 49, 103, 142.
107. *Chagigah* 14a, *Sanhedrin* 93b, Rashi on Exodus 30:3.
108. *Shaar HaPesukim* (Tel Aviv, 1962), p. 5. *Cf. Shaarey Orah*
     63b.
109. *Siddur HaAri: Siddur R. Shabatai* (Lvov, 1866), p. 67b; *Siddur
     Kol Yaakov* (Slavita, 1804), p. 156a, *Siddur R. Ashar* (Lvov,
     1788), p. 59a. See *Shaar HaKavanot* 2:208.
110. *Midrash Tehillim* 31:6 (120a), 78:19 (178b).
111. *Cf.* Chayit 41b. The Sefirot contain the essence of the Divine,
     see *Pardes Rimonim* 4:7.
112. These exercises are actually described by R. Eliezer of Wormes,
     Sodi Razia, p. 41.
113. Ramban B, *ad loc., Yitzchak Sagi Nahor*, line 75.
114. *Shaarey Orah* 37b, 38a, 95a, Yitzchak DiMin Acco, p. 388. See
     note 109.
115. *Sanhedrin* 111a.
116. Ibn Ezra on Genesis 37:5, Gra on Psalms 22:29.
117. *Cf. Yerushalmi, Nedarim* 9:1 (29a), Ramban on Deuteronomy
     22:6, *Sefer HaChinuch* 545, *Shomer Emunim (HaKadmon)* 2:11
     no. 4, *Nefesh HaChaim* 2:4. Also see Job 22:3, Psalms 16:2,
     Radak, *ad loc.*
118. Deuteronomy 26:15, Jeremiah 25:30, Zechariah 2:16.
119. Radak *ad loc., Midrash Tehillim* 90:10, Barceloni, p. 198. See
     Long Version 4:2. Also see *Bereshit Rabbah* 68:10, *Sh'mot
     Rabbah* 45:6, Rashi on Exodus 33:21.
120. See Hirsch on Leviticus 19:26, Deuteronomy 33:27, Psalms
     90:1; *Chotem Takhnit*, p. 177. Others say that the root of the
     word is Eyin, meaning eye, since it is the place from which God
     looks down at the world, Ibn Ezra on Psalms 90:1.
121. Isaiah 65:11, Psalms 83:18, 92:8, 132:14. See Yitzchak Sagi
     Nahor, line 100. Also see *Chotem Takhnit*, p. 200.
122. See *Bereshit Rabbah* 3:7, *Moreh Nevuchim* 2:30, *Ikkarim* 2:18.

123. *Yitzchak Sagi Nahor*, Ramban, *Yitzchak DiMin Acco, ad loc.*, *Otzar Eden HaGanuz* 8a. See *Hekhalot Rabatai* 1:1. *Cf. Tosefot, Megillah* 2b, "*VeOd.*"

124. *Bahir* 88. *Cf. Chotem Takhnit*, p. 111; R. Shlomo Pappenheim, *Yeriot Shlomo*, Vol. 2 (Roedelheim, 1831), p. 44a; Wertheimer, *Shemot HaNirdafim BaTanach* (New York, 1953), p. 136. Also see Targum, Radak, on Isaiah 21:5.

125. *Hekhalot* 1:1. See *Shaarey Orah* 37b, 96a.

126. Some commentators distinguish between *Bazak* and the more common *Barak*, which is the usual word for lightning. Some say that *Bazak* means a spark, *Chakamoni*, Radak on Ezekiel, and in *Sherashim*. Others say that it is sheet lightning, Barceloni, p. 132. See Rashi, Mahari Kara, Abarbanel on Ezekiel 1:14. In talmudical language, Bazak means "to cast" or "throw," see *Bava Bat ra* 73a, *Sanhedrin* 108b. The Talmud interprets Bazak to mean the sparks shooting out of an oven, *Chagigah* 13b.

127. *Bereshit Rabbah* 50:1. According to the first interpretation, the word *Bazak* comes from the word *Zikah*, meaning a meteor. A *Zikah* is also a bubble, *Cf.* Donash. The Kabbalists also say that there is a heaven called *Bazak*, see *Emek HaMelekh, Beriyah* 12 (173a).

128. *Shekkel HaKodesh* (London, 1911), p. 113. This is very much like the *Abubya* mentioned in *Mekhilta* on Exodus 20:4, *Cf.* Barceloni, p. 14. This is an image seen in water, see *Nedarim* 9b, *Tosefta Nazir* 4:7. Such images were worshipped, as we find in *Avodah Zarah* 47a, *Yelamdenu, Acharey Mot*, quoted in *Yalkut Shimoni* 62 on Judges 7:2, *Arukh, Bavoa*. Such reflections were possibly used for idolatrous meditation.

129. *Cf.* Job 28:3, Psalms 139:22.

130. *Cf.* Hirsch on Genesis 41:1; *Shemot HaNirdafim SheBaTanach*, p. 290; *Chotem Takhnit*, p. 198. The *Zohar* states that *Ketz* denotes evil, *Zohar* 1:62b, *Etz Chaim, Shaar HaYareach* 5. When Acher became an apostate, he was said to have cut off (*katzatz*) his plantings.

131. Shlomo Pappenheim, *Yeriat Shlomo*, Vol. 1 (Diherenfurth, 1784), p. 4b.

132. R. Dov Baer, Maggid of Mezritch, *Imrey Tzadikim* (Zitimar, 1901), p. 23d.

133. In *Shaarey Tzion* it is vocalized as *Dabro*.

134. *Midrash Lekach Tov* 1b. See *Toldot Yaakov Yosef, Yitro* (Warsaw, 1881), 54b, Tzaria (92b); *Tzafnat Paaneach* (33b), *Keter Shem Tov* (Kehot, 1972), p. 121. See Abraham Abulafia, *Get HaShemot* (Oxford, Ms. 1658), 95a; Yosef Tzayach, *Evven HaShoham* 94b.

135. Raavad. They are also said to "run" with Metatron, and to "return" with Sanedlfon, *Zohar* 3:229b, Yitzchak DiMin Acco, p. 392.
136. Another possible instance is Ezekiel 43:27, see Rashi, Radak, *ad loc.*
137. *Bereshit Rabbah* 50:1. See Radak, *Sherashim, RaTzaH. Cf. Moreh Nevuchim* 3:2.
138. Isaiah 21:1, 29:6, Numbers 21:14, Targum J., *ad loc.;* Proverbs 10:25, Nahum 1:3, Psalms 83:16. See chapter 6, note 46.
139. The Targum translates this as *Alal*, which means destructive, see *Kelayim* 7:7, Rambam, *ad loc.;* Proverbs 10:25. *Cf.* Radak, *Sherashim, "Sof," Shemot HaNirdafim SheBaTanach*, p. 243.
140. Hirsch on Exodus 2:3.
141. *Cf. Raziel* 36a (123); *Midrash Konen* (in *Otzar Midrashim*), p. 257.
142. See Gra, Malbim, on Nahum 1:3, Psalms 83:16, Hirsch on Exodus 2:3. The Midrash states that *Sufah* comes from the word *Kasaf,* meaning "white," since it makes people blanch in fear, *Shir HaShirim Rabbah* on 3:4.
143. See Abarbanel, *ad loc.*
144. *Chagigah* 2:1. See introduction, note 72.
145. Also see Jeremiah 4:13. See chapter 6, note 46. Also see Saadia, Barceloni, here.
146. This opposes the philosophers who call God the "First Cause." See *Moreh Nevuchim* 1:69. A cause-effect relationship can only exist within the framework of time, and God is above time.
147. See *Maarekhet Elohut* 36a.
148. *Cf.* Yitzchak DiMin Acco, p. 388.
149. To prove that they all meet at a single point, we can imagine the three-dimensional continuum as the surface of a four-dimensional hypersphere. When the hypersphere becomes infinitely large, the continuum becomes flat. Still, all outgoing lines, making "great circles" on the hypersphere, meet on its opposite side. Incidentally, this has nothing to do with the curved space of general relativity, since the entire discussion here assumes an idealized flat space.
150. See *Moreh Nevuchim*, introduction to part 2, No. 16; *Amud HaAvodah, Vikuach Shoel U'Meshiv*, No. 99.
151. *Cf. Shabbat* 89a, *Bereshit Rabbah* 48:11.
152. R. Moshe Luzzatto, *Pitchey Chakhmah VaDaat* No. 3; *Shefa Tal* 3:1 (48a).
153. *Toldot Yaakov Yosef, VaYereh* (17a).
154. *Zohar* 1:4a.
155. *Bereshit Rabbah* 50:2, Targum, Rashi, on Genesis 18:2, *Zohar* 1:127a.

156. *Pardes Rimonim* 6:6. See note 150.
157. *Amud HaAvodah* (Chernovitz, 1863), p. 83c.
158. *Sefer Chasidim* 530, *Sodey Razia*, pp. 9,10. *Cf. Zohar* 1:101b.
159. See *Yafeh Sha'ah* on *Etz Chaim, Shaar Man U'MaD* 4, p. 192.
160. *Nefesh HaChaim* 1:10.
161. See *Shiur Komah* 23.
162. The Mezritcher Maggid uses a similar idea with regard to Israel, see *Maggid Devarav LeYaakov* (Jerusalem, 1971), No. 1, 123.
163. *Zohar* 1:50b, Botril on 2:3. *Cf. Emunot VeDeyot* 6:4. Also see *Maarhekhet Elohut* 36b.
164. See Gra, *ad loc.* See *Shekkel HaKodesh*, pp. 123-124. The *Zohar, loc. cit.,* also indicates that one should contemplate the flame.
165. Gra, *ad loc.* This is the Chashmal seen by Ezekiel.
166. *Otzar Eden HaGanuz* 10a.
167. *Shaarey Orah* 68b. This is the level of Binah consciousness.
168. *Tikuney Zohar* 17a.
169. *Moreh Nevuchim* 1:58, *Kuzari* 2:2, *Ikkarim* 2:22.
170. Thus, music was often used to attain a meditative state, see *Yad, Yesodey HaTorah* 7:4, based on 1 Samuel 10:5, 2 Kings 3:15. However, the Kabbalists write, that the music would be stopped once they reached the desired state. See *Shaarey Kedushah*, Part Four, p. 15b.
171. See note 27.
172. See Abraham Abulafia, *Sefer HaTzeruf* (Paris, Ms. 774), p. 1b. Also see *Razeil* 14b (40), *Get HaShemot* 95b, *Evven HaShoham* 119b. *Cf.* Ramban A, *Yitzchak DiMin Acco*, p. 392, *Otzar Eden HaGanuz* 11a, *Zohar* 3:288b.
173. *Chagigah* 14b. See *Otzar Chaim* pp. 72b, 138a, 200a.
174. This, apparently, was the experience of R. Chaim Vital, see *Shaar HaGilgulim* (Tel Aviv, 1963), pp. 140, 158.
175. At the end of a meditation, Abulafia thus advises the initiate to "eat something, drink something, smell a pleasant fragrance, and let your spirit once again return to its sheath," *Chayay Olam HaBah* (Jewish Theological Seminary, Ms. 2158), p. 18b, in A. Jellinek, *Philosophie und Kabbalah* (Leipzig, 1854), p. 45.
176. *Cf. Zohar* 1:65a.
177. R. Yehudah AlBotini, *Sulam HaAliyah* 10 (Jerusalem, Ms. 8° 334), quoted in G. Scholem, *Kitvey Yad BaKabbalah*, p. 228.
178. *Moreh Nevuchim* 3:49.
179. *Pardes Rimonim* 3:5. However, others say that this is Chakhmah, *Cf.* Chayit 177b. Also see Raziel 10a (23), *Sodi Razia* p. 1, *Mafteach HaRayyon* 31b, *Otzar Eden HaGanuz* 11b, 14b. *Kuzari* 4:25 (57b, 58a) says that this is pure spirit.

180. See *Recanti, ad loc.* Also see Numbers 24:2, 1 Samuel 10:10, 11:6. *Cf.* 1:2.
181. See *Chakamoni,* R. Eliezer of Wormes (3b), Gra, *ad loc.* Also see Raziel 10a (23), 22a (73). Compare this to *Etz Chaim, Shaar TaNTA* 5, from Psalm 23:31, *Nefesh HaChaim* 1:15.
182. It is thus taught that Yesod of Arikh Anpin (Keter) extends into Yesod of Zer Anpin, which is the true Yesod, *Mavo Shaarim* 5:1:16. Also see *Etz Chaim, Shaar Derushey ABYA* 1 (298b). *Cf. Peliyah* 2d.
183. See Gra, *ad loc. Cf. Bahir* 141. Also see *Sefer HaRazim* (Ed. M. Margolius, Jerusalem,1967), p. 108, line 23-24, quoted in *Temirin,* p. 72. Also in *Shoshan Yesod Olam* (Sasoon, Ms. 290), pp. 61-71.
184. *Tshuvot Rashba* 5:51. *Cf. Bahir* 4.
185. *Rosh HaShanah* 32a. See note 5.
186. *Ibid.* See R. Dov Baer, Maggid of Mezritch, *Or Torah* (Kehot, New York, 1972), p. 2a.
187. Also see Raavad on 2:3, Raziel 10b (25), *Sulah HaAliyah* (Jerusalem, Ms. 8° 1302), pp. 11b, 12a, quoted by G. Scholem in *Kiryat Sefer* 22:166.
188. Rashi on Exodus 31:3 states that Knowledge (Daat) is Ruach HaKodesh. Kabbalistically, Daat is the confluence between Chakhmah and Binah. Although Ruach HaKodesh is derived from Keter, it is manifest in Daat. See *Etz Chaim, Shaar Drushey ABYA* 1.
189. See Yitzchak Stanov, *Sefat Emet,* p. 44b. Some interpret the first Ruach to be spirit, and the second to be air, see *Kuzari* 4:25 (58a), *Raziel* 11b (29), 12b (32). Also see Chayit 19b, 53a. Others say that they are Chakhmah and Binah, see commentaries.
190. *Etz Chaim, Shaar HaAkudim* 8, 5.
191. See *Etz Chaim, Shaar Atik* 4, *Shaar Seder ABYA* 1 (356).
192. See Ari on *Sefer Yetzirah.* Also see *Likutey Amarim, Shaar HaYichud VeHeEmunah* 4 (79b).
193. See Donash.
194. *Tikuney Zohar* 17a.
195. *Pardes Rimonim* 10:5, *Kalach Pitchey Chakhmah* 11.
196. It also means writing, see Job 19:24. Also see *Pardes* 16:9, 27:27, Yitzchak Sagi Nahor, line 138.
197. We thus find, "God's" voice carves (chotzev) flames of fire" (Psalms 29:7). There is an indication that this word might indicate a synesthetic process, *Cf. Mekhilta* on Exodus 20:15. See below, 2:6.
198. Gra, *ad loc.*

199. *Etz Chaim, Shaar TaNTA* 5 (p. 70). *Cf. Bahir* 119, *Zohar* 1:32b, *Otzar HaKavod* (Satmar, 1926), p. 37a, Recanti 3b. A similar idea is found in Ecclesiasticus 24:25-31. Also see *Raziel* 12b (33), 14a (39), *Maarekhet Elohut* 12 (167b), Chayit 19b, 165b, Yitzchak Sagi Nahor, line 142.
200. *Sh'mot Rabbah* 15:22.
201. Raavad, *ad loc.*
202. See comment on 1:12.
203. *Taanit* 7a. *Cf. Shir HaShirim Rabbah* 1:19.
204. Hence, a person cannot prophecy at will, see *Yad, Yesodey HaTorah* 7:4, 5.
205. *Kuzari* 4:25 (58b). Also see *Hegyon HaNefesh* 3b. *Cf. Bereshit Rabbah* 4:1, 5:2, *Sh'mot Rabbah* 15:22, *Midrash Tehillim* 104:7, from Psalms 104:3; *Yerushalmi, Chagigah* 2:1 (8b), *Mekhilta* on Exodus 15:11.
206. *Bahir* 2, Ramban on Genesis 1:2, *Hegyon HaNefesh* 2b, 3a; Raziel 12a (32), Chayit 55b, *Etz Chaim, Shaar TaNTA* 5 (p. 70). This is intermediate between actuality and existence, see Raavad, introduction to *Sefer Yetzirah* 2a.
207. Thus, in the Tzimtzum-constriction, the center dot, which is Malkhut, came into existence before the other Sefirot, see *Etz Chaim, Drush Egolim VeYashar* 2.
208. Ramban, *ad loc.* Also see Rashi, *ad loc. Cf.* Chayit 19b, *Pardes Rimonim* 3:5.
209. Chayit 19b, 20a, *Emek HaMelekh* 6b, c; *Etz Chaim, loc cit.;* Also see Raavad of 2:4, Raziel 12b (32), 14a (39).
210. *Pardes Rimonim* 3:5.
211. *Pirkey Rabbi Eliezer* 3, *Sh'mot Rabbah* 13:1. *Cf.* Yoma 54b, *Bereshit Rabbah* 1:6. *Raziel* 14a.
212. *Cf.* Rashi, Malbim, *ad loc., Shabbat* 55b, *Bereshit Rabbah* 98:4. See my *Waters of Eden*, (NCSY, New York, 1976), p. 62. See Pirkey Rabbi Eliezer, *Etz Chaim, loc. cit.*
213. *Bahir* 165.
214. *Etz Chaim, loc. cit.*
215. Raavad, *Otzar HaShem, ad loc.,* but also see *Bava Kama* 4b.
216. *Cf.* Saadia Gaon, p. 125.
217. Radak, Ibn Ezra, *ad loc.*
218. *Raziel* 11b (29); *Tachkamoni*, Raavad, *Otzar HaShem ad loc.,* Barceloni, p. 197. See *Betza* 4:6 (33a), Rashi, *ad loc.,* "Min HaMayim," *Yad, Yom Tov* 4:1, *Bahir* 188.
219. *Cf. BaMidbar Rabbah* 14:12.
220. *Sh'mot Rabbah* 15:22. See *Zohar* 1:32b, 1:103b, Radal on *Pirkey Rabbi Eliezer* 4:3.

221. *Chagigah* 14b, Rashi, *ad loc., Otzar Chaim* 2a. See *Hekhalot Rabatai* 26:2, that the experience is like being washed by thousands of waves of water. Also see *Pardes Rimonim* 23:13 (27b), from *Tikuney Zohar* 40 (80b).

222. See Rashi on Genesis 1:1, *Noam Elimelekh, Chayay Sarah* (Lvov, 1888), p. 11b.

223. *Kuzari* 4:25 (58a).

224. See *Derekh HaShem* 1:5, 4:6:13.

225. See Malbim on Ezekiel 1:1.

226. See *Pardes Rimonim* 23:22 *"Saraf,"* *Kehillat Yaakov "Saraf"* (23a).

227. *Sodi Razia,* p. 8, Raavad, *Introduction to Sefer Yetzirah* 4c, *Kuzari* 4:3 (22b), Ramban on Genesis 18:2, Exodus 3:2, Numbers 22:31.

228. *Raziel* 12a (31).

229. *Bahir* 30.

230. See Raavad, Ramban B, on 3:2; *Etz Chaim, Shaar TaNTA* 7.

231. *Shaar HaKavanot, Kavanot Naanuim* (Tel Aviv, 1962), p. 310; *Siddur HaAri, Siddur R. Shabatai,* p. 100a, *Siddur R. Asher,* p. 381.

232. *Cf. Zohar* 3:243b.

233. The Ten Sefirot were originally derived from five, and this is why they were later divided into five Partzufim. See *Etz Chaim, Shaar HaMelakhim* 5, p. 151.

234. See *Otzar Eden HaGanuz* 20a, *Mafteach HaRayyon* 31b.

235. See *Etz Chaim, Shaar Akudim* 5, *Shaar Penimiut VeChitzoniut* 10, 12. Regarding the five levels, see *Bereshit Rabbah* 14:9, *Devarim Rabbah* 2:9, *Shaar HaGilgulim* 1.

236. It is thus on the level of Atzilut, which is called "nothingness." Therefore, Beriyah, the world below it, is called "something from nothingness."

237. *Sulam HaAliyah* 7 (8a). *Cf. Sefer HaCheshek* 22a, *Otzar Eden HaGanuz* p. 16. See below, 2:6.

238. See Raavad, Moshe Botril, *ad loc.*

239. See Oxford, Ms. 1531, p. 45a (bottom), quoted in G. Scholem, *Major Trends in Jewish Mysticism,* p. 361, note 42. Also see note 43.

240. See note 220.

241. See Abraham Abulafia, *Chayay Olam HaBah* 18a, quoted in *Philosophie und Kabbalah,* p. 45, where such a method is described in detail. This is also related to the method of the *Hakhalot Rabatai,* Chapters 17-26. Also see *Sodi Razia,* p. 32. *Cf.* Chapter 6, note 37.

242. This technique is described in *Shaarey Kedushah,* Part Four, p. 16a. See chapter 6, note 37.

243. *Otzar Chaim* 107a, b.

Chapter Two

1. *Yitzchak Sagi Nahor*, line 243.
2. *Pesikta* 167a. *Cf. Rosh HaShanah* 17a. See *Avot* 2:8.
3. *Avot* 1:6. See *Likutey Moharan* 282.
4. See *Chakamoni*, Barceloni, on 3:1. See *Etz Chaim, Shaar Derushey HaTzelem* 2, p. 13b.
5. Raavad, *ad loc.*
6. *Yitzchak Sagi Nahor*, line 262, *Otzar HaKavod* 39b. Regarding "pillars of Chashmal," see Raziel 14b (40), and compare this to below, 2:6.
7. *Chagigah* 13b (top). See *Or HaSekhel* 4:2 (48b).
8. *Otzar Eden HaGanuz* 54a.
9. See *Sefer Baal Shem Tov, Bereshit* 131-135.
10. *Zohar* 2:54a. See note 54.
11. See Rashi, Yalkut Reuveni, on Exodus 2:14, *Sh'mot Rabbah 1:30.* See *Shaar HaPesukim, Likutey Torah HaAri, ad loc.*
12. *Shoshan Sodot* 72b. Also see *Otzar Eden HaGanuz* 6b. The *Zohar* says that these represent the 25 letters in the verse, "Hear O Israel . . ." (Deuteronomy 6:4), *Zohar* 2:12b, 2:117a, 2:139b, *Tikuney Zohar* 6 (22a).
13. See note 63.
14. See *Or HaSekhel* 7:3 (94), *Get HaShemot* 90a, Chayit 19b. See below, 4:3.
15. See Saadia, *Introduction to Sefer Yetzirah*, Eighth Theory, p. 30. Also see Introduction, note 34.
16. See chapter 1, notes 237, 242.
17. *Chakak* means to write, see chapter 1, note 31. See *Otzar Eden HaGanuz* pp. 160-162.
18. Beginning of *Sulah HaAliyah. Cf. Or HaSekhel* 7:1 (90a).
19. *Evven HaShoham* 12a, *Sheirit Yosef* (Vienna, Ms. 260), p. 2b. Regarding the ciphers, see *Pardes Rimonim* 21:13, 30:5.
20. *Pardes Rimonim* 27:27, *Etz Chaim, Shaar Drushey HaTzelem* 2, p. 12, *Shaar Rashbi* 297. *Zohar* 2:123a supports the assumption that the first two are the gutturals and palatals.
21. See Saadia, Eliezer of Wormes, *ad loc., Tikuney Zohar* 132a, *Zohar* 3:228a, etc. Donash has a third ordering, where the last two are interchanged, see note 36.
22. *Etz Chaim, loc. cit. Cf. Shaar Ruach HaKodesh* p. 113.
23. *Shaarey Zohar* on *Sofrim* 9:1.
24. *Shabbat* 104a, *Megillah* 2b, *Bereshit Rabbah* 1:15, *BaMidbar Rabbah* 18:17, *Tanchuma, Korach* 12, *Pirkey Rabbi Eliezer* 48.

Cf. Chayit 19a. The fact that these letters are not mentioned in *Sefer Yetzirah* may be indicative of its extreme antiquity.

25. *Etz Chaim, Shaar Rashbi, loc cit.* See Barceloni, p. 140, Gra on 1:3 No. 2.
26. *Tikuney Zohar,* Introduction (4b), 70 (135b).
27. *Pardes Rimonim* 21:1.
28. *Tikuney Zohar* 14a, R. Eliezar of Wormes 4b, *Etz Chaim, Shaar TaNTA* 3, p. 66, *Ginat Egos* 24c.
29. Also see chapter 1, note 54.
30. *Pardes Rimonim* 27:27.
31. Hence, "a woman's voice is a 'sexual organ,'" *Berakhot* 24a, *Zohar* 3:142a.
32. *Pardes Rimonim, loc. cit., Etz Chaim, Shaar Derushey HaTzelem* 2, *Shaar Rashbi* p. 297.
33. *Kisey Melekh* on *Tikuney Zohar* 4b (11a). According to the *Tikuney Zohar* 14a, the order of *Pituchey Chotem* parallels the five phonetic families in alphabetical order.
34. Another reason for this order is because they add up to *"Melekh, Malakh, Yimlokh."* See *Shaar HaKavanot,* p. 109a.
35. *Etz Chaim, Shaar HaYareach* 5 (1. 183), *Pardes Rimonim* 13:7. Also see *Yonat Elim,* quoted in *Kehilat Yaakov,* Vol. 2, p. 3a.
36. *Tikuney Zohar* 14a. Significantly, the families then come out like the reverse of Donash's order. See note 21.
37. Raavad, *ad loc.* See *Emek HaMelekh* 6b.
38. *Otzar Chaim* 107a.
39. Saadia B, *ad loc.*
40. Acronym of R. Yitzchak be Asher, died 1132. Scholem, in his *Kabbalah and its Symbolism,* p. 186, claims that this acrostic stands for R. Yishmael ben Elisha. In British Museum, Ms. 754, the abbreviation is R. Tz., which Scholem surmises may be a certain R. Tzadok.
41. Saadia B. *loc. cit. Emek HaMelekh* 9c similarly writes that if one says them backward, he will be swallowed up by the earth.
42. *Chakamoni, Pardes Rimonim* 30:5, R. Eliezar of Wormes, pp. 5a, 17bff; *Otzar Eden HaGanuz* 39a, *Otzar Nechamad* on *Kuzari* 4:25 (61b), *Evven HaShoham* 154b, *Sherit Yosef* 9a, *Shoshan Yesod Olam* No. 454, p. 207.
43. Raavad, *ad loc.* Abulafia presents this system in the name of R. Yitzchak Bardashi, see *Otzar Eden HaGanuz* 16b, 37a; Appendix 5, notes 10, 39. Also in *Kol Yehudah* on *Kuzari* 4:25 (61a). The fact that each array contains 231 pairs, which is 21 times 22, with the letters *AL* in the middle is alluded to in the verse, "Only in You, O God *(Ach Bach El)*" (Isaiah 45:14), see *Zohar* 1:33b, commentaries *ad loc.*, Gra on 6:4.

44. *Emek HaMelekh* 4a *ff.* (see Appendix III), *VaYakhel Moshe* (Zolkiev, 1741), p. 7a, *Shaar Gan Eden* 12a, *Pri Yitzchak* (in *Sefer Yetzirah*, Warsaw, 1884), Vol. 2, page 27a, b. The original source apparently is *Emek HaMelekh*, and he virtually paraphrases R. Eliezer of Wormes in his formula for creating a Golem, see note 61.

45. See chapter 1, note 52, *Shaar Gan Eden* 11c.

46. *Ginat Egoz* 55b, *Otzar Chaim* 108a, *Perush HaNikkud* 48b, 49a, *Evven HaShoham* 154a, 177b, *Tzaror HaChaim* (Jews College, London, Ms. 318), p. 10a, *Gan Yah* 25b. See *Chayay Olam HaBah* 22b.

47. *Bereshit Rabbah* 1:4, *Gan Yah, loc. cit.*

48. *Emek HaMelekh* 6a, *Limudey Atzilut* (Munkatch, 1897), 3a, 22a; *Mikdash Melekh* on *Zohar* 1:16b (Zolkiev, 1794), p. 31b, R. Shneur Zalman of Liadi, *Likutey Torah, Hosafot* on *VaYikra* 53b. See chapter 1, note 32.

49. *Emek HaMelekh* 6b, *Limudey Atzilut* 3a. The sum of the four names *Ab* (72) *Sag* (63) *Mah* (45) and *Ben* (52) also equals 232. It may be that the arrays of the later Kabbalists relate to the Sefirot themselves, while those of the earlier Kabbalists relate to the letters. This would resolve the difference between the two systems.

50. Donash, Barceloni, p. 208.

51. See Saadia, Barceloni, *ad loc.* These mention the reading, but reject it.

52. R. Eliezar of Wormes *ad loc.,* p. 5a. He also cites the previous method in the name of his father, R. Yehudah ben Kolynimos.

53. Raavad on 2:5, from *Yoma* 76a. See *Bet Levi, Emek Halacha, ad loc.,* quoted in *Mitzpah Eitan*, who give other reasons for this number. An elaborate complex calculation is also presented in *Ateret Rosh* on *Eyin Yaakov*. These commentaries obviously were not aware of what the Raavad writes here.

54. *Chayay Olam HaBah* 4b, quoted in Scholem, *Kitvey Yad BaKabbalah*, p. 25, *Otzar Eden HaGanuz* 162b (bottom), *Shaarey Tzedek* (Jerusalem, Ms. 8° 148), pp. 66b, 67a, quoted in *Kiryat Sefer* 1:135; *Sulam HaAliyah* 10 (Jerusalem, Ms. 8° 334), p. 98a, quoted in *Kitvey Yad Bakabblah*, p. 228. *Cf.* Psalms 23:5, 45:8, 109:18, 133:2. It may be more than coincidence that the first two letters of the Hebrew word for oil, *Shemen*, are Shin and Mem, see above, note 10.

55. *Otzer Eden HaGanuz*, p. 34a, *Sefer HaTzeruf* 10a, *Ginat Egoz* 45b (with errors). This is also the system presented by R. Moshe Botril, who apparently attributes it to Hai Gaon. In *Otzer Eden HaGanuz*, Abulafia also apparently attributes it to an earlier source.

56. *Otzer Eden HaGanuz* 38a. On pp. 75b, 76a, he apparently speaks of the 705, 432 combinations of 11 letters.
57. Also see Psalms 37:4, Job 22:26, 27:10. For other sources, see *Yotzer Or*, p. 56.
58. R. Barukh Targomi, *Maftechot HaKabalah* p. 230, *Sefer HaTzeruf* p. 1a, *Evven HaShoham*, p. 177b, *Sheirit Yosef*, p. 168a, *Tzaror HaChaim*, p. 10a.
59. See Barceloni, p. 104.
60. *Commentary on Sefer Yetzirah* 4b, 15b. Also see Raavad, *ad loc., Shoshan Yesod Olam*, pp. 100, 199, 203. *Cf.* Ibn Ezra on Isaiah 26:4, Psalms 68:5.
61. R. Eliezer of Wormes, *ad loc.* 15b, *Emek HaMelekh* 9c. The latter is translated into Latin in Knorr von Rosenroth, *Kabbala denudata* II (actually III): Liber Sohar restitutus (Sulzbach, 1684), pp. 220-1.
62. See Introduction, notes 80-82. Also see *She'elot HaZaken* 97 (Oxford, Ms. Neubauer 2396), p. 53a, quoted by Scholem in his *Kabbalah and its Symbolism*, p. 188, note 1. There also appears to be a similarity between this and the Partzufim mentioned in the Zoharic literature and in the writings of the Ari, a relationship which should be more thoroughly explored.
63. *Or HaSekhel* 8:3 (108b *ff.*) quoted in *Pardes Rimonim* 21:1. Also quoted in *Sulam HaAliyah* 9 (95a ff.), in *Kiryat Sefer* 22:167 *ff.* The Ramak writes regarding Abulafia's teaching: "This is either a direct tradition, given over from mouth to mouth, or else it was revealed by a Maggid."
64. In *Pardes Rimonim* 21:2 there is specific mention regarding using other letters with a similar system.
65. See Raavad, *ad loc.*
66. *Sanhedrin* 38a, *Tosefta* 8 (end), *Yerushalmi* 4:9 (23b).
67. *Chagigah* 12b, *Zohar* 1:82a, 1:186a, 1:231a.
68. Ibn Ezra, *ad loc., Chovot HaLevavot*, end of *Shaar HaBechinah* 4.
69. Raavad, *ad loc.*
70. Donash, p. 68.
71. *Pardes Rimonim* 9:3.
72. *Bahir* 2, Rashi on Genesis 1:2. We thus see that Ben Zomah sat confounded (*Tahah*), *Bereshit Rabbah* 2:4. See Appendix I, notes 4-6.
73. Bachya 3c, *Pardes Rimonim* 3:5, 23:22, *Etz Chaim, Shaar MaN U'MaD* 10 (248b), *Shaar Maamarey Chazal* 15b.
74. *Zohar* 3:27a. *Cf. Bahir* 135. Also see *Notzar Chesed* on *Avot* 5:7.
75. Raavad on 1:1 (beginning).
76. *Imrey Tzadikim* (Zitimar, 1901), p. 19c. See *Chayay Olam*

HaBah 21b, quoted in *Kitvey Yad BaKabbalah*, p. 28. Also see *Sichot HaRan* 40.

77. We find a similar concept in the *Zohar*, that only Moses could assemble the Tabernacle, *Zohar* 2:238b, *Likutey Moharan* 2:6. This is also meant in meditative sense.

78. *Emek HaMelekh* 9c, in his description of how a Golem is made.

Chapter Three

1.   This is the last of Rabbi Ishmael's thirteen Middot, see beginning of *Sifra*. These Thirteen Midot are also in the prayerbook.

2.   *Shavuot* 26a. It is significant that in the opening statement in the *Bahir* (#1), Rabbi Nehunia ben HaKana also makes use of this dialectic.

3.   *Etz Chaim, Shaar Pirkey HaTzelem* 5, p. 336a.

4.   See above, 1:2. Also see *Likutey Shas* (Ari), p. 27a; *Etz Chaim, Shaar TaNTA* 6, p. 72.

5.   The same term is used by Ben Sirah: "In what is mystical (*muphla*) for you, do not probe." See chapter 1, note 17.

6.   Raavad, Ramban B, *ad loc.*, *Etz Chaim, Shaar TaNTA* 7.

7.   *Kehilat Yaakov, "AMSh"* (14a). Also see *Pardes Rimonim* 23:1. *"AMSh." Cf. Otzar Eden HaGanuz* 54b, 70a.

8.   *Noam Elimelekh, Bo* (36). This may be the reason why the *Sefer Yetzirah* can be read in both the third person and in the imperative. It is both a mystical account of creation, and an instruction manual how to parallel it.

9.   *Cf.* Rashi, Ibn Ezra, on Exodus 10:21.

10. See *Midrash Lekach Tov, Sechel Tov, ad loc.* Also see *Pardes Rimonim, loc. cit.*

11. Donash, p. 20, Ibn Ezra on Ecclesiastes 7:19, Radak, *Mikhlol* (Lyk, 1842), p. 72. Also see Donash, p. 45, 48.

12. Saadia B. *ad loc.* This resembles a technique of the Indian faquirs, see *Sefer HaChaim*, Munich, Ms. 207, *ff.* 10d-11a (writ-

ten in 1268), Cambridge, Ms. Add. 643.1, f. 9a, quoted in M. Güdemann, *Geshichte des Erziiehungswesens und der Cultur der Juden I* (Vienna, 1880), p. 169; Menashe Grossberg, notes on Donash, p. 8; G. Scholem, *Kabbalah and its Symbolism*, p. 183.

13. See Introduction, note 99.
14. Raavad, Ramban, *ad loc. Cf. Maarackhet Elohut* 175a, b.
15. See *Yitzchak Sagi Nahor*, line 247.
16. *Zohar* 2:235b, *Tikuney Zohar* 70, 140b. *Cf. Likutey Moharan* 3.
17. See Raavad, introduction (2d), Chayit 9b, *Pardes Rimonim* 2:1.
18. *Kuzari* 4:25 (58a, b) thus states that the "fire" here is the ether (*al atar*). The word *Avir* also refers to space, as in *Gittin* 8:3, *Ohalot* 3:3.
19. *Pardes Rimonim* 9:3.
20. *Raziel* 11b (30).
21. *Bahir* 85.
22. *Tikuney Zohar* 4 (19b). *Cf. Raziel* 11b (29, 30).
23. *Berakhot* 6b. See *Kehilat Yaakov, "Ravayah"* (11a).
24. *Sh'mot Rabbah* 51:7. *Cf. Tanchuma, Pekudey* 8.
25. See my article, "On Immortality and the Soul," *Intercom* (Association of Orthodox Jewish Scientists, New York, May, 1972), p. 6. Also see *Toldot Yaakov Yosef, Bo* (50d) *Keter Shem Tov* 108. *Cf.* Kedushat Levi on *Avot* 2:5.
26. Deuteronomy 11:14. See Radak, *Sherashim*, "*YRH*," Commentaries on Proverbs 11:25.
27. Gra *ad loc., Etz Chaim, Shaar TaNTA* 6, 7.
28. *Mafteach HaRayyon* 26a. *Cf.* Donash, pp. 60, 68.
29. Raavad, *Chakamoni, ad loc., Raziel* 11a (27). *Cf. Avodat HaKodesh, Yichud* 18. Also see *Kehilat Yaakov, "Geviyah."*
30. Barceloni, *ad loc., Tzioni* (Lvov, 1882), p. 4c.
31. *Cf. Zohar* 3:223a, *Pardes Rimonim* 23:3, "*Gaviyah.*"
32. Ramban B, *ad loc. Pardes Rimonim, loc. cit.*
33. *Negaim* 6:7.
34. *Tosefot Yom Tov, ad loc., Pri Yitzchak* here, *Pardes Rimonim, loc. cit.*
35. Ramban, Saadia, *ad loc.*
36. *Tikuney Zohar* 17a. See chapter 1, note 195.
37. *Pri Yitzchak, ad loc., Etz Chaim, Shaar TaNTA* 7.
38. *Minachot* 29b, Barceloni, p. 284. Note that this is stated by Rav Yehudah in the name of Rav, see Introduction, note 82. The statement that the letters *ShOTNeZ GaTz* must have crowns, is also that of Rava, the maker of the Golem in the Talmud.
39. *Ohev Yisrael, VeEtChanan* (Zitimar, 1863), p. 80c.
40. *Etz Chaim, Shaar TaNTA* 1.

41. Chamai Gaon, *Sefer Halyyun*, in *Likutim MeRav Hai Gaon* (Warsaw, 1798), p. 37b, and in A. Jellinek, *Ginzey Chakhmat HaKabbalah*, p. 10; *Kuzari* 4:3 (8b); Abraham Abulafia, *Mafteach HaShemot* (Jewish Theological Seminary, Ms. 1897), p. 58a, *Or HaSekhel* 4:2 (50b). Ibn Ezra on Exodus 3:15, *Or Eynayim* (Lvov, 1886), 9b. In these sources, the Name is spelled in alphabetical order AHVY. It is possible that the original term here was Avyiah (AVYH), but when the Greek derived *Avir* became popular, the latter term was inadvertently substituted.
42. R. Eliezar of Wormes, p. 5d.
43. *Raziel* 11b (28). Cf. *Kol Yehhudah* on Kuzari *4:25 (64b)*.
44. *Sotah* 17a, Rashi, *ad loc.* "Shekhinah."
45. *Ketubot* 64b, *Kol Yehudah* on *Kuzari* 4:25 (56b).
46. See *Raziel* 11b (29, 30).

Chapter Four

1. Also mentioned in *Zohar* 3:255b, *Tikuney Zohar* 69 (104b), 70 (128b).
2. Radak, *Mikhlol* 48a, 57a; Julio Fuerstio, *Concordantiae* (Liepzig, 1840), p. 1363. R. Aaron states that there are only seven cases, see note on *Mikhlol*, pp. 48a, 57a. Also see R. Moshe Kimchi, *Mahalach Shevilei HaDaat* (Hamburg, 1785), No. 10, R. Aaron (ben Moshe) ben Asher, *Dikdukey HaTaamim*, Resh 7 (Leipzig, 1838), R.A. Dablmesh, *Makney Avraham*. Also see *Ben Yehudah, Milin, "Resh," "Dagesh," Otzar Yisrael, "Dagesh." Cf.* Radak, *Minchat Shai*, on 1 Samuel 1:6, etc.
3. The Septuagint thus used a double R in Sarah, see *Gesenius Grammar* (London, no date), p. 43.
4. Saadia, pp. 79, 115, 116; Donash, p. 21; Barceloni, p. 231, *Mikhlol*, p. 81b.
5. *Rosh HaShanah* 31a, b, *Sanhedrin* 12a, *Yerushalmi, Pesachim* 4:2 (26b); *Yad, Kiddush HaChodesh* 5:3, *Sanhedrin* 14:12.
6. Sasoon, Ms. 507. See *Ohel Dawid* (Oxford, 1932), pp. 22-23, plate 2, Sotheby Catalogue, "Thirty-Eight Important Hebrew and Samaritan Manuscripts from the collection of the late David Solomon Sasson", (Sotheby, Park Bernet & Co., Zurich, November 5, 1975), No. 6, plates on pp. 15, 16. Also see Chanoch Yalon, *Pirkey Lashon* (Jerusalem, 1971), pp. 176,

200-201; Alejandro Diez Macho, *Manuscritos Hebreos y Arameos de la Biblia* (Rome, 1971), pp. 15-16.

7. It is thus found in a copy of *Machzor Roma*, written in Pesaro, 1480; Sasoon, Ms. 23. See *Ohel Dawid*, pp. 289-93, plate 38; Sotheby Catalogue No. 28, plates on pp. 92-95. Also used in *Torah, Ketuvim and Haftorot*, Sasoon Ms. 487, written in Seville, 1468, described in *Ohel Dawid*, pp. 15-16; Sotheby Catalogue No. 7, plates on p. 19. Also in *Machzor Roma*, written in Perugia, 1415, Sasoon, Ms. 405, described in *Ohel Dawid*, pp. 276-289, plate 36; Sotheby Catalogue No. 27, plate on p. 89. Also in *Seder Tefilot*, written in Spain, early 15th century, Sasoon, Ms. 59, described in *Ohel Dawid*, pp. 298-299; Sotheby Catalogue No. 25, pp. 84-85. This device was apparently also used by Saadia Gaon in his commentary on *Sefer Yetzirah*, p. 28.

8. *Tikuney Zohar* 5 (20b), Gra (22a), *Nitzutzey Zohar* (35), *ad loc.* Also see *Tikuney Zohar* 19 (39b), *Beer Yitzchak* (54), *Nitzutzey Zohar* (24), *ad loc.*

9. *Tikuney Zohar* 5 (20b), 19 (39b), 70 (128b), R. Yisrael of Koznitz, *Or Yisrael, ad loc.*

10. Gra, *ad loc.*

11. *Bahir* 115.

12. *Etz Chaim, Shaar TaNTA* 5, p. 70. This is said to be related to the *Hevel DiGarmi* in man.

13. *Tikuney Zohar* 70 (128b), *Kisey Melekh, ad loc.* (173b, No. 30). *Cf. Kisey Melek* 58a. Also see *Otzar Chaim* 6a.

14. *Yitzchak Sagi Nahor*, line 313, cites both opinions. See *Peliyah* 39a.

15. *Cf. Sichot HaRan* 77.

16. *Bava Batra* 25b, *Zohar* 1:26b, *Shulchan Arukh, Orach Chaim* 94:2 in Hagah. Seed is to the East, see *Bahir* 156.

17. Gra, *Pri Yitzchak, ad loc.*

18. *Tikuney Zohar* 18 (32a). Also see *Kuzari* 4:25 (53a), 3:17 (24a), Ibn Ezra on Ecclesiastes 11:2.

19. See *Bahir* 70, *Or HaGanuz* on *Bahir* 154; Recanti 1c, Chayit 179b.

20. *Bahir* 117.

21. *Tiferet Yisrael* 2.

22. Radak on Zechariah 4:2, *Ginat Egoz* 38c.

23. See commentaries *ad loc.,* Ibn Ezra on Zechariah 4:10.

24. See Ibn Ezra, *ad loc.*

25. *Cf. Etz Chaim, Shaar TaNTA* 7.

26. Gra, *ad loc.*

27. *Bahir* 70, 177.

28. *Shabbat* 156a.
29. See inset.
30. These are described in detail in *Evven HaShoham* and *Sheirit Yosef.* Also see Israel Regardie, *How to Make and Use Talismans* (Wellingborough UK: Aquarian Press, 1972).
31. Moscow, Ms. Guenzburg 775, unnumberd folios at beginning 32a-33b (pp. 62-64 in my manuscript). These are attributed to Nohaniel Gaon, but no record of such a gaon exists. Also see *Toldot Adam* 158, where these seals are drawn and attributed to the Ramban. They are also found in *Shoshan Yesod Olam*, pp. 268, 322, 460.
32. *Chagigah* 14a. See *Moreh Nevuchim* 2:6.
33. See Bachya, Abarbanel, on Deuteronomy 18:14, *Derekh HaShem* 2:7. Also see *Sotah* 12b, *Tosefot, Shabbat* 156a, *Ikkarim* 4:4. Many writers assume that Maimonides did not believe in astrology at all, based on what he writes in *Yad, Avodat Kokhavim* 11:16 and in *Moreh Nevuchim* 3:37. Elsewhere, however, he appears to admit that, at least to some degree, it can be used to predict the future, see *Yad, Yesodey HaTorah* 10:3, *Sefer HaMitzvot*, Positive Commandment 31. Also see *HaKotev* on *Eyin Yaakov, Shabbat* 156a; *Bereshit Rabbah* 85:2, Rashi, *Sotah* 36b.
34. *Bereshit Rabbah* 10:6, *Zohar* 1:34a, 1:251a, 2:15a, 2:15b, 2° 30b, 2:80b, 2° 171b, 3:86a.
35. *Akedat Yitzchak* 2, *Or HaShem* 4:3 (87a). See *Shaar Rashbi* on *Perek Shirah* (p. 299).
36. See note 32. Also see *Bereshit Rabbah* 78:1.
37. *Bereshit Rabbah* 1:3, 3:8, *Sh'mot Rabbah* 15:22, *Tanchuma, Chayay Sarah* 3, *Midrash Tehillim* 24, 86, 104, *Pirkey Rabbi Eliezer* 4. *Cf.* Barceloni, p. 187.
38. *Bahir* 21. See Radal on *Pirkey Rabbi Eliezer* 4:1, from *Zohar* 1:17b, 1:18b, 1:34a, 1:46b. Also see Radal *ibid.* 4:11. Bachya on Genesis 28:12 reverses this, and states that permanent angels were created on the second day, and temporary angels on the fifth.
39. *Shabbat* 156a.
40. *Niddah* 16b.
41. See chapter 1, note 155.
42. Abarbanel on Deuteronomy 18:14. Also see anonymous *Perush* on *Yad, Yesodey HaTorah* 2:5.
43. *Zohar* 3:269b.
44. *Bereshit Rabbah* 78:4, *Yafah Toar, ad loc.*, *Sh'mot Rabbah* 48:2, *BaMidbar Rabbah* 11:7, *Tanchuma, VaYakhel* 4, Sifri on Numbers 6:26.

45. *Baraita DeShmuel HaKatan* 9, *Bareita DiMazalot* 15; Raziel 17b (51), *Sefer HaKanah* (Cracow, 1894), 86b, *Yalkut Reuveni* 15a.
46. *Pirkey Rabbi Eliezer* 6, 7; Rashi, *Berakhot* 59b *"Shabatai,"* *Shabbat* 129b, *Eruvin* 56a; *Chakamoni* 70c, 72b, *Bareita DeShmuel HaKatan* 3, *Bareita DiMazalot* 7, Barceloni, p. 247.
47. *Yad, Yesodey HaTorah* 3:1, *Bareita DeShmuel HaKatan* 7, *Bareita DiMazalot* 12, Barceloni, *loc. cit.*
48. See Ibn Ezra on Exodus 16:1, R. Shmuel Falkalish, *Seder Avronot* (Prague, 1797), introduction, quoted in *Batey Midrashot* 2:10; *Hadrey Kodesh* (Dihernfurth, 1812), p. 5b. *Cf. Chakamoni* 70c, 72b, R. Eliezer of Wormes.
49. A similar concept is found in *Shabbat* 129b.
50. *Sanhedrin* 65b, *Yad, Avodat Kokhavim* 11:8, *Tur, Yoreh Deah* 179.
51. *Cf. Tshuvot Rashba* 148, 409, *Tshuvot Rashba HaMeYucheset LeRamban* 283, *Tshuvot Mahari Assad* 2:24, *Tshuvot Avney Tzedek, Yoreh Deah* 44. Also see *Yoreh Deah* 179:2, *Nimukey Yosef* on *Sanhedrin* (Rif, 16b), *Sefer Chasidim* 59, *Zohar* 1:169b, 3:234a.
52. *Tikuney Zohar* 70 (128b), *Kiseh Melekh, ad loc.* (58a, No. 18). Also see Gra here. For a different ordering of Sefirot and days, see *Maarekhet Elohut* 183a.
53. See *Pardes Rimonim* 10, 32:2.
54. Raavad, *ad loc.* See *Shaar Ruach HaKodesh*, pp. 86, 145.
55. *Shaar Ruach HaKodesh*, p. 31, from *Tikuney Zohar* 70 (129b), *Sitrey Torah, Zohar* 1:108a.
56. Gra, *ad loc. Zohar* 1:41b-45b, 2:245a-259a, *Pardes Rimonim* 24.
57. *Rosh HaShanah* 31a, *Sanhedrin* 97a, *Avodah Zarah* 9a. This appears to be the opinion of *Pirkey Rabbi Eliezer*, see Radal, *ad loc.* 18:48. Also see *Maarekhet Elohut* 189a, Raziel 15a (43).
58. *Tamid* 7:4.
59. *Sefer Temunah* (Koretz, 1784), 31a, *Maarekhet Elohut* 190a, *Sefer HaKanah* 78b and other places, *Tshuvot Rashba* 423, *Shiur Komah* 83, Radbaz, *Magen David*, Gimel, Dalet; *Metzudot David* 298, R. Yosef Tzayach, *Tzaror HaChaim*, pp. 83b, 85b; *Shaarey Gan Eden, Orach Tzadikim* 1:1. *Cf.* Bachya, Recanti, Tzioni, on Leviticus 25:8, Ramban on Genesis 2:3, *Sefer HaChinuch* 330, Ibn Ezra on Genesis 1:5, 8:22. For a detailed discussion, see *Drush Or HaChaim* 3, at end of *Tiferet Yisrael* on *Mishnayot Nezikin*. This is also apparently supported by the *Zohar*, see Radal, *loc. cit.* This doctrine was opposed by the Ari, see *Likutey Torah* (Ari) *Kedoshim, VeYakhel Moshe* 3a.
60. *Otzar Chaim* 86b *ff.*

61. *Bereshit Rabbah* 8:2, *Zohar* 2:145b. *Cf. Sanhedrin* 97a.
62. See *Drush Or HaChaim, loc. cit.*
63. *Bereshit Rabbah* 1:19, 12:10, Rashi on Genesis 1:14, 1:24, 2:4, *Moreh Nevuchim* 2:30, Ramban on Genesis 1:1, 1:8, 1:24; *Shnei Luchot HaBrit* 1:190b in note.
64. *Bereshit Rabbah 1:12, Yad, Tshuvah* 3:7, Raavad, *ad loc. Emunot VeDeyot* 1:1, 5:8, *Kuzari* 1:67 (41a).
65. *Moreh Nevuchim* 2:28. *Cf. Zohar* 1:138b, *Avodah Zarah* 54b, *Berakhot* 60a.
66. Rashi, Ibn Ezra, Sforno, *ad loc.,* Rambam, *Iggeret Techiyat HaMetim* (Warsaw, 1927), p. 15. Regarding conservation of matter, see *Emunot VeDeyot* 7:1.
67. *Chagigah* 13b, from Job 22:16, Psalms 105:8, *Tosefot, ad loc.* "Tordan," Maharsha, *ad loc.* Also see *Bereshit Rabbah* 28:4, *Kohelet Rabbah* 1:37, 4:4, *Tanchuma, Lekh Lekha* 11, *Yitro* 9, *Midrash Tehillim* 105:3, *Tanna DeBei Eliahu Rabbah* 13 (70a, 72a), 26 (103a), *Tanna DeBei Eliahu Zuta* 10 (15a), *Sefer Chasidim* 1137.
68. *Cf. Berakhot* 61a, *Bereshit Rabbah* 14:3, 4, 10, Ramban on Genesis 1:20.
69. *Moreh* 3:50, *Kuzari* 1:43 (32a); *Pesikta* 105b, *Rosh HaShanah* 10b, *Yerushalmi, Avodah Zarah* 1:2 (3a), *VaYikra Rabbah* 29:1, *Pirkey Rabbi Eliezer* 8 (18a); Ran, *Rosh HaShanah* (Rif 3a) "BeRosh," *Tosefot Yom Tov, Rosh HaShanah* 1:2 "BeRosh," *Rokeach* 200. Also see Rashi, *Sanhedrin* 97a "BeAlafim," *Yad, Kiddush HaChodesh* 11:16; *Avodah Zarah* 8a.
70. *Chagigah* 12b, *Zohar* 3:236a.
71. *Etz Chaim, Shaar Drushey ABYA* 4, 12, *Shaar Tziyur Olomot* 2.
72. *VaYikra Rabbah* 29:11, *Pirkey Rabbi Eliezer* 18 (43a), *BaMidbar Rabbah* 3:8. *Cf. Raziel* 15b (43), 36a (122).
73. *Otzar HaShem, ad loc., Avot Rabbi Nathan* 37.
74. Ibn Ezra on Genesis 1:2.
75. *Bava Batra* 25b.
76. *Bava Batra* 74b. *Cf. Yerushalmi, Ketubot* 12:3, *Kelayim* 9:3.
77. Gra, *Yotzer Or, ad loc. Cf. Zohar Chadash* 78b, 83b, *Zohar* 1:52a.
78. *Bekhorot* 55a.
79. Gra. *Cf.* Radal on *Pirkey Rabbi Eliezer* 18:47. See *Midrash Tanayim* 92b.
80. Gra, *ad loc.* In its entire history, Israel celebrated seventeen jubilees, see *Arkhin* 12b, *Yad, Shemitah VeYovel* 10:3.
81. See *Bereshit Rabbah* 12:6, 26:2, *BaMidbar Rabbah* 13:12, *Tanchuma, Bereshit* 6, Ramban, *Maamar HaGeulah* (in Kitvey Ramban), p. 269, Rambam, commentary on *Sanhedrin* 10:1, *Iggeret Techiyat HaMetim,* p. 11. *Cf. Ketubot* 39a.

82. *Otzar HaChaim* 87a.
83. *Ibid.* 87b.
84. *Otzar Eden HaGanuz* 75b.
85. Raavad, *Pri Yitzchak, ad loc.*
86. See *Sulam HaAliyah.*
87. *Ibid.*
88. *Rosh HaShanah* 27a, regarding the fact that *Shamor* and *Zachor* were said "with one word." *Cf. Yad, Yesodey HaTorah* 2:10.
89. *Otzar Eden HaGanuz* 75b.
90. *Berakhot* 32b. The calculation there yields 1.16434×10^{18}. A variant reading yields 10^{21}. See *Raziel* 18a (54).
91. See notes 43, 44.

Chapter Five

1. Saadia, p. 58, thus says that they include the five senses. See Donash, p. 64. *Chakamoni,* however, interprets it as swallowing.
2. There are various different orderings in the Bible. In Jacob's blessing to the tribes in Genesis 29, the order is Reuben, Simeon, Levi, Judah, Zebulun, Isachar, Dan, Gad, Asher, Naftali, Joseph, Benjamin. In Genesis 46, the ordering is the same, but the sons of Leah's handmaid precede those of Rachel's. In Numbers 1:5-15, the order is the same as in Exodus 1, except that Joseph precedes Benjamin, and the order of the sons of the handmaids is Dan, Asher, Gad, Naftali. In Numbers 13:4-15, the order is Reuben, Simeon, Judah, Isachar, Ephraim, Benjamin, Zebulun, Manassah, Dan, Asher, Naftali, Gad. In Numbers 24:6-29, it is Judah, Simeon, Benjamin, Dan, Manassah, Ephraim , Zebulun, Isachar, Asher, Naftali. (Reuben and Gad are not included, since they remained on the other side of the Jordan.) In Moses' blessing, the order is: Reuben, Judah, Levi, Benjamin, Joseph, Zebulun, Isachar, Gad, Dan, Naftali, Asher. (Simeon is not mentioned, see Rashi on Deuteronomy 33:7.) In Deuteronomy 27:12-13, for the blessings the order is: Simeon, Levi, Judah, Isachar, Joseph, Benjamin; for the curses: Reuben, Gad, Asher, Zebulun, Dan, Naftali.
3. Genesis 30, 35:23.
4. *Otzar Chaim* 201b, Raavad 5a.
5. *Bava Batra* 118b, from Genesis 48:16.
6. *Sheirit Yosef* 12a. *Tzioni* 58c lists them in the order of Numbers

1:20-43, where the camp of Reuben precedes that of Judah. This is also the order in Numbers 26. See note 67.

7.   Numbers 2. In Numbers, 7, this is the order of their offerings. Regarding the reason for the change in order, see *Tanchuma B, BaMidbar* 6a, *Sifri* on Numbers 7:18, Rashi on Numbers 2:2, 7:18, Genesis 50:13.

8.   *Tzioni* 58c, Bachya on Numbers 2:18, *Peliyah* 32a. Also see *Zohar* 2:230a, *Siddur R. Saadia Gaon*, p. 271, *Arugat HaBosem* 1:288.

9.   This is the pairing of the Gra. It is essentially the same as that of the Raavad, except that Levi and Joseph are interchanged by the latter.

10.   Gra, *ad loc.* In the *Bahir* 107, twenty-four permutations are mentioned, since the two letters Heh are differentiated.

11.   *Peliyah* 14a, *Pardes Rimonim* 21:14, *Shoshan Yesod Olam* 126, *Sheirit Yosef* 12a. The same order is also used by R. Abraham Abulafia, *Chayay Olam HaBah* 23b, *Mafteach HaShemot* 62a; and by Isaac of Acco, *Otzar Chaim* 201b. The Lurianic Kabbalists interchanged the permutations for Elul and Adar, see R. Shalom Sharabi, *Or HaLevanah* (Jerusalem, 1925), p. 86; *Siddur R. Shabatai* 2:97a, b; *Siddur R. Asher*, p. 282. In Raavad 5a, 20d, 49b, there are other variations, but all three are different, and they may be due to printing error. Also see *Shefa Tal* 8:3, p. 142b, *Etz Chaim, Shaar HaShemot* 5, *Tzioni* 58c.

12.   *Tikuney Zohar* 9b; *Pardes, Peliyah, Shoshan Yesod Olam, Or HaLevanah, loc. cit.*

13.   Raavad, *ad loc.*

14.   *Yoma* 16b and parallels.

15.   Numbers 2.

16.   See *Maarekhet Elohut* 170b, *Kuzari* 3:17 (24a).

17.   Gra, *Pri Yitzchak*, on 1:2, *Etz Chaim, Shaar TaNTA* 7. See *Yerushalmi, Chagigah* 2:1.

18.   Long Version; Saadia Version 2:4.

19.   Short Version. In *Bahir* 95 the order is similar, but the directions are given as East, West, South, North.

20.   *Bahir* 95. See *Zohar* 2:58b, Gra on *Tikuney Zohar* 64a, *Otzar HaKavod* 13a, *Pelach Rimon* 21:2, 7, 8, 9; *Elemah Rabatai* 3:4:3 (71a).

21.   *Pardes Rimonim* 21:8.

22.   Yerushalmi, Chagigah 2:1 (10a). See *Bahir* 18.

23.   *Bahir* 95.

24.   *Chagigah* 12b.

25.   Also in *Bahir* 95.

26.   Ibn Ezra, Bachya, *ad loc.*

27. *Cf. Moreh Nevuchim* 1:70.
28. See chapter 1, note 41.
29. *Tzioni, ad loc., Bereshit Rabbah* 68:9, Rashi on Avot 2:9. See chapter 1, note 119. *Cf. Moreh Nevuchim, loc. cit.*
30. *Shaarey Orah* 10 (103a).
31. *Etz Chaim, Shaar Arikh Anpin* 3. Also see Rashi, Radak, on Judges 20:43, Habakkuk 1:4, Psalms 22:13; Radak, *Sherashim,* "KTR."
32. *Chulin* 89a, *Sh'mot Rabbah* 38:4. According to Rashi, it is then read, "from under, he is the arms of the universe." It therefore refers to the person who lowers himself to be "under."
33. *Chagigah* 12b. See *Raziel* 14b (40), 15b (44). See chapter 6, note 30.
34. See chapter 1, note 143.
35. *Zohar* 2:81a, 2:131a, 2:203a, 3:227a, *Pardes Rimonim* 25:7, *Shaarey Orah* 5 (50b). These confuse the mind, *Zohar* 3:123a, *Tikuney Zohar* 11b, *Reshit Chakhmah, Shaar HaYirah* 4 (16c).
36. The next verse, "And Israel dwelt safely alone (*badad*), the eye of Jacob," also has mystical connotations. The word *badad* is often used to indicate meditation, see Ibn Ezra on Isaiah 44:25. The verse can then read, "And Israel dwelt safely meditating."
37. *Cf.* Bachya on Genesis 49:26.
38. The third is Habakkuk 3:6. This is a highly mystical chapter, discussed extensively in the *Bahir* 68-79, 147-148, 187-193. The question may arise why the Long Version uses "heights of the universe," which is only in the blessing of Joseph, instead of "arms of the universe," which applies to all Israel. But if Joseph ben Uziel was the author of the Long Version, he may have done this to allude to his name.
39. *Zohar* 1:50a, 1:274b, 2:22a. *Cf. Rosh HaShanah* 11a, *Sifri* on Deuteronomy 33:15. The Ari, however, states that the Twelve Boundaries are in Tiferet, see *Etz Chaim, Shaar TaNTA* 7.
40. Rashi, *Shabbat* 36a, *"Hemsess,"* renders it *Centipellio. Cf. Otzar HaSham* here. Also see *VaYikra Rabbah* 3:4, *Shulchan Arukh, Yoreh Deah* 48:1 in *Hagah.*
41. Saadia, p. 135, *Chakamoni,* Donash, R. Eliezer of Wormes, *Tzioni* 4d, *Arukh, Masass. Cf.* Rashi on Ecclesiastes 12:4.
42. *Kohelet Rabbah* 7:19, 12:3, *Midrash Tehillim* 103:1, Rashi, *Shabbat* 152a, *Berakhot* 61b.
43. R. Aaron of Bagdad, quoted in Botril. *Cf.* Ibn Ezra on Ecclesiastes 12:4.
44. *Zevachim* 65a (bottom), *Torah Temimah* on Ecclesiastes 12:3.
45. *Berakhot* 61b, *Shaabat* 152a. Rashi identifies it with the *Hemsess.* Also see *Avot Rabbi Nathan* 31:3, *Otiot DeRabbi*

Akiba, Lamed; Rashi on Ecclesiastes 12:4, Derishah, Yoreh Deah 75, *Tikuney Zohar* 70 (140b).

46. *Zohar* 2:234b, 2:235a, Raavad 48a, *Pardes Rimonim* 23:19 *"Korkeban."*

47. *Chakamoni*, R. Eliezer of Wormes 10a, 15b, Saadia B, Barceloni, p. 256, *Tzioni* 4d.

48. Saadia, p. 135, says that it is the *Tzam*. In *Sheveiley Emunah* 4 (Warsaw, 1887), p. 42b, we find that the *Tzam* is the portion of the small intestine that follows the duodenum.

49. Donash, *Otzar HaShem*.

50. Barceloni, p. 257, *Sheveiley Emunah, loc cit.* See *Sefer HaKahan* 141b.

51. See *Otzar HaShem, ad loc,. Yoreh Deah* 48:1 in *Hagah.*

52. *Otzar Hashem.*

53. *Chakamoni*, Donash, Eliezer Rokeach 10a.

54. Saadia, p. 135.

55. *Moreh Nevuchim* 3:38, Ramban, Bachya, on Deuteronomy 18:3; Radbaz, *Metzudos David* 271.

56. *Berakhot* 61b, *Zohar* 2:234b, *Tikuney Zohar* 70 (140b), *Pardes Rimonim* 23:19.

57. *Otiot DeRabbi Akiba, Lamed.*

58. See Judges 4:19.

59. *Yoma* 18a. When a person sleeps, his soul warms his body, *Bereshit Rabbah* 14:11.

60. *Berakhot* 61b. Adar parallels laughter, and hence Purim is a time of joy and clowning.

61. *Avodah Zarah* 43a, *Yad, Avodat Kochavim* 3:11. The stars are said to have had the precise shapes of the signs of the Zodiac in the time of the Flood (Bachya 6a).

62. *Cf. Yad, Avodat Kochavim* 1:1 *Brit Menuchah*, beginning. See especially *Midrash Tanaim*, p. 62, qouted in *Torah Shlemah* on Genesis 8:22, No. 108.

63. *Cf. Tosefot, Avodah Zarah* 43a, *"Lo Taasun," Tshuvot Rashba* 167, 525, *Tshuvot Mabit* 2:30, *Sifsey Cohen (Shach), Yoreh Deah* 141:30.

64. The tables are found in the *Almagest* (Great Books, Chicago), p. 234 *ff*. A Hebrew translation of these tables may be found in *Mishpatey HaMazalot*, Sasoon, Ms. 823, pp. 118-138, described in *Magen Dawid*, pp. 1041-1043, plate 32; Sotheby Catalogue No. 15, plates on pp. 40, 53; Moritz Steinschneider, *Hebraische Ubersetzungen des Mittelalters* (Berlin, 1893), pp. 614-616. This manuscript, written around 1350, contains pictures of many constellations.

65. See Gra here.

66. Saadia B on 6:4.
67. Note that the signs here are not in order. If the parallels of the camps are taken, it would come out that the camp or Reuben precedes that of Judah. This is precisely the order in Numbers 1:20-43. See note 6.
68. The entire discussion is taken from Raavad on 1:2. Also see *Sefer HaKanah*, p. 87a, b, *Ateret Tiferet Yisrael, Ki Tavo* (69a *ff*).
69. *Rosh HaShanah* 25a; *Yad Kiddush HaChodesh* 6:2-3, 8:1. In Hebrew, instead of seconds, *Chalakim* are used, where there are 1080 *Chalakim* to the hour. Each *Chelek* is therefore $3^1/_3$ seconds. The 2643 seconds given here are therefore 793 *Chalakim*. Similarly, the 780 seconds below are 234 *Chalakim*, as in the Hebrew original.
70. The order of the Kabbalists, however, is somewhat different than that of the Scripture. It also does not follow the usual order in *Sefer Yetzirah*.
71. *Cf. Zohar* 1:18b, 1:23a. This Name is written on the back of the Mezuzah, see *Raziel* 8a (16), *Tur, Yoreh Deah* 288, *Shulchan Arukh, Yoreh Deah* 288:15 in *Hagah; Hagahos Maimoni* on *Yad, Mezuzah* 5:4 No. 3.
72. *Pardes Rimonim* 21:2, quoting *Maarekhet Elokim Chaim. Cf.* Chayit, 197b; *Likutey HaGra* (Warsaw, 1884), p. 23d. The use of six vowels is also found in Raavad on 2:5 (end), *Shoshan Yesod Olam*, p. 199. The reason why six vowels are used is because six signs of the zodiac are always ascending, and six are always descending, *Raziel* 10b (27). For a discussion of the added Shva, see *Otzar Eden HaGanuz* 151a. Also see *Magalah Amukot* No. 210, *Nefesh HaChaim* 1:1, note *"VeAf."*

Chapter Six

1. For a general discussion, see Shemtov Gefen, *"Teli,"* in *Sefer Zichron fur A.S. Rabbinowitz* (Tel Aviv, 1924), pp. 126-128; Abraham Elijah Harkavy, *"Tli Atalya,"* in *Ben Ami*, January, 1887, pp. 27-35. Many texts vocalize this word as *Tali*, with an initial Kametz. It appears more likely, however, that the initial vowel should be a Sh'va, as in the case of *Gedi* and *Deli*.
2. Targum, Rashi, *ad loc.*, Ibn Janach, *Sherashim, "TLH." Cf. Bereshit Rabbah* 65:13, where it also appears that the root of this word is *Talah*.

3. Targum J., Rashbam, *ad loc.* Both opinions are found in Ibn Ezra, *ad loc.,* Radak, *Sherashim.*

4. *Ginat Egoz* 32b, *Pardes Rimonim* 21:8, *Choker U'Mekubal* 13. *Cf. Zohar* 1:125a, *Or HaChamah, Derekh Emet, ad loc.* This is also identified with the Pole Serpent (*Nachash Bareach*), *Cf. Yesod Olam* (Berlin, 1848), p. 16c. Also see *Bareita DeShmuel HaKatan* 2 (8a).

5. This is possibly based on verse, "He hangs (*talah*) the earth on nothingness (*belimah*)" (Job 26:7). Others say that it comes from the word *Tanin,* meaning dragon, with the nun replaced by a lamed, *Kol Yehudah* on *Kuzari* 4:25 (54b). Another possibility presented there is that it is derived from the word, "to spread." Thus, the Targum on Isaiah 44:25 translates, "He spread the heaven," as *Talit Shamaya.* See *Or HaGanuz* on Bahir 95.

6. *Chakamoni, Bareita DeShmuel HaKatan, Raziel* 20a (63, 64), Ibn Ezra, Radak, on Isaiah 27:1, *Pirkey Rabbi Eliezer* 9 (23a). Also see Ibn Ezra, Ramban, on Job 26:13, Radak, *Sherashim, "Nachash,"* Ibn Janach, *Sherashim, "Barach,"* Mordecai, *Avodah Zarah* 3 (840), *Or HaShekhel* 4:1 (41a). The Leviathan is also mentioned in Psalms 74:14, 104:26, Job 3:8, 40:25.

7. *Seder Rabbah DeBereshit* 17, in *Batey Midrashot* 1:28; *Midrash Konen,* "Fifth Day," in *Arzey Levanon* (Venice, 1601), p. 2b, *Bet HaMidrash* 2:26, *Otzar Midrashim,* p. 254b; *Raziel* 14b (40), *Yalkut Reuveni* 17b; Ibn Ezra, introduction to Torah, fourth method, R. Avraham Azulai, *Chesed LeAvraham* 2:3. In one ancient source, we find that the "world rotates around the fin of the leviathan," *Midrash Aseret HaDibrot* 2, in *Bet HaMidrash* 1:63, *Otzar Midrashim,* p. 450b.

8. *Raziel* 18b (58); Rambam, Bertenoro, on *Avodah Zarah* 3:3; *Mordecai, loc. cit.,* Radal on *Pirkey Rabbi Eliezer* 9:31, Gra here.

9. It is possibly for this reason that the commentaries state that the Teli is in the sphere of the sun, see *Chakamoni,* R. Eliezar of Wormes.

10. Ptolemy, *Almagest* 7, p. 235. This is also used in ancient Hebraic sources, see *Mishpatey HaMazalot,* Sasoon, Ms. 823, p. 118, described above, chapter 5, note 64.

11. *Raziel* 18b (58), *Or HaChamah* on *Zohar* 1:125a. *Cf. Raziel* 21a (97).

12. Rambam, *Mordecai, loc. cit., Sifsey Cohen, Yoreh Deah* 141:18, *Turey Zahav* 141:5.

13. *Otzar Chaim* 6a. Also see *Yerushalmi, Shabbat* 9:1 (57b), *Avodah Zarah* 3:6 (22a), Ramban on *Shabbat* 83b, *"Zeh,"* Ravan 188.

Baal is mentioned in Numbers 22:41, Judges 2:13, 1 Kings 16:31-32, 18:21, 26. Baal and Ashterah might be the male and female serpents, see notes 21, 22. Also see Rashi on Isaiah 27:1, *Sh'mot Rabbah* 3:12, *Tanchuma, VaEreh* 3. An allusion to the fact that the Baal is the Teli may be found in 1 Kings 18:26, in the word *VaYaHaTeL*, which can be rearranged to read *VeHaTeLY* (and the Teli). This serpent may also be identified with the serpent of Genesis.

14. Saadia, p. 60, Barceloni, p. 209, Donash, *Otzar Eden HaGanuz* 55a. This is also most probably the opinion of *Chakamoni*, R. Eliezer of Wormes. Also see *Tzurat HaAretz* 13 (Offenbach, 1720), p. 175, *Sheveiley Emunah* 2 (19a), *Yesod Olam* 2:1 (16a), *Sefer Techunah (Jerusalem, 1967), p. 59; Cheshban Mahalekhet HaKokhavim* 69.

15. Donash, p. 69.

16. *Kol Yehudah* on *Kuzari* 4:25 (54a), *Tosefot Yom Tov* on *Avodah Zarah* 3:3, Anonymous *Perush* on *Yad, Kiddush HaChodesh* 14:1.

17. Saadia, pp. 59, 60; Barceloni, p. 209; Rambam on *Avodah Zarah* 3:3; *Kuzari* 4:25 (55a); Anonymous *Perush, loc. cit.*

18. *Otzar Eden HaGanuz* 55a; *Cf. Peliyah* 30b.

19. *Or HaSekhel* 4:1 (41a); *Cf. Sefer HaCheshek* 10b.

20. *Bareita DeShmuel HaKatan* 2; *Sefer Techunah*, pp. 101-104, Ibn Ezra on Exodus 3:15 (end); Job 28:3.

21. Cf. Rashi, *ad loc.*; *Bereshit Rabbah* 7:4.

22. *Bava Batra* 74b; *Midrash Chaserot VeYeserot (Batey Midrashim* 2:225), *Zohar* 2:34b; *Maarekhet Elohut* 102b; *Raziel* 9b (22); *Emek HaMelekh* 103a; Radal on *Pirkey Rabbi Eliezer* 9:31. Others, however, state that the pole and coiled serpents are identical, since it is coiled around the pole.

23. R. Chananel on *Bava Batra* 74b; Gra on *Sifra DeTzeniuta* 12a; Gra on *Tikuney Zohar* 49 (89b).

24. Gra on *Sifra DeTeniuta, loc. cit.*

25. Ralbag on Job 26:13; *Netzutzey Orot* on *Zohar* 1:125a.

26. *Raziel* 12a (30), 15a (42), 21a (63, 69), 22a (72). This river is mentioned in Daniel 7:10.

27. *Shoshan Yesod Olam*, p. 220 (bottom). Also given is a method of inducing a dream through which communication with the Teli is established, *Ibid.* No. 558, p. 247. *Cf. Etz Chaim, Shaar Kitzur ABYA* 8, p. 403.

28. *Kuzari* 4:25 (55a); *Cf. Etz Chaim, loc. cit.*

29. *Otzar Eden HaGanuz* 55a.

30. *Yerushalmi, Chagigah* 2:1; see Bachya on Genesis 49:26; also see *Raziel* 14b (40); see note 7.

31. See chapter 5, notes 33, 34.
32. *Bahir* 106; see *Kehilat Yaakov, "Teli."*
33. *Chagigah* 14a, *Otzar HaKavod, ad loc. Cf. Sh'mot Rabbah* 8:1, *Tanna DeBei Eliahu Rabbah* 30 (116a), *Yad, Yesodey HaTorah* 1:9. Black hair is associated with youth, see Ecclesiastes 11:10. Also see *Mekhilta* on Exodus 20:2, *Kedushat Levi, Yitro* (Jerusalem, 1958), p. 133.
34. *Etz Chaim, Shaar Arikh Anpin* 5:3. *Cf. Shaar HaKavanot,* p. 46. Also see *Zohar* 3:127b, 3:132a.
35. *Eruvin* 21b, *Zohar* 2:116a, 3:79b, 3:136b, 3:136a, *Zohar Chadash* 6a. A similar expression is found in *Minachot* 29b, with regard to Rabbi Akiba.
36. *VaYikra Rabbah* 19:1, *Midrash Shmuel* 5. *Cf. Shir HaShirim Rabbah* on 5:11, *Torah Temimah, ibid.*
37. *Tanchuma, Bereshit* 1, *Yerushalmi, Shekalim* 6:1 (25b), *Shir HaShirim Rabbah, loc. cit., Zohar* 2:84a, 2:114a, 2:226b, 3:132a, 3:154b, *Tikuney Zohar* 56 (90b). See chapter 1, notes 242, 243.
38. Malbim, *ad loc., Zohar* 3:136a, 3:140a.
39. The word for hair here is *Kevutzah,* and this is the only time in the Bible that this word is used, besides Song of Songs 5:2. The word is very closely related to *Kotz,* meaning a thorn, and also referring to the points and fine details (titles) in the Hebrew letters.
40. Malbim, *loc. cit., Tikuney Zohar* 70 (122a). The thirteen hairs of this Beard are related to the twelve Diagonal Boundaries, see *Elemah Rabatai* 3:4:3 (71a).
41. *Berakhot* 30a, from Song of Songs 4:4. See *Zohar* 2:116a.
42. Ramban, *ad loc., Pirkey Rabbi Eliezer* 35 (82b). *Cf.* Ibn Ezra on Psalms 76:3, Radak on 2 Samuel 24:16, Radbaz, *Metzudot David* 304; *Kuzari* 2:14 (17ab), *Zohar* 1:150b, 2:79a. Also see *Midrash Tehillim* 91:7, *Zohar* 1:131a, 1:72a; *Bereshit Rabbah* 68:5, Radak on Psalms 132:2.
43. *Pri Yitzchak* on 6:3.
44. *Shabbat* 151b, *Bava Batra* 16b, Targum on Job 38:33. *Cf.* R. Aaron of Baghdad, quoted in Botril here, Gra here.
45. *Pesachim* 94b, *Bava Batra* 74a, Radak on Psalms 77:19.
46. See *Likutey Moharan* 5:3.
47. *Bahir* 106.
48. *Ibid.*
49. *Raziel* 11a (27).
50. See Malbim, *ad loc.*
51. *Bereshit Rabbah* 68:12.
52. *Zohar* 1:11b. Also see *Moreh Nevuchim* 2:30, Rashi on Genesis 1:2. *Cf. VaYikra Rabbah* 18:3.

53. See note 37.
54. See chapter 5, note 39.
55. *Peliyah* 45d.
56. *Pri Yitzchak, ad loc., Pardes Rimonim* 9:3.
57. See *Etz Chaim, Shaar TaNTA* 5, p. 71; *Shaar HaPartzufim* 4, p. 115; *Shaar Tikkun HaNukva* 5, p. 160; *Elemah Rabatai* 4:5:3 (140c); *Cf. Zohar* 2:201a; *Tikuney Zohar* 30 (75a); see chapter 1, note 28.
58. See *Kuzari* 4:25 (55b).
59. *Berakhot* 9:5, *Tikuney Zohar* 21 (49b), *Zohar* 1:155b, *Etz Chaim, Shaar Kitzur ABYA* 4, p. 399; Ecclesiastes 10:2, Proverbs 18:2. Also see *Kuzari, loc. cit., Mafteach HaRayon* 26a.
60. *Zohar* 3:47b. *Cf. Chulin* 60b.
61. *Emunot VeDeyot* 1:4, end, introduction to 3, *Or HaShem* 2:6:2, *Sefer HaYashar* 1, *Pardes Rimonim* 2:6, *Etz Chaim, Shaar HaKelallim* 1, *Reshit Chakhmah, Shaar HaTshuvah* 1, *Shnei Luchot HaBrit, Bet Yisrael* (1:21b), *Shomer Emunim (HaKadmon)* 2:13, *Derekh HaShem* 1:2:1. Also see *Zohar* 1:10b, 1:230b, 2:166b, *Sefer HaBrit* 2:1:3.
62. *Esther Rabbah* 10:14.
63. *Midrash Tehillim* 31:7. See *Derekh HaShem* 1:2:1.
64. *Shiur Komah* 13:3 (10b), *Derekh HaShem* 2:6:4.
65. Targum, ad loc., *Yerushalmi, Berakhot* 6:1 (41b).
66. *Moreh Nevuchim* 1:18.
67. *Zohar* 2:42b, *Emunot VeDeyot*, end of 1, *Etz Chaim, Shaar HaKelalim* 1.
68. *Shiur Komah, loc. cit.*
69. *Reshit Chakhmah*, Introduction. *Cf.* R. Yonah on Proverbs 2:5.
70. *Shabbat* 31b.
71. *Berakhot* 6b.
72. *Yad, Tshuvah* 8:7; *Cf. Berakhot* 4a.
73. *Avot* 4:16.
74. *Kiddushin* 39b, *Chulin* 142a.
75. *Avot* 4:17.
76. *Berakhot* 17a.
77. *Yad, Tshuvah* 8:3, *Torat HaAdam*, in *Kitvey Ramban*, p. 307.
78. *Daat Tevunah* (Tel Aviv, 1966), p. 9.
79. *Pardes Rimonim* 2:6, *Shefa Tal*, end of 2, *Etz Chaim, Shaar Derushey ABYA* 1.
80. *Midrash*, quoted in *Shaar HaGamul*, p. 296. Also see *Zohar* 2:166a, *Likutey Moharan* 275, *Sichot HaRan* 134.
81. *Bereshit Rabbah* 12:5, *Chagigah* 12a.
82. *Ibid,. Bereshit Rabbah* 3:6, Rashi on Genesis 1:4.

83. *VaYikra Rabbah* 20:7, *Zohar* 1:135a.
84. *Bava Batra* 10a.
85. *Emunot VeDeyot* 9:5, Ibn Ezra on Psalms 16:11, *VaYikra Rabbah* 30:2.
86. *Berakhot* 34b, *Sanhedrin* 99a, *Yad, T'shuvah* 8:7.
87. *Avodat HaKodesh* 2:18, *Shnei Luchot HaBrit, Bet Chakhmah* (1:22a), *Amud HaAvodah* 101b, *Nefesh HaChaim* 1:12, *Ohev Yisrael, R'eh* (on Deuteronomy 8:16). *Cf. Avot* 4:2, *Nishmat Adam* 1 (Pieterkov, 1911), p. 16b.
88. *Cf. Barceloni*, p. 226, *Get HaShemot* 90a, *Otzar Eden HaGanuz* 16a, 17a.

Appendix I:
Other Versions

1. The order is that of the planets on Sunday morning, the same as in *Shabbat* 156a, *Cf. Hagahot Bet Chadash (Bach), ad loc.*
2. A paraphrase of Ecclesiastes 3:1.
3. Paraphrase of Psalm 93:2.
4. The word *Yarok* is usually translated as green. Rashi, however, identifies Yarok with the Biblical "blue wool" (*Tekhelet*); see Rashi on Exodus 25:4, Numbers 15:33, *Berakhot* 9b *"Tekhelet,"* *Gittin* 31b *"Sarbala."* Also see *Tosefot, Succah* 31b *"HaYarok,"* *Chulin* 37b "Eleh." Also see Rashi, *Chagigah* 12a *"VaYashet."* In *Raziel* 12b (33), this is likened to the green line seen on the horizon, when one climbs the mast of a ship in the middle of the sea. This is also identified as being the same *Klipah* as the stormwind of Ezekiel, see *Tikuney Zohar* 37 (78a), *Pardes Rimonim* 25:7.
5. The Hebrew here is *MePhulamim*. Rashi interprets this as meaning moist (*moisten*), *Chagigah* 12a, *Betza* 24b, *Zevachim* 45a. Also see *Raziel* 11b (29), R. Eliezer HaKalir, quoted in Botril on 1:11; *Yad, Bet HaBechirah* 1:14, *Kesef Mishnah, ad loc.* Since water represents the primeval matter (see chapter 1, note 205), this wetness denotes material existence, see R. Levi ben Shlomo of Lunil, quoted in Botril, *loc. cit.* Others say that the word indicates unknown, nameless stones, from *Ploni Almoni* (Ruth 4:1, see Rashi, Ibn Ezra, *ad loc.*), Raavad, *Otzar HaShem*, on 1:11, R. Aaron of Baghdad, quoted in Botril, *loc. cit.*, Ralbag on Genesis 1:2 (Venice, 1547), p. 9c. Saadia Gaon states that it

means "split rocks," from *MePhulach,* Saadia on 4:6, p. 123. On p. 124, however, he states that this denotes the bedrock of the earth. Another opinion is that these are "ineffable rocks," with *MePhulam* coming from the word *Balam,* since Bet and Peh interchange, Botril, *loc. cit.,* quoting R. Yaakov ben Meir of Gyan in *Tznif Meluchah* (see above 1:8). Others interpret them to be substanceless, ethereal rocks, with the root *Palam* coming from *Belimah,* father of R. Levi ben Shlomo of Lunil, quoted in Botril, *loc. cit.* Others relate it to death, breaking *Polmot* into two words, *Pol Mot, ibid.* The root *Palam* is also related to the English Flume, see *Arukh PLM.* Also see Bertenoro, Rambam on *Shabbat* 22:6 (147a). These can also be seen as "stones of darkness," since this expression in Job 28:3 is rendered by the targum as *Avanim MePhulamim.* These stones are also related to the letters of the alphabet, as in *Sefer Yetzirah* 4:16, see *Tzioni* 3c, *Likutey Moharan* 18:6.

6. *Chagigah* 12a, Ibn Ezra on Genesis 1:2, *Zohar* 2:74b, 2:273b, 3:27a, 3:279a, 3:305b, *Tikuney Zohar,* Introduction (11a), 18 (36a), 37 (78a), *Zohar Chadash* 32c, 55a, 100c, 110a, 119a, *Raziel* 11b (29), 12b (33), 14a (39), *Tshuvot Rama* 6.
7. See chapter 1, note 119, chapter 5, note 29.
8. Peace and evil are seen as opposites from Isaiah 45:7.
9. See *Chagigah* 16a, *Zohar* 1:6a, 2:232a, *Tikuney Zohar,* Introduction (12b), 12 (64b), *Ohev Yisrael, VaErah* (27a).
10. *Cf. Chagigah* 12a.
11. *Cf.* Ecclesiastes 4:8.
12. Paraphrase of Zecharia 14:9.
13. The Hebrew, *MaNedet,* here is obscure.
14. Instead of *Imot,* mothers, Saadia uses *Umot.* This usually means "nations." Saadia, however, translates them as "principles."
15. This is an ancient, obsolete way of spelling the letter Bet. Note its resemblence to Peh.
16. The Hebrew here, *MeChuthal,* is obscure. See Ezekiel 16:4, 30:21, Job 38:9.
17. This was the original designation for the planet Mercury. Later, it was abbreviated as *Kochav* alone, see *Shabbat* 156a. This would appear to indicate that this text antedates the Talmud. Linguistically, this appears to be the most ancient version.
18. In plural. It might denote both the large and small intestines.

Appendix II:
The Thirty-Two Paths

1. Raavad, Introduction (11a), *Pardes Rimonim* 12, *Shoshan Sodot* 33b, 76a, *Peliyah* 48a, *Pri Yitzchak* (Warsaw, 1884), Part 2, 28a.
2. See No. 13.
3. Paraphrase of 1 Chronicles 29:11.
4. Isaiah 25:1.
5. The word is *Me'Atzil*, sharing the same root as Atzilut.
6. Probably alluding to No. 3.
7. This angel is identified as Suriel or Suriah, see *Berakhot* 51a, *Hekhalot Rabatai* 16:4. Also see *Tikuney Zohar* 70 (127b, top). Other sources identify this angel as Sandelphon, see *Zohar* 2:260a, *Zohar Chadash* 38d. *Cf. Kuzari* 3:65.
8. Greatness (Gedulah) is the earlier name for the Sefirah of Chesed, based on the verse 1 Chronicles 29:11. The Ophan is an angel of Asiyah. See *Pardes Rimonim* 1:7.
9. This same idea is found in *Sefer HaIyun* (No. 7) quoted in *Pardes Rimonim* 1:7. Also see *Pardes Rimonim* 12:4, 23:8; Botril on 2:3.
10. See No. 1, 2.
11. See chapter 2, note 7.
12. *Arafaley Tahor* in Hebrew. The expression is found in the Musaf service for Rosh HaShanah at the beginning of *Shofrot*, relating to the revelation at Sinai. Also see *Sefer HaIyun*, in A. Jellinek, *Ginzey Chakhmat HaKaballah*, p. 11, where it is identified with the *Chashmal*.
13. Exodus 20:21, Deuteronomy 4:11, 5:19. *Cf.* Psalms 18:10, 97:2, 1 Kings 8:12.
14. It is therefore a power that surrounds and holds. See Appendix I, note 16.
15. Alluding to Psalm 91:1. See note 18.
16. The verse speaks of the "shadow of Shaddai," the name associated with Yesod. Yesod is called *Chai*, which has a numerical value of 18. This is therefore the 18th state of consciousness.
17. See No. 3.
18. Alluding to Psalm 91:1. See note 15.

Appendix IV:
Editions and Commentaries

1. This edition is not mentioned in *Otzer Sefarim* or in *Bet Eked Sefarim*. It is only listed by Westcott, p. 10, and Waite, p. 3.
2. See *Ne'edar BaKodesh* in part 2.
3. Not in *Otzar Sefarim* or *Bet Eked Sefarim*. Mentioned by Waite, p. 3.
4. The same is true of this edition.
5. Not in *Otzar Sefarim* or *Bet Eked Sefarim*. Mentioned by Goldschmidt.
6. See *Shem HaGedolim*, Samekh 1; Meir Benayu, *Toldot HaAri* (Jerusalem, 1967), pp. 43, 72, 241. Regarding Benjamin HaLevi and his father Shmuel, see *Sinai* 43:100 (1958). Much of this book was taken from *Chemdat HaYamim* (Ismir, 1731). Also see *Ne'edar BaKodesh* (Ismir, 1755).
7. See Amsterdam (1713) edition of *Sefer Yetzirah*.
8. See *Etz Chaim*, Introduction, pp. 19, 20, *Shem HaGedolim, Alef* 11, A. Jellinek, *Litteraturblatt des Orients* (OLB) 1851, p. 425, G. Scholem, *Kiryat Sefer* 4:286 (1928), *Kitvey Yad BaKaballah* 17:7, p. 48.
9. In *Pardes Rimonim* 12:2, the 32 Paths found in the *Raavad* are attributed to Yosef HaArukh. Also see *Otzar Sefarim, Peh* 315; *Shem HaGedolim*, Scholem, *loc. cit.*
10. Especially in his setting up of the 231 Gates. See *Otzar Eden HaGanuz* 16b, 37a; chapter 2, note 43.
11. *Otzar Eden HaGanuz* 16b, quoted in A. Jellinek, *Bet HaSefer* 3:XLII. Also see *Otzar Sefarim, Peh* 316.
12. R. Kirsheim, *Litteraturblatt des Orients* (OLB) 1846, p. 666, quoted in *Temirin*, p. 10, note 8. Also see Ibn Ezra's *Mazney Lashon HaKodesh* (Offenbach, 1791), Introduction.
13. A. Jellinek, *Moses de Leon und sein Verhältnis zum Sohar* (1851), p. 46; G. Scholem, *Kiryat Sefer* 6:387 (1930). However, where R. Yehudah Chayit quotes R. Azriel, this does not fit the printed Ramban, see Chayit 37b, 112b. See note 26.
14. Donash is mentioned by Abraham Ibn Ezra in his commentary on Genesis 38:9.
15. *Revue des Etudes Juives* (REJ), Vol. 105, 107, 112, 113, 119, 121. *Cf.* Munk, "Notic sur Aboul Walid," *Journal Asiatique*, 1850; A. Neubauer, *Catalogue of Hebrew Manuscripts in the*

Bodleian Library No. 1118; Furst, *Litteraturblatt des Orients* (OLB) 1850, p. 897.

16. It would be tempting to identify this with R. Eliezar of Wormes. However, in *Otzar Eden HaGanuz* 16b, Abulafia writes that the commentary of R. Yitzchak Bardashi is unique in its treatment of the 231 Gates. Eliezar of Wormes uses a similar system, and therefore, Abulafia could not have seen his commentary.

17. See A. Jellinek, *Beiträge zur Geschichte der Kabbalah*, Vol. 2, p. 61; Yehudah Leib Dukes, *Nachal Kadomim* (Hanover, 1853), p. 3, Goldschmidt, p. 39; *Otzar Sefarim, Peh* 317. This should be rejected for the reason given in note 16.

18. See Introduction, note 109.

19. See *Tosefot, Chagigah* 13a, *"VeRagley,"* from *Pesikta* 179a. Also see Rosh, *Berakhot* 5:21, *Maadney Yom Tov, ad loc.*

20. See S.D. Luzzatto, *Litteraturblatt des Orients* (OLB) 1847, p. 343; David Castelli, *Il commento di Shabbathai Donnolo*, p. iv.

21. See A. Marx, *HaTzofeh* 5:195, G. Scholem, *Major Trends*, p. 85. Also see Weinberg, in *Jahrbuch der Juedisch-Literatischen Gesellschaft* 20:283.

22. *Otzar Sefarim, Peh* 329, Mordecai Shmuel Girondi, *Toldot Gedoley Yisrael, Mem* 77, Goldschmidt, p. 42.

23. It is significant that in his commentary on 2:3, he uses Abulafia's system for the 231 Gates.

24. See G. Scholem, *Kitvey Yad BaKaballah* 35, p. 93; M. Steinschneider, *Catalogus Liborum Hebraeorum in Bibliotheca Bodleiana* (Berlin, 1852-60), No. 1793; *Toldot Gedoley Yisrael, Mem* 95, *Otzar Sefarim, Peh* 330, Julius Fuerst, *Bibliotheca Judaica* (Leipzig, 1848-63), Vol. 1, p. 187.

25. For a lengthy discussion, see G. Scholem, *Kiryat Sefer* 6:385 (1930). *Cf.* Chayit 48a, 91a.

26. See note 13. Also see A. Jellinek, *Beiträge zur Geschichte der Kabbalah* 1:9, 2:49, *Litteraturblatt des Orients* (OLB) 1851, p. 562. For a counter argument, see Chaim Dov Chevel, *Kitvey Ramban* 2:452. Also see *Pardes Rimonim* 1:4 (end).

27. See *Catalogue Märzbacher* (Munich, 1888) No. 104.

28. Wunderbar, *Litteraturblatt des Orients* (OLB) 1848, p. 737.

29. Raziel was a pseudonym of Abulafia, which he uses in *Sefer HaEdot*, Munich, Ms. 285, published in *Monetsschrift für Geschichte und Wissenschaft des Judentums* (MGWJ) 36:558, and in *HaKabbalah Shel Sefer HaTemunah VeShel Abraham Abulafia*, p. 197. He notes that it has the same numerical value and number of letters as his name Abraham, see *Or HaSekhel* 7:3 (92a), *Chayay Olam HaBah* 7b. Raziel 24a, b actually con-

tains a small portion from the beginning of *Chayay Olam HaBah* regarding the divine Names. It also makes use of the Gematria style reminiscent of Abulafia. See *Otzar Sefarim, Resh* 121. Also see *Batey Midrashot* 1:12.

30. *Cf.* Landauer, *Litteraturblatt des Orients* (OLB) 1845, p. 214; G. Scholem, *Kitvey Yad BaKabbalah* 17:8, p. 48.

31. *Eruvin* 56a, *"VeAin."*

32. There is another manuscript, Parma, di Rossi 399:2, which is also called *Tachakmoni*. This, however, is more of a commentary on the *Bareita of Shmuel HaKatan*, regarding the phases of the moon in 746.

33. The introduction was published separately by A. Jellinek, *Perush Naaseh Adam BeTzalmenu* (Leipzig, 1854), reprinted in *Ginzey Chakhmat HaKabbalah*, Jerusalem, 1969, by A. Geiger, *Paaleh HaPanim* No. 2, Berlin, 1860, and by Zusman Montener, in *Kitvey Refuah*, Jerusalem, 1949.

34. Also see *Otzar Sefarim, Peh* 325; S. Munk, "Notice sur Aboul Walid," *Journal Asiatique* 1850; David Castilli, *II commento di Shabbathai Donnolo*, p. vi; M.H. Landauer, *Litteraturblatt des Orients* (OLB) 1845, p. 562 *ff.* Munich manuscript contains commentaries of Saadia, Yaakov ben Nissan, Shabbatai Donelo, and Yitzchak Yisraeli.

35. See A. Jellinek, *Beiträge zur Geschichte der Kabbalah* 2:39, *Otzar Sefarim, Peh* 326.

36. *Otzar Sefarim, Peh* 322.

37. *Otzar Sefarim, Peh* 323. Also in *Margoliut Tovah* (Amsterdam, 1722), *Cf.* S. Munk, *Notice sur R. Saadia*, p. 16.

38. See Gabrial Falk, introduction to *Chotam Takhnit* (Amsterdam, 1865), p. 7.

39. See note 10.

40. In *Likutey Shas* 32b, there is also a comment on the first Mishnah of *Sefer Yetzirah*. Also see *Etz Chaim, Shaar TaNTA 5-7, Shaar Maamarey Rashbi*, p. 299a.

41. *Cf. Litteraturblatt des Orients* (OLB) 1844, p. 481; *Otzar Sefarim, Peh* 328.

42. There are, however, early citations that do not appear to agree with this published commentary, see Chayit 19b, 198b; *Otzar Chaim* 17b.

43. See *Revue des Etudes Juives* (REJ) 107:109 (1947). Also see Shlomo Yehudah Friend, *Das Buch uber des Elements* (Leipzig, 1884), 8:9.

44. See G. Scholem, *Kiryat Sefer* 4:286-302 (1928). Also see M. Steinsneider, *Catalogue Münchener Hebreischer Handschriften* 115:3. *Cf.* Botril on 2:1, 2:6, 6:1.

45. See note 9.
46. See note 44.
47. L. Zunz, *Zur Geshichter un Litterature*, p. 250; *Otzar Sefarim*, Peh 324.
48. See *Otzar Sefarim, Yud* 384 (published by Yisrael Davidson, Smicha Assaf, and Yisachar Joel, Jerusalem, 1941, 4° 30), 438 pp.
49. For shortcomings in this work, see *Revue des Etudes Juives* (REJ) 29:310-316.
50. According to Fürst and Steinsneider, see Goldschmidt, p. 36.
51. See J.Ch. Wolf, *Biblioteca* (1715), Vol. 1, p. 23, G. Scholem, *Bibliographia Kabalistica* (Berlin, 1933), *"Pistorius," Temirin*, p. 27, note 58. See H. Graetz, *History of the Jews* (New York, 1927), Vol. 4, p. 466.

INDEX

Index

Compiled by Norman D. Peterson.

Entries in bold face indicate chapter and verse references.